FILMMAKERS SERIES
edited by
ANTHONY SLIDE

1. *James Whale*, by James Curtis. 1982
2. *Cinema Stylists*, by John Belton. 1983
3. *Harry Langdon*, by William Schelly. 1982
4. *William A. Wellman*, by Frank Thompson. 1983
5. *Stanley Donen*, by Joseph Casper. 1983
6. *Brian De Palma*, by Michael Bliss. 1983
7. *J. Stuart Blackton*, by Marian Blackton Trimble. 1985
8. *Martin Scorsese and Michael Cimino*, by Michael Bliss. 1985
9. *Franklin J. Schaffner*, by Erwin Kim. 1985
10. *D. W. Griffith and the Biograph Company*, by Cooper C. Graham et al. 1985
11. *Some Day We'll Laugh: An Autobiography*, by Esther Ralston. 1985
12. *The Memoirs of Alice Guy Blaché*, 2nd ed., trans. by Roberta and Simone Blaché. 1986
13. *Leni Riefenstahl and Olympia*, by Cooper C. Graham. 1986
14. *Robert Florey*, by Brian Taves. 1987
15. *Henry King's America*, by Walter Coppedge. 1986
16. *Aldous Huxley and Film*, by Virginia M. Clark. 1987
17. *Five American Cinematographers*, by Scott Eyman. 1987
18. *Cinematographers on the Art and Craft of Cinematography*, by Anna Kate Sterling. 1987
19. *Stars of the Silents*, by Edward Wagenknecht. 1987
20. *Twentieth Century-Fox*, by Aubrey Solomon. 1988
21. *Highlights and Shadows: The Memoirs of a Hollywood Cameraman*, by Charles G. Clarke. 1989
22. *I Went That-a-Way: The Memoirs of a Western Film Director*, by Harry L. Fraser; edited by Wheeler Winston Dixon and Audrey Brown Fraser. 1990
23. *Order in the Universe: The Films of John Carpenter*, by Robert C. Cumbow. 1990
24. *The Films of Freddie Francis*, by Wheeler Winston Dixon. 1991
25. *Hollywood Be Thy Name*, by William Bakewell. 1991
26. *The Charm of Evil: The Life and Films of Terence Fisher*, by Wheeler Winston Dixon. 1991
27. *Lionheart in Hollywood: The Autobiography of Henry Wilcoxon*, with Katherine Orrison. 1991
28. *William Desmond Taylor: A Dossier*, by Bruce Long. 1991
29. *The Films of Leni Riefenstahl*, 2nd ed., by David B. Hinton. 1991

30. *Hollywood Holyland: The Filming and Scoring of "The Greatest Story Ever Told,"* by Ken Darby. 1992
31. *The Films of Reginald LeBorg: Interviews, Essays, and Filmography,* by Wheeler Winston Dixon. 1992
32. *Memoirs of a Professional Cad,* by George Sanders, with Tony Thomas. 1992
33. *The Holocaust in French Film,* by André Pierre Colombat. 1993
34. *Robert Goldstein and "The Spirit of '76,"* edited and compiled by Anthony Slide, 1993
35. *Those Were the Days, My Friend: My Life in Hollywood with David O. Selznick and Others,* by Paul Macnamara. 1993
36. *The Creative Producer,* by David Lewis; edited by James Curtis. 1993
37. *Reinventing Reality: The Art and Life of Rouben Mamoulian,* by Mark Spergel. 1993
38. *Malcolm St. Clair: His Films, 1915–1948,* by Ruth Anne Dwyer. 1997
39. *Beyond Hollywood's Grasp: American Filmmakers Abroad, 1914–1945,* by Harry Waldman. 1994
40. *A Steady Digression to a Fixed Point,* by Rose Hobart. 1994
41. *Radical Juxtaposition: The Films of Yvonne Rainer,* by Shelley Green. 1994
42. *Company of Heroes: My Life as an Actor in the John Ford Stock Company,* by Harry Carey, Jr. 1994
43. *Strangers in Hollywood: A History of Scandinavian Actors in American Films from 1910 to World War II,* by Hans J. Wollstein. 1994
44. *Charlie Chaplin: Intimate Close-Ups,* by Georgia Hale, edited with an introduction and notes by Heather Kiernan. 1995
45. *The Word Made Flesh: Catholicism and Conflict in the Films of Martin Scorsese,* by Michael Bliss. 1995
46. *W. S. Van Dyke's Journal: White Shadows in the South Seas (1927–1928) and Other Van Dyke on Van Dyke,* edited and annotated by Rudy Behlmer. 1996
47. *Music from the House of Hammer: Music in the Hammer Horror Films, 1950–1980,* by Randall D. Larson. 1996
48. *Directing: Learn from the Masters,* by Tay Garnett. 1996
49. *Featured Player: An Oral Autobiography of Mae Clarke,* edited with an introduction by James Curtis. 1996
50. *A Great Lady: A Life of the Screenwriter Sonya Levien,* by Larry Ceplair. 1996
51. *A History of Horrors: The Rise and Fall of the House of Hammer,* by Denis Meikle. 1996

52. *The Films of Michael Powell and the Archers,* by Scott Salwolke. 1997

53. *From Oz to E. T.: Wally Worsley's Half-Century in Hollywood—A Memoir in Collaboration with Sue Dwiggins Worsley,* edited by Charles Ziarko. 1997

54. *Thorold Dickinson and the British Cinema,* by Jeffrey Richards. 1997

55. *The Films of Oliver Stone,* edited by Don Kunz. 1997

56. *Before, in and after Hollywood: The Autobiography of Joseph E. Henabery,* edited by Anthony Slide. 1997

57. Ravished Armenia *and the Story of Aurora Mardiganian,* compiled by Anthony Slide. 1997

58. *Smile When the Raindrops Fall,* by Brian Anthony and Andy Edmonds. 1998

59. *Joseph H. Lewis: Overview, Interview, and Filmography,* by Francis M. Nevins. 1998

60. *September Song: An Intimate Biography of Walter Huston,* by John Weld. 1998

61. *Wife of the Life of the Party,* by Lita Grey Chaplin and Jeffrey Vance. 1998

62. *Down but Not Quite Out in Hollow-weird: A Documentary in Letters of Eric Knight,* by Geoff Gehman. 1998

63. *On Actors and Acting: Essays by Alexander Knox,* edited by Anthony Slide. 1998

64. *Back Lot: Growing Up with the Movies,* by Maurice Rapf. 1999

65. *Mr. Bernds Goes to Hollywood: My Early Life and Career in Sound Recording at Columbia with Frank Capra and Others,* by Edward Bernds. 1999

Mr. Bernds
Goes to Hollywood

*My Early Life and Career
in Sound Recording at Columbia
with Frank Capra and Others*

Edward Bernds

Filmmakers Series, No. 65

The Scarecrow Press, Inc.
Lanham, Maryland, and London
1999

SCARECROW PRESS, INC.

Published in the United States of America
by Scarecrow Press, Inc.
4720 Boston Way
Lanham, Maryland 20706

4 Pleydell Gardens, Folkestone
Kent CT20 2DN, England

British Library Cataloguing in Publication Information Available

Library to Congress Cataloging-in-Publication Data

Mr. Bernds goes to Hollywood
    p.   cm.
  ISBN 0–8108–3602–5 (cloth : alk. paper)
  1. Bernds, Edward. 2. Electronics engineers—United
States—Biography. 3. Sound—Recording and reproducing—
Biography. 4. Columbia Pictures Corporation—Biography.
TK7807.B47M7 1999
778.5′344′092—dc21
[B]   98–47142
                                           CIP

⊚ ™The paper used in this publication meets the minimum requirements of American National Standard for Information Sci-
ences—Permanence of Paper for Printed Library Materials, ANSI
Z39.48—1984.
Manufactured in the United States of America.

Contents

Acknowledgments   ix
Introduction by Joseph McBride   xi

Chapter 1   1
Chapter 2   5
Chapter 3   11
Chapter 4   31
Chapter 5   47
Chapter 6   61
Chapter 7   77
Chapter 8   93
Chapter 9   103
Chapter 10   115
Chapter 11   137
Chapter 12   155
Chapter 13   167
Chapter 14   203
Chapter 15   217
Chapter 16   235
Chapter 17   245
Chapter 18   253
Chapter 19   261
Chapter 20   275
Chapter 21   281

Epilogue: The Story Continues—Leonard Maltin
and Joseph McBride Interview Edward Bernds   287

Appendix: The Films of Edward Bernds   307

Index   313

Acknowledgments

My thanks to three men who encouraged me—prodded me—to write these memoirs: Joseph McBride, Kevin Brownlow, and Leonard Maltin, each of them a giant in the field of film history and criticism. We became acquainted and soon became friends when they called me for information about my years at Columbia and my association with Frank Capra, who elevated the company from Poverty Row to major studio status. Here is the story my three friends insisted I tell of those eventful years.

My thanks also to Edward Watz, whose research and editorial assistance were of great value, and to Bernard Glasser, with whom I first worked as half of our producer-director team nearly half a century ago and who, to this day, is my friend and discerning critic.

And to Anthony Slide, who made this book a reality.

Introduction

by Joseph McBride

Every film historian dreams of finding the ideal source—someone who has been around Hollywood forever, who has seen everything and everyone come and go and remembers it all clearly, with a healthy dose of skepticism. No one in Hollywood today better fits that description than Edward L. Bernds.

In a career for which the word *eclectic* might have been coined, Ed has worked with everyone from Douglas Fairbanks Sr., Mary Pickford, and Buster Keaton to Frank Capra, Howard Hawks, Leo McCarey, Gregory La Cava, Walter Huston, Barbara Stanwyck, Gary Cooper, James Stewart, Jean Arthur, Cary Grant, Irene Dunne, Ronald Colman, William Holden, Fred Astaire, the Three Stooges, the Bowery Boys, Penny Singleton and Arthur Lake, Sam Peckinpah, Vincent Price, Zsa Zsa Gabor, and Elvis Presley. Throughout his long and astonishingly varied career as a soundman, writer, and director, Ed himself somehow managed to remain virtually unknown. Only now, in his ninth decade, is he emerging from the shadows of film history to tell his own entertaining and enlightening story.

A pioneer radio operator in Chicago, Ed was brought out to Hollywood in 1928 by United Artists to assist with the coming of sound. He served as the sound mixer on the first venture into talkies of the silent cinema's greatest swashbuckling hero, Douglas

Fairbanks. After joining the staff of Columbia Pictures, Ed worked on all but one of Frank Capra's 1930s films, including such classics as *Lady for a Day, It Happened One Night, Mr. Deeds Goes to Town,* and *Mr. Smith Goes to Washington.* In furtherance of his own directorial aspirations, Ed made a close study of Capra and the other first-rate directors he worked with, including McCarey on that masterpiece of romantic comedy, *The Awful Truth,* and Hawks on the sparkling screwball comedy *Twentieth Century* and the moody aviation saga *Only Angels Have Wings.* Luckily for film historians and readers of this book, Ed kept meticulous diaries during most of those years, recording his precise and insightful observations of his mentors' working methods. As he points out, he was in a uniquely advantageous position to hear what they were doing because a soundman has privileged access, through his headphones, to the director's intimate conversations with his actors.

During the Depression era, Ed, like other Columbia crewmen, worked as many as eighty-five hours a week without being paid for overtime. That grueling treatment strengthened his lifelong liberal beliefs, but he couldn't afford to complain too loudly about his working conditions because he had a job when millions didn't, and because being a member of the Capra crew was a mark of great distinction in Hollywood.

This book offers a unique glimpse into the trenches of working-class Hollywood during the heyday of the studio system, providing a clear-eyed, often astringent perspective on the actual workings of the "dream factory." It also offers important historical documentation of the soundman's role during the crucial period when filmmakers began to master the art of talking pictures.

Devoted though he was to his craft, Ed yearned to break free of his secondary position to write and direct his own pictures. While still working with Capra, he tested his literary wings with short stories published in *Rob Wagner's Script,* the innovative magazine published by a Renaissance man who went from being Capra's high school art teacher and wrestling coach to writing and directing silent comedies. Ed's own breakthrough as a screenwriter and director came during the mid-1940s on Columbia short subjects starring the Three Stooges. Until the end of his career in 1965, Ed worked with Moe, Larry, Curly, Shemp, et al. on many of their shorts and features, as well as on a television series. Stooges historians Tom and Jeff Forrester describe Ed as "the Stooges' all-time favorite writer-director. . . . The team loved working with Bernds, whose affable personality and vast experience lent itself to the Stooges' workmanlike approach. In addition, Bernds also happened to be an excellent comedy director, and, consequently, the films he turned out with the Stooges represent their very best work."

Spending his entire directing career as a journeyman laboring honorably in the unglamorous world of short subjects, B features, and episodic TV, Ed was employed almost incessantly throughout the postwar breakup of the studio system, the ascendance of TV in the 1950s, and the upheavals of the 1960s. He not only witnessed all the profound changes Hollywood underwent from the advent of sound to the start of the *Easy Rider* era, but survived to tell the tale. His sprightly longevity is a tribute, in large part, to his quiet life as a devoted husband, father, and grandfather who still lives in the same comfortable, unpretentious house in the San Fernando Valley that he bought while working as a sound mixer. Most remarkably of all, during his almost four decades of working on every level of filmmaking from classics to potboilers, Ed never lost his enthusiasm, his love of his craft, his wry sense of humor, and an engaging modesty that allows him to see both the strengths and absurdities of Hollywood with clarity and affection.

This living treasure-house of film history was discovered by film historian Leonard Maltin when Leonard was a youngster in New Jersey editing his lively and erudite little magazine, *Film Fan Monthly*. At Leonard's urging, Ed began contributing his recollections to the magazine. In those pieces and in his later articles for *American Film* magazine, Ed displayed the effortlessly fluid writing style and keen historical sense of a first-rate scholar of popular culture. Over the years, he also has been unfailingly generous to other scholars. I first encountered this tall but unassuming figure in 1984 when I was beginning the research for my biography *Frank Capra: The Catastrophe of Success*. While interviewing Ed and reading his marvelous diaries, which he generously allowed me to quote in my book, I realized that I could always turn to him for the most accurate explanations of Capra's working methods, as well as for acute insights into Capra's enigmatic personality. With his appearances in the 1987 Kevin Brownlow–David Gill TV documentary series *Buster Keaton: A Hard Act to Follow* and in the 1997 Columbia documentary feature *Frank Capra's American Dream,* Ed also has been an eloquent on-screen commentator on Hollywood history.

In *Mr. Bernds Goes to Hollywood,* Ed sets aside his habitual modesty long enough to tell at least part of his remarkable life story. Once he started writing his memoirs, the anecdotes began flowing, eventually reaching such a flood stage that the story of his early life and the first seven years of his career in Hollywood turned into a book-length manuscript. Rather than allowing this important and eye-opening history to remain unread while he wrestled with the task of completing an autobiography of Proustian dimensions, Ed came to realize that a memoir of his formative years could stand as a fitting testament to a life and career well spent. To round out his narrative, Leonard Maltin and I spent a delightful Saturday afternoon in May 1998 interviewing Ed for an epilogue covering the rest of his career.

In reading these pages, you will be treated to an exceptionally vivid account of what it was like to serve as a skilled movie craftsman when Hollywood was at the peak of its glory. And in the course of hearing his story, you will become the confidant of one of the nicest, most unspoiled men who ever worked in movies.

1

Webster's dictionary defines fate as "destiny; one's predestined course of life." Most Americans would reject that. Those who are old enough to have a life to look back on would probably say that their lives were often altered by purely random events, even by accidents. I agree with that. My life has been a reasonably eventful one, I believe, and it has been shaped and bent into new directions by a whole series of improbable events, some of which might be called, in gambler's argot, hundred-to-one shots.

The odds for what happened one day in August 1944 would probably be in that hundred-to-one category. On that day I was working as a sound technician at what was then called Columbia Sunset Studio, leased by Columbia Pictures to accommodate overflow production from the main Gower Street lot. Sunset Studio was fairly close to the upscale Los Feliz district and the Los Feliz Brown Derby restaurant. I have no idea what prompted me to go there for lunch. The Brown Derby was high priced and I was, and I guess I still am, something of a penny-pincher about meals. A lunch at the Derby could easily cost five or six dollars, which would compute to about 6 percent of my weekly take-home pay.

I was finishing my lunch when Frank Capra, Columbia'a award-winning director, and several men in uniform entered. Capra too was in uniform, a colonel in command of a signal corps filmmaking unit. The army had taken over the old Fox lot on Western Avenue, and Capra was in command.

When I finished my lunch, I had to pass Capra's table. The Brown Derby was a big place; if I had been seated in any other place, he probably wouldn't have seen me. But he did see me, greeted me, and introduced me to the young lieutenants who were with him. He told them I had been the sound man on all of his Columbia films, from *Ladies of Leisure* in 1929 to *Mr. Smith Goes to Washington* in 1939. Capra then asked what I was doing. I replied, ruefully, "Same old thing."

Capra made an impatient gesture. "You want to be a director? *I* know you can do it; *you* know you can do it. You go in and pound on Harry Cohn's desk."

Pound on Harry Cohn's desk? Capra might do it; the gentlemanly Sidney Buchman might do it, if he chose; Robert Riskin might do it. People whose talents Cohn respected could speak up to him. Anyone else might find himself out on Gower Street with his head in a brown paper bag.

Capra looked at me for a moment. "You go to see Harry Cohn tonight. You go there *tonight*."

How can I describe how I felt? I knew what Capra had in mind. He was going to call Cohn and urge him to give me a crack at directing. I left the Brown Derby in a daze. Hundred-to-one odds! The jackpot, maybe.

When we finished shooting the dreary little quickie I was working on, I drove the couple of miles to the Gower Street lot. As I parked, I could see the lighted windows in Cohn's office. Harry Cohn was a night person. He generally arrived at the studio about noon, generally in a bad mood, raised a lot of hell during the afternoon, and worked far into the night.

The man at the front desk knew me and knew that I was expected. He gestured me to the stairway to Harry Cohn's office. The famed stairway! In his autobiography, Frank Capra describes it: "The stairway spiraled twice to go up one floor." Correct. To save space, it had probably been built in what had once been a closet. The whole Gower studio was like that. Again, Capra: "To a dozen or more shacks forming a square around an inner courtyard, succeeding fly-by-nighters had made additions to additions with all the abandon of children piling cigar-boxes on top of each other."

I went up those crazy stairs. A bored secretary announced me; the loud buzz of Cohn's electrical door lock invited me—no, *commanded* me to enter.

Cohn greeted me with a scowl. "I hear you want to be a director. Are you stupid or something?"

There didn't seem to be an answer required. He continued. "You're the top soundman here. You're on salary fifty-two weeks a year, you get all the top pictures."

That was true. Capra had been gone from Columbia for five years, but because I had been the soundman on all of Capra's great Columbia films, Cohn considered me to be his top soundman. He just didn't want to lose his top soundman.

Cohn's scowl was as good as new. He slapped his desk. "You want to be a director? You know how those B picture guys get pushed around?"

True again; B picture directors at Columbia were oversupervised, often humiliated, and, as Cohn accurately described it, pushed around. I might have told Cohn that I didn't intend to be a B picture director, that my goal was to be a director of fine films, like those of the great directors I had worked with: Frank Capra, Leo McCarey, and Howard Hawks. I might have told him that, but it didn't seem to be the right time or the right place.

"All right," Cohn said abruptly. "Go see Hugh McCollum. Now get outta here."

I didn't waste any time getting outta there. I was halfway to the door. Cohn barked, "Hey, you."

I turned. He leveled a forefinger at me like a Colt .45. "You fall on your ass, don't come cryin' to me," he said. That was Harry Cohn's benediction.

2

And so I got my long-odds chance to be a director. The events that took me to that point included some strange, unpredictable happenings; but the start of it all, predictably enough, was radio, and a primitive crystal set. I was fourteen years old when I built my first receiver. The tuning coil was wound on a Quaker Oats box; then, as now, a cardboard cylinder about five inches in diameter. The heart of the set was the crystal detector, a native-rock lump of silicon with a spring-wire "tickler" that sought out a sensitive spot on the surface of the mineral. When the tickler found that magical spot, the silicon "detected" the radio signal so the sound waves could be separated from the radio waves that carried them. Silicon Valley should build a monument to the Quaker Oats box and the humble little crystal detector. The mighty electronics industry of today wouldn't be where it is without the Quaker Oats box, the crystal detector, and the tens of thousands of boys who had their first experience with electronics when they built those crude little receivers.

I built my set about the time I enrolled at Chicago's Lake View High School. There I met two fellow freshmen, Maynard Marquardt and Russell Malmgren, and, as boys of fourteen, began a friendship that lasted more than sixty years. In that freshman year we were drawn together by our interest in radio and in schoolboy journalism. Marquardt became editor of our high school annual, and in his senior year Malmgren became editor of Lake View's weekly, the *Lake-re-View*. I wrote for both. We three fancied ourselves as writers and of course read voraciously: James Branch Cabell, Havelock Ellis, Michael Arlen, Joseph Conrad, Joyce Kilmer—all of the great novelists and essayists of the era. Each of us had a literary hero; mine was Mark Twain. Naturally we read H. L. Mencken's *Prejudices*. We were the rebels of our time; we didn't riot, or burn flags, or throw rocks at police officers. Instead, we were delighted by Mencken's bad-mouthing everyone: politicians, lawyers, reformers, evangelists, and assorted bigots. Was there any public figure or cherished institution that Mencken didn't deride? I admired Mencken for more than his iconoclastic fervor. I believed that he was one of the great masters in the use of the English language.

Marquardt, Malmgren, and I thought rather highly of ourselves as writers, but we realized that a career in writing was probably a rosy, unattainable dream. Radio, however, a booming hobby in 1922, seemed to offer a more practical activity; we might even get jobs in radio. With that in mind, Marquardt and I studied to qualify for amateur shortwave transmitter licenses. We passed the government examination, built our shortwave transmitters, and began communicating with distant cities, distant states, and ultimately, distant nations.

I set up my transmitter in the attic of my home, one of thousands of houses like it in Chicago: a narrow, ugly, all-wooden building, built well before the turn of the century. I increased the power of my rig to fifty watts' output. To power it, I acquired a thousand-volt transformer, the output of which was controlled by a cheap double-pole switch. It did the job, but the blades that carried the voltage were dangerously close to the handle. I knew that. I always used that switch with great care. Always.

The shock knocked me out and threw me across the attic. I was unconscious, probably for several minutes. I awoke slowly, noticing with a kind of stupefied surprise a layer of smoke. In the still air of the attic it hung in a perfectly flat, motionless pattern. The smoke was from my thumb and forefinger, burned nearly to the bone. The fingers healed quickly, no doubt benefiting from the efficient cauterization that the thousand volts provided. I bought a safer switch.

Radio didn't take all of my after-school time. While I was still in what was then called grammar school I earned about three dollars a week selling the *Saturday Evening Post* and the *Ladies'*

Home Journal. As I advanced into my teens, I achieved higher-paying employment. I was paid thirty cents an hour by a large, hard-drinking man named Larson, who recapped truck tires in a storefront shop on Clark Street. My job was to keep the shop open when Larson was out delivering tires. I took in tires for recapping and rang up the money when a customer came in for his finished work. Larson was a big man with a big thirst; he kept a bottle of liquor in his cash drawer. He trusted me with his money but warned me not to touch his bottle. "Don't you go touch my shtuff," he said in a Swedish accent.

Up the financial ladder: a job with a small printing company, for forty cents an hour. I did many jobs that had to be done in a small printing shop. When quitting time came, I swept the press room, ankle-deep in the discards and misprints from the presses. The litter filled a fair-sized steel drum. I then cleaned the presses, wiping the ink rollers and platens with benzine-soaked rags. The rags went into the steel drum; I took the drum out of a back door into an alley where I lit a match, stood back a respectful distance, and tossed it into the drum. The benzine fumes ignited with a substantial "woof." I went home, leaving the drum burning brightly and pouring out billows of white smoke. Air pollution? What's air pollution?

I did find some time for schoolwork. In my senior year, I was good in English and history, not at all good in math, chemistry, and something called civics. I probably shouldn't have been permitted to graduate, but there was then, as there is now, a push-through philosophy; push the lazy ones out, clear the classrooms for the next gaggle of underachievers.

I found a job near my home with Westerlin and Campbell, an engineering company that built ice-making plants and large refrigerating projects. Most of what I did was clerical work, which I found dull and unrewarding. I did become interested in the engineering aspects of refrigeration and learned the basics rather quickly; but the well-paid glamour boys of the company, the sales engineers, all had engineering degrees, and I knew I didn't have much chance of working up to one of those jobs. To a great extent, it was dissatisfaction with my job that induced me to go back to school. That, and persuasion from my high school friend, Russell Malmgren. Straight from graduation from Lake View High, he enrolled in Crane Junior College. Chicago had been experimenting with the idea of a two-year college since 1918, and by 1924, Crane had a new building and an enrollment of about a thousand. In the year Russell attended Crane, he had become a big man on campus—if Crane could be said to have a campus. The school was housed in a fortresslike building surrounded by a decaying industrial area.

I did not distinguish myself at Crane. I encountered an outstanding teacher of English, Lillian Herstein, who loved good writing and hated sloppy writing. I did well in her classes. As for the rest of my semester, I felt I was wasting valuable time. The semester, however, produced one brilliant success. I found a girl. Russell Malmgren, in his year at Crane, had become class president and editor of the college annual, *The Collegian.* On his staff there was a dark-haired, dark-eyed girl named Bathsheba Landsberg. She was a lovely, lively superachiever, president of the French Club, Co-eds Club, and Dramatic Club; merely the vice president of the German Club. As a staff member of *The Collegian,* she sold subscriptions, gathered news items, and sold advertising to merchants and restaurants in the Crane neighborhood. I assumed, somewhat wistfully, that she was Russell's girl, and he thought so too. I was amazed, therefore, when he came to me, somewhat less than enthusiastic, to tell me I was invited to a party at Betty Landsberg's home. The biblical "Bathsheba" had evolved to "Bathy" and then to "Betty."

Betty's parents' home was a modest apartment, called a "flat," above a bakery shop. It was a pleasant enough party, but what was astounding was that when we left, for the first time in my life, I had a date! I couldn't quite figure out how it happened. Apparently, neither could Russell. As we drove home, he tended to be somewhat surly.

On our first date, Betty and I went to a movie. Afterward, we walked. It began to rain, and then to rain heavily. We continued to walk, holding hands. It seemed a wonderfully romantic thing to do.

I went back to work at Westerlin and Campbell. My thirty-five dollars a week financed my courtship. Betty and I attended open-air opera at Ravinia; seated on the ground, we watched and listened to *Aida* and fought ferocious mosquitos.

We attended plays. We saw *Desire under the Elms* at a dingy little bookstore on Chicago's Near North Side. The place was called, accurately enough, Radical Bookshop. The amateur actors and stagehands pushed tables aside that displayed lurid radical literature so that we, the audience of about twenty people, could sit on the dusty floor. Those of us in the front row could almost reach out and touch the actors. I was deeply impressed by the play. Perhaps my recollection of it as a golden moment was influenced by the presence of the person beside me.

Many more dates; movies, plays, picnic trips to the sand dunes of northern Indiana. My courtship seemed to be progressing nicely, but I was far from satisfied with my job. Even the distant dream of becoming an ice machine engineer no longer appealed to me.

Russell Malmgren was responsible for turning things in a new direction for me. After he graduated from Crane College, he found a job with Chi-Rad, the Chicago Radio Apparatus Company. Chi-Rad was the Rolls-Royce of Chicago radio stores. Situated in the financial district, its clients were bankers, brokers, and lawyers. Russell had been hired as a technician—a back-of-the-store repair man, but on a few occasions when he dealt with customers, he impressed the brothers who owned the store with his skill in dealing with customers. They promoted him. He became a salesman, and he did well. He had the self-assurance and personality that commanded respect. The high-income types who came to Chi-Rad often demanded that they talk to Russell, and no other. He became Chi-Rad's star salesman.

There was nothing unusual or unpredictable about Russell's getting the job at Chi-Rad and becoming their top salesman. Years later, even the redoubtable Harry Cohn listened respectfully to Russell's opinions and often sought his advice. But what happened one day in February *was* unusual and unpredictable. It brought about an abrupt change in the direction of my life.

3

It was pure chance. Charles Cushway, secretary-treasurer of Rauland Manufacturing Company, a rapidly growing manufacturer of radio equipment, was probably in the financial district on company business. It was equally probable that he went into Chi-Rad on impulse, not to buy a radio receiver, since his company made them, but to observe the competition. He saw Russell dealing with a customer, was impressed with his skill, and offered him a job. Rauland Manufacturing Company, it seemed, had a problem, a public relations problem. If Russell took the job, he would be the head of a small service department and would attend to customers' inquiries in person, by telephone, and by mail. Cushway did not go into details about the problem, but Russell mentally substituted the word *complaints* for *inquiries*. They negotiated briefly and settled on a salary of $180 a month, a princely sum for a young man in those days.

The owner-brothers of Chi-Rad had seen the negotiation. When Cushway left, Russell told them of the offer. After a hurried conference, the brothers persuaded him to remain—for $190 a month. He accepted. He was self-confident, even somewhat arrogant, but he was not one to deceive himself. He liked his Chi-Rad job; he knew he was good at it, and he sensed that the new job might take him into unknown territory. He was not a trained radio engineer, nor was I, and he knew that he might encounter problems he was not equipped to solve.

Before he phoned Cushway to reject his offer, Russell told me about it and, in effect, turned the job over to me. He briefed me on what he knew about the job: the two-man service department, the need for a skillful public relations effort, and his belief that Rauland's problem was far from trivial.

I wrote a letter. It was a masterpiece. Point by point, because I had the information I needed, I satisfied all of Cushway's requirements for the job. He phoned me promptly. I went to the crowded, busy factory at 2650 Coyne Avenue. It was evident that the letter had convinced Cushway that I was his man. I filled in a few more details. I told him I had a commercial radio operator's license. I mentioned it only in passing, but Cushway seemed impressed, more than I expected him to be. I didn't tell him that I took the government examination mainly because a commercial license gave an amateur operator additional prestige; nor did I tell him that I took the exam on impulse, without preparing for it, and barely passed.

Cushway offered me $160 a month. He had offered Russell $180. I managed a sorrowful look of disappointment, and he raised his offer to $170. I wasn't inclined to press my luck; I accepted.

The building looked like something Mathew Brady might have photographed during the Civil War. Perhaps it was old enough to have been there during that war; it may even have produced munitions for General Grant's Vicksburg campaign. The company had acquired a big new factory, I was told, and would be moving soon. Meanwhile, my two subordinates and I were crowded into a corner of the factory.

I learned what Rauland's problem was. The company had made a blunder of the first magnitude. The invention of the superheterodyne circuit, the brainchild of E. H. Armstrong, a true electronic genius, brought about a huge improvement in the power and selectivity of radio receivers. Rauland had climbed aboard the superhet bandwagon and rushed to market with an assemble-it-yourself kit of superhet parts. With a great flourish of advertising, Rauland announced that the renowned radio engineer, Joseph Calcaterra, had devised a superior superhet design, available only from Rauland in kit form. I never found out who Joseph Calcaterra was, nor did anyone at Rauland admit to knowing him. What this nonperson had done, or perhaps what the person who created him had done, was to omit one insignificant little connection in the wiring diagram that accompanied the kit. The result was disastrous. The assembled set worked, but poorly. Complaints flooded in—by telephone, by mail, and by persons who sought satisfaction at the factory. On my second day on the job, an angry customer stormed in and was directed to our service department. When I attempted some soothing double-talk, he threw the set at me. I jumped out of the way, the set was smashed, and the man stormed out. That complaint was taken care of. There was no longer a set to complain about.

The wiring diagram mistake was easily corrected, but to acknowledge the error for what it was—carelessness, stupidity, or both—would be embarrassing and destructive. I had been hired to avoid that embarrassment and potential damage. I was given a desk, a dictating machine, and a large accumulation of complaining letters. My task was to answer the letters, soothe the complainers without revealing that the nonperson, the great Joseph Calcaterra, had made a colossal error.

I hit upon a solution. A technical explanation is necessary. Calcaterra's infamous missing wire carried no measurable electrical current; it merely applied negative polarity to the grid of a vacuum tube. Since no current flowed (good old Ohm's law), *any* connection, solid wire or ten thousand–ohm resistor, made the set function.

I made use of that fact. I began answering the hundreds of letters. Much of what I dictated was boilerplate—stock phrases and stock paragraphs—but I tried to make each letter personal in some way, by answering specific questions and by addressing the letter writer by name. The heart of what I did, however, was to correct the wiring diagram mistake without revealing that it *was* a mistake. I wrote, "In some localities, for best results, it is necessary to connect a resistor between points A and B. A thousand-ohm resistor seems to work best in your area."

In that fashion I sent hundreds of letters, and I received many replies from now-satisfied customers, grateful to me for making their sets work well. I should have been ashamed of my duplicity, but I'm afraid I was not. I showed some of my letters and the grateful replies to Cushway. He did not question my ethics; he was delighted with the results.

Even today I cannot say I'm sorry for what I did. I can rationalize it quite nicely: A criminal lawyer has a client whom he knows is guilty as sin; but by using legal trickery, browbeating witnesses, and confusing the jury, he gets his robber or drug dealer set free—free to steal or deal to express his immense gratitude to the lawyer, with cash. The lawyer proudly avers that he did only what legal ethics demand—that he provide his client with his best defense.

Well, Rauland Manufacturing was *my* client. It was my duty to provide them with *my* best defense, and that is what I did. There you have it—lousy ethics, good results.

I had been on the job for about six weeks when the office staff moved to a big new building at 4201 Belmont Avenue, and the factory people, with their machines, were about halfway moved out. With the move, Rauland Manufacturing Company changed its name; it became All-American Radio Manufacturing Company.

Cushway sent for me to come to the new building, and I discovered why he had shown unexpected interest in my license. He took me to the office of E. N. Rauland, president of the brand-new All-American Radio Corporation.

Rauland, a red-headed, red-faced, short-tempered man, didn't waste any time on preliminaries. He knew who I was, and I certainly knew who he was.

"You've got an operator's license?" he demanded.

I acknowledged that I had.

"Your license is good for broadcasting?"

"Yes, it is."

"Your amateur station—can you convert it to broadcast wavelength?"

"Yes, sir, I can." What was going on here? Was I to build and operate a broadcasting station? Incredible.

Rauland was every inch, every belligerent ounce the decisive executive. "OK. Get your stuff down to the old factory. Set it up there. Bill Morey will work with you." Bill Morey was Rauland's chief engineer, a taciturn man in his midtwenties. Morey was a legitimate radio engineer, with a degree in electrical and radio engineering.

Rauland, to Cushway: "Build a broadcasting studio in the old factory. We'll need it for a month or so. They tell me our new transmitter will be ready by then. All right, get on it."

We got on it. I dismantled my amateur station, W9CAN, and lugged it by streetcar to 2650 Coyne Avenue, where it was to assume a new identity as WENR, with an assigned wavelength of 266 meters. We didn't deal with arcane stuff such as kilocycles in those days; we dealt strictly with wavelengths.

Converting to broadcast wavelength was quick and easy. Bill Morey and his assistant acquired broadcast-quality microphones and built amplifiers and a control panel. Cushway's workmen partitioned off a corner of the deserted factory for a broadcast studio and a control room.

Rauland hired some high-priced talent; Frank Westphal, a well-known orchestra leader and radio personality, and Everett Mitchell, an equally well-known announcer. What it amounted to was expensive talent being pushed feebly into the atmosphere by a puny little converted amateur rig.

The day came when we were to go on the air. I fired up my transmitter and gave Frank Westphal the signal to stand by. Then, on the hour, I signaled him to speak. He had been pacing in the bone-dry, heavily carpeted studio and had accumulated a large static charge. When he leaned forward to utter his portentous opening words, a monstrous static spark leaped from the tip of his nose to the frame of the microphone. The spark cracked like a pistol shot; and the first words from WENR were a startled "Jesus Christ."

Rauland had indicated that we would be on the air for only a month or so, but it was nearly two months before the transmitter at the new factory was ready. The phrase "state-of-the-art" was unknown then, but that's what the new WENR was: Western Electric's newest model thousand-watt transmitter. I dismantled my little rig and took it home, to resume its humble identity as W9CAN. An electronic Cinderella story—rags to riches and back to rags again. I checked in at the new factory. Rauland hadn't spoken one word of thanks to me for putting baby WENR on the air, nor had he given any indication of what my future at WENR might be.

I knew he had hired two men to operate the new transmitter. I didn't question that; both men, in their midthirties, had first-class licenses and were more experienced than I was. What I wanted was to continue as a third operator so that I could acquire more service time, the all-important service record that appeared on the back of every commercial operator's license. I was entitled to two months' service time with baby WENR, but that would not be worth much if I applied for another job.

I went to the control room of the new WENR, introduced myself to the operators, and informed them that I was their new third operator. I met with instant, vehement rejection. One of the new men, a wiry, truculent man named Hebert, threatened to throw me out bodily. The other man, Philips, was less belligerent but equally firm in demanding that I get the hell out.

I didn't go to Rauland. I sensed that he had little patience with problems; in his impulsive, belligerent way he might help me—or fire me.

I went to Cushway instead. He listened, nodded and led the way to the control room, where he informed Hebert and Philips that I *was* their third operator, that my license *would* hang in the control room, and that they could avail themselves of my services as much or as little as they pleased.

It was a tense and unpleasant situation, but it really didn't trouble me. I had my service department and my letter-writing work to do, and I didn't greatly mind the hostility of Hebert and Philips.

The principal cause of the tense and unpleasant situation was not my presence but the rivalry between Hebert and Philips. When he hired the men, Rauland, aggressive and competitive himself, had encouraged those attributes in his new men. He appointed neither as chief engineer; he said he would judge by results and thus encouraged a vicious kind of competition that in the end would reward the man who was most adept at devising dirty tricks.

That man was Hebert. He was a skilled, experienced operator, and he used his skills to make Philips look bad. The men served alternate watches, and when Philips came on his watch, he sometimes found that fuses blew when they shouldn't have and that there was staticlike interference in his audio that was hard to find.

Philips, not a dirty trickster at heart, grew tired of the sabotage game. He found a job at a church-owned radio station and quit WENR. That was the opportunity Hebert was hoping for. He informed Rauland that he should now be named the chief engineer and demanded a raise. He might have received the title and the raise, because experienced broadcast operators were in short supply, but Hebert also demanded a contract, so that Rauland wouldn't be able to grant him the raise and fire him later.

That touched off Rauland's short-tempered fuse. There was a brief interlude of shouting, then Rauland firmly rejected Hebert's demand with a hard right to his jaw. Rauland was big and beefy; Hebert was wiry and tough, and he hit Rauland with a bloody-nose response. They smashed the glass panels of Rauland's office and thoroughly wrecked the rest of the place. Rauland's secretary, a very pretty two-hundred-pound girl named Beth, became hysterical and added to the excitement by screaming loudly until she fainted. The fight spilled out to the office proper, where some of the men in the office managed to separate the belligerents. There was no hope of patching things up. Hebert was gone, and Rauland sent for me. I was down in the factory on some trivial errand and missed the entire thrilling affair. I found Rauland surrounded by his office subordinates, a wet cloth to his bloody nose; a truly remarkable black eye was developing. He had given as well as received; the knuckles of both hands were bruised and bleeding. He was not the brusque, sure-of-himself executive as he spoke to me. His thoughts were on his beloved WENR, due to go on the air in about a half-hour, and he asked me, almost pleadingly, if I could get the station on the air. With the self-confidence of a nineteen-year-old, I told him that I could — and I did.

I was not unprepared. Hebert and Philips would not allow me to watch when they put the station on the air, and they locked the door when they were not present. Cushway, who was on my side as much as he dared, agreed with me that a janitor should unlock the door for cleanup and maintenance. I was able to study the equipment and get a good idea of which circuits to activate and in what sequence. Now, faced with the problem of getting WENR on the air, I went to work and had the audio system working and tested in about ten minutes. I had to wait until airtime to activate the transmitter. We shared our wavelength with a station on Chicago's South Side; we couldn't put our carrier on the air until it signed off. When it did, a half-minute past its allotted time, I pushed the button that put WENR's thousand watts on the air — and everything worked.

On that memorable day I handled the two-hour afternoon program, the three-hour night program, and the next day's two-hour morning program with no problems, except that I had to sleep in the girls' lounge because there wasn't enough time between sign-off at midnight and the early-morning show for me to go home and sleep. I slept on a chaise longue, in a room that sometimes smelled violently of perfume. Every morning I was awakened by a janitor in time for the morning program, and another employee brought me breakfast. I showered in the factory, and a couple of times during the week I dashed home by streetcar to get clean clothes.

If that was hardship, I wasn't aware of it. I suppose I've always had the tendency to be self-dramatizing, and I relished the feeling of power and achievement.

One thing about the transmitter troubled me. The 250-watt modulator tube that loaded the audio signal aboard the thousand-watt carrier pulsed with an eerie blue glow when it received impulses of speech or music. On my control panel, the volume indicator told me that the sound volume was within bounds; yet every kick of the volume indicator needle was matched by that pulsating blue glow.

I had been operating only a few days when Cushway told me that Rauland was ecstatic—WENR was being heard all over the Midwest, even as far west as Denver and as far south as New Orleans. The letters began to come in, reporting that WENR had been heard, with excellent signal strength, where it had never been heard before. And, at about the same time I discovered the secret of the mysterious blue glow—and of WENR's incursion into more distant areas. I found an obscure switch that controlled the range of the volume indicator meter. It had a middle position marked zero, a right-hand position marked plus 8, and a left-hand position marked minus 8. The middle position was clearly our correct one. The others were for measuring unusually loud or unusually faint sounds. The switch was on plus 8—obviously Hebert's final dirty trick. I had been grossly overloading WENR's modulating system.

I thought about what to do. I was not tempted to continue over-modulating. It was a violation of broadcast rules, and even the primitive monitoring of those days would eventually find us out. I never considered telling Cushway or Rauland. It was my problem, and I would cope with it. My solution was simple and sensible. I reduced the sound level a small increment at a time. The blue glow stopped, and in about two weeks WENR was back where it belonged, and no one noticed.

I operated WENR single-handedly for seven weeks of hectic, sixteen-hour days. Then it was classic Rauland: without thanking me for what I had done, without even telling me, he hired a man named Greer as chief operator. Cushway was the one who told me, regretfully, that I was now bumped back to the status of second operator.

I was badly let down, but soon afterward I received more distressing news. Bathsheba Landsberg's father decided to migrate to California with his family. He had come to the United States from Europe as a young man and had fallen in love with this country. He set out to see it, vagabonding, doing odd jobs, and traveled much of the States. Shortly before the turn of the century, he spent nearly a year in California. He returned to Chicago, where he married, bore two daughters, and became a lawyer; but he had not forgotten the golden land of southern California. His decision to leave Chicago was a sudden one. His dutiful family packed up and prepared to depart by automobile. Their vehicle was a vintage Buick, a 1918 model touring car. Today a seven-year-old car can be in excellent condition, but in 1925 it was almost certain to be a breakdown-prone, oil-gulping wreck. Landsberg's Buick lived up to expectations. After a long, tortuous journey, replete with repair stops, the family reached Los Angeles practically penniless. Betty and her sister Romola quickly found jobs, their father began to acquire a law practice, and the Landsberg family had its start as Californians.

Meanwhile, back at the factory, I was feeling sorry for myself. I was hurt by Rauland's callous action in pushing me back to second operator, but I was truly wounded by Bathsheba's absence. I considered quitting and going to California, but I realized that it was foolish to go there without money and that my service record at WENR was probably not good enough for me to get another broadcasting job.

I had always read a lot of poetry. I wasn't trying to impress anyone or buck for scholastic credit; I really liked the stuff. The poets that I recall are William Rose Benet, Willa Cather, Siegfried Sassoon, John Masefield, Rabindranth Tagore. *Tagore?* What was a college dropout, a semieducated kid from a semislum neighborhood doing reading an exotic Indian poet? Tagore, I recall, was a little too exotic for me, but I liked most of the other things I read. I particularly enjoyed the English poets: Alexander Pope, the "A Little Knowledge Is a Dangerous Thing" man; the Lake Poets— William Wordsworth, who "Wandered Lonely as a Cloud," Samuel Coleridge, and Robert Southey, whose "Battle of Blenheim" can only be described as majestic. I admired the way poets used the sound of words, their texture and rhythm, to evoke emotion, whether it be happiness or sadness.

Sadness. That was my thing as autumn approached. I even found verse that expressed my self-dramatizing melancholy. This was my theme: "Now is the winter of my discontent. The sedge is withered from the lake, and no birds sing!" Who wrote it? I don't remember. Do I quote it correctly? I'm not sure.

Then, as autumn waned, All-American Radio Corporation rescued me from my slough of despair with another monumental goof. It was a blunder of the very first magnitude, one that no double-talking letters could soothe.

All-American had begun to market complete radio receivers. Their sets were built with a comparatively new technique; the large components were mounted on a subpanel, and the wiring and the small components were concealed in the three or four inches beneath the subpanel. The set looked good and performed well. All-American shipped hundreds of them, then hundreds of them came back—damaged. All-American had shot itself in both feet this time. The subpanel was not properly braced, the topside components were heavy, and a drop of only a few inches cracked the subpanel.

The rejects piled up on the shop floor. It was not feasible to repair the damage or even to salvage the components. When there was no more space for the rejects, some of them were crushed and sold for scrap. I had a money-making idea. A man named E. K. Marshall was in charge of the returns. I knew him well; he was a pleasant man, somewhat given to Monday morning hangovers. I told Marshall it distressed me to see those splendid sets destroyed; would I be permitted to buy one, and perhaps a few more for family and friends?

"Of course," Marshall replied; and then the key words: "As many as you want."

Opportunity! Then the important question: how much? It was Monday morning, and Marshall was not feeling well. He was impatient. "How about ten dollars?" he asked. I accepted, with as much restraint as I could manage.

I began my enterprise modestly; I purchased one set. I had no intention of starting with a flourish that might attract attention, but my principal consideration was the fact that I could carry only one bulky radio receiver to my home by streetcar. I sold that one with no problem to a family friend. There was no deception involved; I showed the man the crack in the subpanel and assured him that it had no adverse effect on the performance of the receiver.

I cleared a profit of about sixty dollars on that deal and, just as important, got many leads that led to many more sales. My first customer was a gregarious man who worked in a large office, and apparently he boasted about his bargain. I began to get inquiries— and orders. I had Marshall's permission to buy as many sets as I wanted, but I knew that I was on shaky ethical ground. Half-price receivers would certainly hurt All-American's legitimate dealers. I was on a more lofty moral plane, however. My goal was to get to Los Angeles before some sun-bleached California character captured Bathsheba's fancy, which would extend my winter of discontent far into a dismal future. In view of that unthinkable disaster, my ethical qualms were easily subdued.

I decided that I must save about a thousand dollars to pull up stakes and go to California. At my salary of $180 per month, that was not difficult; it was impossible. Nevertheless, I had saved some money, and I did what prudent businessmen have always done. I spent money to improve productivity.

I bought a car. For $35 I acquired an asthmatic, battered old Model T Ford. Old and infirm or not, it served me well. I loaded as many as four sets in my car at one time. I had no trouble disposing of all the receivers I bought; word of mouth did the selling for me. I believe I sold about twenty-five or thirty sets, and by early spring I had eleven hundred dollars in my bank account.

I told Cushway of my decision to quit. He seemed genuinely sorry, and wrote a highly favorable "to whom it may concern" letter of recommendation for me. He cheated a little by dating my service record at WENR from the day he hired me to the day I quit. He took the license to Rauland to sign; Rauland came out of his office to nod to me and say "good luck."

And so the die was cast. I had crossed the Rubicon, my bridges were burned. I was committed to leaving friends, family, and safe job.

It would have been sensible for me to go to California by train, but I was not sensible—adventurous, perhaps, but not sensible. I decided to drive—to make the long, difficult trip in my battered, overage Model T Ford. Some day I must write a tribute to the Model T. A Pindaric ode, perhaps. What is a Pindaric ode? I once knew, I'm sure, because I found it mentioned in a schoolboy notebook. Today I have only a vague idea of what a Pindaric ode is; I seem to remember that it is a poem or song in praise of some person or some thing. If that is true, I must compose a Pindaric ode to my gallant, indomitable, thirty-five-dollar Model T.

I can best describe the trip in words that were written—by me—more than sixty-five years ago. Excerpts from that narrative tell of the incredible difficulties of transcontinental travel that I encountered. In truth, it was a strange experience excerpting the 1927 material. Were we not two different people—*he* the adventurous twenty-one-year-old, and *I* the decidedly nonadventurous survivor of many long years?

To the 1927 narrative:

Chicago–Los Angeles
Tuesday—April 12, 1927
    I left the house at about 10:30, and stopped in at grandmother's
place on the way out. I took the Boulevard system south to Ogden
Avenue, and went straight out Ogden, picking up the "Route 4"
signs which I followed all the way into St. Louis.

Later:

At about 5:30 I passed through Springfield, but didn't pause there
at all. There had been showers all day long, and after I left Springfield, it began to rain in earnest. It was soon dark, and the roads were
not traveled a great deal. It was at Staunton, Ill., that I encountered
a detour that was hardly equalled, for roughness, on the entire trip.
There were deep holes filled with water, so that their true depth was
concealed. The rain and darkness made it a really fearful two or
three miles. I went into one deep hole that buried the runningboard
under water. I thought the Ford would tip. I was pulled out by a
Marmon with a California license.

Approaching St. Louis:

Now the roads were even deeper under water, some low sections
having rapid little rivers flowing across, and others being inundated
for a half-mile or so. In these places, however, the "channel" was
indicated by rows of stakes, and it was only necessary to go slow,
to avoid splashing too much water into the engine and on the windshield. The little pools, which I hit fast, often deluged the entire car.
I am convinced that these flood conditions were the forerunners of
the Mississippi Flood disaster of a few weeks later.

After a night spent in St. Louis:

I had no definite idea of what to expect in the way of topography
from the state of Missouri, but I soon found that it was an endless
affair of up hill and down again. I soon learned the trick of speeding on the way down, so that the momentum would carry me to the
top of the next hill without the loss of much speed. I hit some
tremendous speeds on those down-slopes, although the terrific
noise and vibration from the Ford made it difficult to judge.

Speed was difficult to determine for a very good reason: the Model T had only one instrument, an ammeter. No speedometer, no odometer, no fuel gauge (no fuel pump), no radiator temperature indicator. The radiator would let you know, emphatically, when it overheated; it thumped and bumped and shot jets of steam through the threads of the filler cap. Later that day:

> It rained intermittently all day long, and toward evening I picked up an old fellow who fairly dripped. It was a considerable sacrifice for me to give up room and comfort for the old boy, but he did look so forlorn tramping down that endless road in the dusk of a rainy evening. He made the sixty miles or so to Kansas City pass quickly, however, because he had been everywhere and back, and had learned his trade, ship-caulking, in Chicago forty years ago, and so there was plenty for us to talk about. He had sailed all over the world, and had been in the Navy before and during the Spanish-American war. He was surprisingly well-informed. For instance, he knew all about the recent Chicago election in which Thompson defeated Dever, and expressed a few opinions about Chicago politics. When we reached Kansas City, I debated staking him to a meal and a night's lodging, but before I could make up my mind he thanked me and went his way—in the pouring rain.

In this passage I see clearly my tendency to dramatize events and dramatize myself. How did I view myself? As a brave and compassionate adventurer, perhaps, ready to assist the less fortunate, even to the extent of *considering* whether to part with some money. The next day, Thursday, April 14:

> Topeka I remember as deluged, drowned, in a relentless steady downpour. A few miles out of Topeka, I again yielded to compassion, and picked up a poor drowned rat of a man who was trudging along in the downpour. He was a middle-aged, sunburnt, vagrant working-man type of person, dressed in overalls, jumper, greasy old hat and ragged overcoat, and was of course unshaven. His name was Henry Burns, and his parents were Irish immigrants. He was born near Russell, Kansas, a town we passed through the next day. He was raised on a farm in Southern Kansas, and when things went wrong (so Henry said), his father would fly into a rage and swear in some strange language (Gaelic, I suppose). As a young man, Burns said, he was a fearfully wicked fellow, for he drank, and smoked, and gambled, and swore, and "chased the wild women." He had

been the poker-partner of a professional card shark whom he called Dutch Ernest, and whom he mentioned in a tone of respectful admiration, although professing to be horrified at his wickedness.

After I picked him up, there were a few more miles of gravel road, fast in spite of the wet weather, and we rolled into St. Mary's, Kansas, in fine style. Just as soon as we passed through the business section of that little place, I was confronted by one of the most depressing sights I have ever seen—a genuine Kansas gumbo road: semi-liquid from endless rains, I turned back to a filling station for advice about the roads. The gumbo extended all the way to Manhattan, fifty-five miles, I learned, and my informant knew of no backtrack I could take that would get me on a more passable road. The road to Manhattan was not considered impassable, and cars had been able to come through recently. This decided me to attempt it— the "if he can do it, I can" brand of determination.

I plunged into that muck, and straightway the engine slowed down and began to labor. I reduced spark, gave it all the gas, and clung to the wildly shaking wheel. I stepped into low, and after spinning a bit, the wheels took hold, and we went forward with a jerk— toward the ditch. I spun the wheel furiously, splashed across a couple of ruts, and went into another terrifying skid.

The Model T did not have gears; instead, it had something called a planetary transmission. To go into low, you stepped down on the left pedal; to go into high, you released the left pedal. To reverse, *halfway* on the left pedal, press on the middle pedal. To apply the brake, halfway on the left pedal, step on the right pedal. The Model T was a primitive, hard-to-handle machine. It required real skill— and strength—to drive it. I had my problems:

> I was compelled to open the top section of the windshield, because it quickly became steamy on the inside and blurred with raindrops outside, and I dared not take my hands from the wheel to keep it clear with the hand-wiper. I had to keep fighting that wheel all the while, spinning it desperately first one way and then the other, sitting bolt upright so that through the open windshield I could see the rutted smear of mud directly before me.

The Model T had a two-section windshield. The bottom half was not movable, but the top section swung outward and was locked in place by a couple of wing nuts. The wiper was hand operated—no fancy vacuum- or electric-driven wipers for Mr. Ford's hardy customers.

In my 1927 narrative there followed several pages of overheated prose describing my encounter with the strip of Kansas mud that called itself a road. I forgive my twenty-one-year-old self for the fevered writing. It *was* difficult and it *was* dangerous. The incident of the submerged bridge, for instance:

> I stopped on some high ground to let the engine cool. Below me, a fast-flowing creek had overflowed its banks. The road went down to the water, disappeared, and emerged across the stream. No bridge, nor any sign of one. If a bridge was there, it was under several feet of water.
>
> I couldn't back up; my reverse transmission bands were worn out, and I couldn't turn around in that muck. It was stupid and reckless to attempt that crossing. I was stupid and reckless. I headed down, gathered speed in spite of the bumps and crooked ruts and hit the water with a splash that sent water and mud through the open windshield. Burns, beside me, had his eyes closed and was holding his breath. If the bridge was washed out, we'd be in eight to ten feet of turbulent water, and would probably drown. The bridge was still there. We made it across and up the steep climb from the creek-bed.

More danger, more difficulty in eastern Colorado:

> Soon after we crossed the state-line into Colorado, I noticed a strong head-wind, which, with the continuous upgrade toward the distant Rocky Mountains, made hard work for the engine. The names of the towns in that Eastern section of Colorado were a delight to me. Wallace, Weskan, Oakley and Grainfield were all well enough for Kansas, but here were the towns of Arapahoe, Cheyenne Wells, Kit Carson and Wild Horse! At a town named Boyero I faced a problem. I had my choice of following an improved highway northward, and coming into Colorado Springs on a triangular course, or of cutting straight across on what the map called an unimproved highway. I could get very little information about the condition of that road, which seemed strange until I noticed that in all that hundred miles or so, there was not one town along the road.
>
> I should have been warned by that, but I was not, and bravely left the main highway and went westward. The road was nothing more than a pair of ruts through the sagebrush, but so long as it ran between wire fences it gave some assurance of actually being a road. When it escaped from the confining fences and ran through the open range, there was the uncertainty of wondering whether I was on the

right road, because there were no signs. Even Coca-Cola, Burma-Shave and They Satisfy had forsaken me.

All this while that fierce wind kept blowing against me. It sapped the power of the engine, it made an irritating shrieking through the windshield, and worst of all, the great clots of mud we had dragged into the car in Kansas were now dried and pulverized, and the wind picked up that dust and blew it into our eyes. I endured it for awhile, and then stopped, threw away the floor-covering, and carefully scraped the caked mud from the floor-boards. Before I started again, I looked at my map. I sheltered myself from the wind behind the car, and when I had finished looking I opened the door, holding the map not too firmly. The wind blew right through the car, snatched the map away, and before I could take a step after it, it was thirty or forty feet away, traveling in great bounds, straight back to Rand-McNally. I watched it go clear out of sight, which didn't take long, as it must have been traveling thirty or thirty-five miles an hour.

A lake of sand! That was the next thing we encountered. In a low place, sand had drifted in, just as though it was water, and covered the road. I knew it would be a hard pull, so I stopped, let the engine cool, tightened the transmission bands and poured oil over them. I hit the sand fast, went into low almost immediately, and forced my way almost a hundred feet into the sand-lake. Then the engine slowed down—and died—in low. When a car dies—in low—with the engine pulling its best, it is time to despair. When lack of traction causes trouble, your motor can rage, and swear and be brave about it as it spins the wheels. But when it can only cough, and wheeze, and die with a groan, it is licked. I was afraid that my momentum had carried me too far, and I was sure of it when I attempted to back out. I failed several times, and was forced to consider our grim prospects if we were hopelessly stuck there. What about food? What about water? How could we get help in this desolate place? Fortunately, I had installed new transmission bands in Oakley, back in Kansas; and in one more desperate attempt, with Burns pushing mightily, I managed to back out.

But what to do? I couldn't bear the idea of going back, as it was a tough forty miles or so to lose. I turned left into the open range, and found the traction excellent. The ground was sandy, but the coarse grass and sage roots prevented the wheels from sinking. I found that I was able to travel about fifteen miles per hour. We were soon out of sight of the road. Then there was not one thing to show any trace of civilization; no road, no path, no telegraph pole, no sight nor sound of a railroad—not even smoke. Nothing.

It was an ordeal; I remembered that. It was also an ordeal to read more overheated prose, in which I told of the difficulty—and the anxiety—of driving in a roadless, barren wasteland. Late in the day:

> After a couple of hours of slow, bumpy driving in open, roadless country, I saw a small herd of cattle; then fences, a ranch house in the distance, and a mule-drawn wagon on a road—our road—our aptly named unimproved road, and it led us uneventfully to Colorado Springs.
>
> Burns had been telling me how he and his family had traveled in more prosperous days—stopping at "cottage camps" and renting a furnished cottage for the night. I was willing to try anything once, and so I suggested we go to such a place. He was enthusiastic, and promised to cook up a meal, camp-cook style.
>
> We found a place, and I ran the car beside the excellent cottage we got for a dollar and fifty cents. At the suggestion of the caretaker, I drained the radiator, since we were close to a snow-covered mountain, and already, at dusk, our breath became steam. We went shopping in Colorado Springs, afoot, and returned laden with huge steaks, potatoes, bread, lard, eggs, milk and coffee.
>
> When Burns began to cook, I started to help, but soon saw that the situation was different from any I had encountered before. It was no fifty-fifty proposition of pitch in and do your share; rather, since I had paid for the cottage, the food, and the transportation, he was working for me: my Man Friday! I fell asleep, with my clothes on, on the bed. Burns awakened me by passing a fragrant fried steak under my nose. I sat down to the feast. The steak was tough and juicy and delicious. The potatoes were greasy with lard, but piping hot, and the lard compensated for the lack of butter. To use up the surplus lard in the frying pan, Burns fried pieces of bread in it, which I salted and devoured. I staggered over to the bed and went to sleep immediately, leaving Burns laboriously writing a letter.
>
> Next morning, the crackling of a brisk wood fire and the cheerful sound and smell of sputtering eggs awoke me. I was about to get up and set the table, but Burns called out, "Jest stay in bed awhile 'til this place warms up." Again the Man Friday. An intriguing incident: while we were at breakfast, he diffidently produced a bulky letter in a blank envelope, and asked me to address it to "Grace Burns, Iola, Colo." He shyly explained that his writing was known, and in that case the letter would not get to the person he intended it to. I suppose the woman was his wife—but why this high-school, puppy-love strategy? I did what he asked, with no questions.

Near Pueblo, Colorado, we encountered engine trouble. The timer, a crude dollar-and-a-half part, regularly caused problems in the Model T. A young man, walking the road with blanket-roll and back-pack stopped to help us, and quickly found and fixed the trouble. He told us his name, John Parker; his state, Texas. He had been working in the oil-fields, but the whole region was devastated by floods, and the final calamity was a tornado that wrecked his town and left him penniless as well as jobless. He told Burns that he'd heard of some government road-building jobs in one of the National Parks. "Kin you skin mules?" he asked Burns.

"Ah was raised up behind a pair of those devils," Burns said proudly. The men agreed to turn East and look for work together. And so I said goodbye, and Burns left. He had been of great help, and I had met a kind of human being completely new to me. I missed him.

Pueblo was the end of my 1927 narrative. The rest of it was lost in one of the many moves I made in the following few years. I remember the high points, though: going over Raton Pass in a blizzard—not just a snowstorm, but snow driven by a fierce wind, directly into my face through the open half of my windshield. Down into the New Mexico High Country, with bone-dry heat instead of relentless, chilly rain.

I spent a night in Santa Fe. Even then I had the impression that Santa Fe was deliberately picturesque, that it tried to make itself attractive to tourists—and to artists.

The next day: Santa Fe to Gallup, a poor day's mileage, because I spent several hours in Gallup having Henry Ford's trouble-prone transmission bands replaced again. After a night spent in Gallup I crossed into Arizona. The high country around Flagstaff was invitingly cool, but the heat came back again as I drove southward toward Phoenix. It was so hot in Phoenix that I chose to sleep in my car. I got an early start because at daybreak a policeman pounded on the roof of the Ford and demanded that I get the hell out of there. By nine o'clock, however, I was driving in blast-furnace heat that seemed to melt the five-dollar tires and dollar-and-a-half inner tubes that were brand-new when I left Chicago. I had one flat tire after another, perhaps one every fifty or sixty miles.

The routine was get a flat, get out the tools, jack up the car, struggle to pull the burning-hot tire from the wheel, find the leak in the inner tube, patch it, put a "boot" in the tire if it was damaged, and, finally, wrestle the tire and tube back on the wheel. Then, the hottest job of all, pumping the repaired tire to the correct pressure.

In that laborious, painful, stop-and-go fashion, at about ten o'clock that evening, I reached Needles, a town on the West bank of the Colorado River. Needles was hot beyond belief, but it was in California!

I went to a motel (they called them auto courts in those days) and attempted to get some sleep. No sleep. Needles was not merely hot; it was unbearably humid. Soon after midnight I gave up my attempt to sleep and took to the road again. It was a long, hard rest-of-the-night and following day—more heat, more tire trouble, but the temperature cooled off as I approached Los Angeles. It was well after dark when I climbed Cajon Pass and started down to the Los Angeles Basin. The road was wide and smooth, the grade was steep, and my Model T rattled, clattered, and threatened to disintegrate as it reached unheard of speeds hurtling down that long mountain pass. Later, I rolled serenely on level roads; it was late at night, the air was delightfully cool, and I drove through miles of orange and lemon groves that perfumed the air with their blossoms. The Promised Land!

4

I checked in at the Los Angeles YMCA after midnight and slept until noon. Bathsheba worked in the Los Angeles garment district; I knew when she would come home. This was no time for a conventional reunion: waiting at her home, embarrassed, fidgeting; her parents trying lamely to make conversation.

I waited at the streetcar stop on Brooklyn Avenue. A half-dozen people got off the car with Betty. They were undoubtedly startled by what transpired. It took only a few milliseconds for me to know, surely, that I would not be sorry that I left good old Chicago and the All-American Radio Corporation. When Betty took me to her home, it was not an ordeal. Mama Landsberg was friendly; Papa, who had been an adventurous youth himself, was interested in details of my trip. Betty changed clothes, and we went out for dinner. A special occasion—costly ninety-five-cent dinners instead of adequate forty-five-cent meals. Afterward, we walked and talked. No rain—not in California in April, but even rain could hardly have made the occasion more romantic.

Betty worked for the Betty Brooks Company, a garment district shop that made ladies' dresses. She was the office manager, the accountant, and the supervisor of eight Hispanic sewing machine operators, a few of whom spoke English. Her salary was twenty-five dollars a week. She assigned work, tabulated the wages, and made out the payroll. She then went to the bank for payroll money, put the earnings, in cash, in neat little envelopes, and distributed the envelopes every Friday. She also was the first-aid person. If a

31

sewing machine girl stitched a finger instead of fabric, Betty disinfected it, bandaged it, and admonished the girl, in Spanish if necessary, to be more careful. The job was demanding; it kept her busy, as did rejecting the amorous advances of all four of Betty Brooks' salesmen.

I had time on my hands during the day. I knew I should get down to the business of looking for a job, but I delighted in exploring the golden new world of southern California. There was Long Beach, for instance, with units of the Pacific Fleet anchored in the harbor. In that era when automobiles tended to be ugly, the navy's lean, trim cruisers were beautiful—probably the most beautiful ships in the world.

San Pedro harbor was more in the waterfront tradition: sinister-looking bars, midday drunks lying on the sidewalk, shabby rooming houses with empty whiskey bottles in the gutter.

I drove over Cahuenga Pass to visit the San Fernando Valley. There were old, well-established communities in the valley: Burbank, Glendale, Lankershim (later to be renamed North Hollywood), Van Nuys, and the town of San Fernando, but much of the vast area of the valley was agricultural—hundreds of acres of corn, barley and alfalfa; groves of walnut, oranges, and lemons.

One morning I found a tour bus parked near the YMCA. A pitchman implored passers-by to come with him to inspect a marvelous new real estate development "on lovely high ground, on the shores of the mighty Pacific Ocean." An investment in this newly created paradise, the pitchman said, would undoubtedly make the investor very rich, in addition to that glorious opportunity—free lunch. The free bus trip appealed to me almost as much as the free lunch, and I allowed myself to be loaded into the bus. When we had about twenty passengers, we headed west on Sunset Boulevard. Sunset was well built up through Beverly Hills, but there were more and more open spaces as we went westward. After about a half-hour, our driver took side roads, even newly cut dirt roads. Eventually the bus stopped at the base of a small hill. We were herded out of the bus and climbed the hill, toward a tent with bright-colored pennants fluttering in the breeze. As we walked, we crushed bushy little bean plants, with pods ripe for harvest.

Our pitchman now became the assistant pitchman, because in the tent there was an even more persuasive orator, who assured us that to buy a piece—or pieces—of this incredibly valuable land would ensure wealth and happiness forever.

I did not intend to buy land, beautiful or not. I slipped out of the tent and looked around me. The surroundings *were* beautiful. The air was clean; there was perfect visibility in every direction. Catalina Island was sharp and clear, miles out in the vividly blue Pacific. The Santa Monica Mountains, still green from the winter rains, were a few miles north of where we stood.

A man whom I remember only as "Wise Guy" joined me and told me about the bean crop we had trampled. I had no overwhelming desire to know about the bean crop, but Wise Guy would not be denied.

"Dry farming," he explained. "They plough and disc and make furrows so the ground soaks up every drop of rain that falls in winter. Then, as early as they can, they plant these beans. They grow fast, the pods ripen fast, and you get a crop without ever using a drop of water."

The assistant pitchman came out then, headed us back into the tent, and we listened to more oratory about the immense profits to be made. The price was only seven hundred dollars per lot, one hundred dollars down, easy payments, ten dollars a month, no interest until paid. The land *was* beautiful, and the pitchman was eloquent. If I had been in an investing mood, I might have signed up. Several people did.

"Suckers," Wise Guy said.

I was inclined to contradict him, to speak of the clean air and the wonderful vista of mountains and ocean.

"Suckers," Wise Guy insisted. "These lots are worthless. No water. You can drill a thousand feet and not find water. What are you gonna drink? How you gonna flush your toilet? The suckers will pay for a while and then quit paying, and that sharpshooter in there will get the lots back and sell them to a new batch of suckers."

I ate two of the sharpshooter's box lunches but chose not to eat a third when the assistant pitchman glared at me.

Today, so many years later, I can see, in my mind's eye, the mountains, the ocean, and Catalina, clear in the distance. The angle to Catalina, the distance to the mountains and to the Pacific shore cause me to believe that the worthless land was in Brentwood and that the seven hundred–dollar lot, if one could find a vacant one, would now cost about six hundred thousand dollars.

The term *cash flow problem* was unknown in 1927, but it accurately described my situation. My cash was flowing out much too rapidly. The trip from Chicago had cost $120, car repairs included, but now I was paying an extravagant $1.25 a day for my lodging at the YMCA. I sought cheaper housing in the Boyle Heights area, where Betty lived with her parents. I found a "Room for Rent" sign on a large old house on Brittania Street, atop a steep hill. A small old lady rented me a room in the large old house for ten dollars a month.

I had been in my new lodgings for about a week when something happened that could have been devastating. In parking on Brittania Street, I used the approved steep-hill parking technique, approaching the curb at an angle, turning the front wheels as far right as possible, so that the entire weight of the car pressed the front wheels against the curb. That was supposed to make it impossible for the front wheels to straighten out and send the car careening downhill. That was what it was *supposed* to do.

I had gone to my room for only a few minutes. When I came out, my car was gone. Incredible—who would steal a superannuated Model T? Then I saw a small crowd at the base of the Brittania hill, where it dead-ended into a cross-street. Beyond the crowd, in an empty lot, I saw what seemed to be my car. I ran down the hill. The crowd, mostly women, surrounded me, screaming curses and threats. I learned later that my runaway Ford had scattered a group of children playing on the cross-street and had missed several of them by the narrowest of margins. I pushed my way through the crowd. The lot where my car came to rest was slightly below street level. It had smashed into an eight-inch curb on the cross-street, had become airborne, and landed upright and apparently undamaged. When I examined the car carefully, I found that it was not undamaged. The front tires were blown, and the front axle and steering arms were bent. I pushed through the crowd again and called for a tow truck. The tow truck man was also a mechanic; he straightened the front axle and the steering arms; and the cost, including the towing, was only forty dollars. Two new tires and inner tubes cost $25, and I was on the road again. What would have happened if my runaway car had hit some children? Even today, it is painful for me to think about it.

It took me several days to recover from the shock of the near-disaster and to look for work. I went to the major Los Angeles radio stations; I talked to the operators, trying to learn of any job openings. An operator at KFI, in those days the premier radio station in the Los Angeles area, told me he had heard of a job opening for a radio operator at the *Examiner,* William Hearst's Los Angeles newspaper. At the Examiner Building I learned that the job was with Hearst's newsreel operation. The head of Hearst's newsreel department had the idea that instant communication with home base would improve newsreel crews' efficiency. The radio operator would assist the newsreel cameraman and act as a semi-reporter, describing the content of the film that would be sent in. I pitched hard for the job. I said I was knowledgeable in photography, which was reasonably truthful, and assured the newsreel boss that I was articulate enough to make useful reports. I was sure that I had the job; then, suddenly, I was told that the whole idea was discarded. I was on the job market again.

Once more, making the rounds, I visited radio KHJ in Los Angeles. The station manager told me of a new radio station in Burbank. I did some rapid investigating. The station was KELW, in operation for only a short time. It was in Burbank city territory, but not in the city itself. I had an address: Magnolia Boulevard and Hollywood Way.

Again I drove over Cahuenga Pass, but this time, halfway down, I turned north on Dark Canyon Road. Long ago Dark Canyon Road was renamed Barham Boulevard. I didn't approve of the change. The name Dark Canyon Road had a fine, mysterious sound to it, it *was* in a canyon, and it *was* a road, a steep one, not a boulevard.

Where Dark Canyon Road leveled out, I turned right, past First National movie studio, without the slightest thought that I might one day work there. Then, left on Hollywood Way, about a mile, to the corner of Magnolia Boulevard. The real estate offices of Earl L. White, developer of Magnolia Park, were on the first floor of the corner building. The radio station and offices were in what appeared to be an added-on second floor.

I climbed a narrow stairway and presented myself to a secretary-receptionist. She took me to the manager of the station, a brisk, fast-talking man in his midforties, George Bunton. Bunton took my credentials; glanced at the operator's license, but seemed more interested in Charles Cushway's florid letter of recommendation. He then led me to the radio control room, where I met Stuart Wainwright, who built the radio station and would be my chief if I got the job.

It was a strange job interview. Wainwright studied my license but barely glanced at the Cushway letter. He cleared his throat and appeared to be about to say something, but he was a slow talker and Bunton was a fast talker. It appeared that Bunton had made up his mind to hire me even before I met Wainwright. Now, when Wainwright hesitated, Bunton brusquely announced that I was hired to go to work the next day. Looking at me, he said, "Thirty dollars a week." I nodded. Wages were low in Los Angeles, but the cost of living was also low. I'd get by on thirty dollars a week. Wainwright still looked as though he wanted to say something, but to Bunton, the job interview was over, and he walked out, briskly.

I was left alone with Wainwright. It was an awkward moment. He should have been given the chance to talk to me, to find out whether I was qualified for the job, whether I would work well with him. He should have been given that chance, but he hadn't. That wasn't my fault, but it left Wainwright resentful and considerably less than cordial.

Wainwright, in his midthirties, was medium everything: medium height, medium weight, medium hair color, and medium hair loss. He wore clerk-type metal-rimmed glasses, and when he spoke it was with a marked New England accent.

He showed me the transmitter and control equipment. He had built the 250-watt transmitter; he built it well and was proud of it. I admired the workmanship, and for a moment he almost warmed up, but that soon passed, and he was his unhappy self again.

We arranged a schedule. KELW broadcast four hours in the daytime, 10 A.M. to 2 P.M., and four hours at night, 7 to 11 P.M. Wainwright had been working both shifts, but it made for a long day. It was a light schedule for two men, however, and even with maintenance work it was no more than a five-hour day, six days a week. I was to take the morning broadcast the first week.

And so I began my job as operator at KELW. We were essentially a small-town radio operation, even though Hollywood and Los Angeles were no farther than a twenty-minute drive across Caheunga pass. We broadcast mostly records. Our entertainment was provided by unpaid volunteer performers. We had a number of local advertisers: restaurants, a furniture store, and a Chevrolet agency. The principal advertiser, naturally, was Earl L. White, the owner of KELW.

George Bunton, manager of KELW, was also the principal announcer. He shared the duties of announcer with the program manager, Harry James. The staff of KELW was small. Wainwright and

I, operators; Peggy Orson, secretary-receptionist; George Bunton, manager; and Harry James, program manager, an Englishman. An Englishman in the San Fernando Valley? How did he get there? I never found out. Bunton and Harry James were the announcers.

How Bunton came to KELW was easily accounted for. He was a real estate salesman for Earl White's Magnolia Park development and persuaded White to put him in charge of the radio operation when the station was built. Whenever Bunton was required, by a law that exists to this day, to identify his station every half-hour, he would intone, reverently, "This is radio station KELW, the Earl L. White station, the White Spot of the San Fernando Valley."

It was easy to adjust to Bunton. He was essentially a salesman, a pitchman, somewhat devious, inclined to take the course of least resistance. Harry James was another matter. I had never before had any contact with an Englishman. In my blue-collar neighborhood, in high school and in college, even at WENR, nary a Briton. This first encounter was with an Englishman who was snobbish, intolerant, rigidly moralistic, a ferocious censor at heart. And he was the program manager of our little two-by-four radio station.

George Bunton had one redeeming trait. He wanted KELW to be liked and listened to. He knew that we couldn't compete with the more powerful Los Angeles stations. His aim was for the station to be as neighborhood oriented as possible, which dictated our programming and studio setup.

There was a small open area between KELW's offices and the broadcast facilities. About twenty people could sit on folding chairs in this open area and watch both the studio and the transmitter and control rooms. By Bunton's orders, doors were left open to both places. I believe our little audiences got a sense of participation from the arrangement. Wainwright disliked the setup; naturally I enjoyed it. My door was open; a man named Billy Richards seemed fascinated by our equipment; I invited him to sit in the control room with me. When Wainwright found out about it, he was outraged, apparently he thought there should be something remote and mysterious about us, or it may be that he just didn't like people. Wainwright ordered me not to allow people in the control room. I was prepared for that. I said that Bunton knew of my visitors, approved, and that Wainwright would have to get Bunton's permission to bar visitors. He never pursued the matter; and I suspected that any hope of achieving a rapprochement with Wainwright was now dead.

Billy Richards was short, curly haired, and chubby—so youthful looking that it was difficult to accept the fact that he had been a mechanic and then a pilot in World War I. He was a man of importance in the community, master mechanic of the Glendale Fire Department and a civic leader. He wasn't merely a fan of KELW; he was also a performer. He sang and accompanied himself on his ukelele. It could have been terrible, but it wasn't. He had a good voice, sang with verve, and didn't hit many sour notes.

Very early in my tenure at KELW, I became aware of Harry James's desire to reform the nation's morals, beginning with KELW's broadcast policies. It was remarkable how he found vulgarity and obscenity where none existed.

I held the opinion, and still do, that the lyrics of popular songs were then, and still are, banal and stupid. And I knew, of course, that the popular song phrase "hold you in my arms" was a euphemism for more vigorous lovemaking. Harry James saw it that way, too; he saw the dreadful evil lurking behind the phrase and banned recordings with that dreadful, if remote, suggestion of sex.

Bunton was intensely conscious of public relations. He wanted his listeners to call in with requests; he practically pleaded for them when he was on the air. When a listener's request conflicted with James's arbitrary censorship, I managed through Peggy Orson to refer the matter to George Bunton. The listener won, hands-down. James was not deceived. He knew I was responsible for the setback to his purity program, and I now had another sour-faced sulker arrayed against me.

One interesting visitor to my control room was a young man named Lawrence Butler. He was eighteen years old, a senior at Burbank High School, and, like Billy Richards, was fascinated by broadcasting. He told me his father worked in the motion picture industry. To me the movie industry was remote and arcane, even though I could see the buildings of First National movie studio from our control room window. One day Lawrence took me to his home, a short walk from KELW. He opened the garage door. There, spread out on the floor for the paint to dry, were dozens of miniature French, British, and German World War I aeroplanes and four majestic miniature zeppelins. A wealthy young man was making a film about World War I aerial warfare, Lawrence told me, and was spending enormous amounts of money. The young man's directive to Lawrence's father, who was one of the best-known and highest-paid special effects men of that time, was quite simple: get it as good as you can, as quickly as you can; cost is no object. The well-heeled young man was hiring every pilot and every cameraman who applied. Lawrence didn't know the rich young man's name, but he thought the film was going to be named *Hell's Angels*.

I settled into a routine that was not unpleasant, and my five-hour work day (or work evening) allowed me ample time to pursue my courtship of Bathsheba Landsberg. We did the southern California things: we went to the beach on Sunday, attended concerts at the Hollywood Bowl, saw movies and amateur plays. We even attended a private showing of a film, *The Salvation Hunters*. The director, Josef von Sternberg, spoke after the silent film was shown. In a languid, world-weary fashion, he told us of the obstacles he had overcome, by sheer genius, in making his film. I was impressed. A real, live movie director! Betty said he looked like one of the Betty Brooks Company's amorous salesmen.

At KELW, James continued to be a pain in the buttocks, but his efforts to sanitize everything that KELW broadcast were thwarted by Bunton's dictum that what his listeners requested was what they got.

A couple of records should never have been broadcast. Harry James didn't object to them; he should have. Both were so-called "comedy" records. One was "Two Black Crows," by a couple of blackface comedians, Moran and Mack. The dialog was in the "Amos 'n' Andy" tradition, a pair of woefully uneducated black men trying to impress one another. There was one bit of dialog in "Two Black Crows" that people seem to remember. Moran asks Mack, "How do you spell Ohio?" Mack replies, "Capital O H ten." Brilliant comedy—not! It was dreadfully unfunny, but people requested it, and we broadcast it.

The other record was equally obnoxious. It too was a "comedy" record, "Cohen on the Telephone." It was a monolog—Cohen, a tenant, talking to his landlord, whom we never hear. This brilliant bit of comedy consists of Cohen trying to tell his landlord that a shutter is broken; he repeatedly says, "I do not say 'shut up.' I say 'shutter,' not 'shut up.' " Unfunny? Abysmal, but we got requests for it. One day I saw to it that an accident befell the record. I was able to tell callers, "Sorry, that record got broken."

Billy Richards continued to sing his songs and play his ukelele for us, but not as frequently as before. He was busy with the airplane he bought. Billy had been a mechanic in the Army Air Force—a very good one, by all accounts—and was rewarded by being given pilot training. His great regret was that he qualified as a pilot as the war was ending, and he never had the chance to fly in combat.

It is a disgraceful fact that in World War I, the United States, where heavier-than-air flight was born, did not produce a single plane good enough to fly in combat. American pilots flew British and French fighter planes. The United States did produce the Liberty aviation engine, which was supposed to be a marvel of power and efficiency but was not, and a great fleet of training planes— the famed JN series, affectionately called Jennys. After the war, hundreds of them were sold as war surplus, and Billy Richards bought one of them.

Richards spent many hours working on his Jenny and finally announced that I was going to be his first passenger. We met at an unpaved airstrip in Glendale. One of Billy's helpers spun the prop; the motor roared, and we bumped up the field to our takeoff position. I was in the front seat. Billy pounded the canvas back of my head, and when I turned, he yelled, "Here we go!"

We roared down the field. The Jenny seemed to be trying to get airborne but kept bumping back to earth. As we drew close to the end of the runway, Billy cut the engine and we slowed to a stop. No brakes on a Jenny, I was told later. If you had to stop fast, you pulled hard left or right rudder and lost speed quickly. Billy was disappointed. He pointed to the wind sock, hanging limply like a symbol of phallic disaster.

"Not even a breeze," he complained. "All we need is a little wind to help us get up. We'll try again. I gotta work on the valves."

Try again? When our lives depended on a capricious breeze to help us get into the air? I should have firmly rejected Billy's offer but instead agreed to try again when he finished his tuneup.

Small-townish or not, we had some genuine talent performing for us. Our unpaid baritone was an insurance man from Glendale; our soprano was a housewife whose home was not far from KELW. They sang solos and duets for us, and my opinion was, and still is, that they had good voices. They sang mostly sentimental love songs with syrupy lyrics that Harry James could not find fault with, but some of the music was excellent. It was in the love-song duets that something happened that was poignant and somehow special. They sang their hearts out—to one another. It was in their eyes, in every note of their song. I was sure of it: they were desperately in love, but he had a wife and she had a husband; and at that time Burbank was an Anglo enclave, as strait-laced as any Bible Belt town in Iowa or Nebraska.

Three months passed. I felt secure enough at KELW to get married. Wainwright agreed to take double shifts on Friday and Saturday, and Betty got leave from Betty Brooks. There was a wedding party of sorts at Betty's house in Boyle Heights: her mother, father, sister, and grandmother. Only three of us went to the Superior Court Building in Los Angeles, because only Betty, her father, and I could squeeze into the Ford. A Superior Court judge named Carl Stutsman performed the ceremony. I was not nervous or apprehensive, merely numb.

For our honeymoon, we went to Venice—not the romantic, historic Venice, but the grimy, tacky Venice in California. The view from our hotel room was an electric sign advertising White King Soap that flashed on and off all night. I violated all honeymoon protocol by getting violently sick Sunday afternoon, the last day of our idyll. It was dysentery, the most unromantic of ailments. Betty and I had eaten the same things; she did not get sick. In later years, she sometimes hinted that my illness may have been psychosomatic, caused by my belated realization that I was no longer a free man.

So ended our bargain-price wedding and our less-than-glamorous honeymoon. I have read about weddings that cost tens of thousands of dollars and vastly expensive honeymoons in Paris, Rome, the French Riviera. Then, a few years or even a few months later, equally costly divorces. Our cut-rate marriage fared better. We were stuck with one another, as Judge Stutsman said, until . . .

I packed up and left my hilltop room on Brittania Street and moved into an apartment Betty found just a few days before we were married. Our apartment was a so-called single: a living room, a kitchen, and a bathroom. Our bed was a Murphy in-a-door bed: pulled down, we had a bedroom; folded upward, it disguised itself as a door and we had a living room. Our rent was $22.50 per month, furnished, all utilities paid. We would manage nicely on our combined income of fifty-five dollars per week.

Back to work at KELW. Congratulations, heartfelt and sincere from Peggy Orson, effusive from George Bunton, grudging from

Harry James. Stuart Wainwright didn't even bother to be insincere. He made no comment on my new status and seemed to be a little more disapproving than usual.

Billy Richards continued to perform for us. One evening he announced that his flying machine was tuned up and ready to fly. I met Billy at the airstrip the next afternoon. Again, bumpy ride to the end of the airstrip. Then, roar of engine; we picked up speed, and just before the end of the runway we were airborne. We cleared the high-tension wires a thousand feet from the end of the runway by at least twenty feet. About three weeks later I saw the pathetic remains of a light plane jammed into one of the power-line pylons. But on this day we gained altitude over Griffith Park, skimmed over the tops of the Hollywood Hills, and circled the valley, flying inside the mountains that hem in the San Fernando Valley. Billy then showed me Magnolia Park from the air. Directly over KELW, he banked sharply so that I could look straight down. We were flying so low that I could see the faces of people looking up at us.

We flew over the downtown area of Billy's home base, Glendale. Again he banked the plane, pounded on the canvas skin back of my head to attract my attention, and said something that sounded like "fire."

Instant terror. What can a passenger do when a gasoline-laden wood-and-canvas plane catches fire? But Billy was merely pointing out his workplace, the Glendale Fire Department's Central Station. That moment of terror accomplished something that my common sense had failed to deal with. From that time on I politely declined Billy Richards's offer to take me joyriding in his baling-wire flying machine.

Autumn, the brush-fire season in southern California, is a worrisome time for people who live in the hills. In September, the Verdugo Mountains above Glendale and Burbank erupted in flames. Several years' growth of brush, tinder-dry from a long, hot summer, shot flames into the air that could be seen for twenty miles. Billy Richards came to me shortly after I had finished my daytime broadcast. He asked whether I could broadcast a plea for volunteers to help fight the fire. I didn't hesitate. I could have tried to locate Bunton or Harry James to get permission, but I didn't even consider it. I didn't want any quibbling or delays and, to be quite honest about it, I didn't want to share the excitement—and possibly the acclaim—for what I did. I put KELW on the air and, doing the announcing myself, put out an appeal for volunteer firefighters. Billy, meanwhile, was on the phone with his chief. These were the days long before air drops and tanker planes. It was also before the days of adequate radio communication for police and fire personnel. Billy's chief wanted us to broadcast instructions to his hard-pressed firefighters, on a long and dangerous front, in the hope that KELW's instructions would somehow reach them.

After a frantic half-hour at the station, Billy and I raced to the Glendale Fire Department. The harried chief was issuing orders like a general in the heat of a battle. An embattled fire crew at the extreme northern flank of the fire needed more fire hoses. Would I deliver them? I would! My vehicle was a small utility truck, not a fire-fighting vehicle, but it was equipped with a red light and siren, and I sirened and red-lighted my way at high speed through heavy traffic. It was exhilarating. It was a terrible thing to be in high spirits when the Verdugo Mountains were burning like the fires of hell, but I just couldn't help it.

Of course there were repercussions. Wainwright was too bloodless to be furious, but he came as close to it as his Casper Milquetoast personality would permit. He was incensed because I had acted without permission—from him, from George Bunton, from the district supervisor of radio, probably even from Herbert Hoover, secretary of commerce, the ultimate authority in all things connected with radio.

Harry James was angry and did nothing to conceal his anger. The cause of his anger was plain: he didn't care about permission or legality; he wanted the glory of making the dramatic plea for volunteers. The person whose opinion mattered was George Bunton, and behind him, I suppose, Earl White. Bunton, conscious of public relations as always, was delighted. There were items in several out-of-town papers about our broadcast, and a Glendale daily newspaper printed an interview with Billy Richards and me.

In mid-September I turned the gallant old Model T Ford out to pasture and bought another car. The Ford had not steered well after the accident at the foot of the Brittania Street hill, and Betty, who had learned to drive a gear-shift car, was unhappy with Ford's difficult gearless transmission.

We answered an advertisement in a local newspaper. A clergyman in Pasadena offered a low-mileage 1924 Essex two-door sedan for $135. The 1924 Essex was one of the ugliest cars of that ugly-car era, but we bought it, reassured by the belief that a man of the cloth would not resort to the practice of turning back the odometer or deceive us about the condition of the car.

As we drove the car, however, we began to find evidence that the car had more mileage than the seventeen thousand miles displayed on the odometer, and we discovered that the Essex had a glaring weakness. The man at the Essex factory who designed the engine apparently didn't communicate with the man who designed the chassis. Perhaps they didn't like one another—deadly enemies, perhaps; a quarrel over some girl? Whatever—the Essex was equipped with a large, heavy four-cylinder engine; the front springs were puny, unable to support the weight of that big engine. In the thirteen months we owned the Essex, we had to cope with five broken front springs. Could the Reverend have stiffed us about the mileage and withheld information about the breakable springs? A horrifying thought.

At KELW, James's efforts to purify everything we put on the air were sometimes grotesque. He found fault with Rudyard Kipling's "On the Road to Mandalay." Kipling is neglected today, but he was a poet and novelist of great talent and enormous productivity, and for James to censor an innocuous poem of Kipling's was ridiculous beyond belief.

We frequently broadcast a recording of "On the Road to Mandalay," the poem set to music. Sung by a baritone with pleasing vigor and verve, it was a favorite request among our listeners.

James might have found fault with Kipling's geography—and ichthyology. The first verse, for instance:

On the road to Mandalay,
Where the flying fishes play,
And the dawn comes up like thunder
From Rangoon across the bay.

First, flying fishes swim and fly, but if they play, do they play on a dry, dangerous road? And certainly not on a road to Mandalay, which is, according to a world atlas map, about four hundred miles from the nearest saltwater. That wasn't the basis for James's fault finding, nor was "And the dawn comes up like thunder." There seems to be no record of any person hearing a dawn come up like thunder, but if a person woke up at daybreak with a raging hangover, even the fluttering fall of a leaf—or a sunrise—might seem like thunder. And, finally, a massive error of geography. Mandalay is four hundred miles inland from Rangoon, a seaport at the mouth of the Iriwaddi River. (Try using *that* in a poem or a song.) There is nary a bay between Mandalay and Rangoon. No objection to the geography from James, and I, as a fellow poet, understand why Kipling wrote as he did. He was in love with the sound of Rangoon, Rangoon, Rangoon. What a wonderful, exotic place name to use as a basis for a poem.

What Harry James wanted to censor was another verse, an obviously sinful one:

Somewhere East of Suez
Where the best is like the worst
Where there aren't no ten commandments,
And a man can raise a thirst.

Sinful, according to Harry James. Kipling's words in the poem were presumably those of a British soldier on duty in the Far East. What did "Where the best is like the worst" mean? To me it sounded like poetic double-talk, but to Harry it meant that Kipling was accusing the virtuous British soldier of losing his virtue "somewhere east of Suez." And, finally, the damning words, "where there aren't no ten commandments." James's accusation was that by those words Kipling implied that all moral restraints were off—that the once-virtuous British soldier might even consort with native women. Unthinkable!

James pleaded his case for purity to Bunton, who listened impatiently and said, "All right, if it bothers you that much, we won't play it."

I disliked any victory for James's priggishness, and found a way to thwart it. During the evening broadcast, I answered the telephone and took requests. One of KELW's advertisers asked for the wicked "On the Road to Mandalay." I held the request slip up so that Bunton, in the studio, could see it. Bunton's look, through the glass window, told me "Harry won't like it." I pointed to the name of the listener. My body language said, "Who do we please, Harry or one of our best advertisers?" Through the glass, Bunton mouthed the words, "Play it."

The next day James was furious. Bunton told him that if a listener, particularly a revenue-producing listener, asked for a recording, he would *not* be told he couldn't have it.

James turned to me angrily. "You should have told him you didn't have it; it was broken."

I had him! The supermoralist was scolding me for not lying.

"Mr. James," I said piously, "are you asking me to *lie*? I can't do that."

Bunton was grinning. I knew he was annoyed by James's relentless rectitude, and was not unhappy to see him caught in his own trap—"Hoist by his own petard," is the saying. I believe it translates to "blown up by his own gunpowder." And Harry James, for the moment, was blown sky-high. Bunton ended the discussion by saying, roughly, "If anyone wants the damn record, play it."

I was smug and self-satisfied. I had defeated and humiliated Harry James; it didn't trouble me that he now joined Stuart Wainwright in his fervent desire to get rid of me. I wasn't worried. With George Bunton on my side, I couldn't be fired. But to my shock and dismay, I *was* fired.

5

My abrupt dismissal from KELW was caused by a fire that destroyed a pumpkin. In the 1920s, Los Angeles was notorious for bizarre eating places; a restaurant in a hat (The Brown Derby), a hot-dog stand shaped like a hot dog, a coffee shop housed in a shoe, a steakhouse in a pseudo-castle, complete with pseudo-moat and pseudo-drawbridge.

KELW was on the southwest corner of Magnolia Boulevard and Hollywood Way; there was a drugstore on the northeast corner. Earl L. White sold the lot next to the drugstore to a man who built a nightclub shaped like a pumpkin on it. The real estate transaction included the proviso that KELW would broadcast from the pumpkin, and Wainwright was given a directive to prepare for the broadcast. I assumed that the pickup would be by telephone line. I was surprised to learn that Wainwright proposed to extend a cable across the busy intersection. I didn't like the idea, but I lacked the engineering training to be specific, and Wainwright rejected my weak-kneed misgivings quickly and with more than a touch of contempt.

Dutifully, then, I prepared to help install the cable. Bunton recruited two men from the real estate office to help us. One was stationed on the roof of the drugstore to receive our cable; the other was to control traffic when I dashed across the intersection carrying the cable. The plan worked well. Wainwright lowered the end of the cable from the KELW roof; I took hold of it, waited for a lull in traffic, and ran catty-corner, as we used to call it, across the

47

intersection. I made it safely across, with only one near-miss from a motorist who saw no reason to slow down or stop because a civilian was waving one of Earl White's gaudy display pennants at him. Within minutes the end of the cable was in the pumpkin, and the cable was stretched high above the intersection.

Wainwright took a microphone and an amplifier across to the pumpkin, connected them to the cable, and sent a voice test back to me in the control room. Even in the routine testing, Wainwright's voice seemed to convey a note of triumph, as though he was relishing the victory of his idea over my faint-hearted objections. About a half-hour after the successful test, KELW went on the air with our daytime broadcast. Ten minutes later we heard a commotion, some shouting, and then the sirens of fire trucks. We ran out on the roof. The pumpkin was ablaze. By the time the firefighters arrived, the interior of the pumpkin was gutted.

Wainwright was concerned about the loss of the amplifier and the microphone. I had a more important concern; I was sure that we—KELW—had caused the fire. A technical explanation: when a broadcast is received, five hundred miles from the sending station, only an infinitely small portion of the broadcast power is received. In the immediate vicinity of the broadcasting station, however, there is a large amount of radio-frequency power, and any conducting medium, acting as an antenna, can collect a dangerous amount of radio frequency. At All-American Radio Corporation, my service department was directly under the WENR antenna. When we tested receiving sets, we used an antenna only five or six feet long. If we used a longer one, it picked up so much radio-frequency that arcs would flare up in the spaces of variable condensers. Those arcs were weird; my helpers and I could bend down and hear eerie, distorted speech and music coming from the odd-colored, hot little arcs. WENR's output was a thousand watts and KELW's was only 250, but our cable to the pumpkin became, in effect, an antenna five hundred feet long. It was, without a doubt in my mind, the cause of the fire. When I told Wainwright what I believed, he turned pale and seemed shocked, but recovered enough to tell me vehemently that my theory was false and utterly ridiculous.

When I arrived at KELW the next morning, workmen were cleaning charred rubbish out of the pumpkin. I glanced upward; the long cable was gone. At the head of the KELW stairway, Harry

James was waiting for me, displaying the kind of smile an executioner who loved his work might wear after a job well done. He ushered me into Bunton's office, where I was summarily fired. I was too stunned and hurt to demand an explanation, and none was given. It was a done deal. Bunton had prepared a tepid letter of recommendation, and Wainwright had taken my operator's license from the control room; Bunton had filled out the service dates and signed it.

I didn't need explanations; it had to be the fire. Cause and effect were too close together to be otherwise. But why me? Bunton may have been afraid that I'd go public with my theory about the fire; but it seemed to me that if I were fired, I'd be more inclined to tell the world about my warnings to Wainwright and the five-hundred foot antenna. My humiliation was too painful for me to think about getting even. I left Earl L. White's White Spot of the San Fernando Valley as fast as I could. I didn't tell anyone. Perhaps I should have.

KELW succeeded in covering up the affair of the burning pumpkin. For the coverup to succeed, it was probably expedient, if not honest, for Bunton to get rid of me. His reasoning may have been that I was too talkative and too friendly with people such as Billy Richards and Lawrence Butler to be an acceptable risk. He was probably right.

That evening I told Betty the story of my humiliating dismissal. She assured me that I was blameless and had been terribly wronged. That kind of support is one of the things wives are for. I then told her I didn't want to look for a job in Los Angeles; I wanted to go back to Chicago, where I was sure that I could earn more money. Ruth, in the Bible, said "Whither thou goest, I will go." Bathsheba, in Los Angeles, said, "All right. We'll go to Chicago. I'll have to give Betty Brooks a couple of weeks' notice." She was prepared, with not a syllable of protest, to leave family, friends, and the golden land of California for an uncertain future in not-exactly-golden Chicago.

And so we left Los Angeles. Once more, my life—now *our* lives—were turned abruptly in a new direction by an unpredictable event: the burning of a pumpkin. Gambler's odds on such an event? Perhaps five hundred to one?

We didn't go directly to Chicago; we went first to San Francisco. The federal bureaucracy, moving like a leisurely glacier, apparently considered Los Angeles a small, unimportant town. To take the government examination for radio operator, an applicant had to go to a more important city, San Francisco. My license had a respectable amount of service time, but it was a second-class license, and I knew I'd have a better chance in the Chicago job market with a first-class ticket.

We drove to San Francisco by the coastal route. It is a beautiful trip, even today, but in 1928 it was more beautiful: fewer houses, fewer auto agencies, fewer shopping malls, fewer everything.

In San Francisco, we rented a furnished apartment across the street from the Golden Gate Park panhandle. I enrolled in the YMCA radio school and, for two weeks of four-hour classes, I crammed for my examination. Betty and I had plenty of time to explore and to be enchanted by San Francisco. We went to the usual places: Golden Gate Park, Fisherman's Wharf, the Embarcadero, the Presidio and Fort Point, where approaches to the Golden Gate Bridge now soar high overhead. They were not usual places then; they were not self-conscious tourist attractions.

I passed my examination, receiving my first-class license. We prepared to leave for Chicago but were delayed for a day because the Essex broke another front spring. We lost not only the day; it cost an exorbitant forty dollars to have a surly mechanic remove the spring, weld it, and reinstall it. Then, finally, we were off to Chicago.

We had a final, magnificent view of San Francisco and the Bay as Betty, the Essex, and I crossed to Oakland by ferry. There were no bridges or tunnels then; people, automobiles, and even trains crossed by ferry. I chose a northerly route from Oakland because I didn't want to endure the searing heat of the Arizona-California desert again. It was springtime, however, and we found the temperature decidedly chilly as we began the long climb toward the Sierra Nevada mountain passes. In one deep valley near Emigrant Gap we encountered roads cut through large snowdrifts, and we drove between walls of snow, sometimes eight or ten feet high.

The high passes of the Sierra Nevada were difficult for our car. The thin, high-altitude air decreased engine power; the Essex struggled, overheated, and sometimes ground upward in low gear, but we finally crossed the summit. We made good progress the next few days, but always with the fear that if a spring broke, we might be stranded in some remote, uninhabited place.

Inevitably, a spring did break. Luck was with us; we broke down less than a mile from a small town, Medicine Bow, in Wyoming. A blacksmith named Jim Foley welded the broken spring. When it came time to pay, he asked diffidently, "Does fifteen dollars sound about right?"

It did sound all right, and we were on our way again. We spent a night in Sidney, Nebraska, in an auto court so primitive that the cabins were provided with kerosene lamps, and toilets were traditional Chic Sale[1] outhouses, with crescents carved in the doors.

We arrived in Chicago in midafternoon of our seventh day of travel, to an emotional reunion with my family. We were invited to stay in the house where my brother and sisters and I were born. In those days children of poor families were not born in expensive hospitals. We would have been much too crowded. I had been away for only a year, but I was shocked by how small and cramped our house now seemed. Narrow building lots permitted only narrow houses; there was no room for a hallway. There were three tiny bedrooms. One opened directly into what we called our front room; the middle bedroom opened directly into the dining room; and the back bedroom, the one I shared with my brother, opened into the kitchen, as did the bathroom, an emphatic *no!* in every modern building code. The bedroom my brother and I shared was so small that we had to kneel on the bed to open a dresser drawer; if we stood or sat in front of the dresser, there was no room for the drawer to open. One of Betty's aunts had an apartment with ample room for us. We accepted an invitation to stay with her while I sought a job.

As soon as I had access to a typewriter I composed letters of application to all of the Chicago radio stations. I couldn't wait for job offers to come in; our cash in hand was eroding rapidly.

As an interim measure, I answered a help-wanted ad in the *Chicago Tribune* and was promptly hired by the Grigsby-Grunow Company, manufacturers of Majestic radio receivers. Grigsby-Grunow had made an engineering change that made their receivers wildly popular. They devised circuitry that minimized midrange audio frequencies and greatly increased the low-frequency output of their sets, a change that provided a booming low-note response. Speech was almost unintelligible from a Majestic set; it sounded

---

[1]Chic Sale wrote a book, *The Specialist,* about a man who built outhouses.

like a voice from the bottom of an empty rain barrel, but radio listeners liked the window-rattling strength of the low notes in music.

My pay was $1.35 an hour to design, build, and maintain test equipment. Designing and building test equipment was not demanding. It was the maintenance of the equipment that was traumatic. I fell victim to the scourge of sex harassment. Women who worked on the assembly line *were* a problem. The first time I entered a workroom full of girls, I was greeted by a storm of whistles, yells, and indelicate suggestions. The girls were young, lusty, and uninhibited. Old man Rabelais would have been delighted by them. I retreated and came back with two grouchy, middle-aged men who did the required work.

I eventually escaped the sex harassment hell of Grigsby-Grunow. One of my letters of application brought a response from Howard Campbell, chief engineer of radio station WLS, owned by Sears-Roebuck, "The World's Largest Store."

I presented myself for a job interview. Campbell was a trim, well-tailored man of about fifty, his face pink and unlined, his iron-gray hair carefully groomed. Although he was not a short man, he wore elevator shoes. I handed him my licenses. He glanced at them with an air of bored impatience and pushed them back to me as though they were hardly worth his attention. When he questioned me, his manner was so brusque and condescending that I thought my job chances were somewhat less than zero, that he was merely warming up to tell me to get lost. Instead, Campbell abruptly informed me that I was hired; I would be a vacation replacement for each of the four studio operators. The job would be permanent, Campbell told me sternly, if I met his high standards of good conduct and efficiency. My salary would be sixty-five dollars a week; I would start with the morning broadcast the next day. Tommy Rowe, the chief studio operator, would put the station on the air at eight o'clock, and would spend the rest of the shift with me. With that Campbell strutted out. Campbell invariably strutted. I believe that he would have strutted escaping from a burning building.

I was jubilant when I told Betty about the job. Sixty-five dollars a week was more than twice as much as I was paid at KELW. Betty was delighted too. The nest-builder's instinct emerged; she would go apartment hunting the next day.

My orders were to meet Tommy Rowe at 7:30. I didn't sleep well, and arrived at the studio so early that a janitor had to unlock the studio door for me. I examined the equipment. It was a Western Electric installation, like WENR, but more elaborate. Some of the designations puzzled me, but I knew Tommy Rowe would explain everything.

At 7:30, two announcers arrived, then the organist. I introduced myself as a new operator and said that Tommy Rowe would take charge when he arrived. The reaction of the announcers was strange. The men looked at one another with what seemed to be questioning looks, then one of them looked at the studio clock; it told us it was twenty minutes to airtime. There was a direct telephone line to the WLS transmitter. I called the transmitter operator and introduced myself as a new man, waiting for Tommy Rowe. The man said, "Tommy Rowe? You'd better get started setting up. The announcers will tell you where to put the mikes and where to plug them in; and get that panel fired up, just in case Tommy's a little late."

A little late? Several hundred thousand farmers waiting for crop news, hog-belly prices, future quotes on beef, barley, and soy beans? Anxiety time!

With the announcers' help, I set up the microphones and began to activate the control room equipment, hoping that I was turning on the correct circuits in the correct sequence. Less than ten minutes before airtime, the volume indicator came to life and began to kick, responding to random noise in the studio. The transmitter operator called me. "You're OK. You're coming through."

"I can't hear anything," I told him. "The control room speaker is off and I can't find the switch."

"Don't worry. You're coming through."

Four minutes to airtime. The announcers were accustomed to working with word cues. Since I couldn't hear them, they agreed to use hand signals to cue me when to switch microphones.

At eight o'clock, exactly on time, WLS went on the air. The farm reporter informed his hundreds of thousands of farm listeners about hog prices, beef prices, corn and soybean prices; then he pointed to the newscaster. I switched microphones and the news went out to the waiting world.

Ten minutes later Tommy Rowe strolled in, unhurried, unconcerned. He waved to the announcers, glanced at the control panel and reached up casually to turn on the switch I hadn't been able to find. That was Tommy Rowe. I was angry; fear can readily change to anger, but Tommy said, "Aw, what the hell. You made it, didn't you?"

Betty found an apartment in a new building on Wilson Avenue, in what was then an upscale neighborhood in Chicago's North Side. Our rent was sixty dollars a month, furnished, utilities paid, which was more than double our Los Angeles rent, but I was getting more than double my Los Angeles pay. A Ph.D. in economics could write a scholarly paper about a fact like that.

After my hectic first day at WLS, things went more smoothly. Campbell didn't spend much time at the studio during the morning broadcast. When he did appear, he was imperious and impatient, as though he had business of great importance elsewhere. He would issue a few unnecessary orders, which were generally ignored, and would leave abruptly—strutting.

Before I left California, I wrote to my high school friend, Maynard Marquardt, telling him that I was coming to Chicago to look for a job. Throughout the years of our friendship, starting when we were schoolboys, we had a history of helping one another—a kind of young-boy network. When I was operating as chief operator at WENR, I used some high-octane tactics to help Maynard get a job at WCFL, Chicago. Now Maynard returned the favor. He got me the offer of a job as transmitter operator at WCFL, with permanent status and a salary of seventy-five dollars a week.

When I gave Campbell notice that I had another job offer, he reacted with anger and disbelief, as though I had repaid his kindness and generosity with treachery. I told Campbell I was prepared to stay at WLS as long as I was needed, but he replied coldly that he would do nicely without me, and I was invited to leave, immediately. As I left I felt certain that never, ever, to the boundaries of infinity would I get another job offer from Howard Campbell. I accepted the WCFL job offer quickly—and gladly.

Radio WCFL was owned by the Chicago Federation of Labor. It had considerable political power in Chicago, which may be why WCFL was enabled to install its transmitter on city-owned Navy Pier, which extended a mile into the waters of Lake Michigan. The WCFL studios were in downtown Chicago, a short run for the telephone lines that carried programs and an open-line telephone between studio and transmitter.

My assignment was night transmitter operator, on the air from six o'clock until midnight. There was no stress or anxiety during my first night on the job. The man assigned to instruct me was on time, meticulous in demonstrating equipment and procedures, and left me a checklist that included measures to take in an emergency.

The job of transmitter operator, if everything went smoothly, was not demanding. There was a routine: call the studio on the phone line, test to be sure the audio from the studio was of good quality, warm up the transmitter, put it on the air at the precise moment of airtime, and signal "go" to the studio. From then on, boredom was the enemy. A man who is lonely and bored needs friends, and I discovered that I had friends. Day-shift operators brought paper-bag lunches to work. They were careless with the food, leaving crumbs on the floor and half-eaten sandwiches in wastebaskets. At night, my friends appeared—mice, about a dozen of them, a happy mouse family enjoying abundant food and a peaceful environment. They were fascinating to watch. There was a wire-mesh wastebasket in the control room that was like a child's jungle gym to them. One after another they would climb up the wire mesh, reach the top, tumble in, and eat their fill of someone's discarded half-sandwich. One large mouse, possibly Papa Mouse, would climb up to my control panel desk and stare at me for a long time, probably wondering what I was doing there. *I* knew what I was doing there—I was enduring boredom for seventy-five dollars a week.

The boredom ended suddenly one night. Late in September there was a rainstorm that inundated Chicago. Our telephone lines from studio to transmitter began to fail as they were flooded. The last words I got from the studio manager were "Keep the station on the air, any way you can."

Keep the station on the air? How? I had a microphone, and I could go on the air with it, but what was I supposed to do—sing, tell jokes, dream up a brilliant monologue? There was one thing I might do: play records, if I could find some. I broadcast a hurried "Please stand by." In a storeroom I discovered an obsolete record player and a pile of ancient records. I wired the reproducer head to an amplifier and started spinning a record on the turntable. I was too busy to be nervous. I picked up my microphone and told my audience something like this: "I'm the transmitter operator here at WCFL, and the big storm we're having has cut us off from the studio. My orders are to keep the station on the air. I've found some old records and I've got one spinning now. I don't know what it is; I was too busy to look. Let's find out."

The random choice was a fortunate one. The record was old and scratched, but it was Irving Berlin's "Over There," a great favorite in the rousing days of World War I. There was a nostalgia factor there that the scratchy sound could not damage and might even have enhanced.

I had about forty minutes to sign-off time. I selected more records, picking the ones I could comment on. I praised the good songs, made fun of the corny ones, and called attention to the idiotic lyrics of some of them. As I drove home, I wondered what the studio bosses' reactions would be.

They reacted favorably. Most of the people at the studio said I did well. An officer of the Chicago Federation of Labor told the program director that he liked my ad-lib stuff better than some of the material that was usually broadcast.

I received a more solid mark of approval a few days later. I was asked to come to the studio for a meeting with one of WCFL's sportscasters, who began our meeting by telling me that everything we spoke about was confidential; I must agree to complete secrecy. Cloak-and-dagger procedures, in broadcasting? I agreed: secrecy, silence, sealed lips, Omerta—whatever.

The sportscaster asked whether I knew baseball, whether I had ever played the game. I told him that I had grown up just a stone's throw from Cubs' Park, that I had gone to many games before it *was* Cubs' Park, when the home team, the Chicago Whales, were members of the outlaw Federal League. Then, proudly, I told him I had been a member of the 1922 Lake View High School baseball team. I didn't tell him that I had been a benchwarmer until our catcher was hurt and I was pressed into service as a catcher. I had been a mediocre third baseman; I became a spectacularly bad catcher.

Repeating the need for secrecy, the sportscaster said that WCFL was negotiating with the Chicago White Sox baseball team to broadcast home games the next season. "We're just starting to talk deal," he said. "Any publicity right now might bollix it."

That's what he said: "Bollix it." The term "blow it" was not in use then. "Bollix it" conveyed the thought quite well.

The sportscaster continued. "Look, this is not an offer. It's just a would-you-be-interested thing. If we make the deal, we'll need an operator to handle the remote —you, maybe—and if you could fill in as announcer, do some play by play, maybe even take over during rain delays, it would be a good operation. Are you interested?"

Of course I was interested! I assured the sportscaster that I was not merely interested, I was enthusiastic; and that his secret was forever safe with me. We shook hands and I went on to my nightly rendezvous with the WCFL transmitter and my friendly little mouse family.

Betty shared my enthusiasm for my promising new job prospect, but our pleasure was tempered by the fact that we missed California—the clean air, the wide, uncrowded streets, the blessed sunshine. We had to be practical, however. We could save money from my WCFL wages, and one day we might return to California, but in 1928, a year of sudden change, events moved rapidly. I began the year at KELW. After my ego-bruising dismissal, we spent two weeks in San Francisco, and made the long cross-country trip to Chicago. I worked three weeks for Grigsby-Grunow and six weeks for WLS. Then, in my seventh week at WCFL I received a phone call—a most unlikely phone call—from Howard Campbell. His manner was brusque and impatient, as usual, but without rancor; he was businesslike and almost friendly. He informed me that he was chief engineer of the brand-new sound department at the United Artists movie studio, and he offered me a job, in Hollywood. I agreed quickly.

We were in the midst of preparations; Betty had bargained with our landlord to buy out our lease; I was loading household goods into the Essex when we received a telegram from Campbell. It informed me that he had hired Harold Witt, a WLS operator whom I knew, and suggested that we travel together. It was not merely a suggestion; it was an order.

I phoned Witt. Every operator at WLS had been offered a job, Witt told me; he was the only one who accepted. He too had received a telegram. It ordered him, in terms even stronger than in mine, to join with me and travel, as it were, in convoy. Witt was not happy with the order. He had a splendid new Nash roadster and he knew that I had a trouble-prone, aging Essex. He complained that he would be slowed down by traveling with us. And, he demanded, what right did Campbell have to dictate how we were to travel? Why would he, in Witt's words, "butt in with something stupid like that?"

"Because he likes to give orders," I said.

We discussed routes. Witt favored a southern route, through Missouri, Arkansas, and Texas. I believed that the southern route was longer and the roads probably not very good, but I didn't object. Witt was unhappy that his fast new car would have to "poke along," as he described it, with my plodding, box-on-wheels Essex; I chose not to add to his unhappiness by arguing about a route.

We left Chicago on October 10. I drove at my best speed, about fifty-five miles an hour. Occasionally, after following tamely for a time, Witt would lag behind, then speed up and pass us at a speed of perhaps seventy-five miles an hour. It was childish, Betty said. We knew his car was faster than ours; he didn't have to risk his neck to prove it.

Slow and steady may win tortoise versus hare races; it also allows travelers to achieve respectable mileage numbers. We made good progress down through Illinois, across southern Missouri and into Arkansas. Witt had stopped complaining. Then, inevitably, one of those misbegotten front springs broke. It happened in Benton, Arkansas. Benton was a sizable town, but in 1928 it was the quintessential southern town; no sweat, no strain, no hurry.

A mechanic at the Hudson-Essex agency told me that he could get me a new spring in a couple of weeks. A welder, the only man the mechanic knew who could repair the spring, had gone fishing. His wife didn't know where he went or when he would return.

Crisis time. Witt now had a good excuse to go on without us. We would have to sell the Essex and persuade Witt to take us with him. Betty set out to sell the Essex; I remained close to Witt. I appealed to his better nature, asking him whether he would really abandon us in this far outpost of civilization. His reply: "Damn right I would."

Betty found a buyer—a farmer, whose car had been demolished in a collision, had just been released from a Benton hospital. Limping, his arm in a sling, he drove a hard bargain. He offered twenty dollars for the car and everything in it. Betty protested that our household goods were worth more than a hundred dollars, but the farmer was adamant: twenty dollars. The deal was made. Witt's Nash was filled with his own possessions; we were able to take only a few things other than the clothes we wore. Crowded into the roadster, we resumed our journey.

Witt drove fast—much too fast. As it grew dark, he announced that he intended to drive all night, to make up for time lost in Benton. Betty and I were concerned, but there seemed to be only two

alternatives: get out and walk, or take control of the car from Witt
by force. Neither seemed to be an attractive option.

Some time after midnight, somewhere in East Texas, Betty fell
asleep. Then I fell asleep, and so did Harold Witt.

I felt a jolt, heard a thump, and awoke to find my face full of
leaves. We had gone off the road, into an area of tough, brushy
growth. Witt and I climbed up to the road. It was elevated, about
eight feet above the surrounding terrain, probably because the low
area was flooded during heavy rains. We saw, by the light of a quarter moon, that the road behind us went straight to the horizon. In
front of us, the road curved. Witt had kept to his straight course, left
the road, and had been airborne for about twenty feet before coming down to a relatively soft landing in the brushy thicket. Whatever those ground-hugging bushes were, they saved our lives. On
bare ground we would probably have rolled over, and with no seat
belts and only a canvas top over our heads, all three of us might
have required the services of some small-town Texas coroner.

Witt and I, on the ridgelike road, waited for help. Just after daybreak a farmer driving a tractor appeared. He attached a steel cable to the Nash and pulled it back on the road. The car was
scratched and dented, but thanks to our miraculous soft landing,
was otherwise undamaged.

On the road again, Witt drove more carefully, but he was alarmingly groggy with fatigue. In a small Texas cow town we stopped
to buy gas. Witt dozed off waiting for the fill-up. That convinced
him. In midafternoon we checked into an auto court; it proved to
be a noisy one. We discovered that the rip-roaring Old West was
not quite dead. Cattlemen, it seemed, and some 1928-model cowboys were having a boisterous get-together. They whooped it up,
noisily, played poker, noisily, and entertained ladies, noisily. We
were not kept awake very long. A typhoon couldn't have kept us
awake very long.

After a late start, we were on the road again. Witt no longer drove
aggressively, and I stopped asking him to let me share the driving.
We were not exactly comfortable, three of us crowded into a seat de-
signed for two, but at good speed the miles rolled behind us. New
Mexico and Arizona were surprisingly temperate, and three days af-
ter our brush with disaster in Texas we arrived in Yuma, Arizona.
California was a few miles away, across the Colorado River, with
Hollywood one day's drive before us. The Promised Land regained!

6

Our last day on the road: from Yuma to San Diego, our route took us close to the Mexican border, a hot and desolate journey; then, halfway to San Diego we encountered mountains with steep, winding roads. From San Diego to Los Angeles we had good roads and to the west, the cool, blue Pacific. We arrived in Los Angeles in early evening. Witt took us to the home of Betty's parents.

The next morning we borrowed Papa Landsberg's venerable Buick. Betty drove me to the United Artists studio and drove on to find a house for us. I crossed Formosa Avenue and entered the UA main gate. I was keyed up; I was entering a challenging and glamorous new field and a future full of uncertainties. My first encounters were with bureaucracy, not glamour. I was directed to the office of Sam Hill, studio superintendent, who gave me a studio pass identifying me as a sound technician. Next, to the payroll office, where I was told that I would be on the payroll as of that day. I was grateful for the twelve dollars and fifty cents I earned so easily. I would need many more twelve-fifties to buy clothes, household goods, and a car.

I phoned Campbell's office. His secretary informed me that Campbell would not be available that day. I was free to do as I pleased.

The streets and walkways of the UA lot were crowded with actors and extras dressed in the costumes of the French monarchy. Douglas Fairbanks was making a film, *The Iron Mask,* a sequel to his classic *The Three Musketeers.* Here, at last, was glamour.

61

When the actors and extras were needed, an assistant director ordered them back to work, and soldiers, priests, swashbucklers, and even Cardinal Richelieu obeyed his command. I was confronted by a sign: "Positively No Visitors Allowed." I was not a visitor, I told myself; I was a sound technician—my studio pass said so. I entered and no one challenged me.

What I saw was stunning; a huge set, a street of old Paris, filled with people, lighted by hundreds of arc lights. The big ones were called sun arcs, but the light they produced seemed whiter and bluer than sunlight. It was a noisy, crowded set; there seemed to be a dozen things happening at the same time. I tried to discern whether there was some sort of order in this chaos. My attention was drawn to a man who seemed to be in charge. He shouted orders in a strong, commanding voice, and men obeyed him; I learned that he was the boss electrician, called, appropriately enough, the gaffer. Then I saw that another man exerted a great deal of authority: Lucky Humberstone, the assistant director. Finally, I discovered that the gentleman sitting quietly in a canvas chair was the director, Allan Dwan.

I found myself wondering how we, the sound people, could fit into that turbulent new world and what changes we would bring. For one thing, the sun arcs would have to go. The heart of each arc light was an intense, white-hot electrical fire. The flames were fed by carbon rods; these had to be rotated—driven by electric motors—to ensure even burning. The stage was filled with the grinding noise of the motors and the high-pitched whine of the flames.

I watched for Douglas Fairbanks to appear. He had been my boyhood idol, when I spent my hard-earned ten cents to see a Saturday matinee at the Buckingham Theater on Clark Street in Chicago. Doug did not appear; a crowd scene was being made without him. After much order shouting and many rehearsals, the scene was filmed—several times—until the director was satisfied and called out, "Print that one."

The arc lights were switched off; the house lights seemed feeble and yellow after an hour of blue-white glare. The extras drifted out of the stage; I drifted with them.

I found our new sound building. It was not quite complete; workmen were putting finishing touches on the structure, and inside the building workers were opening crates of sound equipment. In what would become the recording rooms there were large cement pedestals; I was told that the recording machines were to be mounted on them. It seemed to me that we were many weeks from being able to go to work as soundmen.

That evening Betty told me that rents were low and many good houses and apartments were available; it was merely a matter of selecting the best one.

The next day I called Campbell's office; again I was told that he was not available. I was free to take the rest of the day off, if I wished. I did not wish; what I wished was to get started on what promised to be a demanding new job.

I went back to Doug Fairbanks's *Iron Mask* set. The mob of extras was still there in that huge street set; and on this day Doug was working. I moved as close to him as I thought was prudent, and I was able to see, at close range, the man whose muscular forearms I had admired on the lobby cards of the Buckingham Theater. I could not only see Doug but also hear him talk to his fellow workers, and I learned that he was an incorrigible prankster. One of Doug's diversions was the use of the electric chair, a canvas "director's chair," left invitingly unoccupied and connected to a Ford spark coil. When the victim was comfortably seated, he—or she—would be given a substantial shock and generally leap up with a startled scream. Great fun.

Doug's favorite prank, however, was to touch, or cause to be touched, someone with a sensitive rear—a practice known indelicately as goosing. One of those touched that day was a prop man named Kenny, who had the habit of gobbling like a turkey when his privacy was invaded. I was scandalized. It seemed to me that such conduct might be expected from a gaggle of sniggering schoolboys but that it was not proper entertainment for the greatest movie star of his time, a veritable king in Hollywood. But Doug's *droit du derrière* was not as deadly as the favorite pastime of his fellow monarch, Ivan the Terrible, who delighted in tossing peasants from the roof of the Kremlin to the pavement below. Doug's peasants merely cried out, or gobbled like turkeys, or tossed whatever they were carrying high into the air. I was told of a propman who was carrying a roasted piglet with an apple in its mouth. When he was skillfully touched, the propman shrieked and threw the pig a remarkable distance into the air.

"Can you imagine the mess?" my informant asked. "A nice greasy pig splattered all over the set? That made Doug enjoy it more than ever."

The following day I went to Campbell's office. His secretary told me that Campbell was still not available. Dorothy Roux had been Campbell's secretary at WLS and had come with him to Hollywood. She had many of Campbell's mannerisms: an air of impatience and a lack of civility. On this morning Roux informed me that Campbell might not be able to see me for several days. I was free to go home and take the rest of the week off—in effect, get lost.

I didn't choose to get lost. I wanted to see more picture making. In addition to *The Iron Mask,* two other silent pictures were filming at United Artists: *New York Nights,* directed by Lewis Milestone, and *Lady of the Pavements,* directed by D. W. Griffith. After the bedlam, excitement, and horseplay of the Fairbanks set, the *New York Nights* set seemed almost sepulchral. The scenes I saw were low-key dramatic scenes. There was sideline music: a violinist, a cellist, and a pianist who played on a small portable piano. There had been sideline music on the *Iron Mask* set, but the musicians performed only between scenes. It was obvious that mood music would not be helpful as Doug sprang from balcony to balcony or jumped from a lovely lady's window to pursue and climb aboard a fast-moving carriage. A full-fledged symphony orchestra might be appropriate, playing Wagner—loudly—with clashing cymbals, but not a hearts-and-flowers trio playing "Humoresque."

On the *New York Nights* set, Norma Talmadge and Gilbert Roland were filming a love scene. The musicians scratched out sentimental music. Lewis Milestone didn't coach his players during the scene, as directors of silent films were presumed to do; he sat beside the camera, watching closely.

I could hear bits and pieces of what Talmadge and Gilbert Roland were saying as the scene was shot. In silent films it didn't matter what the actors said, and there are many tales about outrageous things players did and said during what were supposed to be tender love scenes. It didn't matter what they said, unless some sharp-eyed viewer lip-read their X-rated ad-libs.

I listened as best I could. Talmadge was barely audible and, while emoting vigorously, spoke a kind of mundane double-talk—something about new clothes and a coming holiday. Gilbert Roland, however, a spectacularly handsome young man, responded eloquently with genuine love talk, in a fervent mixture of English and Spanish.

D. W. Griffith was making *Lady of the Pavements,* with Lupe Velez and William Boyd, who later became early TV's Hopalong Cassidy. I knew Griffith was a legendary figure, one of the great men of the early cinema. *Lady of the Pavements* was a costume drama, set in the Paris of about 1850. The set Griffith was filming that day was the interior of a dive called "The Smoking Dog."

Lupe Velez finished a scene, and Griffith told her to change her costume. The wardrobe woman had Lupe's costume ready and started to lead her to her dressing room. Lupe said, "We don't need no dressing room," took off her dress, and posed provocatively for a moment before she put on her new costume. People on the set took the episode in stride, but I was shocked. Not that Lupe had revealed much flesh—the swimsuits that innocent high school girls wear today reveal far more epidermis than Lupe did that day. Nevertheless, I was shocked. I suppose I was born square, and the sharp corners had not yet rounded off. As for Lupe, I believe she was merely trying to live up to the publicity department's selling of her as a tempestuous, uninhibited Mexican pepperpot.

Days later I was summoned to meet Campbell. There were no friendly preliminaries, no "Did you have a good trip?" or "Welcome to Hollywood." Instead, he complained about the pampered, entrenched movie people, the producers, directors, and cameramen. "They don't like us," Campbell said. "They don't like sound; they wish we'd go away, but we're not going away." His theme was that if you gave those motion picture autocrats an inch they'd take a mile. His response was that we would not give them that inch. I was troubled by Campbell's intransigence. I felt that it would make the transition from silent to sound film more difficult and certainly more abrasive.

The day I received my first paycheck, Betty and I rented a small house at 1305 N. Sycamore Avenue in Hollywood, a ten-minute walk to the studio. It was unfurnished, except for a stove and an icebox; the rent was thirty-five dollars a month. That afternoon we bought furniture from a secondhand store: a bed, a kitchen table and four chairs, two carpets, and an alarm clock. We loaded them in the Buick; since it was a so-called touring car, without its canvas top it made an admirable truck. We then shopped for bedding, kitchen utensils, and clothing, which we piled on top of the furniture. We probably presented a Beverly Hillbillies image long before the TV series was even a gleam in the producer's eye.

Betty cleaned the house vigorously; I scrubbed the stove and icebox with equal vigor; and when I invested twenty-five cents in a chunk of ice for our icebox, we were a functioning household. We needed a place for our clothing and our linen. Betty piled three orange crates atop one another, and with a colorful towel to decorate the top, we had an open-face substitute for a chest of drawers. We never considered installment buying or borrowing. We adhered to a simple economic principle: if we couldn't pay cash for it, we couldn't afford it.

Back at the studio after the move-in weekend, I saw redoubled activity in the sound building; more men opening more crates and more electricians pulling more wires through conduits. A man in a business suit was also watching. He shook his head and turned away as though what he saw pained him. "Lots going on in there," I said.

"There certainly is," the man replied. "On overtime." His name was Dent, and he was a member of the UA accounting department. His responsibility was cost control, and he was not happy about skyrocketing costs. It was the fault, he said, of the UA partners, who wrangled and complained and failed to agree on a plan of action. Joseph Schenck, the executive the stars had taken in as a partner, had given an interview in which he said that sound pictures were a mediocre novelty and predicted that they would not last more than three or four months. Dent credited Mary Pickford, whom he regarded highly, with forcing her partners to stop bickering and come to a decision. She was convinced, Mary told them, that sound was not going to fade away; and, much as she disliked doing so, she would vote to convert to sound. Her partners agreed, reluctantly, but their indecisiveness had caused the loss of three or four valuable weeks. "Now we're trying to catch up," Dent said. "On overtime."

In the back-lot area of United Artists studio, an old set was torn down and a new one began to take shape. It was to be a mountainside set, the construction foreman told me, for an added scene for the film *Eternal Love,* directed by Ernst Lubitsch. It took only a few days for the framework of lumber to be transformed into a plaster-of-paris mountainside. A wire-mesh cylinder was installed above the set; it provided snow, the foreman told me. It would be filled with bleached corn flakes; shaken gently, the device would produce a light snowfall. Shaken vigorously, it would produce a blizzard. The scene to be filmed called for an avalanche, which would crash down when several large bins, loaded with corn flakes, gypsum, and chunks of white-painted cork, would be dumped on the actors below.

On the day of the filming, I was one of a crowd of spectators. United Artists studio, unlike many in Hollywood, permitted visitors. This day there were a dozen middle-aged, prim-looking ladies, probably members of a club. Arc lights glared, and a battery of wind machines, powered by World War I airplane engines, stood ready to blast the set with blizzardlike wind. The star players appeared, John Barrymore and Camilla Horn. The scene called for Barrymore to carry Horn up the mountain trail. For the rehearsals a double for Barrymore carried a double for Horn. They rehearsed the scene many times, for Lubitsch and for the cameraman; with heavy snowfall, light snowfall, and no snowfall. The avalanche was not rehearsed. It would take several hours to refill the bins.

Finally, everyone was ready. An assistant director, armed with a pistol, was stationed to fire blanks and stop everything if the scene had to be cut.

The take: glare of arc lights, roar of wind machines; Barrymore, carrying Horn, struggled up the path, then stumbled and nearly fell. Lubitsch rose from his chair and called out to cut the scene, but no one heard him; and the assistant with the pistol forgot the pistol, forgot what he was supposed to do, and the blizzard raged on. The men on the avalanche bins heard no shots and dumped their bins. Barrymore and Horn were engulfed in a gritty, dusty mess. Finally, one by one, the wind machines were shut down. Barrymore struggled clear of the corn flakes and the gypsum, leaving the beautiful Miss Horn to fend for herself. In his splendid Shakespearian voice, he went into the questionable ancestry of everyone concerned; the main thrust of his remarks was what he intended to do to the assistant who had failed to fire the gun. He proposed, with somewhat earthy terms, to take the gun from him and thrust it forcibly into his rectum. Not feasible, of course, but threatening to do so may have soothed some of Barrymore's outrage. And what of the visitors, the prim and proper club ladies? They were scandalized, of course, but titillated as well. They'd have something to talk about for weeks to come.

The sound building was finished. The swarm of workmen departed, and Western Electric engineers began to test the recording equipment. Since that equipment and the way it was used had a significant effect on the quality of the early sound films, a look at the four sound systems in use in 1928 might be of value.

There were the Warner Bros., with Vitaphone. They lit the firecrackers that caused the film industry to stampede to sound; and they did it with a system, disc recording, that was impractical for motion picture production. Disc recordings could not be edited; it was one thing to put a recorded song on a disc, with an ad-lib by Al Jolson at the end of it; it was quite another to edit a fast-moving melodrama, in which there might be a dozen short scenes—"cuts"—in one minute of film. And using disc sound in the theater was trouble-prone. A projectionist had to possess keen eyesight and a steady hand to place the stylus on the correct starting point. If he missed by only one groove the movie was grotesquely out of sync, which generally caused the audience to laugh or to yell angrily and throw things. The Warner Bros. saw the light and changed quickly to sound on film.

The Fox studio had its sound system, Movietone, first used in newsreel cameras as a "single system"; sound and picture were recorded on one negative in the camera. The heart of this system was a gas-filled tube, called an AEO light, that, when activated by an audio input, responded by producing sound-modulated light that could be photographed. When the AEO light was used in a separate recorder, the film could be edited, but the quality was poor, and the Fox-Case system soon went the way of Vitaphone and the carrier pigeon.

The RCA system, Photophone, was also an optical sound system. It employed a galvanometer-type device in which a tiny mirror twisted and turned in response to sound waves and photographed those sound waves on film. This produced a negative, white on black, in which the profile of the sound resembled a mountain range with many peaks and valleys. Printed, the mountain range became black; the background white. Photophone could be edited and development and printing of the film was not critical.

The United Artists studio used the Western Electric variable-density sound system. The sound image was recorded not as a black-on-white mountain range but as a series of black, white, and gray bars of infinite complexity and accuracy. The heart of the system was a brilliant invention called a light valve. A pair of ultra-light metallic ribbons provided a slit through which a strong source of light was focused on the film as it passed through the recording machine and photographed the sound. The Western Electric light valve had one significant advantage over the RCA mirror-galvanometer: the light-valve ribbons were so light that they had no measurable inertia. The RCA mirror, although it was made as light as possible, had an appreciable degree of inertia, so that it resisted modulation by faint sounds and tended to overmodulate loud sounds, a flaw generally called volume expansion. It was not a serious problem; RCA variable area sound and Western Electric variable density sound served well until magnetic sound—tape recording—replaced them in film production.

The man who invented the light valve may have been a genius, but the engineers who designed the other Western Electric equipment were decidedly not. Everything they provided for us was oversized and overweight. They must have come straight from designing battleship hardware, because, for studio use, they made liberal use of bronze, which resists saltwater corrosion but is heavy. Saltwater corrosion is not a serious problem in Hollywood. The engineers' masterpiece was a portable mixing panel. It was made not of bronze but of steel, and it was portable, after a fashion; it had a pair of handles, and two strong men, chancing the peril of hernia, could carry it.

The cables and cable connectors were also grossly overweight. We called the bronze connectors "pineapple connectors," because they were roughly the size and shape of large pineapples. I have a personal grudge against them. A pineapple connector broke my nose. We carried coils of cables on the roof of our sound truck. I stood on a ladder to take down one of the cables. When I lifted it, a connector, not properly secured, swung free and smashed my nose. I dropped the cable and nearly fell off the ladder. Had I fallen, I might well have broken my neck, my head, or both. A studio driver took me to a doctor, who stuffed my nose with cotton, told me to use an ice pack, and assured me that my nose would heal straight. A prizefighter's bend might have made my unremarkable nose more interesting.

It was inevitable that the microphone Western Electric provided for us would also be heavy. Officially, it was called a condenser-transmitter-amplifier, or CTA for short. The nature of a CTA required that an amplifier be a part of the device; this added to bulk and weight, so that the CTA weighed about eight pounds;

and, naturally, it was encased in bronze. The result was that this electronic heavyweight, which should have been light, agile, and capable of quick movement, proved difficult to move. Because of its size, it was even difficult to conceal in the benighted days when we hid microphones in flower arrangements and behind curtains.

The size and weight of the equipment may have added to the difficulty of making the first sound films, but it was the manner in which we used that equipment that affected, for better or for worse, our first productions. Too frequently, our methods were not helpful. Western Electric people finished their tests and turned the equipment over to us. We began testing, but our tests were essentially useless; there was no consideration of the way the system would ultimately be used. Several of the infamous camera booths had been built; we could have requested a camera crew and actors for a full-fledged camera and sound test, but we did not. In short, we were given no training in actual picture making.

The time came—inevitably—when we had to begin the work we were being paid for. In the beginning, there were sound and photographic tests of actors and actresses, talking prologues for otherwise silent films, and talking-picture segments for those abominable hybrids, part-talking films.

I worked on several of these fragments. Their dates are of interest; it would be helpful to have such a record. I had one, but it is lost. When I came to United Artists, I needed only a few days to realize that what we were doing was of importance to the movie industry, to the people who went to movie theaters, and, incidentally, to me. I began to keep a day-by-day journal, not a "Dear Diary" affair of secret thoughts and weighty opinions, but a bare-bones account of what we did and how we did it, day by day.

In 1973, the Motion Picture and Television Library of the University of Wyoming solicited documentary material from me. I was flattered by the request and contributed scripts, photographs, correspondence, and my diary, with the understanding that the material would be available to me at any time. When I asked for the diary, I was told, regretfully, that it could not be found; it was lost, gone, vanished.

I sorely need the dates and the facts that were in the diary. Without them, I can only guess at the sequence of events and perhaps forget some of the happenings of that turbulent time.

Tests of actors and actresses probably came first in our ventures into sound-and-picture shooting. We tested two beautiful young actresses, Camilla Horn, who starred with John Barrymore in *Eternal Love,* and Vilma Banky, a star in many of Sam Goldwyn's silent films. The lovely ladies were early casualties of sound. Middle European accents can be charming and sexy, but Camilla Horn, German, and Vilma Banky, Austrian, had less-than-charming Teutonic accents, the kind of exaggerated accents the so-called "Dutch" burlesque comedians used. The careers of these beautiful ladies were severely damaged. Camilla Horn made a few films in England; Vilma Banky made no more films but starred in another field of endeavor. She married actor Rod La Rocque, became an outstanding golfer, and won many tournaments.

Another series of tests brought distressing results. Mary Pickford's cameraman was Charles Rosher, one of the great cinematographers of the silent era. Rosher began his association with Mary in 1918, and photographed most of her hit films that solidified her position as America's Sweetheart. Mary was concerned about her screen appearance, and with good cause; she had bought the successful play, *Coquette,* and chose, as her first talking-film role, that of Norma Besant, a flirtatious, headstrong southern belle. She made tests, first silent, with an open camera, then with sound, the camera in one of the hated camera booths. Mary, a dedicated, hard-working filmmaker, was aware that the camera booth was a formidable handicap; it robbed the camera of its mobility. Worse, it caused inferior photography; shooting through a pane of plate glass caused superb lenses to become mediocre ones. A young camera assistant told me, "You shoot out of one of those damn booths, and what you get is flatter than a platter of pea soup." I think he said pea soup.

After a series of sound tests, Mary was dissatisfied with the way she was photographed. In what must have been a bitter confrontation, she ended her long, productive association with Charles Rosher. Perhaps Mary discharged Rosher, or he may have lost his temper and quit. The opinion in the studio was that Mary had fired him. It must have been a heart-wrenching decision, but Mary's career, inexorably, came first; her future depended on how she looked as a very young woman.

In Scott Eyman's excellent book, *Mary Pickford, America's Sweetheart,* he tells us that Mary discharged Rosher because he called "cut" during an emotional scene when a shadow fell across her face. Apparently Mary told this version in an interview years later. This version is not accurate. Apparently Mary could not face the pain of telling what really happened, so she created a spontaneous, emotional reason for her break with Rosher rather than admit to a calculated, career-motivated decision.

Mary's version does not fit the facts. Rosher photographed only tests; Karl Struss was the sole *Coquette* cameraman. As for the emotional scene Mary spoke of: she would not have chosen to play such a scene in a photographic test. Whatever the cause, her loss of Rosher added one more heavy burden. It followed the death of her mother the year before, and there was the looming menace of sound, which threatened her place in the hearts of millions of fans.

There were more tests; then, finally, we began to work on film that would go into theaters, film that people would pay money to see—and to hear, such as sound sequences inserted into silent films.

One of the monstrosities of those days was the part-talking picture, such as *New York Nights*. I didn't work on the sound sequences, but I saw the result. The film came on, silent, with a recorded musical score, the photography beautiful, the music reasonably good. Then suddenly, with a jolt, the talking sequences came on, the photography flat (those damned camera booths), and the sound raucous, scratchy, and much too loud. I could understand why the old-line producers and directors hated us, with our obnoxious microphones and two-ton camera booths and camera motors that ran backwards. We were interlopers, a bunch of young upstarts who were destroying the beautiful art form they had spent years perfecting.

My first work on made-for-the-theater film was a talking prologue for Doug Fairbanks's *Iron Mask*. I saw Fairbanks at his carefree, prankish best during the silent filming of *The Iron Mask*. Then I saw what the coming of sound did to him when we filmed a talking prologue for the picture. A ten-foot-high blowup of a page of the Dumas novel, simulating ancient parchment, was mounted in a frame. Doug slashed through the page with his sword, sprang into the foreground, and delivered his prologue speech. We did the scene over and over—and even after all these years, I can remember Doug's lines: "Out of the shadows of the past, as from a faded tapestry dim and vast, I bring you a tale of long ago."

Finally, we got a complete take, and, as was the barbaric custom in those days, we played it back. Sound equipment was touchy and inefficient then. Sometimes speed would go out of control. When we made that playback for Doug, we had a "runaway" on the wax playback machine, just fast enough to give Doug a girlish falsetto. Mercifully, somebody pulled the loudspeaker plug, but I think Doug never really recovered from the shock of hearing that gibbering runaway version.

There is something of a mystery about that prologue. My research assistant, Edward Watz, has provided me with a videotape of *The Iron Mask* and a review of the film from *Variety* of February 27, 1929: "His [Fairbanks's] direct vocal address is in the form of minute and a half appendages as prolog [*sic*] to the first and second halves of the show. There is no other dialog at any time." The videotape, a 1940 reissue with spoken commentary to replace the on-screen titles, opened with a prologue in which Doug appeared in a sylvan setting with his three comrades. I'm mystified; what happened to my sword-slashing version, my first foray into ticket-selling production?

The first all-talking picture to go into production at United Artists was *Alibi,* a crime melodrama. There was an unfortunate breakdown in communication between camera and sound, director and film laboratory. Nobody told the camera crew that they had to give up part of their film area to make room for the sound track. In silent filming, the cameraman could use the entire 35mm width of his film, with the traditional aspect ratio of three to two. Sound on film, however, required that the sound track be printed beside the picture and that the 4mm width of the sound track had to be taken away from the cameraman. He not only lost the left edge of his negative; he also lost his 3-by-2 aspect ratio. The remedy was to use a new, smaller aperture in the camera that maintained the classic 3-by-2 ratio and, of course, ceded the left edge to the sound track. But no one informed Ray June, the cameraman, or Roland West, the director. The cause of the communication meltdown may have been that many studio people were thinking of Vitaphone, of sound-on-disc, in which optical sound track would be re-recorded on disc for theater release. That technique had been abandoned by most of the Western Electric–equipped studios, but no one told anyone.

About half of *Alibi* was shot before the error was corrected. The result was that well-composed camera angles became poorly composed, and scenes in which there was action close to the left frame line lost that action. Some of the damage was replaced by close shots, retakes, and inserts, but June was disconsolate. Many of the scenes on which he spent time and effort were still mutilated.

I worked with the great one, D. W. Griffith. The film was *Lady of the Pavements,* the production in which I had seen Lupe Velez do her semistriptease. We recorded a few scenes to make it one of those odious part-talking pictures. The old master didn't seem to be awed by sound; he took the sound sequences in stride and handled them with skill and assurance. Having worked with D. W. Griffith, I have a claim to fame. In fact, from time to time I have suggested that my left shoulder be designated a historical object, because that shoulder was the one that the master patted as he assured me, in his rich, theatrical voice, "I understand, my boy. I quite understand."

To replace a soundman who had the flu, I worked for a few days on the all-talking film *The Locked Door,* directed by George Fitzmaurice, starring Barbara Stanwyck and William Boyd, who was known in Hollywood as "Stage" Boyd, to distinguish him from the Bill Boyd who would one day become Hopalong Cassidy. Despite his Irish name, Fitzmaurice was a Frenchman, a portly man with one of the reddest faces I have ever seen—a magnificent example of what we used to call a bourbon blush. Fitzmaurice had directed *Son of the Sheik,* Rudolph Valentino's last film, and the hugely successful wartime drama, *Lilac Time.* He was noted for his visual style, but his visual style was of no help with his camera locked up in a glass-fronted tomb. Fitzmaurice seemed to be nervous rather than excitable, as a proper Frenchman is supposed to be. He appeared to be confused by sound, and his strong French accent hindered communication with his cast. Even Barbara Stanwyck wasn't able to do much with the lifeless material. In release, *The Locked Door* suffered a sad fate. At a time when almost any film that talked or made noise was successful, it was a solid flop.

One of those who truly hated the new medium was Sam Goldwyn. We soundmen in those days used monitor booths—glassed-in rooms suspended from the walls of the sound stages. The men who designed the early sound systems thought we needed a full set of theater-type speakers to monitor the sound quality properly, a far cry from the featherweight set of earphones the soundman uses today.

I was in one of those monitor booths during filming of *Bulldog Drummond,* Goldwyn's first talking picture, starring Ronald Colman and Joan Bennett. Goldwyn and his aide, Mike Levee, completely ignoring the presence of the soundmen in the booth, argued violently about continuing to make sound pictures. Goldwyn disliked the way *Bulldog Drummond* was going. He said that Colman's acting was ruined by sound, and that Joan Bennett, "such a beautiful girl, she don't look so good when they have to photograph her out of those goddamn doghouses." Mike Levee argued that sound was here to stay and that sound and picture quality would improve. Not a bad prediction.

I had done many bits and pieces of film, but I lacked even one complete picture credit. I attempted to talk to Campbell about it, but his autocratic attitude was beginning to cause problems and he was in no mood to listen to complaints. Campbell had clashed with a man whose ego was just as gigantic as his own. The man was Dr. Hugo Riesenfeld, UA's musical director.

7

When the stampede to sound picked up speed in the summer of 1928, the Hollywood studios had millions of dollars' worth of silent films on their hands. As more and more theaters installed sound equipment, the studios, including United Artists, attempted to salvage what value they could by providing recorded scores for silent films, calling them Sound Pictures.

UA had a half-dozen of such silents. Three of them—*Woman Disputed* with Norma Talmadge, *Revenge* with Dolores Del Rio, and *The Awakening,* produced by Samuel Goldwyn and starring Vilma Banky—were scored in New York by a formidable composer-conductor, Dr. Hugo Riesenfeld. When the UA sound equipment was ready, we prepared to record music for our Hollywood productions. Campbell welcomed the opportunity to supervise the scoring of UA films. To musicians at radio WLS he had been a dictator. Microphones were placed where he said they were to be placed, and bands and orchestras were arranged as he ordered. Campbell expected to exercise the same kind of authority at UA, but at the first scoring session he was confronted by Dr. Riesenfeld, a musician with Albert Einstein hair, a Charlie Chaplin mustache, and a fiery temper. They did not establish a cordial rapport. The doctor insisted that *he* would place the microphones, *he* would arrange the orchestra, and *he* would instruct the man in the monitor booth how to handle the mix of three microphones.

The men argued, nose to nose. It seemed that affairs were at an impasse, but Riesenfeld called in his heavy artillery. He proposed to invite Doug Fairbanks, Mary Pickford, and Joseph Schenck to arbitrate the issue. Campbell hastily backed away from the confrontation. He had been told that the doctor was held in high esteem by Doug and Mary, but he had been too self-assured to consider the consequences of a clash with Riesenfeld. He retreated to his office, while the doctor placed the microphones where *he* wanted them, and the scoring proceeded more or less serenely. Advantage: Riesenfeld.

There were further consequences of the Campbell-Riesenfeld imbroglio. Another doctor appeared, one J. P. Maxfield, a Ph.D. in architecture, his specialty: acoustics. He had been hired by the UA partners to assist Riesenfeld in obtaining the best music-recording quality.

Maxfield arrived and went to work immediately. Attended by Riesenfeld and his entourage and Campbell and his people, Maxfield began what to us seemed to be a weird routine. He went to the center of the empty scoring stage, clapped his hands, then quickly cupped his ear to listen for reverberations. He repeated the process from all points of the stage. We soundmen, with not a single Ph.D. among us, wondered whether this was a sober, scientific procedure or a gigantic practical joke. Finally, we were informed that the doctor had found the best places for our microphones: he called them "nodes." Riesenfeld expressed his approval of Maxfield's microphone placement; the UA partners thanked Maxfield for his contribution to better UA music. It was another defeat for Campbell. Advantage: Riesenfeld—again.

Maxfield should have quit when he was ahead. Roland West, director of *Alibi,* was an interested observer of Maxfield's tests. The men talked. Maxfield asked about the on-the-set recording techniques and was appalled when West told him that the soundmen positioned their microphones over the actor's heads, as close as the camera line would permit. That was wrong, Maxfield said. The ears of the audience were not above the actors. Their ears—the microphones—should be where their eyes—the cameras—were. Roland West welcomed that idea. He told Maxfield that he stood beside the cameras and was able to hear every word spoken by his actors. Maxfield was triumphant, his theory was vindicated. He was so enthusiastic that the UA studio heads asked him to make a test, and one was arranged, with hired actors and a full camera crew.

Maxfield set up his microphones, two of them—"two ears," he said—and placed them close to the camera booth. To complete his setup, he fastened them to a medicine ball, to simulate a man's head.

Maxfield's idea ignored one important fact. The cameras, his "eyes," might not move, but the lenses could be changed. With a 75mm lens, a camera, from a distance of about twelve feet, could get an excellent close-up of an actor's teeth, if he smiled and if he had teeth. With a 50mm lens, the actor would be seen in a nicely composed medium close-up. With an 18mm lens he would be a distant figure. The camera people didn't mention the lens change problem. They probably wished so fervently for relief from the obnoxious overhead mikes that they hoped, somehow, that Maxfield's theories could be implemented.

When the test was run, the next day, it was a disaster. Even when the actors faced the camera their voices were weak and indistinct; when they turned away, their voices had a distant, voice-in-a-barrel quality. The embarrassing test film was quietly taken out of circulation, and Maxfield was seen no more.

Campbell was not exactly vindicated, but he behaved as though he had been; he again became the impatient, autocratic order giver. One of his directives was to create what he called production teams: a mixer (he called him a monitor man) and the man on the stage floor (who he called a stage technician). The formation of teams was not a bad idea, but Campbell added a proviso that was not good. He decreed that the monitor man and the stage technician would exchange jobs, on a weekly basis. It was a thoroughly bad idea. The monitor man was the one who listened to the scenes and passed judgment on them; he negotiated with the director and was, by the nature of the job, the boss of the sound crew. The arbitrary changing of jobs was bound to be disconcerting to the director, the actors, and the soundmen themselves.

I was teamed with David Forrest, well dressed, well mannered, about thirty years old. Unlike most of us, he had a degree of sophistication and a knowledge of the motion picture business. His principal assets were his charm and his persuasiveness. Though he joined the UA sound department after most of us had been hired, he soon was high in Howard Campbell's esteem. Soon after Dave and I became a team, I had to face the fact that Dave might take over as the dominant member of our team. During the Pickford tests, for instance, it was Dave whom Mary consulted and deferred to. If the job rotation plan failed, I might find myself mired solidly in second place.

Forrest had worked in the movie business for about eight years, he told me, in a variety of jobs—as a production assistant for the Christie brothers, makers of two-reel comedies, and as a publicity man for various stars and starlets and some Poverty Row producers. In 1928 he was not doing well financially and decided that the advent of sound might provide an opportunity. Friends helped him to get a low-pay, nontechnical job in the Paramount sound department. The job didn't enable him to learn much in his few months at Paramount; in spite of that, he was able to persuade the head of the Paramount sound department to recommend him to Campbell. Howard Campbell was vulnerable to charm and to flattery; Dave Forrest possessed the charm and used the flattery. Now he was both my partner and my competitor.

Dave and I were assigned to *Coquette,* Mary Pickford's venture into sound. It was UA's most important picture, Campbell told us, and we were his number one team. I didn't tell him that I would prefer to be number one on a small film than number two on a big one.

Two talking films had been made before *Coquette, Alibi* and *Bulldog Drummond.* There hadn't been much improvement in production efficiency. Camera booths were still used, and we, the sound people, were still hiding microphones in flower arrangements and hanging them from sound-stage catwalks. We heard rumors that sound booms were being used in other studios, but Campbell was adamant: mikes were not to be swung around recklessly. They would be placed carefully and judiciously, and the actors would be instructed how to play to them. He had other anti-boom arguments: a heavy CTA at the end of a long boom arm would be dangerously prone to tipping, and the camera booths and the lights monopolized the front of the set; there was no room for a clumsy, tip-prone mike boom. Some of us were not convinced. We felt that a boom could be counterweighted, and if we could demonstrate the need, room would be found for us in the front of the set. I was beginning to see things from the point of view of the filmmakers. There *was* a need for a microphone that could follow the actors and give the directors and actors the ability to stage scenes the way they, and not the soundmen, wanted them.

The filming of *Coquette* began in mid-December 1928. It was Mary Pickford's gallant struggle to retain her hold on the hearts of millions of her fans. It was a struggle against long odds, against cumbersome sound techniques and the inferior photography that sound imposed on the cameramen. In the silent era, Mary had been in control—filmwise, camerawise, and storywise. She no longer had that control. Scenes were shot with agonizing slowness; we, in sound, took too much time setting our microphones. A grip would go high up to the stage catwalk and drop a rope to us. We would tie a microphone to it; it would then be raised to clear the top frame line of the widest-angle camera, and ropes from the light platforms would be used to pull the mike into position. It was laborious and wasted time, and if the staging of a scene or the camera setup was changed, our mikes had to be repositioned in the same cumbersome way.

The problems of the camera people were even more time-consuming. The loss of camera mobility and photographic quality was unavoidable, but the camera booths caused other difficulties. Sam Taylor, the director, used multicamera setups—two, three, and even four cameras. That multiplied the cameraman's problems; lighting that was good for one camera angle was not necessarily good for another. The camera booths took up space that should have been available for front lighting, and there was the maddening problem of "kicks"—elusive, hard-to-find reflections on the glass fronts of the booths. A cameraman and his gaffer would spend valuable time looking for these kicks, and a weird array of devices, called shutters, snoots, goboes, and cutters, were devised to combat the troublesome reflections. The problem existed even inside the booth. The cameraman, his camera operators, and assistants wore long black robes, like judges, because light-colored clothing reflected on the glass *inside* the booth. When the camera crews came piling out of their booths after a long scene, gasping for air (the booths had no air supply during takes) they looked like a panel of Supreme Court justices conducting a fire drill.

The multicamera technique hurt our sound. The clumsy, nondirectional CTA mikes had to be as close as possible to actors to get good close-up sound. In one of Sam Taylor's four-camera setups, the top line for our mike was set by the camera with the widest-angle lens, probably a medium long shot, and our microphone might be seven or eight feet from the actors, too far for good close-up quality. This was particularly damaging in close-ups of Mary; her voice—and her performance—suffered from the distant-mike handicap. Mary had what Douglas Fairbanks called "a small, tight voice," a voice that needed to be caressed by a microphone close to her, one that would not require her to strain that small voice to reach a too-distant mike. Everyone in the cast spoke loudly; scenes of tenderness and intimacy between Mary and Johnny Mack Brown were spoken much too loudly. Despite Mary's efforts, "Sid," in his review of *Coquette* in *Variety,* April 10, 1929, wrote that "certain passages had the male voices normal and Miss Pickford's very weak."

It seemed to me that Sam Taylor, the director, did very little to guide Mary's performance, that he was more concerned with camera setups than with performances. There was a man on the set, Earle Brown, whose title was "assistant drama director." His role seemed to be someone who would rehearse with Mary. "Assistant drama director?" The title speaks volumes about the lack of a strong guiding hand.

In an interview years later, Mary described the filming of *Coquette* as a painful experience. Restrictive sound and camera techniques and frequent equipment failures, she said, made it impossible to create good scenes. That may well be, but as Sid wrote in his review, "The script is the culprit. The film neither grasps nor holds the imagination as did the play for three pretty fair reasons—cast, change in story and a repeated tendency to become too talkie and motionless."

Sid was relatively kind in his review. He might have said that a good story, well paced and well written, is the bedrock of a good motion picture and that *Coquette* was a poor choice for Mary Pickford's venture into sound. It was fatally slow paced, overwritten, and grossly melodramatic.

In release, however, *Coquette* was a box office success. It grossed nearly a million and a half dollars in domestic revenue, more than three times its cost; and, of great importance to Mary, it won the Academy Award for Best Actress. *Coquette,* however, was not a good film. The Academy Award was a salute to the past, a tribute to Mary's years of glory. The box office success was, in effect, a farewell by millions of fans to their idol of past years; they wanted to see how Mary performed in the new, demanding era of sound-film production; and having seen, they wanted no more. In time, Mary recognized that heartbreaking fact.

When Dave Forrest and I finished *Coquette,* we were given "time off," which meant that we could do as we pleased, were not required to report to the studio, and were paid for our idleness. Campbell kept one crew ready at the studio, should there be an unexpected call for a test; the rest of us were given alternate days off, then alternate weeks off. Most of my fellow soundmen considered the arrangement an employment utopia, but it worried me. I felt certain that one day UA, moneyed though it was, would realize that it had not twice as many soundmen as it needed, but nearly three times as many—and that would be the end of "days off" and "weeks off" and the beginning of unlimited time off—with no pay.

Dave and I were assigned to the next film to go into production, *Lummox,* to be directed by the eminent silent-film director, Herbert Brenon. Again I protested to Campbell that I wanted a picture of my own. His response, in his brusque, impatient manner: if I didn't like the assignment, I might consider looking for work elsewhere. I needed the steady seventy-five dollars a week, because Betty and I knew that in December we would need cash for diapers, baby food, a crib, and other necessities. We intended to save money to pay the doctor and the hospital. The baby would arrive COD.

The film *Lummox* was a cinematic soap opera, a tale of a poor scullery maid who bore up nobly despite cruelty and injustice. At that time UA tended to make such pictures. Perhaps talk in films suggested a relationship with the theater, which in turn suggested *drama.* To the UA people, drama seemed to mean slow, soggy, and relentlessly downbeat films.

After *Coquette, Lummox* was more of the same, but Herbert Brenon was a new kind of director. He was an Irishman, a top director of silent films; he had directed the original *Beau Geste* and was very much a hands-on director. He dictated every move and demonstrated, by reading the lines, how every line of dialogue was to be delivered.

The leading lady was Winifred Westover, wife of the superstar of early-day Westerns, William S. Hart. Hart was reputed to have semipartnership in UA. Nepotism may have played a part in casting Westover as the lead in *Lummox;* she was not a star and was not well known; she tried hard, was badgered and scolded by Brenon, and suffered, suffered, suffered—both *in* the film and making it. What she (and Brenon) achieved after much painful effort was the tale of a servant girl so oppressed, so downtrodden and so noble in the face of abuse that it bordered on nauseating. A militant feminist of today would throw beer bottles at the screen if she saw the film and had some beer bottles. The script of *Lummox* was adapted from a novel by Fannie Hurst. The author visited our set several times during the filming, and I spoke to her. She told me she had received fifty rejection slips before she got a single twenty-five dollar acceptance.

Brenon worked at maintaining his image—that of a demanding, flamboyant director. There was the episode of the roses. The propman had dressed a set with roses, good-looking artificial ones. Brenon demanded real roses. The cast and crew waited while the propman hurried to find genuine red roses. The ones he found, however, wilted rapidly in the hot lights, so he had to find more of them, and they had to match.

In another sequence, Winifred Westover, a servant in the house of rich playboy Ben Lyon, is seduced by him. When she tries to tell him she is pregnant (racy drama in those days), he threw money at her feet and walked out. The script called for Westover to grovel on the floor in anguish and to tear the money with her teeth. The propman had a supply of authentic-looking stage money. Brenon decreed that the money had to be genuine. The propman emptied his wallet, borrowed money from the crew, and hoped that the scene could be done in one take. But Brenon, the hands-on director, had to *show* Westover how to do it; *he* groveled, *he* tore the money to bits, and he used real money.

In release, *Lummox* was not treated kindly by film critics. In *Variety,* March 26, 1930, "Waly" wrote, "There are stretches as lethargic as the dray-horse type that Westover personifies— drab kitchen life is carried to the extent that it depresses and bores." And, "What is intended to be a dramatic highlight becomes ludicrous because flowery lines are forced on Ben Lyon by the script. Noting Westover's bare feet in the garden dirt, Lyon likens them to Magnolia blossoms."

That kind of metaphor may have been acceptable in a novel, but it was deadly in a motion picture. When I saw *Lummox* in a neighborhood theater, it caused a storm of derisive laughter.

The release date, March 1930, is significant. It was considerably later than the usual UA release, which seemed to indicate that UA knew it had a poor picture on its hands and that it was, as old-timers used to say, "sneaked out" rather than released.

When we finished *Lummox,* Campbell told us that we were to do Shakespeare's *Taming of the Shrew,* a film of great importance to United Artists, since it starred Douglas Fairbanks and Mary Pickford.

Meanwhile, I enjoyed the delightful alternate weeks of pay without work. I still had misgivings; I felt that this working man's utopia would one day be done in by harsh financial considerations. Some of our soundmen were of the same opinion. It is well known that even in Hollywood the Devil will find work for idle hands. There were too many men for too few jobs. Cliques were forming; the core of one of them was the group of five men whom Campbell recruited from radio station WCCO in Minneapolis. Campbell's abrasive manner had earned him few friends and many enemies. Dave and I suspected that members of the WCCO clique bore tales of Campbell's mistakes to the management people of the studio.

We began filming *Taming of the Shrew* early in July 1929. Sam Taylor still used his multicamera setups. There was no longer a problem editing soundtracks, nor could his objective have been economy of time, film, or money. The one constant in Doug and Mary's policy was the striving for excellence, and they were willing to pay for it. Mary kept a watchful eye on production costs, not to save dollars but to be sure that those dollars were used to put quality where it would be seen, on the screen.

If Sam Taylor had any thought of changing his methods, the problem of the massive camera booths probably deterred him. It was not difficult to use the camera booths in the front of the set, with a 28mm long-shot lens on one camera, a 40mm medium-shot lens on another, and a couple of 75mm lenses for close-ups.

It was much more difficult to push the elephantine camera booths back and forth in the set for the close-ups.

The problem of too-distant microphones confronted us again, as it had in filming *Coquette.* The sets for *Taming of the Shrew* were larger, and because the walls and floors were bare, they were more reverberant. We soundmen didn't use the word *reverberation* much. We called the acoustical properties of a set "roominess," which seemed less pretentious. Maximum roominess might be encountered in a marble or tile bathhouse, and the minimum in a carpeted, heavily draped room, such as the old-fashioned broadcasting studios.

The *Taming of the Shrew* sets were not only high walled and reverberant; they were architecturally magnificent, so that Sam Taylor tilted his long-shot camera upward, to capture the beauty of the graceful arches and dramatic stairways of the William Cameron Menzies sets—and our microphones were forced even higher.

Doug (Petruchio), Edwin Maxwell (Baptista), and Joseph Cawthorn (Gremio) had excellent voices. Legend has it that Doug's voice didn't record well, that it failed to live up to his virile image. That was not true. It seemed that the playing of Shakespeare demanded that all lines be declaimed, loudly, and not merely spoken. The men, with their strong voices, reached our microphones with reasonably good intelligibility. Mary, with her "small, tight voice," did not fare so well. Her role of Kate, the shrew, required her to scold, stridently, but because our microphones were generally too far away, her voice had a distant reverberant quality that sometimes made her hard to understand.

There were no indications that Doug was apprehensive about sound. He was the same exuberant prankster he had been on the *Iron Mask* set. Kenny, the propman, flinched nervously if anyone approached behind him, and Doug's electric chair was once more in use. The problem was that all regulars on the set were wary of the hot-wired chair and never sat in one that had a telltale wire attached to it. Doug and his people needed a new, unsuspecting victim, and they got one. He was a fan magazine writer, gathering material for an article about *Taming of the Shrew*. He was an ideal victim, because he seemed to have a high opinion of himself and exhibited a self-important manner.

The writer was persuaded to sit in the director's chair, shocker switch in hand, with instructions to wait until his victim was comfortably seated and then give him his jolt. When he did so he gave *himself* the shock. He jumped up with a scream and stormed out of the studio vowing vengeance to Doug and his people. The episode had the satisfying element of comedy; persuading the man to electrocute himself made it a most successful caper. Shattered dignity and outraged self-importance added zest to the jest.

Doug could never be the victim of his electric shock setup because he never sat in one of the director's chairs. He used a bicycle seat, mounted on a pedestal; when he sat on it his legs were fully extended. Doug did so, his wardrobe man told me, because in many of his films, Doug wore tights, and if he bent his knees to sit down, his tights would become baggy at the knees, and that would never do; Doug's legs had to look good at all times. It seemed to me that Mary was tolerant of Doug's sometimes destructive pranks. Often it was a mild reproof: "Oh, Doug, please; let's get on with the scene."

There were undoubtedly cross-currents of ambition, resentment, and jealousy on the *Taming of the Shrew* set, but I was engrossed with the demands of my job and the realization that I was about halfway to becoming a rookie father, so I was not aware of them. In later years Mary described the making of the film as a disastrous experience, speaking of troublesome differences between Doug's temperament and hers. She also expressed resentment toward Sam Taylor, accusing him of having a condescending attitude toward her. I saw no such attitude on the set. It is not likely that a director would be condescending to an actress who was, in effect, his boss.

Doug and Mary worked hard to make *Taming of the Shrew* a good film. There was no self-indulgent coming to the set late, unprepared, and leaving early. They tried hard, but the film had flaws. Stripped of its credentials as a classic, the work of the hallowed Shakespeare, and judged solely as a motion picture story, the *Taming of the Shrew* seemed to be a poor choice. Consider Doug's character, Petruchio, for instance, who is shown in the film as a mercenary and cruel adventurer. One might argue that *Shrew* is a comedy, that all is in fun, but apparently the great American movie audience did not see it that way. Petruchio always carried a whip, a stark symbol of cruelty, and in the scene that introduces him he tells his friends, Hortensio and Gremio, that he came to Padua to marry for money, no matter how ill favored the bride is. Later, he bargains shamelessly with Baptista, Kate's father, for a large dowry and twenty thousand pounds in cash. On their wedding night, Petruchio pushes Kate into a wallow of mud, which she shares with a pig. Later, when Kate has put on her wedding gown, Petruchio explains how he will degrade and humiliate her, telling it to Troilus, his dog. Try that on an honest, unsophisticated Midwestern audience; he tells how he intends to torment her—to a *dog*. There is no doubt that Doug's career declined after *Shrew*. It is possible that unsophisticated audiences, without really being aware of it, transferred dislike of Petruchio to Doug. Certain movie stars must never play odious persons. John Wayne never did, nor did Jimmy Stewart, and Douglas Fairbanks should not have done so. Fundamental, of course, was the fact that *Coquette* and *Taming of the Shrew* were wrong for Doug and Mary. They fell into the trap of believing that the advent of sound oriented them toward the theater rather than allowing them to continue doing the things that had brought them their tremendous success: making movies—film that *moved* and told stories that their millions of fans wanted both to see *and* to listen to.

Contemporary reviewers were kind to *Taming of the Shrew.* "Sime," in *Variety* of December 4, 1929, wrote, "A money picture, easily, for it's worth 75 cents for anyone to see Mary Pickford and Douglas Fairbanks do this extravagant burlesque of Bill Shakespeare." A later-day reviewer, in a film-for-TV book, called the film "A static version of the Shakespeare classic, defeated by its lack of pacing."

Better sound, better camera work, better editing, and, of course, better directing would have resulted in a better film, but that would not have saved the careers of Doug and Mary. In release, *Taming of the Shrew* earned a profit, for the same reason *Coquette* did; people wanted to see how Doug and Mary worked together, and having seen, they wanted no more, and the royal couple were royal no longer. Doug made a few undistinguished films; Mary made three: *Forever Yours* (1930), which Mary decided was not good enough to release, *Kiki* (1931), and *Secrets* (1933), both critical and financial failures.

We finished *Shrew* early in August. *Condemned,* with Ronald Colman and Ann Harding, was about to go into production. Dave Forrest thought we might be assigned to it, but something happened that would bend my future into a challenging new direction. Campbell was fired. He was sacked because he offended Mary Pickford, and at UA that was the kiss of death.

Mary had made some tests. When they were delivered to the UA projection room, Campbell ran them, was dissatisfied with the sound, and in his usual autocratic manner, ordered Bill Bridge, the projectionist, not to show the tests to anyone until sound reprints were made. Campbell could not have intended that his high-handed order would apply to Mary Pickford, who was merely one of the owners of the studio, and Bill Bridge would certainly have disobeyed Campbell's order if Mary chose to run the tests. Soon after Campbell's departure, however, an apprentice from the editorial department came and took the film away. Then, like a well-timed entrance in a stage play, Mary arrived. Bridge broke the news that the film was not available; Campbell had taken it away. The projectionist was a good-looking young man from the South. When he was agitated, his accent became pure Dixie.

"When I told Mary this Campbell fella took the film," Bill said, "she just looked at me. She didn't scold, didn't say anything, just looked. And when I saw that look, I knew that fella Campbell was daid—he just ain't fallen down yet."

And that's the way it was. Campbell was indeed "daid." Mary, the businesswoman, the hard-headed professional, made sure of her legal ground, was assured that a new sound department head had been selected—and Campbell was gone. A security man drove Campbell's car around to Santa Monica Boulevard, where a fire door that hadn't been used for years was forced open. Campbell's possessions were loaded into the car, along with his secretary, Dorothy Roux, and he drove away. None of us ever saw him again.

The man chosen to replace Campbell was John Hilliard, a member of the WCCO clique. That meant instant trouble—for Dave, because he had been a Campbell favorite, and for me, because I had developed a hearty dislike for John Hilliard, and he was not at all fond of me. It was time for me to abandon ship—to leave United Artists, but I didn't know how to go about it.

Dave Forrest did know. He offered his services to several studios and got job offers from Warner Bros. and Columbia. Warners were big-time; Columbia was just emerging from Poverty Row. Dave took the Warners job and turned the Columbia job over to me. It was almost a replay of the All-American job that Russell Malmgren helped me to get four years before. Dave told me what Columbia was like and what I might expect from John Livadary, head of the Columbia sound department. Livadary, Dave told me, was a man of Greek ancestry, raised in Turkey, who came to the United States as a student and graduated from MIT with a degree in electronics and a reputation as a near-genius in mathematics.

"He may be a genius," Dave said, "but he sure gets nervous when he talks to one of those tough Columbia bosses. I gave him a big buildup about you. When he's nervous, he talks, so let him do the selling. I told Livadary you wanted eighty-five a week."

"That might spoil the deal," I protested. "I've heard that some of their men get only sixty. I want that job."

"You'll get it. Columbia is trying to get out of Poverty Row. They've got a couple of the best cameramen in Hollywood, and they pay top price for them. More money, more respect. That's the way it is. You stick to eighty-five." I agreed, with misgivings.

I drove to Columbia. I drove. A few weeks before, for $150, I had bought a year-old car in excellent condition. It was, of course, a Model T, and it was the last model year of the cranky, eccentric, beloved Flivver.

Gower Street was being repaved that day in August. I parked on Beechwood Drive and walked toward Sunset, along Poverty Row, with shabby, ramshackle offices and cutting rooms on both sides of the street; then turned left on Sunset, with a short walk to Gower; left again on Gower, with historic old Columbia Drug Store on the corner. That was Gower Gulch, a short stretch of sidewalk where movie cowboys waited to be picked up for jobs. That day, even midmorning, a half-dozen cowboys were there, hoping to be picked up to work in some long-forgotten Poverty Row Western.

I gave my name to Cap Duncan, the man at the Columbia front desk, who looked like a solid, dignified bank president. He phoned John Livadary, who came to the lobby to meet me. That was not Hollywood protocol; the job seeker was expected to go to the job giver. Perhaps Livadary thought I might get lost in the confusing maze of corridors that Frank Capra described in his autobiography.

Livadary greeted me—nervously—and we mounted the notorious ingrown stairway. To the right was Harry Cohn's office; to the left, the offices of Sam Briskin and Sam Bischoff, the executives who helped Harry Cohn run Columbia.

We went to Sam Bischoff's office. He greeted me with a curt nod and cut Livadary's introduction short.

"You want this guy?" he demanded.

Dave Forrest was right. Livadary was intimidated by the Columbia bosses. Speaking rapidly—and nervously—Livadary told Bischoff what an excellent mixer I was, with credits on some of United Artists' most important pictures. I was shocked. I would never have had the nerve to make those exaggerated claims for myself. Bischoff broke in on Livadary's recital of my achievements. He was a man of few words—rough ones. "How much?" he demanded.

"Eighty-five dollars. He . . ."

Another interruption. "Your top guys get seventy-five?"

"Yes, except Blanchard. He . . ."

Bischoff cut him off in midsentence. He pointed to me. "This guy goes in at eighty-five. Now all your guys want eighty-five." The way Bischoff said it, financial ruin threatened.

Livadary pleaded. "Mr. Bischoff, I need an experienced mixer with good credits." (I winced inwardly when I heard that.) "We're starting two pictures . . ."

Bischoff interrupted again. Livadary didn't get to finish a single sentence during our meeting. "All right," said Bischoff. "He comes in at seventy-five, so there's no squawks from your guys. He does a good job on two pictures, he gets eighty-five. He does one not so good job, he's out." He glared at me. "OK?"

I nodded. No need to speak. I'd be interrupted anyway. Bischoff, briskly: "OK, let's go see the boss."

We were announced, we entered the lair, and I had my first look at the fabled, fearsome Harry Cohn. He was at his desk, on a slightly raised dais, at the end of a long, rather narrow office. A beautiful girl sat beside the desk, displaying an eye-catching pair of silk-clad legs, and a man stood beside her—an agent and a starlet, probably. Cohn didn't allow us to get more than halfway into the office. "OK, OK!" he said impatiently, "put him on." And, harshly, to me: "You better be good."

I had the job!

8

My first assignment at Columbia was *Song of Love,* a backstage drama starring Belle Baker, a nightclub singer popular in New York. The start of filming was delayed for additional recording of Belle Baker's songs, and I was able to get acquainted with Columbia, the studio, and the people.

The Columbia lot, as Capra described it, had been built patch on patch. One corridor, where several small structures had been joined together, presented several levels—up a couple of steps, down a short ramp, up a few steps, then down again.

The lot was small, even smaller than the UA lot. It was L-shaped; Columbia's property that faced Beechwood Drive extended almost to the cross street, DeLongpre Avenue, but on the Gower Street side the lot was only a few hundred feet long. Columbia's new sound department building was on the Gower Street property line; beyond that Gower was lined with squat, rustic-looking California bungalows that probably dated back to Hollywood's earliest days. From the window of the sound department toilet, I could look into a neighbor's chicken coop, where an arrogant rooster lorded over a harem of a dozen hens and crowed loudly from time to time.

Columbia had two fair-sized sound stages and one small one. The sound equipment, like UA's, was Western Electric; it presented no problems. Also like UA, Columbia had two sound channels—the main amplifiers and recording machines were in the sound building; at both studios the channels were linked by underground cables to "upstairs" monitor booths.

I visited the set of a film in production, a blood-and-thunder story of villainy at sea. It was low-grade filmmaking, but what interested me was that the mike man was using a crude wooden boom, and the camera, wonderful to relate, was not in a ponderous camera booth but encased in a small padded box, which allowed it to pan and dolly and move much as it had done in silent films.

The scenes being filmed may have been melodramatic junk, but it was the speed and efficiency with which the scenes were shot that impressed me. The crew—electricians, grips, propmen—functioned at high speed. The director also worked at top speed; scenes were set up fast and shot fast. With the use of his boom, the mike man got his mike into position quickly and without argument from the camera crew; apparently they had decided that the presence of the microphone was inevitable and that cooperation was better than conflict. The mike man communicated with the script clerk, the camera crew, and the director. The mixer didn't appear during the half-hour I spent on the set. He conferred with his mike man by interphone and remained in his "upstairs" monitor room. That wasn't the way I intended to work.

That afternoon I was given my copy of the *Song of Love* script. It was a story, with music, about show-business people. I learned later that Harry Cohn had once been a song plugger in New York, with strong ties to Tin Pan Alley, and favored stories about music and musicians. Not brainless musicals, not the multimillion-dollar Busby Berkeley spectacles, with hundreds of chorus girls executing kaleidoscopic patterns in elaborate sets. Columbia made stories *with* music: *The Jolson Story,* for instance, and the story about Chopin, *A Song to Remember.* There were the Fred Astaire–Rita Hayworth films, *You'll Never Get Rich* and *You Were Never Lovelier,* the Grace Moore pictures, and Bing Crosby's *Pennies from Heaven,* an appealing story with Bing's music.

Song of Love was the story of Belle Baker and Ralph Graves, vaudevillians, and their eight-year-old son, who is a part of their act. Graves dallies with a beautiful chorus girl. Baker is heartbroken, leaves Graves, and goes on to great success as a "single." Their son, portrayed by a precocious young actor named David Durand, reunites his parents for the mandatory happy ending.

Song of Love was not a high-budget film, but it was important at Columbia because Harry Cohn had a personal interest in it. That was why Joseph Walker was assigned to photograph it. He faced a formidable problem. Belle Baker was short and plump, and Joe's directive was to make her look glamorous.

I approached our first day of production with a degree of anxiety. A great deal depended on my first Columbia picture. Not only baby clothes and baby furniture were at stake; Betty had found a house and was negotiating to buy it. We wanted that house.

The first day went smoothly, thanks to a great extent to Joe Walker, a great cameraman and a true gentleman. He was the inventor of the first zoom lens and devised the padded "blimp" that restored the camera to its silent film freedom. He knew that I was a newcomer and saw to it that we got our microphone where we wanted it, even if it required changes in his lighting.

Joe Walker and the director, Erle Kenton, did not use multicamera setups. When a close-up was filmed, the camera was close, the microphone was close, and Joe's lighting units were close at hand, where he could work his magic with them and make short, plump Belle Baker look glamorous, like a somewhat well-rounded angel.

I disliked being exiled from the set in one of Western Electric's glass cages, the "upstairs" monitor room. Western Electric had a number of not-quite-brilliant ideas about movie equipment, and the upstair's monitor room was one of them. The Western Electric people thought that we, the mixers, needed a full set of theater-type speakers to monitor the sound properly. They instructed the studios to build glass-fronted booths high up on the sound stage walls. Theoretically, the sets would then be built facing the monitor booth, so that the mixer could look down on the scenes he was recording. That notion probably lasted only until the first production meeting, because at any studio—colossal M-G-M, aristocratic UA, or Poverty Row Columbia—stage space was precious, not to be squandered merely to afford the mixer a view from on high. Orienting sets to be visible from the mixer booth might waste as much as 40 percent of the stage space. The result was that the mixer frequently had an uninspiring view of the back of some set.

The first day of production of *Song of Love* went smoothly, and so did the days that followed. The film presented few problems; the members of the cast had good voices, there were no frantic dolly shots or complicated stagings, and each day the rushes were satisfactory.

There were six Belle Baker songs in the film. One of her songs was her most popular number, her "trademark" song, as *Variety* called it: "Atlas Is Itless Tonight." It told the sad story of a wife whose husband, Atlas, is "itless" (impotent) that night. The song was just raunchy enough to be titillating, but not raunchy enough to be censored.

The role of the chorus girl who seduced Ralph Graves was played by a young actress, Eunice Quedens. In her skimpy chorus-girl costume she was truly gorgeous and drew the admiring—and perhaps even the lustful—attention of the crew members. Later, Eunice Quedens became Eve Arden. Her agent, Ray Milland, visited her on the set from time to time. On the last day of production, I was handed the script of my next assignment: *Wall Street,* whose shooting title was *Wolf of Wall Street.*

Wall Street was what Columbia called a "program picture." That implied a short schedule, a tight budget, and bare-bones production values. The director was Roy William Neill; the cameraman was Ted Tetzlaff, an excellent cinematographer and as young and good-looking as any of the leading men he photographed. Neill was an Irishman. His speech was that of a well-educated Englishman, but with a touch of Irish lilt. His true name was Roland de Gostrie, an odd name for an Irishman; but history tells us that one of Napoleon Bonaparte's best generals had the equally unlikely name of McMahon.

From the start, *Wall Street* proceeded smoothly. The leads, Ralph Ince and Aileen Pringle, had good voices, and though Roy Neill's staging and camera movement were more complex than Erle Kenton's, they caused us no difficulty.

Wall Street was a run-of-the-mill film, easily forgotten but for what could have been what show-business people call a bad laugh: a cruel, derisive laugh at what is intended to be a tender or dramatic moment. Some bad laughs are legendary in the movie business. A film of the 1950s provided a classic example: in a World War II story of naval warfare, the stern of a destroyer is blown up by a torpedo. It becomes a shambles of wreckage and wounded and dying men. The skipper, Richard Widmark, phones aft. "Are you all right back there?" he asks. The audience with whom I saw the film howled with laughter. They had witnessed an example—though unintended—of the comedy of understatement. Bing Crosby was the master of understatement. In one of his *Road* films, in an

African witch-doctor's hut, he comes face to face with a skeleton. "This chap has had a nasty accident," he tells Bob Hope.

There was a scene in *Wall Street* that could have been a huge bad laugh. In the film, a tough ex-steelworker, Ralph Ince, has become a ruthless Wall Street tycoon. A man who faces ruin because of Ince's tactics pleads for mercy; he threatens to kill himself if Ince doesn't relent. Ince roughly tells him he hasn't the courage to carry out his threat. The man dashes from Ince's office, runs to a window, and jumps out. Ince hears screams, rushes to a window, and looks down. He tells his secretary, "I didn't think he had the guts."

There was a spontaneous roar of laughter from the crew; it was a reaction to the incongruity of commenting on a victim whose intestines were presumably on display twenty floors below. Roy Neill was bewildered. He wondered why members of his crew were laughing. Ince tried briefly to explain, then said, "Suppose I just say, 'I didn't think he'd do it.' " We filmed it that way, and *Wall Street* and Neill were spared a humiliating horse laugh in the theater.

In my job interview with Sam Bischoff, John Livadary mentioned a man named Blanchard, who apparently was paid more than other Columbia mixers. I didn't encounter Blanchard until filming of *Wall Street* was nearly finished. Blanchard, a stocky, florid man in his midthirties, came to my monitor room and told me, condescendingly, that I had been doing reasonably good work and that he would help me to improve in the future. I tried to look properly grateful. He told me my next assignment would be *Murder on the Roof,* with director George Seitz.

Clearly, something was amiss. Was John Livadary the boss or was he not? He was a naive, mild-mannered man. Perhaps he had delegated authority to Blanchard; perhaps he had not. I chose not to make an issue of the matter. I felt that I was vulnerable if the phantom credits Dave Forrest created for me were questioned. Until I was more solidly entrenched at Columbia, I didn't intend to make waves. Blanchard had one solid achievement in his favor. He had been the sound man on Columbia's most ambitious film, *Flight,* the story of Marine Corps flyers pitting their new weapon, the fighter-bomber, against guerrillas in Central America. The director of *Flight,* named Capper, made the important films at Columbia, and Blanchard was his soundman. I had heard of Capper; I had seen him, a quick-moving, dark young man, not much older than I was. In time, I learned that his name was not Capper but Capra.

Murder on the Roof was assembly-line melodrama, with the same small budget and the same tight schedule as *Wall Street*. It told the story of a lawyer, William V. Mong, who is framed for murder and sent to prison. It was remarkable how many Columbia films used unjust imprisonment as a plot device. It was a quick, easy way to establish conflict; the wife, the daughter, the son, the brother—as the case might be—then labored mightily and braved deadly peril to spring the innocent victim. The director, George Seitz, had been in the movie business since pre–World War I days and had directed and acted in the famous Pearl White serials, the Saturday afternoon cliffhangers that had thrilled me as a ten-year-old. As a director, he worked briskly, without undue haste; he stressed tempo and movement—of actors and of the camera—and avoided the slow, stand-still-and-talk syndrome of some of the Columbia pictures.

Murder on the Roof was finished on budget and on schedule. Another credit for me; three of them in less than seven weeks. They were B picture credits, but they were *mine*.

The finish of *Murder on the Roof* coincided with two important events. Sam Bischoff had promised me a ten-dollar raise after my second film. I didn't ask for the raise then, but when I finished *Murder on the Roof* I spoke to Livadary about the promise. He reacted nervously, as he did whenever he had to deal with Columbia's executives, but he phoned Bischoff and reminded him of the promise. There were some angry noises from the phone; Livadary handed the phone to me. "Don't you tell anybody about the ten bucks," Bischoff said harshly. "All the guys will want it."

The raise was a welcome event, and it came within days of another: we bought our house. We would have made the deal even if there had been no raise, but the job security the raise signified made our plunge into home ownership seem less venturesome.

Our new home, at 8749 Clifton Way, Beverly Hills, was a modest two-bedroom house. We were not aware that a Beverly Hills address was a status symbol—it was simply a house that we liked and could afford. It was not in the Beverly Hills prestige area; we were actually astride the Beverly Hills–Los Angeles boundary line. Every year we received two tax bills, a sizable one from Beverly Hills and another small one from Los Angeles for the ten feet of our back yard that was its territory. The price of our house was $8,500—eight hundred dollars down, with the mortgage payable to an insurance company in Kentucky at $250 per quarter and 8 percent interest.

I went to work on *Mexicali Rose,* again with director Erle Kenton. The locale of *Mexicali Rose,* a Mexican border town, was somewhat unusual in a program picture, but the principal story element, a scorned mistress who seeks revenge, was used many times. In *Mexicali Rose* a gambling casino owner, Sam Hardy, discards his mistress; she gets revenge by marrying Hardy's young brother. Barbara Stanwyck was the vengeful mistress. It was a thankless role in a cheaply made film, and Stanwyck was unhappy about it. Later, in an interview, she called *Mexicali Rose* "an abortion."

During the filming of *Mexicali Rose,* we received our first professionally made microphone boom, the Mole-Richardson model MR103, affectionately called the clam digger. There is no such machine, so why was our tall, odd-looking contraption called a clam digger? Simply because it had to have a name, and movie crews often created weird and wonderful names for the unique devices they used in filmmaking. Consider the kookaloris, for instance, a device electricians use to project patterned light on an otherwise blank wall. A reasonable person, inspecting the strange device, would undoubtedly agree that it deserved to be called a kookaloris. Then there was the "Barney," a padded camera cover, used to reduce camera noise for exterior filming. Why "Barney"? Because in the 1920s there was a popular comic strip and song that told of Barney Google, who dearly loved his horse and provided him with a well-fitted quilted coat. The camera also wore a well-fitted quilted coat; therefore, it was called a Barney. Perfectly simple and perfectly logical.

The Mole-Richardson microphone boom, the MR103, was a huge success from the day it was put into service. It was so well designed hundreds are probably still in service around the world. Made of steel, the clam digger was heavy and tall, making it capable of reaching over the front-lights usually clustered around the camera. It did the job—superbly—that it was designed for. The mike man now had three functions to work with instead of two. The third function, the MR103's smooth, quiet in-and-out capability, enabled the mike man to follow an actor whenever he went within the reach of the boom, and the clam digger had a wonderfully long reach.

I finished *Mexicali Rose* and was assigned to *Acquitted,* directed by Frank Strayer, who later directed many of the early "*Blondie*" films. I remember *Acquitted* as the worst of the Columbia films I worked on. The *Variety* review of December 11, 1929, called it "utterly silly."

In mid-November 1929, I persuaded my friend of school days, Russell Malmgren, to come to Hollywood. When he arrived, Betty and I had just moved into our new house, and we gave him lodging, amid our moving-day clutter, until he found a place for himself. During that time, I gave him intensive briefings about the Western Electric sound system and, most important, about John Livadary. It was the mirror image of the way Russell had briefed me for my job-winning interview with Charles Cushway of All-American Radio, five years before, and it was equally successful. Russell was hired as a maintenance supervisor.

My son, Edward Junior, was born December 9, 1929, at Hollywood Presbyterian Hospital. I suppose I had thoughts on that great occasion, but I recall them as bewildered emotions rather than thoughts. Three thousand years ago, on the banks of the Euphrates, a Chaldean merchant may have felt just as I did when he contemplated the miracle of his first child. That evening my brother Bill and Russell Malmgren took charge of me. They seemed to think that in my bemused state I might wander in front of a speeding streetcar. They took me to dinner and then home. It sticks in my memory: the three of us, sitting in my new house, cartons of household goods still unpacked. We sat for a long time, saying very little. Around midnight Bill and Russell went home and I went to my lonely bed. The show had to go on, and so did the eighty-five dollars a week, now that I had a wife, a son, and a mortgage to provide for.

My next film, *Personality,* was a comedy about a young couple, Johnny Arthur (the Don Knotts of his day) and Sally Starr, his wife, who get into money trouble by overspending his forty-dollar a week salary. The director—and writer—was Victor Heerman. That was something new to me—a director who wrote his own script. He directed with what seemed to me to be a good touch for comedy. "Char," in his *Variety* review, February 26, 1930, wrote, "*Personality* is well done in a light comedy manner. It's a domestic narrative with plenty of humor." Char also gave me a good review—of sorts. He wrote, "Clear recording and photography throughout."

A week before *Personality* wrapped up, Frank Capra began filming *Ladies of Leisure*. It was an event of considerable importance at Columbia. Since the advent of sound, Capra had made the films that enabled Columbia to prosper. If *Ladies of Leisure* was a success, Columbia could grow; if it was a failure, Columbia might well revert to its penny-pinching Poverty Row days.

I wondered about Barbara Stanwyck being cast as the lead. *The Locked Door* had been an early talking-picture flop, and *Mexicali Rose,* an inferior B picture, seemed to guarantee a quick ticket out of the movie business. Capra may or may not have seen film from *Mexicali Rose*; if he did, he made no mention of it. In his autobiography, he relates that he cast Stanwyck after he viewed a three-minute test: a scene from the play *The Noose.*

Ladies of Leisure had been filming about two weeks, with all going smoothly. My next assignment was to be a steamy melodrama with an African locale, *Vengeance.* When I read my script, I recognized it as a sanitized version of *White Congo,* a play that had scandalized Chicago and fascinated me when I was a teenager. I was not to work on *Vengeance,* however. Abruptly, Blanchard informed me that I was to take his place for a night of location filming at Malibu Lake, in the Santa Monica Mountains. I checked with Livadary. Blanchard had asked to be relieved so he could attend to pressing personal business. That seemed incredible to me. I wondered whether Blanchard was self-indulgent, seeking to avoid the discomfort of an all-night shoot in midwinter.

Joe Walker, his camera crew, and I made the long trip to Malibu Lake in one of Columbia's ancient Lincoln limousines. To me, that was VIP treatment; on B pictures only the director, the first cameraman, and the leading actors rode in cars; the rest of us crowded into the noisy, rough-riding crew bus. During the long ride, Walker gave me hints about working with Capra. "Never cut a scene," Joe told me. "Let the scene finish, no matter what goes wrong, then tell your troubles."

I couldn't quarrel with that. I knew that, despite flaws, parts of a good scene could be salvaged. But even more important, the momentum of an intense, well-played performance might be lost when a soundman, using his loudspeaker, bellowed midscene from his glass cage, "Cut, NG [no good] for sound!"

At Malibu Lake I reported to Dave Selman, assistant director. Capra acknowledged my presence with a nod. I had my own work to do but was able to watch Capra organizing the night's filming. He was young, about thirty years old, but he had the poise and decisiveness of a veteran director. The term *leadership* is often misused, but that quality does exist, and I believe I saw some of it that chilly night at Malibu Lake.

For sound, the night's work was not demanding. There were a few dialogue scenes and a long-shot scene that could have presented a problem. Stanwyck, rowing ashore to escape a wild party on a yacht, calls out to Ralph Graves on the shore. My microphone would have to be at least fifty feet from Stanwyck if I tried to record the scene. My mike man, a large young man named Win Brotmarkle, asked, "Are you gonna try to record it? Blanchard would have been hollering that he couldn't do it; they'd have to bring the boat in where he could reach it."

I decided I would not holler. I knew that Capra was going to film the scene in close-up, and the close-up soundtrack could be used over the long shot if necessary. I had Brotmarkle tape a microphone to a post on a pier, as far as possible from the camera, which wore the customary "Barney" for location filming.

When we shot the scene, Stanwyck's voice, from the distance, barely moved the volume indicator needle. I had learned, however, to trust my ears; if I heard something, it recorded. Stanwyck's voice sounded the way a voice heard from a distance should sound.

It was a long, cold night. Stanwyck wore an evening gown. The wardrobe mistress kept her covered with blankets until she was needed for a scene; then, arms and shoulders bare to the cold, she did her scene, uncomplaining.

We finished filming at about four o'clock Sunday morning. Scheduling night exterior filming on Saturday was standard studio practice. The rationale was that crews who worked long past midnight had all day Sunday to sleep and be ready to resume their daytime schedule on Monday.

On that Sunday morning there was the long ride back to the studio, a quarter-mile walk to where my car was parked, and a weary drive home. I was having breakfast at noon Sunday when John Livadary called. Capra had requested that I continue on *Ladies of Leisure*.

I was surprised—and elated. It occurred to me that this could well be another sudden, and promising, turn in the road.

9

I reported early Monday morning. Capra was on Stage 2 before me; he sat quietly, script in his lap, studying the set we were filming that day, mentally staging the scene in that set. Capra gave me the slightest of nods, acknowledging my presence. I got the message: I was there because he had asked for me, but I had better deliver.

In my monitor room, between scenes, I read my *Ladies of Leisure* script. I was disappointed. I knew the script was based on a play, and it seemed, like *Coquette,* to be overdramatic in the manner of a stage play and, like *Lummox,* to make a virtue of noble and hard-to-believe self-sacrifice.

What Capra did with his material, I soon found out, was different from the treatment Sam Taylor and Herbert Brenon gave theirs. Taylor more or less accepted what his actors gave him; Brenon demanded that his people deliver their lines exactly as he demonstrated them. Different methods, but the same result: less than satisfactory performances. Capra employed a low-key kind of indirection; he explored motives and emotions behind a scene rather than discussing the words of the scene itself. I had been in the movie business for less than a year and a half, and I was certainly no authority, but it seemed to me that first day that Capra's scenes were better than they were written, and that the film we were making might be a very good one.

After wrap-up of the day's filming, we ran dailies of our Saturday night work at Malibu Lake. Joe Walker's photography was excellent, and the dialogue scenes were well recorded. Our long-shot lake scene came on the screen, and we heard Stanwyck's voice, clearly, far out on the lake. "Interesting effect," Capra said.

Ladies of Leisure was two-thirds finished when I came aboard. The work of defining the characters and the discussion of the relationships had been done, but Capra continued to remind his people of the thought and the emotion behind each scene. He frequently stressed "honesty" to Stanwyck; I suppose he meant honesty in acting—no emotional tricks—and it worked. Scenes that might have been mawkish became moving and believable.

In his autobiography, Capra writes, "Stanwyck gave her all the first time she tried a scene, whether in rehearsal or in unused long shots. All subsequent repetitions were but pale copies of her original performance. I had to tap the heart of the scene, the vital close-ups of Barbara—first, and with multiple cameras so that she would only have to do the scene once."

That was true to an extent. Capra was fanatical in protecting Stanwyck's sacrosanct first take, but he was ferocious in protecting the performance of all his actors. Stanwyck went along with his methods because she knew that with his guidance she was giving a fine performance, but she was no tender, delicate actress who needed support and protection. She had been through the Broadway grinder; she had been a chorus girl, made the painful climb to be an actress, and achieved hard-won success in the play *Burlesque*.

Capra did use two cameras frequently, one of them always a close-up of Stanwyck. Close shots filmed in this manner tended to be profile close-ups; they had value, and many of them were used, but there were times when Capra (and the audience) wanted to see Stanwyck full-face, to see both eyes and get the full impact of her performance. These full-face close-ups and the close, over-the-shoulder two-shots Capra was fond of could not be filmed as part of the usual two-camera setup. The camera had to move deep into the set to get a suitable angle for such shots, and Stanwyck displayed no letdown when she filmed those highly important scenes.

In the matter of rehearsals, Capra's autobiography tells us, "On the set I would never let Stanwyck utter one word of a scene until the cameras were rolling. Before that I talked to her in her dressing room, told her of the meaning of the scene, the points of emphasis, the pauses."

That is not as I recall it. The scene could be rehearsed by members of the cast and Stanwyck's stand-in. The camera moves, the cast positions, and the lighting could be set, after a fashion; but then, would a completely unrehearsed Stanwyck be thrust into the set, cameras rolling, to ad-lib her movements and her interaction with the other members of the cast? It could not work that way, and did not work that way. She did rehearse, at half-speed, as it were, and, as Capra writes, "never blew a line, never forgot anything." And it was certainly true that when the cameras rolled, she responded with searing emotional intensity.

In his autobiography, Capra (or his collaborator, Eugene Vale) may have stretched facts to add to the Capra-Stanwyck mystique, but there can be no quarrel with results: *Ladies of Leisure* was a huge hit in the theaters, and Barbara Stanwyck became an instant star.

After *Ladies of Leisure,* I sensed that I had gained status. John Livadary, who had not been particularly happy when Capra selected me to finish his film, was cordial, and his assistant, a pint-sized martinet named Eddie Hahn, was downright deferential. Hahn had been Harry Cohn's chauffeur and had, in effect, been awarded a pension—a job in Columbia's sound department. He aspired to be a miniature Harry Cohn; he was harsh to the rank-and-file sound people, but because he knew nothing about sound or moviemaking, he was somewhat in awe of mixers, and we were spared his tirades. I learned later that he had broken in as a soundman on Capra's difficult *Flight* location in the San Diego back country. He had been a helper then, a rookie, and Harry Blanchard had given him a bad time. If I was to be the new number-one mixer, Hahn was apparently in favor of it.

What of Blanchard? He had disappeared, and so had one of Columbia's valuable microphones. No one could say he took it—it disappeared from a locked room; it merely vanished the same time Blanchard did.

It was pleasant for me to feel that I had earned a step up in the eyes of my bosses, but I wasn't inclined to flaunt it. When we finished *Ladies of Leisure,* Capra gave me no indication that I would be on his next film. Studio rumor had it that there would be a next film, soon—a circus picture, a big, expensive one.

The next film I was assigned to was not scheduled to start for a week. Columbia did not have a generous policy of "go home, take a trip, take a week off" as UA did; every penny of Columbia's payroll money had to be charged to something, even if it was make-work such as testing microphones or reporting to the dubbing room to assist the re-recording mixer. That's where I found myself two days after I finished *Ladies of Leisure,* and the mixer I was assigned to assist was my friend of schoolboy days, Russell Malmgren.

Three months earlier, to help Russell get the job at Columbia, I had briefed him about Livadary and Columbia. I knew that if he got the job, he would do well—and he did. From the beginning he had earned Livadary's confidence. Mild-mannered and professorial, Livadary wanted someone self-confident and aggressive to depend on, and Russell was decidedly self-confident and aggressive. His first challenge was the problem of the film editors' unreliable moviolas. Film buffs know all about editors and moviolas; they can fast-forward their reading and get past the technical detail.

Columbia employed about a dozen film editors. Each editor had a cutting room furnished with film racks, a work table, a splicing machine, and the film editor's indispensable tool, his moviola. Each moviola was a small film-viewing and soundtrack-reproducing machine. Controlled by a foot treadle, the moviola could be run fast or slow, forward or reverse. The corridor outside the row of editors' rooms echoed with a cacophony of electronic sound. The machines themselves produced a loud clatter; to override that noise, the editors turned up the volume of the sound track they were listening to. Run fast, the sound became a shrill gibberish; run slowly, it moaned and groaned. Running his film repeatedly forward and reverse, the film editor was able, through the viewing lens of his machine, to select what he hoped was the perfect frame of film for his cut. Because each moviola was equipped with a miniature sound system, maintenance was delegated to Columbia's sound department, and the sound department's record of reliability was not good. Livadary assigned Russell to solve the problems, and with a few commonsense measures, he did solve it.

Livadary's next task for Russell was to improve Columbia's re-recording procedures. Re-recording, always referred to as dubbing in those days, was—and is—an important step in sound-film production, but in the first few years of sound, the re-recording mixer was not recognized as a skilled specialist. At UA as well as at Columbia the dubbing was done, often poorly, by production mixers between film assignments.

Russell quickly improved dubbing efficiency, and when no be-tween-assignment mixer was available for dubbing, he persuaded Livadary to let him try his hand at the job. He was successful from the start, and so I found myself with the make-work job of assist-ing him at the mixing panel. I didn't mind being an understudy. It was a pleasure to watch the skill and the finesse of his work. Fi-nesse? On a Buck Jones Western? That's what we were working on, but even on a Buck Jones Western I saw skill—and, yes, fi-nesse. For many years Russell was considered the best re-record-ing mixer in Hollywood, and that made him, it might be argued, the best in the world.

Status or not, my next assignment was another B picture. Top-notch cameramen such as Joe Walker spurned cheap films, but we soundmen couldn't afford to do so. I certainly couldn't; it was De-pression time, and there was no social safety net—no unemploy-ment insurance, no Medicare, no Social Security. Families sur-vived the old-fashioned way; if one member of a family had a job, all his kinfolk had food.

My new assignment was *Guilty?,* which had a morbid, dull script; the principal plot element was a self-sacrificing suicide that backfired and nearly got the leading man hanged for murder. George Seitz was a pretty good director, but he seemed to be dis-heartened by the downbeat script. "Waly," in his *Variety* review, wrote, *Guilty?* is a poor scramble of conventional things—one of the slowest motion pictures ventured by a Broadway house this season. There is no such thing as suspense because the picture has a leaking plot—a kindergarten effort."

I finished *Guilty?* to be greeted with the news that Capra's cir-cus film was no longer a matter of rumor; preparations were well under way for a full-sized circus layout in the San Fernando Val-ley. There were no indications that I would get the assignment. Meanwhile, my next job was to be on one of Columbia's low-bud-get westerns, starring Buck Jones, to be directed by a man who was already a bull-in-the-china-shop legend, D. Ross Lederman. The script was packed, as all Columbia's Western scripts were, with fist fights, gun fights, and chases. I wondered how it could be filmed on schedule. I was not destined to find out. Eddie Hahn playfully snatched the Buck Jones script out of my hands and presented me with the script of Capra's circus film, *Rain or Shine*. Word had come down; I was to be assigned to *Rain or Shine*.

For the *Rain or Shine* circus, Columbia leased the famed Jim Jeffries ranch, owned by the man who was the heavyweight boxing champion of the world from 1899 to 1905. With his prizefight earnings, Jeffries bought a sixty-acre ranch in the San Fernando Valley. He built a large barn on the property, installed seats and a prizefight ring, and sponsored weekend amateur fights. The film community was a tight-knit group then, and it was the thing for the Hollywood elite to do on a weekend: come to Jim Jeffries' barn and watch a couple of local boys batter one another. Because they were amateurs, they were paid by dividing the money thrown in the ring. More blood, more money, and there were some bloody fights at the barn. Our circus was set up not far from the Hollywood Hills and the Los Angeles River, where the Disney and NBC studios are now.

The *Rain or Shine* script was unlike any other script I'd read. Based on a successful Broadway musical, it had romance, treachery, thrills, spectacle, and comedy. The triangular romance was well worn but serviceable. Joe Cook, "Smiley," star of *Rain or Shine,* loves Joan Peers, "Mary," owner of the circus, but Mary prefers "Bud," William Collier, a wealthy young man who joins the circus to court Mary.

The treachery: Mary—and her circus—are the targets of a dastardly plot. Mary's villainous ringmaster and her equally villainous lion tamer conspire to drive the circus into bankruptcy and acquire it on the cheap.

The romance may have been run-of-the-mill, but the thrills and the spectacle were not. There was the glamour and excitement of the circus and the treachery of the ringmaster, who foments a riot of dissatisfied customers and causes a fire that burns the circus to the ground.

The comedy in the script was a strange mixture of slapstick and what seemed to be stand-up vaudeville routines; they probably were holdovers from the Broadway musical. The routines, a half-dozen of them, tended to be repetitious; in each, Joe Cook, with Tom Howard, "Amos," demonstrates that he, Cook, is a fast-talking con man and that Amos is an incredibly stupid country bumpkin. This was not movie comedy; it was more Broadway than Hollywood, and in Hollywood Joe Cook was an unknown quantity. I wondered what induced Columbia to stake its future on a Broadway musical that no longer was a musical and on an actor/comedian/acrobat who did stand-up routines filled with outrageous non-sense. In 1920s Broadway parlance, Joe Cook was labeled a "nut comic," a term that suits his style perfectly. I learned later that Cook was one of the favorites of the famed Algonquin Round Table, haunt of the New York literary elite, and that drama critic Percy Hammond called Cook "the funniest man in America." Brooks Atkinson agreed, calling him "one of the greatest comedians of our time." Robert Benchley, a funny man with every syllable and every gesture, also agreed. He said that Cook is "entirely mad at heart, and sheer madness is, of course, the highest possible brow in humor."

The *Rain or Shine* circus sequences were big-time, big-expense items. Sam Bischoff bought an entire circus and moved it to the San Fernando Valley. Performers, clowns, and roustabouts were housed in their own wagons and fed by their own chuckwagon. Columbia hired crowds of extras, huge by Columbia standards, who had to be transported, fed, and paid every day. It could have been a costly, chaotic madhouse, but from the first day Capra took charge. He was confident, even buoyant, as though he welcomed the challenge of bringing order out of what easily could have become chaos.

On my memorable night location at Malibu Lake, I thought I saw in Capra evidence of that intangible quality, leadership. On our circus location I became sure that he possessed it. He was the center of everything; people came to him from all directions, to ask questions, to get decisions. He seldom seemed impatient or showed signs of stress. He was the man in charge.

Capra liked to use rain in his films. He used it in *Ladies of Leisure,* but the rain was outside a window; our microphones and cables were safe and dry inside. In the opening scenes of *Rain or Shine,* Smiley's circus wagons, in a typical Capra downpour, are bogged down in a sea of mud. Smiley, riding an elephant, shouts orders to his crew, trying to get his wagons out of the mud. We had to get our microphone into that deluge to record Smiley's orders. There were no operating manuals from Western Electric telling us what to do; we had to invent something, and we did. Our cables were waterproof; it was the connectors that were vulnerable. We cut pieces of innertube (there were no tubeless tires in those days), encased the connectors in them, and taped the ends tightly. We protected the microphone the same way. With the use of the wonderful old clam digger boom and the rubber-booted mike, we recorded Smiley, high up aboard the elephant, with no difficulty. In a later scene, the troupe's six hundred–pound fat lady falls out of her wagon into the mud and rain. Four strong men try to boost the fat lady back into her wagon. They can't do it. Smiley, on Pansy, his elephant, comes to the rescue and pushes the fat lady back into her wagon. Again we recorded Smiley's lines with no difficulty.

In the next scene, the script called for another wagon to bog down. Horses were unable to pull it out; Smiley ordered that Pansy be hitched to the wagon in their place. Our still photographer, a small man with large ears, decided to photograph the scene. In those days there were no flashbulbs; photographers used traylike flash guns in which they poured a charge of flash powder. Our man needed a great deal of light; he loaded the tray of his flash gun with all the magnesium powder it would hold. Placid, powerful Pansy was starting to move the wagon when our still man fired his over-loaded flash gun. The burst of light was enormous, and so was the powerful "woof" of the explosion. Pansy did not like the blinding flash of light; she snapped the wagon tongue like a matchstick and took off for the hills—the Verdugo Hills. The electricians manning the arc lights followed her with their beams of light. From high vantage points we could follow Pansy's route by observing the headlights of automobiles as motorists made panic stops, a prudent thing for them to do when a brightly illuminated elephant stampeded across their paths. Pansy's trainer, a tough little man named Murph, found Pansy the next day, contentedly grazing in the Verdugo foothills above Burbank, where brush fires had raged three years before.

Pansy's escapade caused a delay in production, but no other harm was done. There was a more serious accident. Capra wanted a high platform for a long shot of the entire circus. Our grip boss improvised a camera tower: three standard-sized camera platforms atop one another. It was improvised but not unsafe; it was secured by guy lines from each corner of the tower to stakes driven into the ground. Capra, Joe Walker, and our assistant director had been on the tower. They came down to organize the action, leaving an assistant cameraman, Fred Kaifer, alone on the tower with two cameras. A truck blundered into the area and snagged one of the guy lines. Men yelled, but the driver of the truck didn't heed the warning. A guy line snapped and the tower began to fall. I heard the yelling and looked out of my sound truck. I saw Fred Kaifer trying to keep his cameras from falling. The tower seemed to be at a balance point, as though it might right itself, but then it crashed, and Kaifer was badly injured. Our first-aid man tended him as best he could, but it was a long time until an ambulance arrived. When Freddie was released after months in a hospital, he was not the strong, cheerful young man we had known; he was a morose, bitter cripple.

On *Ladies of Leisure,* an intense, emotional film, Capra had been one kind of director; on *Rain or Shine,* a different kind of film, he was another kind of director. His manner with the crew was lighter, with good-natured banter, a display of camaraderie. His relationship with the New York actors, Joe Cook, Tom Howard, and Dave Chasen, was cordial from the beginning. There seemed to be a feeling of trust and respect between Capra and his New Yorkers.

On location, I was close to the action. Instead of being isolated in an "upstairs" monitor room, I took my mixer panel out of our sound truck and placed myself where I belonged, on the set, where the action was. I was able to listen in on plans for the next scene, the next sequence, or the next day. I had more contact with Capra; I felt that I was gaining acceptance. Some of the contact was forced on us by airplane noise. Even in 1930 there was considerable air activity in the San Fernando Valley. Lockheed airport was north of us, and the little dirt-strip airfield from which I had flown with Billy Richards in 1927 had developed into a commercial airfield, called Glendale Airport, with a paved runway. Later, when a handsome new passenger terminal was built, it became Grand Central Airport. Planes going north flew directly over our circus location. On some scenes, moderate plane noise could be covered by music or dubbed-in crowd noise, but some scenes would not be covered, and Capra was patient and cooperative in filming those scenes. He was, in fact, patient and tolerant if there were unavoidable mishaps, but he would not tolerate carelessness or inattention. There was the case of John Silver, hired as an extra camera operator when Capra was filming with four cameras. John Silver was the victim of viewfinder parallax. Camera experts know all about parallax; they may fast-forward if they wish.

The lens and the viewfinder of the Mitchell camera were about eight inches apart. The finder could be adjusted so that it displayed the same image as the lens *at a given point.* On a close-up, for instance, because the lens and the finder viewed things from a slightly different angle, they had to *converge* on the close-up; beyond that point they *diverged,* and in the background the lens and the finder were no longer looking at the same thing. John Silver failed to check his lens: he relied on his perfidious viewfinder, and when the dailies were run, in the background of Silver's shot an electrician stood nonchalantly beside one of his lamps. Silver may have gone to sea, perhaps even to the Spanish Main; that is not known. What is known is that John Silver worked for Frank Capra no more.

When we made *Ladies of Leisure,* scenes played better than they were written, and that is what happened on *Rain or Shine.* It didn't always occur like that; on some B films, directors and actors managed to make scenes play worse than they were written. Capra gave scenes animation and tempo. His emphasis was not on more speed but on the *correct* pace for each scene. He used various methods to achieve, usually by indirection, a brisk tempo in a scene that required it. In many of his films he used a phrase that worked well: he told his actors, "Remember, every word is the last one." He didn't elaborate, and didn't have to. Actors interpreted it as I did: "There are no lines in the script. You're making up your lines then and there, thinking about what you're saying. If you're the listener, every word is new to you, and you have to think about how to respond." A cumbersome lecture like that was never necessary. Actors thought about what they were saying, and they listened and reacted when spoken to.

Joe Cook's vaudeville-type routines surprised me. In the script I thought they might be too frequent, too long, and at times downright silly. When we filmed them, I could understand why they were successful in the Broadway musical. The performances of Joe Cook and Tom Howard had been polished by hundreds of performances, and Joe Cook displayed a personality that made him likable when a lesser man might have seemed obnoxious. His tour de force was a long discourse about the technique of eating cornflakes. The payoff of the outrageous routine was his conclusion that eating cornflakes without milk was not pleasant. It took a remarkable personality to make that routine work. What is the word for it—bravura? Webster says *bravura* is "daring, brilliant performance," and that's what it was.

There were interesting scenes of the circus and its performances; then came the black-hearted conspiracy—and trouble.
Capra seemed to relish the challenge and complexity of the action.
When the ringmaster incited the crowd to riot, Capra orchestrated
a most convincing riot. When the circus people responded to the
"Hey, Rube!" call to arms, we had a genuine Donnybrook, with
many contusions, abrasions, and some bloody noses.

The fire that destroyed Smiley's circus was the big climax of *Rain
or Shine*. Capra planned it like a general preparing to do battle; he
planned every detail, gave orders to everyone involved. He intended
to film his fire in one grand conflagration. Many directors, then and
now, preferred to use a series of controlled fires and film their holocaust one scene at a time. By using gas jets, fires that looked deadly
could readily be controlled; but Capra's fire was to be one big, expensive, no-second-chance conflagration. Capra was calm, decisive,
with no indication of concern or anxiety. He was a small man, but
he commanded many big men; electricians, grips, camera operators,
and stuntmen. They listened, and obeyed, because he was their
leader, and he would lead them to victory—a movie-business victory, a moneymaking film that would lead to more jobs, more food
on the table, more rent money, and more car payments for all.

Capra supervised the placing of eight cameras. Two of them were
linked to our sound truck: they were to photograph and we were to
record scenes in front of the blazing big top. The other six cameras
were "wild"—each had its own power supply. Capra's orders to the
six camera operators were simple: each one of them was on his own.
He was free to move his camera, change lenses, use his best judgment
in filming his part of the fire. When everything was rehearsed, discussed, and ready, Capra turned to Sam Nelson, our assistant director, to give the order to start the fire. Joe Walker told me later that Sam
looked worried, but Capra calmly told him, "OK, Sam, light 'er up."

No controlled series of fires could have duplicated what Capra's
grand conflagration did. The long-shot cameras showed wind-
whipped flames; large pieces of burning canvas flying high, borne
up by the intense updraft; the big tent poles crashing down. The
camera operators on the ground, urged to use their initiative, did so;
if flames got too hot, they retreated; if the flames subsided, they
moved in again, and some great film was shot in that fiery half-hour.
Of course there were pickup shots. There was no way that the
scenes of Smiley rescuing Mary from the burning big top could be

done safely. They were done—and done well—with controlled fires, and after the rescue Smiley turned Mary over to Bud. They presumably lived happily ever after.

There was a scene after that, another of the Joe Cook–Tom Howard routines. I was willing to concede that Cook was brilliant and could make outrageous material work by sheer force of personality, but about four minutes of nonsense, it seemed to me, was much too long when the audience sensed that the story had been told and it was time to go home.

"Sime," in his July 23, 1930, *Variety* review, had kind words for *Rain or Shine*. "It's a much better than average circus picture," he wrote. "It's a well-handled mob scene, as in the big fire right after. Frank Capra's direction is marked throughout the picture." Sime, however, found fault with the ending of *Rain or Shine*. "Toward the finish the story does go a little ragged and without a smooth finish."

Smooth finish or not, *Rain or Shine* didn't lack earning power. In release it was a rousing moneymaker. At Columbia it was said that every time Frank Capra made a picture, Columbia built a new sound stage. After *Flight,* Columbia built Stage 3; after *Ladies of Leisure,* Stage 4; and when the box office money from *Rain or Shine* came in, Columbia acquired two new stages, not by building but by buying them.

One of them became Columbia's Stage 6. It was an ancient stage, probably one of the first built in Hollywood, located between Columbia's offices and Sunset Boulevard. James Cruze, director of the silent classic *The Covered Wagon,* had just finished his first talking picture, *The Great Gabbo,* on that stage when I came to Columbia in August 1929. The other acquisition, which became Stage 7, was on Beechwood Drive, across the street from Columbia's main lot. It had been a rental stage, serving Poverty Row producers, and there were times, veteran electricians told me, when porno films were made there; they were called "stag reels" in those days. Stage 7 was tricky; there were some secret exits. If the place was raided, the juicers told me, cast and crew generally got away.

Columbia was growing—more sound stages, more production, and two new mixers with good credits were taken on as regulars, which meant more competition. I had an unofficial number-one status, but I knew that I must not turn in less-than-good work, even on the cheapest of B films; and B films were what I would work on until the next Capra picture.

10

There were nearly four months between the finish of *Rain or Shine* and the beginning of *Dirigible*. I was kept busy working on one B picture after another. It was week after week of twelve- and fourteen-hour days, six days a week. We endured an institution known as the Columbia Frolic; we worked from early Saturday morning until dawn Sunday, and we, the sound people, along with the script clerks and the assistant directors were not paid overtime. The Columbia Frolic lost some of its charm when the actors made the ridiculous claim that if they worked after midnight they were entitled to another day's pay, and they won their point.

My first films at Columbia are distinct in my memory because so much depended on them. After *Ladies of Leisure* and *Rain or Shine,* I was more secure, and the films I worked on became less memorable. I wish I had kept a diary during those first years at Columbia. Perhaps, unlike my UA diary, it may not have been lost. I would have a solid anchor in facts, names and dates. Walter Kerr, in his excellent book *The Silent Clowns,* has a most perceptive comment about memory: "The trouble with memory is not that it fails, but that it so generously creates." True. In autobiographies, and in interviews and letters that become the material of biographies, there is an overwhelming temptation on the part of the person whose story is being told to bend his account of events in his favor; to make them more exciting or more interesting, and to make himself more witty, more intelligent, and more courageous. So much for memory. Mine may fail, but I will try not to allow it to create.

Any such omissions and creations may be hard for movie buffs to document. It was long ago, and the Columbia B films of the early 1930s were of such little importance, even then, that the most dedicated film buff might not find films with which to challenge my omissions—or creations. To my knowledge, those B films have never been shown on TV and are not available on videocassettes. Perhaps Columbia destroyed the negatives or allowed them to disintegrate. None of them are listed in Leonard Maltin's *Movie & Video Guide,* and that is an almost certain indication that they have gone to the great incinerator in the sky.

Here is a grab bag of my films after *Rain or Shine: Prince of Diamonds,* director, Karl Brown—poor picture, good actor, Ian Keith. *Royal Romance,* director, Erle Kenton; Clarence Muse was excellent, the rest of the cast was not. *The Squealer,* director, Harry Joe Brown. The man cast as The Squealer was Louis Natheaux, perfectly typecast as a cowardly, double-crossing mobster. He was a treacherous crook in Roy Neill's *Murder on the Roof* and Erle Kenton's *Mexicali Rose.* He was the quintessential rat fink, and he's not even listed in Leslie Halliwell's *Filmgoer's Companion!* In *The Squealer,* Louis Natheaux is machine-gunned by Earle Bunn, doubling for Jack Holt. More about Earle Bunn later.

Also among my credits was *Pagan Lady.* The director was John Francis Dillon, and the locale was a waterfront dive. The script required Wallace MacDonald, portraying a Latin lover, to sweep Evelyn Brent off her feet and lift her to the top of the bar. He was unable to do it. John Francis Dillon was cruel; he forced MacDonald to try, many times. Brent attempted to help Wally by executing a little jump when he picked her up, but it didn't work. MacDonald didn't suffer a hernia, but he did suffer acute embarrassment. I was to encounter MacDonald later—twenty years later.

Erle Kenton, director of my first Columbia film, was typical of the veteran directors who made the transition from silent to sound film. Kenton had a silent-film history that went back to early Mack Sennett days. Like many silent-film veterans, Kenton referred to lines of dialogue as "titles." To them, the spoken words were merely substitutes for the printed titles shown on the screen, and some of the directors didn't pay much attention to how well or how badly those lines were delivered.

When I did *Song of Love,* my first Columbia film, Kenton's demeanor seemed arrogant and condescending. I had worked with

Herbert Brenon and George Fitzmaurice, famous silent-film directors, and with D. W. Griffith, greatest of them all, and the manner—of all of them—was far less pompous than Kenton's. I didn't realize until my second film with Kenton that his lordly manner was only that—his manner—and that he was not condescending and only moderately arrogant.

When I made *Mexicali Rose* with Kenton, I believe some of Barbara Stanwyck's hatred of the film was caused by what she perceived to be Kenton's patronizing attitude. Stanwyck knew she was a good actress; she tried to do her best with poor material, but to have Kenton talk down to her made the film a painful ordeal— "an abortion," as she called it. She once referred to *Mexicali Rose* as one of the worst pictures ever made.

After *Rain or Shine* I worked again on a Kenton film, a gangster movie, *The Last Parade.* Kenton had progressed as a director. From time to time he still called a line of dialogue a "title," but he now paid attention to how those lines were delivered. *The Last Parade* was a good picture and earned Kenton some favorable reviews. "Sime," in *Variety,* March 4, 1931, wrote that *The Last Parade* was "a box-office picture—a very well-made film." The name of Earle D. Bunn appears in the cast list as the character "Lefty," but Earle was more than a bit player; he was Columbia's resident machine-gun man. Earle was a World War I veteran who was severely wounded and lost a leg. When a one-legged man was needed in a film, Earle generally got the job, and he developed into a reasonably good actor. His main job in *The Last Parade,* however, was to be Columbia's machine-gun man. He was an expert with the Thompson submachine gun, the infamous "Tommy gun" used by mobsters of the era. Earle was one of the few men in Hollywood who could rig a Tommy gun to fire blanks reliably.

The script called for Jack Holt to be ambushed by a hit man. A door frame inches from Holt's face was to be shattered by a blast from a Tommy gun. Live ammunition was to be used. A steel plate, faced with four-inch planks, was placed out of camera range to stop the bullets before they ricocheted out of Stage 3, perhaps into Sunset and Gower, where they might have winged some unsuspecting cowboy waiting for a job.

The scene was done split-screen. Half of the camera aperture was covered, and Jack Holt's reaction to the volley of bullets was photographed. The film was rewound in the camera; the aperture cover was moved from the door frame part of the scene to the Holt portion. Earle Bunn prepared to shoot. He cradled his Tommy gun on the back of an upholstered armchair, knelt on the seat of the chair, and fired a full magazine. The noise was awesome, and the door frame was blasted into a blizzard of dust and splinters. There were no casualties; the steel and wood backstop caught all of the bullets.

The scene was run in the dailies the next day. Jack Holt reacted beautifully; the timing was just right, but when Earle Bunn's Tommy gun slugs tore up the door frame, the cloud of dust and splinters stopped abruptly at the split-screen line. It was a weird effect; it was like one of the force fields the science-fiction people are so fond of: an invisible, powerful barrier capable of stopping a speeding bullet, a speeding artillery shell, or a speeding leading man. The film editor salvaged the scene by double-exposing flying debris over the clear portion of the split-screen.

And, finally, there was Roy William Neill, the Irish director with the French-sounding name. Crew members called him "Rocking Chair Neill" because, on every film, he demanded that the propman provide him with a rocking chair. He differed from other Columbia directors in many ways. He was not quick-tempered or profane, as some of them were, nor was he imperious, as Kenton was. He did not refer to lines of dialogue as "titles"; he had stage experience, and took pains with the way lines were delivered. I liked Neill but disliked working with him because we invariably worked long hours on his films. In the morning Neill was an artistic, painstaking director, working as though he had a generous A picture schedule. At the lunch break the production office would discover that Neill had used one-half of his time to film one-third of his scheduled day's work. The production office cracked the whip; Neill tried to become a fast, efficient B picture director, but he didn't know how to be fast and efficient. We invariably ended up working far into the night, while Roy Neill rocked, gently, in his rocking chair.

Neill was a gentleman, courteous and considerate of people with whom he worked. I hadn't heard a harsh word from him until we made a deep-sea drama, *Fifty Fathoms Deep*. The story involved the sinking of a submarine. Working from photographs of a U.S. Navy sub, our set builders constructed the interior of the submarine. The control panel, the periscope, and the huge diesel engine were woodworking masterpieces. All was well until the submarine was rammed and began to sink; water poured in, and men floundered in shoulder-deep water. It was exciting and dramatic; but suddenly the big diesel engine, the wooden masterpiece, pulled loose from its hold-down nails and floated to the surface. Gentlemanly Roy Neill used some coarse language; whether he learned the words in Ireland, England, or Hollywood is not known, but he used a number of vigorous Anglo-Saxon expletives that day.

Dirigible, with Frank Capra, was going to be an adventure. We would start production in New Jersey, at the Lakehurst Naval Air Station, home base of the dirigible *Los Angeles.*

Many of our studio people came to the old Southern Pacific station to see us off. We were not a full crew; the New York unions had decreed that most of the jobs had to be filled by their people. We were allowed a propman, George Rhein, and a script clerk, Tess Gilbert; Frank Capra was allowed one assistant, Sam Nelson. Joe Walker had one assistant, George Kelly, and the aerial cameraman, Elmer Dyer. The camera operators and their assistants would be New York people, and there were times when we would use eight cameras. There were two of us soundmen. At Lakehurst we would be joined by two men from New York. The man John Livadary chose for the trip was Russell Carpenter, a man so versatile and so skilled that he could do any job in the sound crew and do it well. Livadary's decision to send Carpenter on the trip was a good one. Without Carpenter, we would have been in deep trouble.

Train travel was a glorious way to travel. No plane can match the feeling of ease and luxury we had in the first-class trains of sixty years ago. One memory of the trip stays with me. It was my first night in a Pullman sleeper. I woke up in the small hours of the morning; the train was roaring along, and there was a great sense of speed and power. I looked out of the window; we were somewhere in Arizona. I saw a desolate landscape, like the surface of the moon, bright in the moonlight. The scene remains clear in my memory, probably because I was unsophisticated, I was embarking on an adventure, and I was twenty-five years old.

We entered the Midwest, past well-cared-for farms and small towns—the nation's heartland. We changed trains in Chicago. Everyone changed trains in Chicago. I'd heard it since I was a child that no train ever went *through* Chicago. My family—my hard-working, uncomplaining parents and my two sisters—came to see me during the short time between trains. It was apparent that my parents were proud of me, but we were not a demonstrative family; there was emotion, but it was beneath the surface.

On the road again, the final day took us down the Hudson River Valley. A memorable day—the river, the small towns, and the cities, the place names of American history.

We were met in New York by a contingent from the Columbia New York office. A man named Ben Schwalb was assigned to be our liaison with New York, and thus I became acquainted with him. Just as Wallace MacDonald would cross my path twenty years later, so would Ben Schwalb—even later.

Schwalb loaded us into a bus; we crossed the Hudson River and went into New Jersey. We were bound for a town called Toms River, about sixty miles from New York—a slow sixty miles. About halfway, we ate dinner in an old house that looked like the Bates house from *Psycho,* except that it was on flat land, near a saltwater estuary rather than on a hill. We were served "shore dinners," wonderful food, featuring an abundance—a superabundance—of seafood. We arrived in Toms River after dark; our rooms were ready.

The next day was Friday. Our rented sound truck was to have preceded us to Toms River, so that we could test the equipment and be ready to work on Monday, but it hadn't arrived, nor did it appear on Saturday. Schwalb phoned; he was told that the truck had left New York as scheduled, with a driver and two sound technicians aboard. No truck. Schwalb told the Columbia office; it was AWOL somewhere in New Jersey. It was panic time in New York, and a massive lost-truck search was laid on, as the British would say. Finally, late Saturday evening the truck—and the men—were found. The men had done some serious drinking early in the trip, and the driver managed to lose his way. The men were in jail, and the truck was impounded in a small town near Trenton, New Jersey, forty miles off course, where the driver had smashed into a couple of parked cars. Trenton is famed in history because George Washington crossed the Delaware River there and defeated England's Hessian mercenaries. It was not an interest in history that brought our men to Trenton; they were there, Ben Schwalb said, because they were "stupid, stinkin', fall-down drunk."

Schwalb set out on a rescue mission. He chose our propman, George Rhein, to go with him, but his most powerful persuasion was in his pocket—a thousand dollars in cash. Rhein related their adventures to me. They routed a local magistrate out of bed. He was furious but listened when Schwalb hinted that financial transactions might take place. Ben agreed that the driver should be held, but he insisted that the truck and the soundmen should be released. The magistrate disagreed; he didn't believe any nonsense about movies and a sound recording truck; the vehicle was clearly a clandestine radio transmitter, communicating with bootleggers operating off the New Jersey coast. Logic didn't help, documents that proved that we were a legitimate movie company didn't help, but the persuasive currency in Ben Schwalb's pocket did help. The magistrate sent for a police official; they bargained, became somewhat more wealthy, and released the sound truck and the two hung-over soundmen.

The truck and the men reached Toms River midmorning Sunday, and the men went straight to bed. Carpenter and I opened up the sound truck. It was a shambles. The vehicle had been slightly damaged in the accident, but the jolt had knocked amplifiers from their racks; the box of delicate light valves and the equally vulnerable microphones were on the floor. When Ben Schwalb saw the damage, he was shocked. The damage seemed too great to repair, and there wasn't another sound truck available in New York. While Ben Schwalb agonized about what to do, Carpenter examined the wreckage. After a time he said, "I can fix this thing."

He began immediately. The light valves, protected by the case that held them, were not broken. The CTA mikes, the monsters that had vacuum tubes in them, had some shattered tubes but were otherwise unharmed, and Russell found a cache of spare tubes. He refused my help. It was a one-man job, he said; there wasn't room for two men, and, besides, there was only one soldering iron. Russell worked all day Sunday and into the night. He slept for a few hours on the floor of the truck and began working again. He was not quite finished Monday morning, but the rains came and our call to work was canceled. Russell finished the work, and we were able to make a complete test of the equipment.

That afternoon we met our wayward soundmen. The recordist was named Cameron; I never learned his given name. He was a competent recordist when he was sober, but he was often not sober. The man hired to be our mike man was named "Tilly"; Carpenter and I never learned his surname. Tilly's value to us can be summed up in one word—useless. He disappeared whenever he chose to do so, and when he returned, he usually brought a bottle for Cameron.

Our first day at Lakehurst Naval Air Station was a day of overpowering spectacle. The navy put its lighter-than-air fleet on display. The New Jersey sky was filled with free balloons, captive balloons, small blimps designed for antisubmarine patrol, and the majestic dirigible *Los Angeles*.

Our work that day was not demanding; we recorded sound effects: blimps and airplanes passing overhead, the cheering of a large crowd. When the *Los Angeles* came slowly into view, its engines were turning so slowly that they could hardly be heard.

Our repaired truck functioned well, but I found another cause for concern. The mike boom supplied with the truck was poorly designed and poorly built. It had a too-small base; when it was used with the heavy CTA, it tended to be dangerously unstable. Ben Schwalb promised to find a Mole-Richardson boom for us. When I told him that Tilly was useless and ought to be fired, he was horrified. He pleaded with me not to fire Tilly, or even to reprimand him; it might cause a strike. We had to make do without Tilly, which was, in any event, better than making do with him.

In the days that followed, Joe Walker shot some spectacular film, such as the *Los Angeles* hovering over the airfield, demonstrating that it could abandon ship, if necessary, like any other navy vessel, with a twenty-man parachute jump. With multiple cameras, Joe filmed the docking of the *Los Angeles* to its mooring mast, a maneuver that demanded wonderful precision and teamwork. Joe, no youngster, made the dangerous climb to the top of the mooring mast to photograph the actual locking-in of the *Los Angeles* to its movable mast. New York cameramen had spoiled several shots, mostly aloft, where Joe couldn't check on them, and Joe climbed the tower to be sure he got the close shot of the docking process. We filmed an impressive night takeoff; as part of our *Dirigible* scenario, the airship was departing on a rescue mission to the South Pole. It was big-time, the biggest of big-time, millions of dollars' worth of the navy's airfleet, working for us.

Inevitably, we, the sound crew, had to do some unspectacular but necessary work; record dialogue scenes. Fortunately, much of what we did were scenes that required little or no microphone movement. Russ Carpenter functioned well as our mike man.

Some of our work at Lakehurst was to be filmed in the navy's enormous hangar, a structure so lofty that it created its own weather; we were told that at times, clouds formed in the hangar and rain fell. To Columbia, it was a valuable production asset. In Hollywood, every production manager and every assistant director tried to provide a cover set, an interior set that served to keep production moving when a troupe on location was driven indoors by rain. The hangar was our cover set.

Rain came to Lakehurst in midafternoon one day, and we moved into the hangar. I was spotting our sound truck where it would be needed when I was jolted by a hard blow to my shoulder. I turned—it was Jack Holt, drunk, angry, and incoherent. He was angry at sound—and therefore at me—and not without reason. On a film with Jack, earlier that year, my boom operator had been a little slow in his reactions. On two occasions Jack, seated, rose quickly and cracked his head on the heavy CTA microphone. Jack gave me another strong push—the traditional invitation to put 'em up—to fight. Out of the corner of my eye I could see Capra, concerned, wondering whether to intervene. One more push—Jack had done the scene in many films. If the coward wouldn't fight, hit him; make him fight. It was time for action, and I went into action—verbally. I recited an entire litany of mea culpas. I touched all bases. I said that I had been negligent, careless, didn't do my job well, and deserved his righteous anger. I begged his forgiveness, promising that I would perform better in the future. Jack listened, befuddled by my torrent of apology. "All right," he growled. "You just watch it." With that, he turned and walked away, square jaw, square shoulders, square everything. He was so drunk he couldn't talk straight, but he did walk straight—the exaggerated stiff walk of the veteran drinker. Capra came over to me. "You did the right thing," he said. "You handled it just right."

Jack Holt did not drink again during work hours, but he did go pub crawling with three navy men. The navy officer who was driving made an alcohol-induced navigation error and crashed his car into a bridge abutment. The navy men were all badly hurt, but Holt escaped with a cut on his forehead, and Columbia was spared a financial disaster. I overheard Capra and Sam Briskin discussing it. Briskin was vice president of Columbia and ordinarily worked in Hollywood, but he came to New York to oversee production of *Dirigible* and from time to time visited us at Lakehurst.

"When I called Cohn to tell him about the accident," Briskin said, "he bawled me out for letting Jack get hurt. I told him I was here to help with the production, not to be a nursemaid to Jack Holt. Anyway, all he got was a cut on the head; we won't miss a day." "Columbia luck," said Capra.

Columbia had more luck as we neared the end of our scheduled stay at Lakehurst. Some aerial shots of the *Los Angeles* flying over New York had been made, but the weather had not been ideal, and background shots, which we called "plates" in those days, were needed for process shots to back up the scenes in the dirigible's navigating bridge. A few days before we were scheduled to leave Lakehurst we had perfect weather over New York City, and the *Los Angeles* and a fleet of camera planes took off to photograph the great airship and the great city. Joe Walker, aboard the *Los Angeles,* roamed the ship, carrying a hand-held Eyemo camera. He told me that he ventured down a tiny, retractable ladder so that he could descend from the belly of the airship and photograph the city straight down: The Battery, Times Square, Broadway, and Central Park, with nothing but three thousand feet of air beneath him. A wealth of fine footage was shot that day, but something happened that hurt Joe Walker deeply. Some cameramen turned in only a part of their footage and sold choice shots to newsreels and film libraries. Joe, the most honorable of men, was hurt because he thought of his New York cameramen as friends as well as fellow photographers.

In the huge hangar we filmed the scene in which Commander Bradon (Holt) addresses the officers and men of the Lakehurst Naval Air Station, telling them of the rescue mission to the South Pole. The scene contained vital strong information, but in the script it seemed formal and static. As Capra and Walker filmed it, it was far from static. Capra asked the navy officer in charge to have his men assemble in the hangar at top speed. It may not have been the way the navy ordinarily did it, but our navy people complied; the men rushed into the hangar, a thousand of them, with all-out, disciplined speed wonderful to behold.

The first time Capra and Walker saw the immense hangar, they were determined to film an extreme long shot in it. In the Antarctic briefing scene, they made such a shot. They sent a camera crew up to a catwalk, just under the roof of the hangar, with instructions to use a wide-angle lens to get the longest shot possible. In the rushes we saw the white-clad enlisted men, in a long, straight line, the men so small they appeared as tiny white figures. Capra used the long shot sparingly, but it was most effective; it gave Holt's presentation of the South Pole mission drama and importance.

Our work at Lakehurst was finished, and we packed and left Toms River. We had one more day's work in New York City, on the steps of the city hall, where Jack Holt, commander of the Antarctic mission, is given a hero's welcome on his return. We spent the night in a hotel in New York. The next morning we found that our sound truck made the trip from Toms River safely, with our makeshift boom lashed to the roof. We had to make do with that boom, and to function as a two-man sound crew as well, because Cameron and Tilly disappeared as soon as they reached New York.

Carpenter and I should have been dismayed, but we were not; we found it exciting—a challenge. I felt exhilarated, much as I'd felt when I was careening through the streets of Glendale, siren screaming, while the Verdugo Hills were ablaze. Carpenter told Sam Briskin of our short-handed plight. Briskin had been with us at Lakehurst and was now functioning as chief worrier, concerned about the high cost of filming in New York. Carpenter and I did have a problem. There were two of us, and there were three jobs to be done. Carpenter could handle the mike boom or operate the recording machine, but not both. His solution was simple and direct; he drafted the vice president of Columbia Pictures, Sam Briskin, to handle the boom. "No problem," Russ Carpenter told me. "Mr. Briskin was worrying about cost. He can worry just as well while he's making sure that boom doesn't tip and crack somebody's head."

Everything we did in our filming at city hall was designed to match the newsreel footage of the ceremony honoring Admiral Richard Byrd for *his* aerial flight over the South Pole the year before. Holt was dressed in navy white, as Byrd had been; Columbia hired actors who resembled Mayor Jimmy Walker and his famous greeter, Grover Whalen. Everything else matched the Byrd ceremony: the radio announcers, the navy band, and the crowd of celebrities on the steps of the city hall. Columbia even found the Packard touring car that had carried Admiral Byrd on his triumphant parade.

For us, the two-man sound crew, everything went well. The few scenes we recorded were short, simple, and didn't require mike movement. When the mayor asks Holt to sit on the back of his seat, "Where the people can see you," that too produced a perfect match; Admiral Byrd had perched just so during his parade. And so, thanks to newsreel footage, Columbia had a parade with a cast of half a million people and a blizzard of ticker tape.

So ended, successfully, our epic trip to New Jersey and the great city of New York. The trip was successful for us—for sound, thanks to Russell Carpenter. I sometimes wonder what happened to him. In the late thirties, war clouds were beginning to gather. I was away on location when Carpenter announced that he was leaving Columbia "to work for the government." That was all he would say; apparently he had been warned to say nothing about this job, not even to say that it was secret. There were rumors that Russ had been recruited to work for the navy in a antisubmarine warfare base on the East Coast. We sound people at Columbia expected to hear from him when the war was over, but we heard nothing. I hope he survived the war. If the navy got Russell Carpenter, the navy got a very good man.

Our trip home was even more pleasant than the trip to the East; there was a feeling among us of a job well one. In the dining car, one day, I had the opportunity to ask Capra why he had demanded that I finish *Ladies of Leisure* instead of Blanchard.

"Blanchard was a four-flusher—you know that, don't you?" Capra said. I replied that I did know that. "He was a prima donna," Capra continued. "I'd tell Joe what the next scene was. Ten minutes later Blanchard wanted to be told, *personally,* what the next setup was. Then he'd bend my ear telling me how good he was. That night at Malibu Lake you listened, and when Joe was ready you were ready. What happened to Blanchard?"

I was able to tell him. In San Diego I met a man named Otto Benziger, a probation officer for San Diego County. "We had one of your people here," he had said. "A fellow named Blanchard. I don't suppose you know him?" I had assured Benziger that I did know him. "He passed some bad checks here," Benziger had said. "I was his probation officer. He reported a couple of times, then failed to show up. I was told that he went back East somewhere." "I'm not surprised," Capra said. "All ego and no brains."

And so we returned to Hollywood, to our home base at Sunset and Gower. While we were at Lakehurst, the South Pole was being constructed for us at Arcadia, California, on the site of an abandoned World War I balloon school. Crews were trained there in the operation and maintenance of observation balloons, used for artillery spotting on the Western Front.

Our principal interior sets were built on Columbia's Stage 1, which meant I was exiled once more to my upstairs monitor room, with an uninspiring view of empty light platforms and the back of an unused set. The scenes we filmed were "story" scenes, long and carefully rehearsed, much different from the short, fast-moving scenes we shot at Lakehurst. I had time to marvel at the remarkable success Columbia—and Capra—had achieved and, with *Dirigible,* would again achieve, using the same two-men-and-a-girl story for the third time—and with the same actors. In *Submarine* Jack Holt and Ralph Graves are deep-sea divers, comrades, until a woman, Dorothy Revier, comes between them. They become bitter enemies, but when Graves faces death in a sunken submarine, Holt rescues him. In *Flight,* Holt and Graves are Marine Corps flyers, and again a woman comes between them, Lila Lee, a navy nurse. Holt thinks Graves double-crossed him to gain the love of the luscious Lila Lee, but when Graves, bombing guerrillas in Central America, is shot down behind enemy line, Jack Holt rescues him from certain death. And now, in *Dirigible,* Jack Holt, commander of the navy dirigible *Pensacola,* loves Fay Wray, but she is married to his best friend, Ralph Graves, a publicity-loving naval aviator. Honorable, square Jack Holt wouldn't dream of making a pass at beautiful Fay Wray, but when she asks him to kick her husband off of a lighter-than-air expedition to the South Pole, Holt agrees, reluctantly. When Holt gives Graves the bad news, the showoff pilot is enraged; he accuses Holt of ditching him because Holt wants all the glory for himself. Graves then organizes his own flight to the South Pole and, arriving there, impulsively decides to land at the pole instead of flying over it. "It's perfect for a landing," he says, but the South Pole is *not* a perfect landing place; the showoff pilot lands—and crashes. And, of course, Holt, with his new airship, the *Los Angeles,* rescues him from certain death, turns him over to his forgiving wife, and rides with an aching heart in a ticker-tape parade in his honor.

It's not hard to scoff at the story recycling, but a few facts should be noted. All three films did well. They were not merely successful, they were legitimate box office hits. Capra gave them something that lifted them out of the ordinary, and the box office dollars and the prestige the films earned for Columbia gave the studio a strong push upward from Poverty Row. Capra was probably aware that the triangular love story with the military background had run its course; he never made that kind of film again. His next four films—*Miracle Woman, Platinum Blonde, Forbidden* and *American Madness*—were all different from one another and completely different from the Holt-Graves epics.

In the studio, several of our sets were on our newer stages, and there I was released from the infamous upstairs monitor booth. When the Columbia people built the new stages, they knew that the upstairs booths were expensive to build and inefficient in operation, so old camera booths were pulled out of Columbia's scene dock, cleaned up, and equipped as monitor booths, to be used on the stage floor. It was a big improvement; I could pop out of my booth and in a few seconds view a rehearsal, instruct my mike man, or, if necessary, confer with the director. And, from time to time, I did confer with the director. I felt that I was gaining acceptance with Capra and even, on occasion, ventured an opinion—diffidently, of course.

We were to go to Arcadia for our Antarctic sequences, leaving some of our interior sets available as cover sets. Cover sets? To protect against the possibility of rain, in September, in the San Gabriel Valley? Sunstroke, perhaps, but not rainfall.

Our move to Arcadia was delayed because we had to conform to navy scheduling. We were to spend a day filming aboard the giant aircraft carrier *Saratoga*. We had two sequences to film. The first was a rendezvous at sea with the *Saratoga* when Jack Holt tethers his dirigible, the *Pensacola,* to the deck of the *Saratoga* for refueling. In our story, the *Pensacola* is destroyed by a hurricane soon after the refueling and goes down at sea. The *Saratoga* responds to the *Pensacola* SOS and rescues the survivors. The second sequence aboard the *Saratoga* was to show the arrival of the rescued men.

That first sequence was most interesting. We were to shoot scenes to be intercut with official navy film. The navy film was described in a paragraph in our *Dirigible* script, scene 205: "The following scene is based upon a section of film now in the Navy Department files, and if a copy of this film is made available it will never be necessary actually to bring the *Los Angeles* and the *Saratoga* together in the filming of this scene."

Jo Swerling, who wrote the screenplay, had apparently seen the film, because it was broken down in our script, scene by scene, exactly as it was to be intercut with the film we would film aboard the *Saratoga*. For instance: Navy film: "The crew and officers are watching the approach of the dirigible; dirigible settling down, background of open sea." Our film: Interior *Pensacola* control bridge, process shot, in studio. Holt: "Drop forward lines, stop engines." Navy film: "Men are picking up the lines dropped from the *Pensacola*." The entire sequence was shot in this fashion. Our close shots, with our actors, were carefully matched to cut with the navy film. End of sequence, scene 218: Officer (our actor): "All OK, Jack, good luck." Holt, scene 219, process shot in control bridge: "Let go all lines. Drop forward ballast." Navy film: "Water ballast is let out, a great volume of water douses the crew of the *Saratoga*."

That was the way our script required us to film, and that's the way we shot it. The day aboard the *Saratoga* was a memorable day for me, made even more so because I was introduced to the captain of the *Saratoga*. Capra, Joe Walker, and Sam Nelson were discussing the next setup, and I was listening. I did a lot of listening in those days. An officer approached us. He told us that the captain of the *Saratoga* would like to greet us. "Would you and your senior people come with me?" he asked. I wasn't sure I was included, but Capra gave me a kind of quizzical look and said, "All right, *senior,* let's go," and I went. We met the captain, a lordly figure, almost as lordly as Erle Kenton. He introduced his executive officer and his air officer, two formidable three-strip commanders. It was informal—no handshakes, just an exchange of names. Capra reeled off Joe Walker's name, Sam Nelson's—and mine. I had been introduced to the captain of the mighty warship *Saratoga*. It would have made a much better story if the *Saratoga*'s captain had been Ernest King, who was admiral of the fleet during World War II, chief of naval Operations, and commander of the greatest fighting fleet the world has ever known. In Capra's autobiography, he writes that he met Ernest King in 1929 when he filmed scenes for *Flight* aboard the *Saratoga*. But Ernest King never commanded the *Saratoga,* so the captain I met was not the illustrious wartime admiral. Ernest King was captain of the *Sara*'s sister ship, the *Lexington,* in the late 1920s. Perhaps Capra met him aboard the gallant *Lex,* sunk in battle, lying deep in the waters of the Coral Sea.

In the finished film, the refueling sequence was not used. It could not have been Columbia's decision; the sequence would have been of great pictorial and great story value. The navy probably exercised that "if" mentioned in scene 205 of our script. Perhaps some crusty old admiral, a lighter-than-air advocate, learned that in our story our airship, the *Pensacola,* was destroyed by a hurricane only a few hours after the refueling rendezvous and decided, angrily, that Columbia couldn't have the film.

We moved eastward, where dozens of men, working many weeks, created our Antarctica in the San Gabriel Valley. They spread a great quantity of raw burlap and pegged it to the hard ground; a thick slush of hard-drying plaster was put atop the burlap. When it hardened, it effectively prevented Arcadia's dirt from discoloring the pristine white of our South Pole. Gypsum and marble dust, collected from the waste bins of many marble cutters, provided the fallen snow. For our snowstorms and blizzards we used bleached cornflakes; about a ton it was on hand. To provide a background, and to hide the palm trees and orange groves a half-mile away, a snow-covered range of mountains was built. It was an excellent set, in concept and in construction.

We first filmed scenes at the base camp from which the flamboyant "Frisky" Pierce (Graves) would take off for his flight to the South Pole. The *Dirigible* script specified that the base camp he built exactly like Admiral Byrd's; Graves's plane, a Fokker Tri-Motor, was similar to the plane flown by Byrd. Perhaps Columbia hoped to use some of the Byrd scenes as stock shots, but none were used. Perhaps the Byrd people were disgruntled because *Dirigible*'s fiction was a great success, while the real-life Byrd film was not.

The temperature at the base camp was supposed to be subzero, and it troubled Capra that there was no frosty breath. He experimented with little wire-mesh cages that held a small piece of dry ice, to be placed in an actor's mouth. The theory was that cold breath in hot air would produce the same effect as warm breath in cold air. It didn't work that way. Condensation was so slight that it could hardly be seen, and actors could only mumble with the troublesome little cages in their mouths. Hobart Bosworth, the veteran actor cast as the eminent explorer, Rondelle, swallowed his piece of dry ice and was violently ill. There were no more of the dry-ice experiments, and no critic pointed out the lack of frosty breath as a flaw.

It was hot in Arcadia that September. Actors and extras, stripped to shorts and shoes, groaned when Sam Nelson called, "All the men in furs." They reluctantly put on fur parkas, heavy padded pants, mittens, and high-topped boots; and when Capra got a good take and said "OK, print that one," the parkas, pants, mittens and boots came off very quickly. An added ordeal was "frost on the puss." Many of the men at the base camp were bearded. In the bitter cold of the Antarctic, a man's warm breath condensed and froze on mustache and beard; hence Sam Nelson's call: "Frost on the puss." Our makeup man, Norbert Miles, brushed melted paraffin on beards and mustaches, and the men were properly frosted.

We encountered few problems in the base camp scenes. On location, in bright sunlight, there can be trouble for sound: microphone shadows. When a cameraman or a director chose to shoot in flat light—direct, over-the-camera sunlight—the mike-shadow problem is sometimes insoluble; it is difficult to use a "cutter" on the sun. Walker and Capra disliked flat light, Joe because it made for flat photography and Capra because a harsh front light was not consistent with sunlight in a polar region. In an interview about the filming of Antarctic scenes, Joe said that he always used some diffusion to soften the harshness of our California sun.

The Fokker plane was the center of many of our base camp scenes. It was a genuine plane, but not airworthy. Columbia bought it to wreck it, and wreck it we did. The engines of the Fokker had been replaced by electric motors; they turned the three propellers almost noiselessly, which helped our recording of scenes with the plane in the background, propellers turning.

We filmed the crack-up of the Fokker plane. The crash had been shot in miniature by Hollywood's best special effects men of that time, William Butler and Ned Mann, assisted by my teenage friend of KELW days, Lawrence Butler, working with his father. We met from time to time when the special effects team brought film for us to see, and Larry and I agreed that much had happened since he sat with me in the cramped little control room of KELW.

Capra wanted the plane crash to be as realistic as possible, and so, with the help of a gigantic crane, we flipped our plane, a horrendous somersault, with four cameras turning. We patched up the damage and crashed the plane several times, with different camera angles and different camera speeds. Most of the cameras were undercranked to speed up the crash, but Capra overcranked some cameras for a slow-motion effect, to make the crash seem more ponderous. Overcranking was seldom used in those days. Perhaps our use, in *Dirigible,* foreshadowed the use of over-cranking as it was used in *Butch Cassidy and the Sundance Kid* when Butch and Sundance dash out, in dreamlike slow motion, to meet their fate.

To the eye, none of the crane-assisted crack-ups were impressive, nor was the miniature or the undercranked and overcranked scenes we saw in the projection room. Capra acknowledged the problem. "We'll have to fix it in the cutting room," he said.

It *was* fixed in the cutting room. In his *Variety* review of the film on April 8, 1931, "Sime" wrote, "The crack-up is a tenser all the way. How Columbia did it is its own secret. There's no process to explain that." Capra's film editor, Maurice Wright, could have explained. It was a cutting-room shell game, quick cuts that made viewers see things—and believe what they saw—without knowing exactly what they *had* seen. It was the same film-cutting technique that Hitchcock employed in the famous shower murder scene in *Psycho.* Maury Wright had taken a few cuts of blurred, rapid movement, one of them a fragment from the Butler-Mann miniature, and used those quick cuts between the start of the full-sized plane's crash and its finish. Even if a person ran the film repeatedly, he couldn't be sure what he saw.

From the crash onward, the story of the crash victims is one of misery and death. Of the four men aboard the plane, the explorer, Rondelle, dies soon after the accident. Graves's mechanic, McGuire (Roscoe Karns), sustains a broken leg; it becomes infected, and in a harrowing scene, Graves amputates it. McGuire, realizing that he is holding back Graves's attempt to walk back to the base camp, crawls out into a blizzard to die while his companions sleep.

There is skillful editing throughout *Dirigible.* D. W. Griffith, who invented the technique of parallel action, would have approved. The plight of the victims of the crash—the deaths of two of them, the desperate attempt of Graves and his radioman Hansen to walk to the safety of the base camp—is intercut with scenes of Fay Wray's reaction to her husband's mortal peril and with scenes of Jack Holt pleading with an admiral for permission to fly to Antarctica on a rescue mission. We see the plight of Graves and Hansen grow worse; Graves becomes snow-blind. He drags the heavy sleigh, laden with their tent and their meager food supply, guided by Hansen's directions. Again, back to Lakehurst: Holt asks for volunteers for the rescue mission.

In Antarctica, Graves and Hansen skirt a terrifying crevice; exhausted, Hansen fails to warn Graves and the edge of the crevice breaks away. Graves barely saves himself from falling to his death, but the sleigh is lost. Now they have no food or shelter, and their plight is hopeless.

From that point on, the parallel action gains speed. The cuts are shorter, creating an air of urgency. Finally, the men are sighted by lookouts on the dirigible and are rescued by parachutists, who hoist them aboard.

With the rescue, we finished our work at Arcadia and returned to Columbia to shoot two sets: the control bridges of the two airships of our story and the huge, cavernous interiors.

From time to time, with a touch of nostalgia, I think of our adventures at our South Pole in Arcadia. The famous Santa Anita racetrack is about a mile from where we filmed, and the land we transformed to Antarctica is now part of the Santa Anita golf course.

For scenes in the control bridges of our airships we used the famous Dunning process. Before the advent of back-screen projection, Dunning was the only means of providing moving backgrounds in the studio for automobiles, trains, and aircraft. Our aircraft, the *Pensacola* and the *Los Angeles,* had complete semicircles of viewports. With the Dunning process, our audience would be able to see the New York skyline, the storm clouds of the Carribean, and the frozen wastes of Antarctica.

Dunning is a complex and difficult process. Explaining it is also complex and difficult, but I'll try. Aerial scenes of New York were photographed during our stay at Lakewood. Stormy skies and snow-covered mountains were filmed by aerial cameraman Elmer Dyer, flying over California's High Sierras. All were shot for background use, as "plates."

The prints of the plates were not made in the usual way. With a special dye process, yellow images were produced, called "straw-colored" by the Dunning people. They took the straw-colored plates to a darkroom, where they wound the plates, emulsion to emulsion, with unexposed negative film, in what they called a bipack. This required great care and complete darkness. With panchromatic film, not even the traditional dimmed red light could be used. When the bipacks were loaded into camera magazines, the Dunning process was ready to be taken to the set—a weirdly lighted set.

The control bridge of each airship was illuminated by strong, straw-colored light, as were the officers and men in the bridge. Outside the ship, there was a large backing of brilliant blue, with arc lights focusing their intense blue light on the backing.

This is the way the Dunning process worked: the yellow-lighted control bridge and the man in it printed through the yellow images on the plate. When nothing lit with yellow intervened, the blue glare of the backing combined with the straw-colored image of the plate and the background—the plate—printed through. Done properly, Jack Holt and his crew would be looking out at New York City, viewing stormy skies over the Carribean, and scanning the frozen terrain of the Antarctica.

Filming with the Dunning process was slow and required great care. Even a small amount of blue light could cause a "ghost." The Dunning men carried little bags of straw-colored powder; they liberally dusted anyone or anything that might reflect blue light into the camera. One important scene had to be retaken that contained a logbook, suspended on a chain, turning slowly. At a certain angle it reflected blue light into the camera, and a ghostly vision of New York appeared on the logbook cover.

Our dirigible hull was an impressive set. Columbia was only a few years removed from Poverty Row, but even in leaner times Columbia's back-lot people had been first-rate. In his autobiography, Frank Capra tells of Columbia in 1927: "Within the incredibly small back lot, miracles were created—department heads welcomed the challenge to make do with little or nothing—decorwise Columbia was a junkyard; but brain-wise it was a gold mine."

Columbia made many low-budget pictures, and the back-lot people built many low-budget sets, but they were always as good as the budget allowed; and when they were called on to create Grade A sets for Grade A films, Columbia's art directors and construction crews responded with sets as good as any in the movie industry.

Our dirigible hull was huge; a narrow catwalk ran the length of the set, through a maze of girders and fuel cells. Columbia's special effects department did an excellent job in a climactic sequence, the destruction of the airship *Pensacola* in a hurricane.

In the control bridge we filmed a scene in which Jack Holt, his airship in grave danger, decides to go aft, into the hull of the ship to look for damage. He discovers a rip in the outer skin of his ship, then he is alarmed when one of *Pensacola*'s girders begins to buckle. The girder twists—and breaks. Other girders fail; Holt races up and down the catwalk, ordering his men to abandon their stations and go forward. As more girders fail, Holt follows his men to the forward part of the ship. The *Pensacola* breaks in two; the aft portion plunges into the sea. The forward portion makes a less destructive descent and floats, and the *Pensacola* crew members are rescued.

The twisting and breaking of the girders were effective and realistic. The girders were made of lead; at each end of a failing girder, out of camera view, a muscular special effects man, with ample leverage, twisted his girder in one direction, while his fellow efects man twisted it in another.

In his *Variety* review of April 8, 1931, "Sime" was impressed. He wrote, "For picture houses of any class this spectacular film will be a heavy draw and money picture." For Sime, however, all was not milk and honey: "*Dirigible* is a purely commercial, highly fantastical [*sic*], and often silly story." *Silly* seems to be an overly harsh word, but Sime does have a point; there are some king-sized unplausabilities in the *Dirigible* story. But then Sime attempts to explain why he predicts that the picture would be successful. "Still of interest in its way," he writes in his review, "and quite interesting if you don't try to dig in. The story, of course, is the worst of it all. Adaptation and dialog, latter especially, all right for what it's framed around. With the acting doing a great deal, accepting that Frank Capra did everything that could have been done in the direction." Sime's prose was tangled, but his reasoning was on target: Capra's skill as a director made *Dirigible* a success. Capra had the ability to make scenes play better than they were written and induced audiences to believe them. His action scenes were fast-paced and exciting because he had a feel for tempo and action.

Sime was right; *Dirigible* did earn a great deal of money and prestige for Columbia. No new sound stages were bought or built, but production boomed, and I went back to the grind of low-budget films, some of them quite odd—and quite interesting.

11

After the action and excitement of *Dirigible,* I was again given a slow-paced make-work assignment in the dubbing room. Russell Malmgren was now solidly established as Columbia's top re-recording mixer. He told me about Columbia's newly hired mixers, Lodge Cunningham and Glenn Rominger. They were excellent mixers, Russell assured me; if I considered myself Columbia's number one production mixer, he said with mock concern, I had better be aware of my new competition. Russell was a needler; he had been even when we were fourteen-year-old schoolboys. Webster defines the verb *needle* as "to tease, heckle, or annoy." Sometimes Russell annoyed me, but I knew there was a solid foundation of friendship beneath his sometimes heavy-handed needling, and I seldom retaliated.

I was assigned to an odd kind of film, *Africa Speaks.* Some film historians refer to it as a documentary film, but it was far from being one. A cameraman/promoter/adventurer named Paul Hoefler raised money in Colorado and went to Africa to make a film; he called his venture "The Colorado African Expedition." Hoefler shot a great deal of footage of African wildlife and African natives. He had a story in mind, but the film was not well organized and needed connecting scenes to give the material a coherent story line.

Hoefler sought to market his film and entered a partnership with a producer, Walter Futter, who brought the deal to Columbia. It was a low-cost, low-risk project; Columbia bought it, agreeing to shoot connecting scenes and to provide for finishing costs, including scoring, dubbing, and editing. There was no script. Hoefler and Walter Futter had notes outlining what we were to film.

I was assigned a new boom operator for *Africa Speaks.* Bus Libott had been a mike man for only a few months, but in those few months he had become a skilled one. Bus didn't have the Mole-Richardson boom to work with on *Africa Speaks,* because on low-budget films there was no room for the large, heavy clam digger on the grip truck, nor was there enough manpower to move the top-heavy boom over rough ground. To solve the mike-boom problems, Bus, with the help of our maintenance shop, rigged a makeshift boom. His contraption consisted of an old camera tripod fitted with a counterweighted wooden arm. The camera legs telescoped to about six feet, and the tripod head could pan and tilt. Makeshift though it was, it was better and more stable than the boom Carpenter and I had to use at Lakehurst. Bus called his creation a Goldberg, in honor of Rube Goldberg, a famous cartoonist of his day, who drew cartoons of weird, wildly complicated machines that performed simple tasks.

Africa Speaks was an odd project. The filming was unusual; with no script, it was an ad-lib kind of production. We shot on location, in Sherwood Forest, so named because Douglas Fairbanks filmed his silent-film classic *Robin Hood* there, in what is now an area of million-dollar homes, Westlake Village.

Futter and Hoefler would consult their notes, confer, then set out to find "lion country." The entire troupe would follow: a caravan of sound truck, grip truck, camera truck, and a truck acquired to match the one Hoefler used in Africa. It bore the lettering "Colorado African Expedition," and the entire procession bumped over the rough terrain. When we found "lion country," we filmed connecting scenes that made no sense to us, and then we were off again, in search of "gorilla country." For a long time afterward, when a director on location was searching for a setup, someone who had been on the *Africa Speaks* crew would say, "He's looking for gorilla country."

I saw *Africa Speaks* after it was edited and scored, with a narration by Lowell Thomas. Our film matched the African film; our Sherwood Forest lion country was a good match with the African lion country. *Africa Speaks* was not a documentary film, a film of reality; some scenes, to put it bluntly, were faked. A ferocious lion, for instance, is supposed to leap up and attack a group of natives. It was a quick cut, but viewed at slow speed on a moviola the lion is seen to be lying down, relaxed, not at all belligerent. After a few scenes of the approaching natives, the lion gets to his feet, a very short cut. Hoefler reacts with alarm, fires at the lion and kills him. On the moviola, run frame by frame, it can be seen that the lion is not aggressive; when he gets to his feet, he acts as though he expects someone to feed him. I believe Hoefler shot a tame lion.

My next assignment was a Buck Jones Western. A half-year before, I had been assigned to one of his Westerns, but the *Rain or Shine* job intervened. My boom man, again, was Bus Libott. When we filmed interiors, and Bus had the use of a Mole-Richardson boom, it was apparent that he was going to be an excellent mike man. The director, as before, was to be D. Ross Lederman, the man with the volcanic temper.

I never knew the title of that Western. The title of Columbia's low-budget Westerns didn't necessarily tell what the content of the film was, but there was an unbreakable rule: the title must identify the film as a Western, and no other; and so the three-hundred low-budget Westerns Columbia produced between 1929 and 1955 always bore titles with "western" words, used in endless combinations: Outlaw, Range, Sheriff, Gunfight, Raid, Ambush, Ranch, Six-Gun, Vengeance, Rider, Desert, Apache, and, of course, western place names such as Abilene, Dodger City, Texas, Durango, Arizona, Rio Grande, Santa Fe, Wyoming, and Tombstone. The scripts we were given often bore no titles; they were identified by production numbers. Titles were frequently decided on just in time for the filming of the main title.

Ross Lederman was a large, handsome, ruddy-faced man with big shoulders and a big torso. He had the top-heavy look of some athletes and, in fact, had been an outstanding athlete in his youth, in the young and growing city of Los Angeles before World War I. He began his movie career as a propman at the old Mack Sennett studio in Edendale.

We began production at famous old Iverson's ranch, an area of weird rock formations and rugged terrain near the summit of the Santa Susana Mountains. Movie pioneers found Iverson's ranch early in their pilgrimage from New York to Hollywood, and it had been used to film Westerns since the earliest days of Hollywood. An old-timer told me how it was in those days. The roads that gave access to Iverson's were so rough and so steep that the primitive trucks and buses of the day couldn't negotiate them, and cast and crew rode the last few miles on horseback. They lived in tents and were served meals from a chuckwagon, cowboy-style. In the years that followed, so many Westerns had been made at Iverson's that even in the most remote area, brass and copper shell casings could be found, some of them green with the patina of many years, relics of long-ago gunfights in long-forgotten Westerns. Today, Iverson's has been destroyed as a movie location; the Simi Valley Freeway slashes through the heart of it. The place we called Garden of the Gods, the most spectacular of Iverson's jumbled rock formations, is a few hundred yards from the speeding flow of traffic.

Our cameraman was Ben Kline, small, slender, assertive—and talented. He had been the cameraman on our strange hybrid film, *Africa Speaks,* and I was impressed by his speed and by the quality of the film he shot. Kline's first assistant, a hard-bitten veteran named Fred Dawson, told me about Ben. He said that he was good enough to film the most important films made in Hollywood but that he preferred the fast action and lack of pretentiousness in making Westerns. Ben could shoot better film, Dawson said, with his grip crew and their reflectors, than any (expletive) stuck-up, high-priced M-G-M cameraman with a crew of electricians.

Ben Kline did use only reflectors on location; he had to. The budget of a Columbia Western did not provide money for a generator, lights, and electricians. The reflectors were part of the equipment the grips carried in their grip truck. Their arsenal of reflectors contained mirrors, tins, silvers, golds, and leads. Mirrors were used rarely, in special circumstances. Tins were panels of bright, shiny metal—a harsh source of light, used to throw light on foliage or dark buildings, never on people. The most useful reflectors were the silvers and golds. They were, like the mirrors and the tins, panels about four feet square. When they were mounted on lamp stands, they could be raised or lowered, turned or tilted to catch the sun. A silver produced a powerful key light, but it was punishing to an actor's eyes. Gold reflectors were used for players who couldn't tolerate the silvers; and leads, the least powerful, were used for performers who couldn't endure even a gold. Often, such a person was a starlet, a contract player sent out to gain acting experience in a Western.

There was an element of danger in the use of reflectors. A

sudden gust of wind could topple a whole battery of them, threatening skull-fractures and broken bones. I witnessed many narrow escapes. I was not present when a script girl was seriously hurt by a falling reflector.

Later, on another Western, I saw how Ben Kline and his grips used the mirrors. The director was Lambert Hillyer, a tough, bow-legged little man who began directing Westerns with one of the first and greatest of cowboy heroes, William S. Hart. Hillyer needed a shot of his leading lady hiding in a stable, sought by a half-dozen dog heavies who meant to do her harm. In Westerns the unshaven, uncouth henchmen were called dog heavies. The leader, the smooth, sinister boss villain, was called the lead heavy. Hillyer wanted a shot of his leading lady, frightened, hiding in a horse stall, but the stable was dark. With their mirrors, Ben's grips bounced sunlight into the dark stable, where another mirror bounced the light to a silver reflector, positioned to provide a key light for the leading lady. Freddie Dawson, as usual, had a word or two to say. At M-G-M, he said, one of their (expletive) cameramen would have used two hours and a dozen electricians to get the shot. Ben did it in about fifteen minutes—with mirrors.

Some time later I was working on a Buck Jones film in which a simple scene might have become deadly. It was the mandatory fist-fight in the lead heavy's saloon. Buck's opponent was a circus strongman turned actor, Joe Bonomo. The script called for Buck to beat the strongman in a fistfight, whereupon the strongman was to resort to unsportsmanlike conduct and throw a chair at Buck. The chair was a solid, heavy saloon chair; no breakaway could be used. Made of balsa wood and held together by glue, a breakaway would have come apart the moment Joe Bonomo attempted to throw it. Buck wanted the scene to look good; he wanted the chair to fly over his head with inches to spare. He coached the muscle man. "I'm standing there at the window," he told Bonomo. "You throw the chair right at me. Don't worry, I'll see it coming and I'll duck, but when I go to the floor, *don't look at me.*" Realizing that Joe had probably developed muscle power at the expense of brain power, Buck repeated his instructions: "Keep your eyes on where I *was*; don't look at me when I duck, Joe. Have you got it?"

Joe nodded—he had it. The scene started. Joe picked up the chair and threw it; but despite Buck's instructions, his eyes followed Buck to the floor, and the throw of the chair went with the eyes. The chair hit Buck in the back, inflicting a deep, bloody wound. If it hit his head it might have killed him; if it hit his spine, he would almost certainly have been paralysed. A first-aid man was called to bandage the wound; he urged Buck to go to a hospital for treatment and X-rays. Buck refused to go. It was not bravado; he had taken many a hard knock in his life and was satisfied that the wound could be endured. He comforted Joe Bonomo. I had never before seen a 250-pound strongman cry. Buck told Joe that he had no hard feelings, that accidents sometimes happened. The wardrobe man produced a clean shirt to replace the bloody one, and Buck Jones finished the day's work.

Many actors are heroes on film, but Buck was a hero in real life. The world knows that Buck Jones died saving lives in the catastrophic Coconut Grove fire in Boston in 1942. Buck, with producer Scott Dunlap, was in New England on a War Bond tour; they were within a few days of finishing their tour and returning to California when they made the fateful decision to go to the Coconut Grove. In the mid-1950s I worked with Scott Dunlap, a producer at Allied Artists Studio. He told me of that tragic night. He and Buck were burned but escaped from the building; Scotty bore the scars of his burns on his hands and face. When Buck heard that people were trapped inside, however, he went back into the inferno in an attempt to guide them to safety, but fire seared his lungs and he died.

I was next assigned to a low-budget film, *Subway Express,* directed by Fred Newmeyer. The entire film was about a murder in a New York subway car, and the attempt by Jack Holt, a police inspector, to find the killer. All of the action was in one set, and the scenes of Holt questioning suspects were poorly written, slow paced, and repetitive.

It can be asked, Why did Columbia make such an obviously dull film? The proper question is, Why did Columbia buy the play and spend money to have a screenplay written? Once the script was written, going into production was almost automatic. In 1931, nearly thirty B pictures and Westerns were made, and the Columbia head men were not particularly worried if a dull, static script was made into a dull, static film. Neither, it seemed, were the buyers of the film, the exhibitors. In the days when people went to a movie, ready to accept whatever was shown, an occasional poor film seemed to be no cause for concern, by the producer or the exhibitor.

Frank Capra was preparing to make a film, *The Miracle Woman,* based on the career of the famous evangelist Aimee Semple MacPherson. MacPherson collected millions of dollars from the devoted members of her Four Square Gospel Church. Then sensational headlines appeared: She was the victim of a dastardly kidnapping, but there was no kidnapping; it was faked to cover the preacher's love tryst with the operator of her radio station. Barbara Stanwyck was to play MacPherson.

As the start date of *Miracle Woman* grew closer, I expected to be told I would be assigned to it. Then the blow fell. One of the sound department's new men, Glenn Rominger, was given the assignment. I was crushed. I thought I had established a solid rapport with Capra. I didn't know then why I didn't get the *Miracle Woman* assignment, and I don't know now. The important thing was that when it was announced that Capra's next film would be *Platinum Blonde,* with Jean Harlow, I was told that I would be assigned to it.

We began production of *Platinum Blonde* on August 3, 1931. I was determined, that first day, to maintain an attitude of dignified reserve, to give no indication that I had been hurt by not being a member of the *Miracle Woman* team. That attitude lasted one day. On the second day Joe Walker and I were conferring about the next setup. Capra approached and made a joking reference to something that happened at Lakehurst, where, on occasion, we used actors to portray navy officers. The enlisted men there took no chances; they saluted anyone who wore the insignia of rank. I had engaged one of our actor-officers in a long conversation about movies and show business. The man seemed confused; he *was* confused—he was not an actor, but a genuine lieutenant commander. Embarrassment, and now a needle—a gentle needle—from Capra. That demolished my attitude of dignified reserve; we were back where we had been when we finished *Dirigible.*

Platinum Blonde was a new kind of script but not a new kind of story. It was not particularly original. Robert Riskin's structure of scenes and his sharp dialogue, however, *were* new.

The story: Stewart Smith (Robert Williams) is a star newspaper reporter. His "pal," Gallagher (Loretta Young), is also a reporter—a sob sister, Smith calls her. Gallagher adores Smith, but he is oblivious; she's only his pal and co-worker. That must have been difficult for an audience to accept, because Loretta Young was a stunningly beautiful girl. In the script, Stew is given an assignment to visit the aristocratic Schuyler family, to check on the story that the young man of the family has fallen into the grasp of a predatory female. The editor tells Stew that there are rumors of blackmail and a payoff. Stew visits the family and, in a well-written scene, outwits the haughty family, displays a breezy, witty style, and gets his story. The playboy's sister is Anne Schuyler (Harlow). She turns her charm on Stew Smith, pleading with him not to use the story. He resists her plea and phones the story in, but her high-octane sex appeal has churned up his libido. *That* was believable. Harlow, whatever she did, on screen or off, sent shock waves of sex appeal rocketing off in all directions. Anne Schuyler, in turn, is intrigued by Stew Smith. By well-written love scenes and carefully conceived time lapses, the audience is persuaded to accept the fact that haughty, aristocratic Anne Schuyler marries the fiercely independent Stew Smith.

Gallagher is heartbroken but bears up bravely. The marriage, however, is soon on the rocks. Schuyler wants to remake Stew Smith into a respectable member of her upper-crust set. The marriage crashes, and Stew Smith and Gallagher become more than pals; they find love together, and presumably pursue scoops and hot stories happily ever after.

The story of *Platinum Blonde* was not new: man marries wrong girl, discovers his mistake, scuttles the marriage, and goes back to the right girl. One of Columbia's B pictures a year or so before had essentially the same plot, but it did not have the snap, crackle and pop of Riskin's dialogue. It can be argued that *Platinum Blonde* was the first true romantic comedy made by Columbia, the first of a whole generation of romantic comedies that served Columbia well for many years.

The cast, at first glance, might seem offbeat, but in Capra's hands it seemed exactly right. Loretta Young, only eighteen years old in 1931, had a role that was subdued and passive compared with the roles of flamboyant Robert Williams and incandescent Jean Harlow, but her passiveness was inherent in the structure of the story. She played her part well—and she was beautiful.

Harlow, in the role of the aristocratic Anne Schuyler, was certainly not typecast, but by hard work and Capra's painstaking direction she made the role of the high-society aristocrat believable. On the set, Harlow was pleasant, modest, and unassuming. In an interview, Capra said that he had no qualms about casting Harlow as Anne Schuyler, and added that she was "one of the hardest-working and unaffected actresses I have ever worked with."

Robert Williams was a phenomenon; an actor who came to Hollywood virtually unknown, starred in *Platinum Blonde,* and was promptly labeled "can't miss" for stardom. Bob Riskin's writing fitted Williams's on-screen personality perfectly, and he played his scenes with wit, verve, and style.

I didn't particularly like Bob Williams. As justification, I could quote the following, written three hundred years ago, by the English writer Thomas Brown:

I do not like thee, Dr. Fell.
Why this is I cannot tell;
But this I know, and know full well,
I do not like thee, Dr. Fell.

What Brown seems to mean is that it is not necessary to justify a dislike; it happens, and need not be thrust aside, whether it is reasonable or not. My lack of affection for Williams was not arbitrary or unreasonable. In their book *The Films of Frank Capra,* Victor Scherle and William Turner Levy quote Frank Capra about Harlow: "She wasn't popular with the other actors, however, because they were jealous of her. Her photo was on every movie-magazine cover, and the other actors resented that."

I disagree with Capra. The "actors"—Bob Williams and Loretta Young—were not jealous; they were flagrantly rude. They became engrossed with one another; between scenes they giggled and flirted like a pair of high school adolescents, and they completely ignored Harlow. Loretta Young might be excused since she was only eighteen years old in 1931, but Bob Williams was then about thirty years old and should have acquired some degree of respect for fellow actors. Harlow showed no signs of resentment, but the flagrant discourtesy must have hurt her. I resented the discourtesy, and because of that I was not overfond of Robert Williams. I *liked* Jean Harlow; I did not lust for her, as many of my fellow workers did . . . well, perhaps I did, just a little, in a purely theoretical way.

Platinum Blonde did well in release. Again, box office gold poured into Columbia's treasury. In spite of good reviews, Capra deprecated the film, referring to it as an unassuming little picture, filmed to recoup losses on *Miracle Woman* and fill the gap in production when Barbara Stanwyck demanded a raise in pay and refused to report for work on *Forbidden.* In 1929, Stanwyck signed a contract with Columbia for $2,000 a week, a respectable sum for an actress who had made one poor picture for United Artists and an equally poor film, *Mexicali Rose,* for Columbia. That film might well have ended her career, but then, miraculously, she achieved overnight stardom in *Ladies of Leisure* and received critical acclaim for her work in *The Miracle Woman.* She was then undoubtedly worth more money, but Harry Cohn maintained that a contract had to be honored, and he refused to raise her salary. The term "playing hardball" was not known then, but it was decidedly Cohn's game, whatever it was called in 1931. He offered *Forbidden* to Helen Hayes, and when she refused the part, he announced that he would scuttle the project and abandon *Forbidden.* Stanwyck capitulated and Harry Cohn, having won his victory, promptly gave her the raise she wanted. The script was finished and the sets were designed, so *Forbidden* went into production just one month after *Platinum Blonde* wrapped up.

Forbidden was a different kind of film, a departure from the fast pace and humor of *Platinum Blonde,* and Capra again became a different kind of director, intense and demanding, as he had been during the filming of *Ladies of Leisure.* Now, making *Forbidden,* he was even more protective of Stanwyck's first take. The legend of Stanwyck's no-rehearsal first take may have been born during *Ladies of Leisure,* but it grew to full size during *Forbidden.*

The plot of *Forbidden* was similar to that of Fannie Hurst's novel *Back Street.* It was the story of Lulu Smith (Stanwyck) hopelessly in love with a married man (Adolphe Menjou). Al Holland (Ralph Bellamy) was the newspaperman whose obsessive hatred of Menjou was a driving force in the story and caused Stanwyck, in a scene of tremendous dramatic impact, to murder him. It was heavy drama all the way.

The rehearsals that were not quite rehearsals were even more muted than they had been on *Ladies of Leisure.* Capra and Stanwyck walked through the moves together, Stanwyck almost inaudible as she spoke her lines. Actors sometimes resent special treatment given to stars, but there was no indication of resentment as Adolphe Menjou and Ralph Bellamy performed dutifully in the

With Jimmy Stewart (left) on the set of *You Can't Take It with You*
(1936).

Filming *Carnival* with the snake lady.

The United Artists sound crew, 1928 (Bernds is in the middle row, second from left).

In the water, filming *Girls' School* (1938).

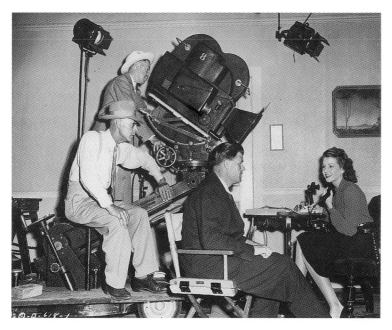

Directing his first film, *It's Murder*.

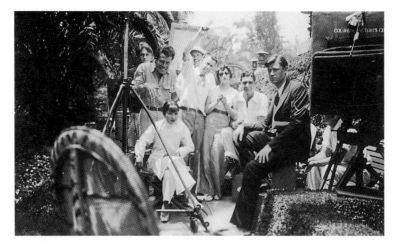

On the set of *The Bitter Tea of General Yen* (Bernds is on the far right).

At Lakehurst, New Jersey, filming *Dirigible* (1931) with Russell Carpenter.

With Shemp of the Three Stooges and Tom Kennedy.

On the set of *Harem Girl*.

The Capra crew on *It Happened One Night*. From left to right, bottom row: still photographer Irving Lippman, propman George Rhein, Frank Capra, and assistant director C. C. (Buddy) Coleman. Middle row: mike boom Irving (Buster) Libott, assistant cameraman George Kelley, cinematographer Joseph Walker, dialogue coach Gene Reynolds, and Edward Bernds. Top row: gaffer George Hager, head grip Jimmy Lloyd, best boy Al Leetz, and electrician Jim Bakely.

The first night of filming *It Happened One Night,* at the old Greyhound bus depot in downtown L.A. (Bernds is on the extreme left, in bright light, next to the sound boom).

Carole Lombard in *No More Orchids;* the inscription reads, "For Eddie the pal. How's it for sound?"

Bernds with the Three Stooges, on the set of *Three Arabian Nuts* (1950).

On location at Busch Gardens, Pasadena, during the filming of *It Happened One Night*.

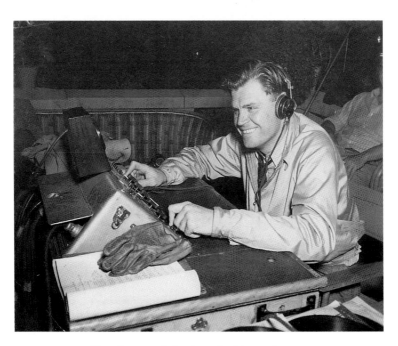

Bernds at a mixing board with earphones.

"One for all!" with the Three Stooges (from left to right, Shemp Howard, Larry Fine, and Moe Howard) and producer Hugh McCollum (far right). They are receiving a Movie Exhibitor's Award for Best Comedy Short Subjects (1951).

The zany comedy team of Bert Wheeler (left) and Robert Woolsey in the first big musical number Bernds ever recorded, "Goodbye America, Hello Africa," from *So This Is Africa* (1932).

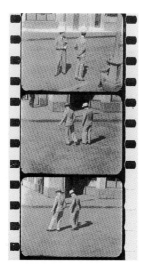

One-of-a-kind 35 mm snapshots that Bernds took of Wheeler and Woolsey rehearsing their dance steps on Columbia's back lot for *So This Is Africa* (October 30, 1932).

A birthday party for Irene Dunne, with the crew of *The Awful Truth* (December 20, 1936). From left to right, Cary Grant, Leo McCarey (holding the cake), and Miss Dunne. Bus Libott is hiding behind Cary Grant, and Bernds is in back of McCarey.

strange, subdued rehearsals. When the cameras turned and Stanwyck responded with searing, emotional performances, they responded brilliantly.

Adolphe Menjou was a fascinating man. He loved to declaim, to make speeches to no one in particular between scenes. It was a kind of vocal aerobic exercise. He would suddenly begin a spiel, imitating a patent-medicine pitchman, that went something like this: "Ladies and gentlemen, we have here this marvelous elixir, nature's own remedy, composed solely of fruits, roots, barks, and berries." It sounded mad, it was outrageous—and it was delightful. The words "fruits, roots, barks and berries" came sonorously from his lips; he loved the sound of them. He was also fascinated by the name of a prizefighter of some renown who came from Argentina, named, as I recall, Enzo Escobar Fieramonte. The name delighted Menjou; he used it many times as he told crew members, in his rich, theatrical voice, of the mighty victories of Enzo Escobar Fieramonte.

Poets like the sound of some words. I liked the sound of some words. Adolphe Menjou liked the sound of *his* words. I should, therefore, have liked Adolphe Menjou, but I did not, because he was a rabid, intolerant right-winger.

In 1931, the Depression was worsening. President Hoover wanted no radical solutions; he believed the government must not intervene; the economy would soon cure itself. 1932 was a presidential election year, and Menjou was worried that the "communists" (Democrats) would win the election, raise taxes, destroy the value of the dollar, and deprive him of some of his wealth. There was a persistent rumor that a new administration would abandon the gold standard and require all citizens to surrender gold to the government for thirty-two dollars an ounce. Through my microphone I heard Menjou tell Capra, "I've got gold stashed in safety deposit boxes all over town—they'll never get an ounce from me."

I was disappointed that Capra didn't object to Menjou's intention to defy the law of the land; by his silence, he seemed to tolerate Menjou's extreme right-wing attitude.

In release, *Forbidden* was a box office winner. Some critics called the story unoriginal and oversentimental, a variation of *Back Street*. Almost all critics agreed, however, that Stanwyck's performance was superb. "Sid," in *Variety,* January 12, 1932, as usual gave *Forbidden* sour with the sweet: "*Forbidden* is really a conglomeration of many pictures. There's a little bit from numerous past features included, but in directing Frank Capra has woven it into entertaining fabric dominated by Barbara Stanwyck. It's the best film Miss Stanwyck has made for Columbia. She has at no time looked so well on the screen. This may be due to Joseph Walker's camera work or, finally, to Miss Stanwyck herself." Sid does not explain why or how Stanwyck took over Joe Walker's camera duties. Sid probably had something in mind, but perhaps facing a tough deadline, he didn't have time to explain it.

Platinum Blonde was released late in 1931, *Forbidden* early in 1932. They provided a potent one-two punch at the box office, and again impressive quantities of cash—Capra-cash—flowed into Columbia's treasury.

At 8749 Clifton Way, Beverly Hills, life went on, as it will. Edward Junior was nearly two years old and growing fast. We furnished our house and bought a second car—in cash. Every three months I sent a check for $250 to the Insurance Company in Kentucky for our house payment, pleased that the balance we owed grew steadily smaller.

Our second car was a 1928 Hudson Super-Six, manufactured by the Hudson-Essex company. It had a large, sluggish six-cylinder engine and was undoubtedly a gas-guzzler. That was of no great concern, however; gasoline sold for about sixteen cents a gallon, except when service stations displayed lurid signs such as GAS WAR. Then gasoline sold for as little as eleven cents a gallon.

The 1931 holiday season approached. It was marked by Columbia's Christmas gift to each employee, a ten-dollar gold piece. It was also a time of uninhibited parties on Christmas Eve, not at Columbia alone but at all of the Hollywood studios. Many departments at Columbia held open house, with abundant drinks for all comers. It was bootleg liquor, of course; the repeal of Prohibition was still in the future.

Columbia tradition demanded that Harry Cohn receive, in person, Christmas greetings from his employees. For the ordeal, everything movable was taken from Cohn's office, and the carpet and desktop were protected against cigarette burns and spilled drinks by sheets of plywood. I made the climb up the notorious double-jointed stairway with a horde of stumbling well-wishers. Cohn stood behind his desk, unsmiling, enduring the ordeal as he would a root-canal procedure. As they passed in front of him, some employees offered a simple Christmas greeting; others scolded, or complained, or even insulted the boss. The insults were forgiven; that too was part of the tradition. When I reached the front of the desk, Cohn looked at me, surprised. It was, in fact, a miniature double-take. His look at me seemed to ask, "You're sober. What are you doing here?" I moved on. That concluded my participation in Columbia's annual Saturnalia, and I went home to a quiet Christmas Eve.

There were injuries arising from the Christmas party. The most serious was to a stocky, sandy-haired assistant cameraman named Jim Goss. Jim drank at the party then, wisely, decided he should not drive; he persuaded a friend to drive him home. Unfortunately, the friend had also been drinking. He started his car, gunned it forward, and smashed into the car parked in front of him. Jim Goss was thrown forward and broke the rear-view mirror with his left eye. The sight of the eye was destroyed, and for all the years I knew him, Jim's sightless left eye peered out of a grotesquely smashed-in eye socket.

Columbia seemed to be doing well. Production boomed in 1931, and profits from *Platinum Blonde* and *Forbidden* were strong, but early in 1932 all production at Columbia came to a jarring halt. Everyone but a few department heads were laid off. It came as a shock to me; suddenly I was off salary for the first time in nearly five years. My status as Capra's soundman didn't help; Capra was enjoying a vacation in Europe.

The cause of the shutdown was a power struggle for control of Columbia. Jack Cohn and Joe Brandt of the New York office were allied against Harry Cohn in Hollywood. Brandt and Jack Cohn didn't want to gamble on big pictures that might entail big losses. Harry Cohn wanted to throw the dice with big pictures that had the potential for big profits and big prestige. It was brother against brother; Jack Cohn and Joe Brandt schemed to depose Harry Cohn as head of production. A. P. Giannini, giant of California banking, learned of the scheme and warned Harry Cohn. There was a bitter power struggle and Joe Brandt, weary of the quarrels of Harry and Jack Cohn, sold his shares of Columbia stock to Harry Cohn for a half-million dollars.

The shutdown occurred at an awkward time for me. I discovered that we were going to have added expenses; we would have another child, to arrive about October 1.

Fortunately, the halt in production didn't last very long. Columbia Studio was back in business, but not everyone went back to work immediately; it took time to get films into production. There was one positive aspect to the shutdown, an improvement in Columbia's infrastructure: the back-lot corridor was paved. The corridor was the product of Columbia's geography; the studio was long and narrow, compressed between two city streets, Beechwood Drive and Gower Street. The corridor was narrow; it too was compressed, bounded by cutting rooms, the sound department and Stages 3 and 4 on the Gower Street side, and by the mill, where sets were built, and by dressing rooms, the electric department, and the payroll office on the Beechwood Drive side. It was a wide walkway for people but a narrow one for vehicles. There was no turnaround room; a trucker who wanted to deliver lumber to the mill had to back up the entire distance, about two hundred yards, from the Beechwood auto gate to the mill loading platform. Before the shutdown, the corridor had been unpaved, and when it rained it became a six-hundred-foot-long mud puddle. Duckboards and planks were put out to bridge the bigger puddles, but there were times when leading ladies, wearing delicate high-heeled shoes, reported to the set with mud up to their ankles.

Our first assignment after the shutdown was a Tim McCoy Western, directed by Ross Lederman. Westerns tended to be alike; there was little to distinguish one from another. On this Western, however, there was an incident that was memorable. We filmed a scene in which outlaws were pursuing a stagecoach. The coach swerved out of control and toppled over. The driver jumped and was not hurt; the out-of-control horses dragged the coach on its side for a hundred feet before wranglers dashed out and stopped them. The passengers in the coach, three men and one woman, were extras, accustomed to working in Westerns. They reacted correctly; they went to the floor of the coach. If an arm or a leg or a head had gone out of the downside coach window, that arm, leg, or head would have been torn off. The passengers were helped out of the coach. One of the extras, a feisty lady about sixty years old, got a big laugh when she accused one of the men of "copping a feel," as she called it, when the four people were tangled together on the floor of the coach. The little lady got her laugh, the crew put the coach back on its wheels, and we went on with the day's work.

There were big events in 1932. The Depression was getting worse and there was to be a crucial presidential election, probably the most important one since the Civil War. We, the sound people, had an event that was of no interest to the rest of the world but was important to us: in 1932 we got rid of the clumsy, overweight CTA microphone and were given Western Electric's new dynamic microphone, which was smaller, lighter, and more directional. We needed a device to take advantage of the directional capability of the new mike. Bus Libott and our maintenance people devised a method of turning the mike: it made use of a rotating disc, cord, some pulleys, and a suspension of rubber bands. It was baling-wire engineering, but it worked. Western Electric would probably have spent two years and eighty thousand dollars to invent something that didn't work as well as our home-grown gadget. With it, the mike man now had one more function: he could pan the mike, raise and lower it, move it in and out, and now turn it, to aim it at an actor, to pick up more of the valuable high frequencies that made speech intelligible. Bus Libott quickly became master of the four-function mike boom; he handled complex scenes flawlessly. I acknowledged to myself, wryly, that Bus could probably do my job well, but without his excellent reflexes and hand-eye coordination, I could probably not do his. I kept such dark thoughts to myself.

We were assigned to the film *Faith,* starring Walter Huston. Later, when the picture was about to be released, it was given the title *American Madness.* The director was Allan Dwan, the first director I had ever seen inside a movie studio, the man who sat impassively on the set of *The Iron Mask,* Doug Fairbanks's last silent film.

We began filming the first week of April 1932. In 1928, Dwan had sat impassively on the set of *The Iron Mask.* In 1932, he sat impassively on the set of *American Madness.* He chose camera setups, then accepted whatever the actors gave him in performances. With excellent actors, that approach sometimes worked well, and Walter Huston was certainly an excellent actor, but in this case it did not work at all. Something was needed to spark intensity, to make the problems posed by the story believable. Bus Libott and I agreed that *American Madness* was not going to be a good picture. After several days of shooting, Harry Cohn came to the same conclusion. He shut down production and dismissed Dwan. For Cohn, it must have been a wrenching decision. It was the same problem he faced when he replaced the veteran director Irvin Willat on *Submarine*. In both instances, failure was intolerable. *Submarine* was Columbia's first venture into A-grade production; it was imperative that it succeed. *American Madness* was Columbia's first important film after Harry Cohn's victory in the bruising battle for control. There was no alternative; *American Madness* had to be a good film, and both times Cohn called upon Frank Capra to avert a disastrous failure.

After a hiatus of a few days, Capra took over, and it was the return of the conquering hero, the U.S. cavalry arriving just in time to save the wagon train. Capra refilmed everything Dwan had shot; scenes that had been slow picked up pace, characters came alive, and everyone, cast and crew, began to believe that we were going to make a good film.

Capra was at his best. He did not wait patiently for whatever the cast gave him. He animated the crew, as he always did, and worked with the cast; he threw himself into rehearsals with energy and enthusiasm, trying not for perfection in the words spoken but for the attitudes and the way the words were spoken that made the characters seem real. From the beginning, Capra's rapport with Walter Huston was good; I saw in Huston a respect for Capra and confidence in his methods.

In Capra's autobiography, *The Name above the Title*, there is a strange omission. He fails to mention that he replaced Allan Dwan. He had not been reticent in telling of his takeover of *Submarine*, when he replaced Irvin Willat. When I first read Capra's book, I thought he omitted the mention of Dwan out of consideration for the veteran director. Joseph McBride, in his magnificent book *Frank Capra: The Catastrophe of Success*, presents a different explanation. McBride theorizes that Capra, in his autobiography, wanted to claim credit for cowriting *American Madness*. In his book, Capra writes, "Riskin and I concocted a wild story about a bank president (Walter Huston) who is filled with youthful optimism and a cheerful trust in men. Riskin wrote the screenplay, marking the beginning of a Capra-Riskin collaboration that would last for years."

To make this claim, McBride argues, Capra could not admit that the script was written for another director—written, in fact, while Capra was traveling in Europe. I found this theory disturbing. The Capra I knew in 1932 was generous, open, and displayed no overt signs of ego. Bob Riskin visited our set often during the filming of his script. What I saw in Capra and Riskin was two men who genuinely liked and respected one another. If there was any credit grabbing, it must have come later—much later—perhaps in the years when Capra's autobiography was being written.

In the *Variety* review of *American Madness,* unlike the review by "Sid" of *Forbidden,* there was only sweet, no sour. "Abel," in *Variety,* August 4, 1932, told his readers, "*American Madness* is a money picture. That goes both ways. It's about money and banks and spells dough for the box-office. It's timely, topical, human, dramatic, punchy and good entertainment at one and the same time. Film's appeal is strong. It's swell propaganda against hoarding, frozen assets and other economic evils which 1932 Hooverism has created." And, finally, praise not only for Capra but for me and my sound crew: "Capra's direction throughout is big time. Same goes for everything from casting to sound and production." A pat on the back for us from *Variety!*

American Madness was a landmark film, for Capra and for Columbia. The Depression was on the minds of millions of people, and *American Madness* voiced daring ideas about money, banking, and politics. Hard-shelled Hooverites denounced Capra for advocating dangerous radical ideas, but he did not create those ideas; they were—and remained—Bob Riskin's. Capra merely filmed them, brilliantly.

Capra voted for Hoover in 1928.

12

We finished *American Madness* late in April and were assigned to *Hollywood Speaks*, directed by Eddie Buzzell. Buzzell had been a song-and-dance man on Broadway. Harry Cohn, who liked popular music and musicians, brought him to Hollywood. In 1930 Cohn gave Buzzell his start by assigning him to direct a series of one-reel comedies, "Eddie Buzzell's Bedtime Stories," and in December 1931 assigned him to direct his first feature film, *The Big Timer*.

Hollywood Speaks was written by Jo Swerling and Norman Krasna. Each had done good work and would do so again, but *Hollywood Speaks* was not a good script. Perhaps Jo Swerling was too prolific. He began his career at Columbia in 1929, writing the screenplay for *Ladies of Leisure*. From then on he was amazingly productive. In 1930 he had seven writing credits, including two Capra films, *Ladies of Leisure* and *Rain or Shine*. In 1931 he had another productive year — six writing credits, including three Capra films, *Dirigible*, *Miracle Woman*, and a cocredit on *Platinum Blonde*. His other three scripts were not of top quality. Apparently Jo Swerling had the newspaperman's attitude: given an assignment, he did the best he could with it, turned the story in, and went on to the next job.

After *American Madness*, *Hollywood Speaks* was a letdown. Where Capra would have been forceful and sure-handed, Buzzell was tentative and uncertain. Dialogue that might have been acceptable with perceptive direction became slow paced and stilted.

In Beverly Hills, in our modest home on the unglamorous boundary of Beverly Hills and Los Angeles, the impending growth of our family required growth in our living space. We hired a carpenter, a Mr. Hammet, to add a room to our house. For six hundred dollars he built a large new bedroom. The added room enabled us to hire live-in household help. These were Depression times; the going price for household help was fifteen dollars a month. We paid twenty dollars, but it was the food and shelter that were important.

At the studio we working people argued; was Herbert Hoover responsible for the Depression? Many of my co-workers thought so. As spring moved on to summer in 1932, they no longer had to content themselves with being anti-Hoover. They now had a champion, Franklin Delano Roosevelt, a man of enormous appeal, unflappable, supremely confident, who could turn aside the most venomous attacks with devastating wit and good humor.

Columbia was busy the summer of 1932; production had to be stepped up to make up for the time lost during the shutdown earlier that year. With only a few days between pictures, Buster Libott and I were assigned to a film *War Correspondent*, starring (again) Jack Holt and Ralph Graves, directed by Paul Sloane, whom I had not seen before and would not see again.

War Correspondent was another recycling of the Holt-Graves rivalry that was the principal story element in Capra's *Submarine*, *Flight*, and *Dirigible*. It was used again in Columbia's *Hell's Island*, in which Holt and Graves, in the French Foreign Legion, contend for the love of Dorothy Sebastian. And now, in *War Correspondent*, with the background of civil war in China, Holt and Graves vie for the affections, once more, of Lila Lee. In the film, Jack Holt is a pilot, a mercenary, flying for a Chinese warlord, and Ralph Graves is a war correspondent. As usual Graves wins the lady, but Jack Holt loses his life. Again, the script was by Jo Swerling.

As a director, Paul Sloane was short-tempered, impatient, not efficient as a director of B films should be. Because of his time-wasting methods, we worked brutally long hours, even by Columbia standards. In the script there was an episode in which a warlord bestows a medal for valor: the Order of the Golden Dragon. Bus Libott, brash, unawed by authority, conspired with our prop man to create his own medal. With cardboard, gold foil, and fake jewels they created likenesses of the Order of the Golden Dragon.

Buster called his medal the Order of the Asses Draggin'. To enlighten the uninformed: when one's ass is dragging, one is tired, exhausted, beat, worn out, and pooped. That's what we were, on *War Correspondent*. Bus distributed the medals to members of the crew, who wore them proudly. Sloane fumed and spoke of getting people fired, but nothing came of it.

In the studio, in Los Angeles, in the nation, the presidential campaign was heating up. The newspapers—all of them—were against Roosevelt. The people I worked with understood that; newspapers were Money, and Money didn't like Democrats or Roosevelt. There was much name-calling; Roosevelt was called a dangerous radical who would destroy the nation's economy.

In July 1932, we began production of Frank Capra's *Bitter Tea of General Yen*. In his autobiography, Capra writes that he chose *Bitter Tea* in an effort to get an Academy Award for Best Picture and agreed with Harry Cohn that only "arty stuff" had a chance to win. *Bitter Tea* was certainly different from anything Capra had done in the past. Adapted from a novel by Grace Zaring Stone, it told the story of a young American missionary, Megan Davis (Barbara Stanwyck), who came to Shanghai to marry a dedicated missionary, Dr. Strike (Gavin Gordon). In the chaos of civil war in the streets, Stanwyck is knocked unconscious. She awakens aboard the troop train of one of the embattled warlords, tall, elegant General Yen (Nils Asther). He takes her to his province, ostensibly to wait until he can safely send her back to Shanghai, but secretly he is fascinated by her and intends to keep her. His American adviser, the excellent actor Walter Connolly, protests Yen's decision. Stanwyck, against her will, is attracted to General Yen and attempts to convert him to the Christian concept of mercy and forgiveness.

Megan befriends Mah Li, General Yen's concubine, who confesses her love for Captain Li, General Yen's aide. Connolly, however, discovers treachery: Mah Li and her lover have sold out to Yen's enemies. He informs Yen, who proposes to deal with the traitors the efficient Chinese way, by killing them. Megan pleads with Yen to spare their lives. Yen responds to Megan's pleas, spares Mah Li and Captain Li, but his conversion to the notion of mercy and forgiveness costs him his province, his trainload of gold, and his life. As he dies, having imbibed the "bitter tea"—poison—Megan realizes that she loves General Yen.

For me, *Bitter Tea* is unforgettable. There were battles in the crowded streets of Shanghai, and there was a dramatic night sequence, an attack on General Yen's gold train made possible by Mah Li's treachery. The night sequence was a tremendous spectacle—the scene called for two complete freight trains, drawn by steam engines, panting as old steam engines did, emitting clouds of smoke and occasional jets of steam. There were dozens of arc lights, projecting their powerful beams of blue-white light. Then, the clash of battle as General Yen's troops are surprised and fight a thousand enemy soldiers.

Capra was in his element, as he had been when he staged the riot and burned down the circus in *Rain or Shine*. In the *Bitter Tea* battle scenes, he was again the man in charge; there were questions, problems, decisions to be made, and he made the decisions quickly and confidently.

There is a curious error in Capra's autobiography about the filming of *Bitter Tea*, just as there was about the writing credit for *American Madness*. In his book, Capra describes the battle of the warlords' trains. He tells how Walter Connolly, cast to play the part of Jones, Yen's adviser, was rushed from New York by plane, met at the Los Angeles airport by an assistant director, who hurried him into a studio car and drove him straight to the train robbery location. Connolly arrived, breathless, awed by the spectacle before him. Capra asked him to jump from a slow-moving boxcar where a camera was to photograph him. In his book Capra says that Connolly jumped, broke his leg, and played the rest of the picture with his leg in a cast. Not so. I was there. Connolly said, "Mr. Capra, I'm just recovering from a hernia operation. If I jump, I'm afraid I'll tear out all the stitches." Capra changed his plans, and with some deft film editing got Connolly out of the boxcar with no stitches torn. The proof that there was no broken leg is in Capra's book. On page 150 is a picture of Barbara Stanwyck, Nils Asther, and Walter Connolly, and Connolly is standing firmly on two good legs.

In 1939, during the making of *Mr. Smith Goes to Washington*, Capra told me that *Bitter Tea* was his favorite film. "It's got more real *movie* in it than anything else I've done." *Bitter Tea* remains sharp in my memory because it truly did have more "movie" in it.

We finished *Bitter Tea* in mid-August and were assigned to *Virtue*, to be directed by Eddie Buzzell. It would be another credit for me. At United Artists, for nearly two years, I longed for just one solo credit. At Columbia, in three years, I had credits on about forty films. I was quite willing to go from one film to another; to maintain the flow of paychecks. The arrival of the new member of our family was going to cost nearly four hundred dollars for hospital and doctor, and again we proposed to pay cash on delivery.

A few days before *Virtue* was to begin, I was in Columbia's main projection room, watching dailies. At Columbia the dailies— the film shot the previous day—were generally shown in mid-morning. Dailies were an excellent way to observe a director's methods; the film was shown just as he shot it, from first shot in the morning until wrap-up at night. It showed, for instance, how he coped with the problem of an actor who repeatedly blew lines. Perhaps he employed the print-and-pickup technique, or he may stubbornly have tried for an error-free take, with the slate showing double-figure scene numbers.

That day I was watching the dailies of *Washington Merry-Go-Round*, a political expose-type film starring Lee Tracy, Walter Connolly, and Alan Dinehart, directed by James Cruze, famous for directing the silent-film classic *The Covered Wagon*. I sat next to Jo Swerling, writer of the screenplay. All went well for a time, then one of the actors was required to use the word *grandiose*. He pronounced it "grandoysie." Jo Swerling jumped up as though he'd been stuck with a long, sharp needle and stormed out, cursing. I learned then that Jo was not a take-the-money-and-run writer but one who cared about what happened to his words after he wrote them.

Virtue could have been a bad picture but was not. It told the old, tired story of the prostitute with the heart of gold (Carole Lombard), redeemed by the love of a good man (Pat O'Brien). There were misunderstandings, complications, and much anguish, and Lombard is even accused of murder. But Pat O'Brien believes in her and, by tireless effort, wins her vindication. *Virtue* was no cinematic gem, but it wasn't the maudlin mess it might have been, because the screenplay was by Bob Riskin, Carole Lombard was talented and beautiful, and Pat O'Brien performed his hard-to-believe role with skill and conviction.

Virtue was Lombard's first film for Columbia and my first encounter with her. Profanities and obscenities were not as common then as they are now, but many a dainty leading lady of that day would, on occasion, cut loose with some earthy x-words. Carole used them all, at the top of her lungs, and strangely, because of her uninhibited exuberance, they seemed no more than an expression of high spirits. If that's a convoluted defense of her unique vocabulary, so be it. Square I was, and square I may still be, but I liked Carole Lombard wholeheartedly.

We crew members regularly went from one film to another, but stars usually did not. Our next assignment, however, was *No More Orchids*, starring Carole Lombard; she had the same interval between films that her sound crew did: five days. Joe Walker apparently didn't choose to go quickly from one assignment to another. He photographed *Virtue*, but another cameraman—a very good one—Joseph August, photographed *No More Orchids*.

Orchids was a heavy-handed romantic melodrama. Anne Holt (Lombard) is a rich, spoiled young woman. She desires Tony (Lyle Talbot), a poor but proud man who spurns her because she is too rich. Buster Libott observed, wisely, that any man, in any film, who spurned Lombard was a completely unbelievable character. That, however, was the way the script was written.

I disliked the *Orchids* script because it used the morbid, overworked device of self-sacrificing suicide. Lombard's father (Walter Connolly), president of a failing bank, wants to save Carole from marriage to the wrong man, Prince Carlos, a wealthy, obnoxious character, whose wealth can rescue Connolly's troubled bank. Connolly deliberately crashes his plane and is killed; the insurance money saves the beleaguered bank, and Carole gets the right man, Lyle Talbot. The wrong man, Prince Carlos, portrayed by Jameson Thomas, has the mission in the film of creating dislike with every word and every gesture, to leave no doubt in the minds of the audience that he *was* the wrong man. He did his job so effectively in *Orchids* that he was cast, a year later, in *It Happened One Night*, as the obnoxious King Westley, Claudette Colbert's wrong man. For Jameson Thomas, a notable achievement: the wrong man for two beautiful stars, Carole Lombard and Claudette Colbert.

My mind was not wholly on *Orchids*. My thoughts kept going to B-day—baby day, about October 1, the doctor said. On September 29, 1932, there was a downpour of rain in Los Angeles. The nurses at the hospital, my wife told me later, said, "There's nothing like a big storm to bring out a lot of babies." My Scottish brother-in-law rushed my wife to the hospital, and our wonderful baby daughter, Elsa, was born there, in midafternoon, when the hospital was in a turmoil because the basement was flooded.

The heavy rainfall did bring out the babies. Three babies were born on that day, September 29, 1932, to members of the *No More Orchids* crew. A son was born to Sam Nelson, our assistant director; his wife shared a room with my wife at the old Cedars of Lebanon hospital in Hollywood. Charlie Granucci, our propman, had a daughter born that day at another hospital. A dedicated horse player on our crew, who thought always in terms of odds, called our three-in-a-day a hundred-to-one shot.

Carole Lombard shrieked when she heard about our triple-header; and when Carole shrieked, wine-glasses shattered and wine bottles were at risk. "Three kids!" she screamed. "Three kids the same day!" And then, referring to the long hours we spent on the job, "When did you bastards find time to do it!"

No More Orchids finished shooting the first week in October, and Betty and Elsa came home from the hospital soon afterward. It was new regime with our new family member. Our household helper proved to be—the clichéd term—a jewel. She was a large young woman named Ella, an affectionate, caring nanny and an expert cook, who taught Betty much of the art of Southern cooking. I had about a week to settle into this new regime, and then it was back to work, assigned to the film *So This Is Africa*, with the comedy team of Wheeler and Woolsey.

I read my *So This Is Africa* script with considerable interest. Columbia hadn't made a film with comedians as stars since I came to the studio in 1929. Joe Cook was a comedian and a star, but in *Rain Or Shine* his comedy was incidental; *Rain or Shine* was primarily a love-triangle film with a melodramatic circus background. In *So This Is Africa* our stars were Robert Woolsey and Bert Wheeler, vaudeville and musical comedy veterans who had made a highly successful series of films for RKO studio. In the *So This Is Africa* script, Wheeler and Woolsey are introduced as a pair of vaudevillians with an animal act featuring half a dozen lions. The supposedly ferocious lions are lethargic, and the act is so bad that the boys are fired after only one performance.

The script then takes us to a conference at a movie studio, where management faces a grave crisis. The studio hired a noted authority on African wildlife, Mrs. Johnson Martini, to make a film in Africa. (Her name is a wordplay; Mrs. Osa Martin and her husband, Martin Johnson, were notable African explorers and filmmakers.) Mrs. Johnson Martini, however, returned from Africa with not a single frame of film—because she was afraid of wild animals. It was a terrible dilemma; what was the studio to do? An office boy tells the studio executives about Wheeler and Woolsey and their listless lions. "We're saved!" the president exclaims. That story thread, tenuous though it was, eventually got the boys to Africa, despite a succession of feeble comedy routines. In Africa the real story began, and there were laughs and some genuine comedy, but most of it was blue—the bluest of blue—sexy, salacious, sensuous, and censorable.

The writer of *So This Is Africa* was twenty-three-year-old Norman Krasna. He had been a secretary to the Broadway columnist Walter Winchell and impressed Columbia's boss, Harry Cohn, as a bright, witty young man. He had one shared screenplay credit, *Hollywood Speaks*, written in collaboration with Jo Swerling. He pleaded with Cohn to give him a chance to write a solo screenplay, and Cohn gave him the *So This Is Africa* assignment.

When Cohn read Krasna's script, he realized that the script was vulnerable to censorship, and he must have dreaded the prospect of forty-eight censor boards in forty-eight states slashing his film, but he accepted the assurances of Norman Krasna and Eddie Cline, the director, that the scenes in question would be handled with good taste. Good taste? It would be interesting to observe how good taste would soothe the censors when a shapely, amorous native girl, Tarzana (Raquel Torres) forces Bert Wheeler into her treehouse and presumably makes love to him all night long. In another part of the forest, Woolsey too is being seduced. More good taste would be required; Mrs. Johnson Martini displays unbridled passion for Woolsey. From the script:

Mrs. Martini hugs Woolsey violently to her. She talks passionately, thru gasping breaths.
   MARTINI
I want to smother you with kisses. I want to keep you in my arms!
   WOOLSEY
You stop that! All you girls are the same—that's all you think about. Stop it! What if I faint?
   MARTINI
I'll resuscitate you.
   WOOLSEY
If you do you'll have to marry me!

Later:

> *Martini hugs him, almost climbing on him. Her knee is practically*
> *in his crotch.*
> WOOLSEY
> Ow! Ow! You're hurting my cuticle!
> *Woolsey gradually gives in to passion, sinking down on the grass,*
> *still in the kiss. Mrs. Martini is lying practically on Woolsey.*

And, one wonders, how would good taste deal with evidence that
Josephine, a large, lecherous female gorilla, madly desires Woolsey
and presumably has her lustful way with him.

Later in the script, Martini tries to protect the boys. They are the
captives of a tribe of beautiful Amazons.

> MARTINI
> These women seem peaceful now, but at nightfall they become
> wild! They'll kill you with love!
> WOOLSEY
> Well, I want to be killed by that little one on the end there.
> MARTINI
> You don't understand! They'll love you to death!
> WOOLSEY
> Death, where is thy sting!
> *The Amazons dance, and the camera features a rear view of the*
> *writhing, wriggling, well-shaped dancers.*
> MARTINI
> Please! We must leave!
> WOOLSEY
> Not yet. I want to study their backgrounds.

Harry Cohn must have known that the script, as written, was a
minefield of censorship problems, but he was in a hurry to go into
production, even with a script that needed more work. He was in
danger of losing the lucrative deal he had made with the boys, because RKO wanted Wheeler and Woolsey to come back. They left
RKO because David Selznick hurt Bert Wheeler's tender feelings;
now RKO offered them a money-laden deal, but Wheeler, still
sulking, made exorbitant demands. Paramount was also interested
and was preparing to make an offer.

Cohn had to act quickly. He had caught Wheeler and Woolsey
on the rebound from their hurt feelings at RKO and persuaded

them to accept a deal that was pure gold—for Columbia. In mid-October Cohn learned that Paramount was about to make a firm offer to Wheeler and Woolsey, reported to be four films at $75,000 each and a substantial share of profits. It was imperative that Columbia get Wheeler and Woolsey firmly committed by having them in a film in production. Filming began on October 17, 1932.

When I read the script, I thought the opening sequence was dull and unfunny. When we shot the vaudeville scenes, my reaction was worse. Woolsey's pitch to the audience about the lions was inane, and Wheeler's gags were weak and predictable. There was, for instance, the ancient gag: an applause machine is cranked by Wheeler to produce loud applause. The theater manager discovers the fraud, and the boys and their lackluster lions are fired. The only story point in the long, dull sequence is that the boys have a very poor act.

We next filmed Wheeler and Woolsey in their hotel suite. They have called a doctor, who is shocked to discover that his patients are the boys' languid lions. "Your lions are in bad shape," he tells the boys, "because they miss the wilds, the jungle, it's in their blood. They need a rest—a vacation—in Africa."

At last there was a story thread, although it took a long, not very amusing sequence to disclose it; but just when it seemed that the story might gain momentum and go somewhere, it was shoved aside by a silly and distasteful routine. The doctor also recommends that the lions be fed horse meat, and Wheeler and Woolsey, equipping themselves with a rifle and a large bear trap, set out to slaughter a horse for the lions to eat.

The script created two story threads: Wheeler and Woolsey's listless lions need a trip to Africa, and the movie studio needs such supine lions. The story threads are nearly lost in the witless horse hunt, but eventually they come together. The boys, fleeing from a vengeful mule they attempted to slaughter, run for refuge into the lobby of their hotel. There they find Mrs. Johnson Martini and the president of the film company, who persuade the boys to go to Africa. There follows a long, elaborate musical sequence with a "going to Africa" theme, and Wheeler, Woolsey, and Mrs. Martini are conveniently lap-dissolved into the jungles of Africa.

In the African film there is some genuine comedy, but much of it is deep-blue comedy—censorable situations, censorable dialogue, and censorable dances by amorous Amazons wearing censorable costumes.

And so it came to pass, when the film was released, there was a tidal wave, a firestorm of censors' outrage. The National Board of Review rejected the entire film. "Nothing so salacious has ever come before the board in eight years of viewing—it outrages every common standard of decency." Will Hays warned, "If *So This Is Africa* is released in its present form, nothing can stop the censorship bill pending before the Nebraska legislature from passing." Even *Variety* took pot-shots at *So This Is Africa*. In *Variety*, April 23, 1933, "Rush," almost certainly not a blue-nosed censor type, wrote, "Some of the stuff is extremely raw, notably recurrent passages with the female impersonator twist—stuff like this will likely offend women—there is also a generous amount of hip waving by half-dressed girls that only emphasizes the general vulgarity."

So This Is Africa was a remarkable film, for one dubious distinction; it set a record as the most censored film of its time. Countrywide, it brought about a frenzy of film slashing.

When the mangled remains of his film were dumped on Harry Cohn's doorstep, what was left was too short to be released as a feature film. In the original editing, the film editors had wisely decided not to use much of the weak early footage; now they had to put it back to qualify *So This Is Africa* as a feature film.

In spite of that, and perhaps because of the publicity about the film's censorship problems, *So This Is Africa* was a solid moneymaker for Columbia. Harry Cohn's hunch and hurry-up production panned box office gold, but Wheeler and Woolsey received not a penny of it. For years at Columbia, when a distant, mysterious noise interfered with production, an old-timer would say, "That's Wheeler and Woolsey, looking for their share of profits."

Franklin Delano Roosevelt was elected president of the United States when we were at about the halfway point in the production of *So This Is Africa*. We were elated by his victory but not surprised; our crew voted for him almost unanimously. We looked forward to the new year with new hope and confidence.

I chose not to attend Columbia's 1932 Christmas party. I left the studio early in the afternoon to spend Christmas Eve with my newly enlarged family. We knew that the coming year would be an important and exciting one. Just how important and exciting it would be we could not have foreseen.

13

We were off to a quick start in 1933, assigned to *When Strangers Marry* with Jack Holt, directed by Clarence Badger. Badger was a veteran director of silent films; he directed many of Will Rogers's best silent pictures. In the script, Holt is a rugged construction boss who meets a woman (Lillian Bond) in Paris, falls into a hasty marriage with her, and takes his bride to Malaya, where he's building a railroad. Holt's new wife is spoiled, pampered, and discontented. A dastardly villain appears and not only attempts to steal Holt's wife but plots to destroy his railroad project as well. He is done in, not by Holt, but by Holt's errant wife.

When Strangers Marry was a run-of-the-mill B film, not at all memorable, except for what the elements did to Columbia's production plans.

Most of the picture was to be shot on location: the jungle, the railroad construction site, a bridge over a fair-sized stream. Our location-hunting people found an ideal place, and Columbia put a good portion of the film's construction budget into an area of swamp and a slow-moving stream. It was what we now call wetland, with trees and underbrush and tall clumps of bamboo—an ideal location except that southern California often gets its heaviest rainfall in January; and our wetland was wet because rainfall drained to it for several miles around. When we had several days of heavy rain, our bridge and our railroad were flooded, and our access road was impassable. We had to shoot our interiors, our cover sets. It was every production manager's bad dream; we used up our cover sets, and cast and crew waited, on salary, for the location site to dry out.

Because of the flooding delay, *When Strangers Marry* took more than a month to finish. Within a few days we were assigned to *The Woman I Stole*, again with Jack Holt, this time with Fay Wray and directed by Irving Cummings. The story of *The Woman I Stole* had a respectable lineage; it was adapted by Jo Swerling from Joseph Hergesheimer's novel *Tampico*. At one time it had been scheduled as a vehicle for Frank Capra.

The film, as we shot it, seemed to be just another Jack Holt tough-guy vehicle, not memorable except for earth-shaking events that occurred during filming. The first event, of course, was Roosevelt's inauguration on March 4, 1933, as president of the United States, an event of supreme importance, to the nation and to the world. The next day, Roosevelt announced that all banks would be closed from Monday, March 6, through Thursday, March 9, the famous "Bank Holiday." It was a bold, statesmanlike move; it prevented bank runs, which thrived on rumor and hysteria, but most of all, it assured the nation that something was going to be done. The Bank Holiday was a time of euphoria, a feeling that things would be better. If we had no cash, we signed IOUs. No one refused IOUs, and when banks reopened, no one refused to pay.

The great events of March 1933 were not quite finished for us. On Saturday, March 10, one day after the end of the Bank Holiday, the earth shook—literally. It was the disastrous Long Beach earthquake. It struck shortly before 6 P.M. With Irving Cummings, Ben Kline, and the rest of the *Woman I Stole* troupe, I was in Columbia's main projection room viewing dailies. The quake hit—and hit hard. We all dashed for the exit; Cummings, in his midforties, showed remarkable agility in getting out first. I was close behind. The projection rooms and the cutting rooms at Columbia all had iron balconies, a practical arrangement; projectionists and film editors could take a few steps to smoke or get fresh air. I dashed out to the projection room balcony. I saw a tall power pole swaying like a cornstalk in a high wind. That was dangerous; high up on the pole were a couple of high-voltage transformers. As I watched, wondering whether the power pole was going to snap, Denver Harmon, Columbia's chief electrician, came running around a corner. He ran so fast that he skidded, hopping little sideways steps—the kind Charlie Chaplin used for comic effect. Harmon had no comic intent, however. He ran to the base of the pole to cut off the high voltage. After what seemed to be a long time, the earth stopped shaking and I began to breathe again.

I hurried home. The streets were full of anxious people hurrying home. Traffic was chaotic; many traffic signals were knocked out. I found Betty, Ella, and the children safe, but Betty, usually calm, was shaken. She had been in a market on Wilshire Boulevard when the quake struck. Ella was in our car with Eddie and baby Elsa. As cans by the hundreds fell from shelves and bottles smashed, Betty dashed to our car. It was parked beneath a large sign that was snapping to and fro, threatening to fall. Betty drove the clumsy old Hudson out of the parking lot—fast. That night there were two aftershocks. The chimney of the apartment building across our street had been damaged by the big shock, and all night long we heard bricks falling, dislodged by aftershocks.

When I went to the studio Monday morning, I found that although the city of Long Beach had been hit hard, with hundreds of buildings damaged or destroyed, Columbia had suffered very little damage. Some lights had fallen from the light platforms and were smashed, but no one was hurt. A quake story was making the rounds. One of our propmen said his son was in the bathroom when the quake struck. The terrified little boy ran out of the bathroom, crying "All I did was flush the toilet!"

In April, we were assigned to a low-budget film, *Dangerous Crossroads*, directed by Lambert Hillyer, with a cast that included Jackie Searle, a ten-year-old boy who helps his father, Preston Foster, solve a baffling series of train robberies. *Dangerous Crossroads* was memorable because of the way we shot it. Since much of the action takes place aboard a moving train, Columbia rented an entire freight train and loaded all of our production gear aboard the train: cameras, grip equipment, props and wardrobe. Our sound truck was loaded on a flat car, securely tied down. Aboard the train, we were taken to a little-used branch line, where we steamed back and forth, through rugged, deserted country, filming fights, narrow escapes, dramatic scenes while the train was under way. *Dangerous Crossroads* was the quickest of quickies, but I remember it fondly because of the unusual and adventurous way it was shot—a "real movie," as Capra described it.

We finished *Dangerous Crossroads* on April 24; we began production of Frank Capra's *Lady for a Day* on May 9. When I read my script, I was certain that it would be another good picture. The story of *Lady for a Day* is probably familiar to every film buff: Apple Annie, a beggar woman, sells apples on Broadway. She has an illegitimate daughter who she sent to Spain as a child to be educated in a convent. The beggars and grifters and con men of Broadway contribute to Apple Annie's expenses. Then disaster threatens: Annie learns that her daughter is going to be married to a young Spanish aristocrat and that she will come to New York with her husband-to-be and his father, Count Romero, to meet the supposedly upper-crust Mrs. E. Worthington Manville.

A Broadway character, Dave the Dude, a gambling man in the best Damon Runyon tradition, cannot allow Annie to be destroyed by the collapse of her deception, because the apples he buys from her bring him good luck. He therefore organizes a gigantic masquerade and transforms the ragged, unkempt Apple Annie into the socially prominent, well-heeled Mrs. E. Worthington Manville. The wildly improbable scheme escalates; it survives countless perils and involves, finally, the cooperation of the mayor, the police commissioner, and the governor of New York. The daughter marries her man, Count Romero is satisfied that his son has made a good marriage, the couple and count return to Spain, and Apple Annie once more sells apples on Broadway.

Lady for a Day was a fairy tale, so fragile that one not-quite-right scene might cause the whole delicate fabric of the story to be torn apart. There seemed to be no problem in the writing; Bob Riskin's script was brilliant, his ear for dialogue so true that the script was a delight to read. Frank Capra would bring Riskin's words to life, getting every bit of value from them. The casting, however, had to be exactly right. The part of Apple Annie was the key, and May Robson was wonderful in the part. It was said that Columbia tried to borrow Marie Dressler from M-G-M, but Louis B. Mayer would not part with her. She may have been excellent as Apple Annie, but could not have been better than May Robson. We heard rumors that W. C. Fields had been considered as the billiard-playing con man, Judge Blake. That casting would have been disastrous. *Lady for a Day* would have become a W. C. Fields picture, and the judge would have been a semicaricature. Capra also thought of casting Jimmy Cagney as the superstitious gambler, Dave the Dude. Apparently Capra, Riskin, and others realized that Cagney could not shed the image of a strong, streetwise tough guy to play a sentimental gambler who concocts a wildly unworkable masquerade.

The cast that went before the cameras the first week in May was superb: May Robson; Warren William, a fine actor, as Dave the Dude; Guy Kibbee as Judge Blake; Glenda Farrell as a brassy nightclub owner, Missouri Martin; Nat Pendleton, large of muscle and small of brain, as one of Dave the Dude's henchmen; Ned Sparks as Happy, the vinegar-faced pessimist; and in a triumph of casting against type, Walter Connolly as Count Romero. Connolly? He was perfect in the part.

Capra cast small parts carefully, but I disagreed with one of his selections. I learned that he intended to cast an actor named Wallis Clark for an important role as New York police commissioner. I had worked with Clark on a Buck Jones Western and thought he was unbearably hammy, so I undertook to tell Capra about it. It was presumptuous, of course; even a B film director would have been outraged, but Capra listened. When I told him that Wallis Clark was hammy, he said mildly, "You could be right. But many politicians are hammy—maybe we can make it work for us." I didn't overhear how Capra did it, but Wallis Clark performed very well as New York's police commissioner.

Early in the production I heard Capra tell Guy Kibbee, "We can't reach for laughs too early. The audience has to believe Apple Annie and care about her. When we've got that, we can go all-out for laughs." Capra took great pains with May Robson's performance. They rehearsed quietly, apart from other cast members. Much of the time it seemed to be discussion rather than rehearsal. Robson listened eagerly, nodding agreement from time to time. She demonstrated gestures she planned to use: a shaky hand drawn across her mouth, a futile attempt to brush back her wispy, unkempt hair.

In the *Lady for a Day* script, Apple Annie bribes a doorman at a luxury hotel, the Marboro, to steal hotel stationery so she can write to her daughter, keeping up the pretense that she is wealthy and socially prominent. Then, returning to the hovel where she lives, Annie prepares to write the letter. To prepare herself for the task, she takes a bottle of gin from her pocket and gulps down a couple of stiff drinks.

Rehearsing, Capra demonstrated how Apple Annie would react to the drink; a painful grimace as the raw liquor goes down, then a quick, open-mouthed gasp for breath to cool a fiery mouth and throat. A trifle, a small thing, perhaps. But May Robson's performance consisted of many things, great and small. It may well be that the small things—the short step and shuffling gait, the lumpy costume, the shapeless felt hat, and the reaction to strong drink—all contributed to the audience's perception of Apple Annie as a person they would accept and caused them to hope fervently that Dave the Dude's preposterous scheme would succeed.

May Robson had two scenes early in the film in which the fate of *Lady for a Day* was in her hands: the one in which she writes the letter to her daughter and one in which she tells Dave the Dude of her tragic dilemma. The scenes were highly emotional—vulnerable, as such scenes tend to be. One false note, one touch of bathos instead of pathos, and the story of Apple Annie might well be destroyed. But with Capra's patient, perceptive direction, Robson made audiences believe in Apple Annie and care about her, and Capra and the other members of his cast were free to go all-out for their laughs. Capra's rehearsals with Dave the Dude and his Runyonesque henchmen were high-spirited and informal. Capra did very little directing, in the usual sense, but his light-hearted bantering and occasional small joke seemed to create a relaxed atmosphere in which Bob Riskin's well-written comedy scenes were polished and perfected.

Lady for a Day had a third ingredient, an important one—it had a chase. Not the hero dashing through the woods to save the heroine from a fate worse than death; not the U.S. cavalry riding hell-bent to rescue the wagon train. The chase in *Lady for a Day* was the odds-on certainty that Dave the Dude's improbable scheme would collapse and destroy poor old Apple Annie. When it did not, audiences sighed with relief; it was the fairy-tale ending they wanted.

In release, *Lady for a Day* was a rousing success. Nationwide, the public and the critics loved it. It was nominated for Academy Awards in four categories: Best Picture, Best Director, Best Screenplay, for Robert Riskin, and Best Actress for May Robson. None of the nominations won, but *Lady for a Day* got a call, as horse players say; it had been in contention, and a visit to the winner's circle, for Frank Capra and Columbia, was not an impossible dream.

After the excellence of *Lady for a Day*, there was a bumpy descent: assignment to one of Columbia's series of Westerns. The Westerns of 1933 were shot so fast that there was no time for a try at quality. It wasn't the fault of the directors, because in 1930, when Columbia began to make the series westerns, the schedules ranged from fifteen to twenty-two days. But by 1933, the Buck Jones and Tim McCoy Westerns were being filmed in seven to nine days. They were long, hard days, worked at top speed; even so, I preferred working on Westerns to the dull B films that were often overdramatic and boring to work on.

Series Westerns tended to look similar on the screen; they were also much alike in the way they were filmed. The seven- to nine-day schedule was about half interiors and half exteriors. They were hastily staged, hastily shot, and poorly acted. There was a reason for the poor acting; the supporting cast—the lead heavy and his "dog" heavies, and our hero and his friends—had fights as well as acting to do. Many actors refused to do their own fights; they wanted doubles, and the budgets on a Columbia Western just didn't provide for that kind of expense. If they did agree to do their fights, they were not good at it and actually were quite likely to get hurt. Therefore, stuntmen became actors. They were often poor actors, but it was a compromise the director had to make. Since fistfights and gunfights and chases were more important to the film than the quality of the acting, the job generally went to the stuntmen-actors.

It was typical that four or five frantic twelve-hour days were spent on interiors. Then we had the typical Western exteriors. Generally, the call for outdoor shooting required the crew to leave the studio at 6 A.M.; in winter we checked in while it was still dark, stamping to keep our feet warm. The assistant director was impatient, checking the crew in and angry because some latecomers were delaying the departure of the crew bus. When the laggards were loaded aboard the bus, it took off, usually for Iverson's ranch, just as the sun was beginning to rise.

The bus took us over Caheunga Pass—the old, steep road, not the multilane freeway that is there now. Then the bus went across the northern San Fernando Valley and made the steep climb up the Santa Susana Pass, then a right turn to a narrow dirt road, and we were at Iverson's. At Iverson's there were rock formations and a sizable level area for running shots, with a camera car racing ahead of the madly galloping outlaws and the posse. We spent a long day of chases, gunfights, fistfights, and more chases.

Out on location, dialogue scenes were generally saved for last, because in filming close shots we could "chase the sun." Chasing the sun was a classic Western maneuver. Because of the mountains that surrounded Iverson's ranch, the sun began to leave us sooner than if we had been photographing on level terrain. There was usable sun, photographically, but we had to go to higher ground to take advantage of it. The director would generally shoot the master shot of a dialogue scene first and leave the close-ups for later. In close-ups, the background didn't matter a great deal—it was all rock and rush, out of focus. Late in the day we would climb a hill, find some sun, shoot close-ups, and when the shadows came up to the actors' shoulders, we'd pick everything up and dash farther up the hill—high enough to get more sun and shoot more close-ups. The sun would finally disappear behind the Santa Susana Mountains about the time we got our last shot.

Loading the trucks after a long day was hard work. When it was done, our procession of trucks and the crew bus would grind its way out of Iverson's down Santa Susana Pass, across the vast, open stretches of the San Fernando Vlaley. After a long, hard day; usually everybody fell asleep. On one trip I woke up; the road was rather rough, and I looked around. Twenty or so people were in the bus, all sleeping. Their heads were lolling, and every time there was a bump, their heads would all snap. I was a little alarmed; a neck could break if it snapped hard enough. If we hit a really hard bump, twenty necks might snap and the bus would roll into the Beechwood gate of Columbia with twenty dead men aboard. I worried about this for about ten seconds, and then I fell asleep.

I was on just such a Western in mid-June 1933. We returned to the studio long after dark. As I climbed out of the crew bus, Eddie Hahn, the assistant head of the sound department, took hold of me and pulled me aside. "You gotta go to England," he said. "Right away."

I was startled. I had, like most of the crew, slept much of the time during the long bus ride. I wasn't sure I was awake. "England?" I asked. "Right away? When is that?"

Hahn calmed down a little. "I don't know," he said. "We got a cable from Harry Cohn in London. He wants you and Joe Walker there as soon as possible. I guess that means as quick as we can line up Walker and get you passage on a boat."

I broke the news to Betty when I got home. She didn't like it. She said she wanted me to be home. She was always a little concerned whenever I went away for some length of time, as I did on *Dirigible*. I considered that flattering—a good mark on my report card. I had mixed feelings about going on the trip, and about leaving the children. Eddie Junior was three and a half years old, active, and full of "why" questions; I wouldn't be there to answer them. Baby Elsa was nine months old, and I'd miss several months of her progress as a bright, affectionate little girl. There was no choice, however; the absolute monarch of Columbia, Harry Cohn, had commanded, and we, the vassals, had to do what vassals do: obey. Even Joe Walker was a vassal, although he was a high-priced one. He had to obey, too, but he was not to be rushed; Joe wasn't ready to leave until the end of June.

Joe and I left Los Angeles on the evening of Saturday, July 1, on the Achison, Topeka, & Santa Fe's crack train, *The Chief*. I found travel by train to be just as exhilarating as it had been two years before, when we were on our way to Lakehurst to film *Dirigible*. One pleasure that Joe and I shared was spending time on the observation platform of our train. In the heydey of train travel, the last car of a top passenger train had an ornate back platform, that had room for about a dozen people standing, or four or five seated. Observation platforms have a role in the political history of the nation. In the early days, a special train would be chartered to carry a presidential candidate, his staff, and a carload of newsmen. It would make many stops, at towns and cities, large and small. A crowd would gather at the railroad station, a presidential candidate would make a speech, the crowd would cheer, the train would move on to the next town, and at the end of a long day the candidate might've made a dozen or more speeches from the observation platform of this special train. It is a political legend that Harry Truman, by vigorous, grass-roots campaigning from his campaign train, defeated aloof, overconfident Governor Thomas Dewey in the 1948 presidential election.

Joe and I enjoyed sitting out on the observation platform, watching the landscape spinning away from us to the horizon. One hot and humid evening, we were sitting on the observation platform, our train pounding through some rich bottom lands in eastern Missouri. There had been rain, and water glistened in the ditches beside the track. As we roared through the lush greenery, fireflies by the thousands—by the *tens* of thousands—disturbed by our passage closed in behind our train with a display of lights as far as our eyes could see.

Again we changed trains in Chicago, where I spent far too short a time with my parents and my sisters. In midafternoon, July 5, we arrived in New York. There we were met by people from the Columbia office, who took us to dinner and delivered us to our ship, the Cunard liner *Aquitania*, just in time for its six o'clock sailing.

The *Aquitania* was the pride of the Cunard line, a magnificently luxurious liner, elegant in appearance and designed for speed. When founder Samuel Cunard received the international mail contract back in 1840, he resolved to maintain a dependable delivery schedule with superior-powered vessels. Our ship had the distinction of being the *R.M.S Aquitania*, the "R.M.S." standing for "Royal Mail Ship," which gave it special status.

Joe and I remained on deck as tugs shoved our ship out into the Hudson River. We steamed past the Statue of Liberty, and, when we dropped the pilot, I turned to Joe and said, "Now I believe it. We're really going to England to make a picture."

We remained on deck until we passed the Fire Island lightship. It was dark then; we headed out into the Atlantic. A steward guided us to our cabin—and to shock and disappointment. The cabin was small, cramped, and "inside"—it had no portholes. Joe asked the steward, "Is this a first-class cabin?" The man hesitated. "Uh, why, yes sir," he said. Joe and I remembered that hesitation. "It will not do," Joe said firmly. "Take us to someone with authority to change this." The steward took us topside to a man with thin gold stripes on the sleeves of his uniform. Joe again asked if our cabin was first-class. Again there was a split-second of hesitation, but the man assured Joe that it was first-class. Joe was firm: he repeated that he would not accept the cabin.

The thin-striped man tried to be stern with Joe; he protested that there were no other first-class cabins available, and that in any case he had no authority to change anything. "Then let me speak to someone who *does* have that authority," Joe said. "We'll wait in the lounge." We sat in the lounge. Presently another officer came to us, this one with wide gold stripes on the sleeves of his uniform. The lounge was full of people; the man looked around nervously, so concerned was he that our complaint would be noisy and attract attention. Joe, however, speaking quietly and firmly, said that his contract called for first-class travel. Wide-stripe protested that the cabin in question *was* first-class, but he seemed to lack conviction. He consulted a slip of paper. "We can't get in touch with your company," he said. "The Columbia Company, I believe. Obviously, we can't contact them until Monday. Until then, please use the cabin assigned to you . . ."

Joe interrupted him, quietly and firmly. He said, "We will not spend a night in that cabin." The wide-striped officer thought about it for a moment. I think he saw in Joe an unwavering resolution, and he surrendered abruptly. "Very well," he spoke to the steward who had come with us, "please take the gentlemen to 18A." The steward led us to an elevator that took us up several decks, to what must have been one of the finest cabins on the ship. Cabin? It was much more than that. It was a stateroom.

Our baggage arrived soon after we did, and we reveled in the spaciousness and luxury of that stateroom. Joe and I developed some theories about the whole affair. First, why was this stateroom vacant? Joe theorized that the Cunard Line kept such a luxury cabin available in case there was a last-minute booking from, perhaps, a cabinet minister, a member of the royalty, or an earth-shaking tycoon. Not an ordinary VIP—first-class was full of them—but instead a very, very VIP. When such a last-minute request was not made, the stateroom remained empty when the *Aquitania* sailed. Now, thanks to Joe's quiet insistence, *we* had it.

Once we were settled in our deluxe cabin, the voyage was a delight. The great ocean liners no longer provide the only pathway across the north Atlantic; air travel has driven most of them from the sea. There are still great ships—cruise ships—that match the ships of the past in size and power, but they sail aimlessly; they do not carry on the business, the diplomacy and the politics of the world. They sail to amuse and divert and pamper the people who sail aboard them.

The next morning, after a truly spectacular breakfast, a cable arrived from Columbia's New York office, addressed to Joe. It was an abject apology for the poor cabin we'd been offered, and it used the word "misunderstanding."

In the *Aquitania's* ornate first-class dining room, Joe and I were put at a table for two in an obscure corner, because Joe, a man of simple tastes, had not bothered to buy formal dress. I had done so; I knew that first-class passengers "dressed for dinner," so I bought what we called a tuxedo in those days—all black, with a stiff collar, a shirt with an armor-plated front, trousers with a strip of black satin sewn on the side of each trouser-leg.

Joe was sedate and spent a lot of time in the stateroom reading or sitting on deck, but I was active and explored our great ship. I asked to see the engine room and was taken down many decks; from a high, iron gallery, I looked down the *Aquitania's* immense engine room. There were no pumping up-and-down pistons the way movies of that time often portrayed the engines of a steamship. The *Aquitania* was driven by four immense steam turbines turning the ship's four propellers.

In a brochure about the ship's facilities, I discovered that the *Aquitania* had a swimming pool modeled after a Roman bath. I went down many decks and found the pool; an attendant supplied me with swimming trunks, and I went in. I was all alone in it; the water was just the right temperature, and it moved gently as the ship rolled. The *Aquitania* had antiroll devices, sort of wings out from the inside of the ship that cut down on the rolling motion. But apparently it could not do much about the fore and aft movement—pitching, I believe they called it—when the boat dipped into waves head-on. After a while, the motion of the water increased some, then began sloshing back and forth a little more violently. I was enjoying it, being rolled back and forth by the movement of the water in the pool. The force got stronger, and I became even more delighted with it. Just as I was beginning to get a bit concerned, an attendant ran in. Forgetting the usual deference of the ship's staff, he ordered me to come out of the pool, and was quite emphatic about it. I sensed the urgency in his voice, made for the ladder that took me out, and a big surge of the water in the pool nearly tore my hands off the ladder. I got out; there was another surge that slammed water clear out of the pool. The attendant held the door open, yelled for me to come through—I dashed in and he slammed the door shut behind us. The door had a glass window reinforced with wire; we looked in and saw a couple of really monstrous surges that smashed one way and then the other. I would've been helpless in it; I had been bruised and scraped by surf at Topanga Beach and Malibu Beach, but this would have been deadly. One surge might have broken my head; in the other direction, it could have broken my back. I would have been another unlikely victim of the sea. Somewhat chastened about the whole thing, I dried off, dressed quickly, and got up on deck. The ship was indeed pitching quite strongly.

On the late afternoon of July 11, we made our first landfall: just small dark objects across miles of stormy sea. They were the Scilly Isles, a sailor told us, and he pronounced it "silly." There were about 140 of these islands, the sailor said, but only five of them were inhabited; the rest of them were little more than granite rocks thrust up from the bottom of the sea. I relished the wonderful place names; the Scilly Islands were off the coast of Cornwall — *Cornwall*, that had a splendid sound. And there were the Scilly Isles' neighbors: Penzance, Lizard Point, Newquay, Torquay, and Dartmoor. Dartmoor — Scotland Yard, Sherlock Holmes, and foul deeds, out on the desolate moor. Dinner interrupted; soon the tiny granite islands were no longer in sight. After dinner, Joe and I saw Lands' End in the last of the long summer twilight.

That night, I sensed that we were steaming at reduced speed, probably because we were in the heavy seaborne traffic in the English Channel. I was awakened at daybreak by the sensation that we were no longer under way. I put on robe and slippers and went on deck to a gray, rainy dawn. The *Aquitania* was anchored far out in Cherbourg harbor, perhaps a mile from the nearest shore. A lighter was alongside taking aboard passengers, baggage, and freight to go ashore. The lighter, named *Alsatia*, was a sizable steamer but it was dwarfed by the great size of the *Aquitania*. I roamed the deck for my first look at a foreign country. There were fishing boats with red sails heading out to sea; in the harbor, men in small boats pulled up lobster traps. Ashore I couldn't see much — red roofs barely visible through rain and fog.

It took two hours to complete the *Aquitania's* business in Cherbourg, then it was up anchor and off to England. I hadn't kept a diary since the one I maintained during my United Artists days, but going to England was such a great event for me that I began to keep a diary again. From the diary as we approached the English coast: "Isle of Wight, a trio of warships — destroyers — heading out, tramp steamers, fishing boats with red sails."

We entered what our sailor called "solent water." Spithead and Portsmouth were on our right — little towns with red roofs — and white cliffs were on the left. Cowes was also on our left, and an airfield, Calshot. A seaplane, flying low, passed us at tremendous speed and was out of sight in a few minutes. My diary didn't go into detail about the seaplane, but I remember it vividly. In 1933, there was an international flying event, a race for seaplanes, called the Schneider Cup. Apparently, Schneider (or whoever sponsored the event) thought that the future of the airplane was in the use of flying boats and seaplanes employing the lakes and oceans of the world as flying fields. This speeding seaplane was the first aircraft that I had ever encountered that outran its own sound. The plane seemed to speed in silence, pursued, at a distance of a couple of hundred yards, by the noise of an immensely powerful engine. (Of historical note, it is generally accepted that the British Schneider Cup racer of the mid-1930s, and its powerful Rolls-Royce engine, was the ancestor of Britain's great fighter plane of World War II, the Spitfire.)

We docked at Southampton at noon, just as factory whistles sounded in the town. A large factory lay a quarter of a mile from the ship, and as the whistle sounded, what seemed to be a thousand men poured out . Some of them walked, but most of them rode bicycles, and a mass of men spread out in all directions. I learned that in England, Wednesday was called "Early Closing Day," a half-holiday for many factory workers.

When I returned to our stateroom, I found Joe with a man named Harrington, from Northern Transport Company, hired by Columbia's London office to assist us in getting through customs. Harrington took charge of dealing with the customs people; it seemed to me that he did more harm than good. Joe had brought with him many of his beloved lenses, filters, and diffusion devices. In his quiet, courteous way, he would probably have passed customs with no problem. Harrington, however, was arrogant and demanding; as a result, clearing customs was controversial and time-consuming. Finally, Joe had to sign a document promising that if he didn't take every lens and filter back to the United States with him, he would have to pay a substantial penalty for every item that was missing.

Finally, we were aboard the boat-train. Not *a* boat-train—*the* boat-train; in most countries, a crack train was scheduled for one purpose: to transfer shipboard passengers and their baggage to the nation's capital or its principal city. The train was barely underway when I noticed that Harrington was troubled about something. He'd steal a glance at me, then look away quickly. Finally he nerved himself. "Sir," he said to me, "I hope you don't mind . . ." Don't mind?

About what? Harrington beat about the bush, apologized about seven times, and finally blurted out what was bothering him. "Your attire, sir. Sport clothes in London on a weekday. It's not done, sir!" Well, it was true. I was wearing sport clothes: a blue jacket with brass buttons and a fake yacht club emblem on a breast pocket, white trousers—Betty and I called them "ice cream pants"—and black and white saddle shoes. I thanked Harrington for his advice. I might have been embarrassed or concerned about being a non-conforming dresser in a foreign land, but I was not. I didn't care what foreigners thought about my attire. But wait a minute, I told myself; now *I'm* the foreigner. I still didn't care.

At Waterloo Station, we were met by Joseph Friedman, chief of Columbia's European operations; two of his English assistants, who were to be our contacts with the London office; and George Seid, head of Columbia's film laboratory in Hollywood. Seid was a longtime ally and friend of Harry Cohn's, and Cohn had conscripted him to come to England to help in supervising the film we were going to make. He was not a very pleasant man and was not at all happy about being in England. He was away from his family and his beloved labs and, as he told Joe, "This damn British food is killing me."

With our welcoming delegation, we crowded into Joseph Friedman's chauffeur-driven Lincoln limousine, which seemed huge in a traffic jam of tiny British cars. We were on our way to Wardour Street to Columbia's London offices. On the way, Friedman said he was going to give us a quick sightseeing tour in the heart of London. We crossed Waterloo Bridge, saw the Embankment, Charing Cross, Trafalgar Square, and the Mall. We approached St. James' Palace, and one of our English hosts called our attention to it: "St. James' Palace," he said with a touch of pride. "It looks like a brewery," George Seid said sourly. Joe Friedman winced, and the British men reacted with something like anger, which they quickly concealed. George Seid ran the best film laboratory in Hollywood, but he was not a particularly satisfactory person to be an ambassador of goodwill. Actually, Seid was right; St. James' Palace *did* look like a brewery—the Germans and Austrians who built breweries in the United States a century ago tended to admire the architecture of Old World palaces—and that's the way they built them.

At Wardour Street, Friedman took us to an office where Harry Cohn was waiting for us. Gower Gulch or Wardour Street, it was

the same rough, imperious Harry Cohn. There were no preliminaries, no polite "How was your trip?" Instead, he told us
brusquely what we were going to do: make a picture at British and
Dominion Studio in Elstree with American efficiency—*Columbia*
efficiency. Cohn then turned to me. "Now, you," he said, in the
gentle, kindly tones of a Marine drill sergeant displeased with an
inept rookie. "I didn't bring you here just to twist any goddamn di-
als. I can hire twenty guys here to do it. I brought you here because
you've got American ears. I listen to people here and sometimes I
can't understand half of what they're saying. Sometimes I can't
understand *any* of it! We're making a picture with an all-British
cast, and it's up to you to make sure that people in the U.S. can understand every damn word that's said. If they can't, don't bother
to come back to Columbia."

The trip suddenly seemed much less of an enjoyable adventure.
I'd been on a British ship for six and a half days and on British soil
for only half a day, but I was already aware that some English accents were almost unintelligible to Americans. The British actors
with whom I had worked in Hollywood hadn't prepared me for
that unwelcome fact. I suppose that living and working among
Americans had caused them, even those portraying cockneys or
north countrymen, to alter their accents subtly, so that they were
perfectly intelligible, but no less British.

After our conference, Joe and I were taken to our quarters at the
Park Lane Hotel. After dinner at the hotel, we were free for the first
time to explore London. My diary tells me that we "walked around
Hyde Park, saw Scotland Yard, Embankment, Houses of Parliament, Westminster Abbey, Birdcage Walk. Joe shared my delight
every step of the way."

There were some steps that weren't exactly a delight. I'd grown
up in Chicago, a notoriously tough and lawless town, and spent
several years in Hollywood, which everyone knows is very sinful.
But I had never encountered prostitutes—streetwalkers—on the
street before. Joe and I were accosted about a dozen times on Piccadilly and Park Lane. The ladies usually made their pitch to Joe—
a tribute to his seniority, I suppose. "Hi there, Yank—show you a
good time?" was the usual opening ploy. They were never wrong;
they invariably spotted us as Americans, even though I was no
longer wearing my blue blazer and my ice cream pants. I let Joe
carry the ball and watched, amused and a little touched—because

Joe, the ultimate gentleman, couldn't be rude to anyone. One girl was very persistent; Joe then made up an excuse and politely told her that he was very sorry, but we were late for an appointment. The young lady remained undeterred: "Have you all through in no time at all, sir." Some time later, when Joe encountered languid salesmen in a London camera store, who didn't seem to care whether you bought or not, he said wryly that the streetwalkers of Picadilly were the only enterprising salespersons he had encountered in England.

We returned safely to our Park Lane Hotel. Joe had a fine room with a window that overlooked Piccadilly. With less seniority, I suppose, I had a smaller room in the back of the hotel, overlooking a narrow little street called Brick Street. I delighted in British place names anyway, and this one seemed to me to be a splendid one. I had just fallen asleep before midnight when I was awakened by screams and shouting. I opened my window and looked down on Brick Street. A couple of prostitutes had been thrown out of a low-life pub just below me, literally thrown out. A burly bouncer or bartender had pushed them out so violently that one of them fell down. Then I heard curses the like of which I had never heard before. I heard—and recognized—"bastud" several times. The pubkeeper replied in kind, and after a time the girls went away and I went back to bed. It had been a most eventful day: July 12, 1933, my twenty-eighth birthday.

The following morning, Joe and I had breakfast in the hotel grill. Joe was what my mother used to call a "picky" eater. He was vaguely dissatisfied with his food; I thought it was excellent, and ate everything in sight—including some of Joe's jam and toast. Joe called a waiter and asked for a glass of orange juice. The man looked startled, and hurried off to see his manager. The man came quickly. Joe repeated his request for orange juice. "Are you ill, sir?" the manager asked. Joe didn't get the orange juice. The Park Lane, one of the truly good hotels in London, simply didn't have any. For a long time afterward, back in Hollywood, Joe told the story: "Are you ill, sir?"

After breakfast, George Seid picked us up in Friedman's Lincoln limousine and took us to the Mayfair Hotel where Harry Cohn was staying. He joined us, and we were driven out to Elstree to get acquainted with the people we would work with. London to Elstree took about two hours by car. I sat behind the driver, a very small man. It seemed that he could barely see over the steering wheel. It was raining hard and he drove far too fast, it seemed to me, *and* on the wrong side of the road. Of course I knew that the left side of the road was the correct side in England, but instincts take over, and I flinched every time a vehicle moved up in the rain, head-on to the left of us.

As we were driving to the studio, Harry Cohn told us—almost casually—that a strike had shut down all production in Hollywood and that a strike had started at Columbia. Joe and I wanted to know more about it, but the London newspapers carried only a few two-line items in the weeks that followed.

At British & Dominions Film Corporation (B & D), Joe and I met our production manager, a man named Cunningham; the head of the sound department, Overton; and the art director, Berndorff. Harry Cohn left us at Elstree and returned to London in the Lincoln limousine. After a couple of hours spent with the B & D people, Joe and I were driven back to London in a small, cramped little English car. When we returned to the Park Lane Hotel, we were handed a message: "Go at once to St. James Theater." An employee met us at the curb of the empty theater and ushered us backstage. Harry Cohn was there. He introduced us to Gilbert Miller, who was to be our director, and Leslie Howard, our leading man. They would be available for tests at Elstree the following Monday. Cohn then told Miller what he had told me: that I was to be responsible for the intelligibility of every syllable in the picture. During Cohn's colorful—and profane—account of his difficulties with British-style English, I happened to catch Leslie Howard's eye. My expression must have told him, "This isn't my idea. I don't like it." He gave me the slightest of nods. I like to think it meant, "I understand. We'll work it out."

Joe and I had three days to ourselves before we were to film tests at Elstree. I wanted to see the docks and the mean streets of London, as well as the traditional places of interest. So Joe and I separated; I went to the Tower of London, but Joe was more interested in making the rounds of Mayfair's famous camera shops. The cryptic notes in my diary are, "Boarded a top-heavy double-decker bus. Went by way of Oxford Street, Holborn Viaduct, Newgate, Cheapside, and Eastcheap Street to the Tower of London; Tower Bridge, shipping in the river, cannon on the bank. Tickets, one shilling and sixpence (about thirty-seven cents). Went through the

Crown Jewel Room and then were shown the prison rooms, which had a dank, musty smell, three hundred years' old. In the court-yard—youthful soldiers of the garrison." In the Chapel of Saint Peter Ad Vincula, one of the top-hatted, red-coated yeoman warders gave a cheery little talk about the aristocrats who were beheaded and buried beneath the flagstones of the chapel. The yeoman stationed himself at the door as we filed out. People gave him tips; I had no English coins, so I gave him what I had: several U.S. dimes and a couple of Buffalo nickels. He glanced at the nickels suspiciously, and then with surprise and admiration he exclaimed, "What ho! Bison!"

I crossed Tower Bridge and walked along the river. In my diary, I noted the "appalling poverty. Thin, pale little English boys—no energy—don't shout and run like kids should." Here were the meanest of mean streets. Tall, drab tenement buildings, crowded close to the narrow street. It seemed to me that the streets were so narrow and the buildings so high that the meagre London sun would probably never reach into the windows of those tenements. On one such street, I found something that shocked and disturbed me. A small storefront funeral parlor had in its window an infant-sized coffin with a crude sign, "Child's Funeral, ten-pounds, six-pence." In that grim neighborhood, people expected children to die.

I heard music and walked toward it. I came upon a good-looking young man, a street singer, performing for pennies that were thrown down to him from the building. I thought his voice was excellent—the acoustics made his voice seem powerful and eloquent. The man finished his song, then a few people opened windows and threw down coins. I didn't have any coins, so I handed the singer a ten-shilling note. As I walked away, he called out in his Cockney-accented voice, "Thankee, thankee, sorr. Gawh' bless ye, Yank." The Londoners never missed! It was as though Joe and I had "U.S.A." tattooed on our foreheads.

I went home to the Park Lane by a new route: on the south side of the Thames by Bridge Road, which changed its name without warning to Kent Road and then to St. George's Road, across Westminster Bridge, and on to the incomparable sight of the Houses of Parliament and Westminster Abbey in the late-afternoon sunset. Joe was waiting for me somewhat impatiently. We had been invited by Harry Cohn (and that meant we had been *ordered*) to attend a press showing of *Lady for a Day* at a place called Great Tower Street. After dinner we boarded a cab, gave the cabbie our destination, and were taken on what my diary called "a wild goose chase." Our driver took us miles in the wrong direction to deliver us to a street with a name similar to the one we had given him. That destroyed the myth that every London cabdriver knew every obscure little street and alley in London. We arrived at the theater just in time to see the opening scenes of *Lady for a Day*. Joe was not satisfied with the quality of the picture image. He blamed poor projection—the film was not quite in focus. I didn't like the sound quality, either. It sounded muffled, lacking in the high frequencies that gave it intelligibility. When the picture was finished, a crowd of distinguished British filmmakers (including Alexander Korda) and most of London's film critics surrounded Harry Cohn and Joe to congratulate them.

I woke up to heavy rainfall the next morning. I gave up plans to take a train to Ramsgate, a resort town at the mouth of the Thames, and decided instead to do something about my literary career. I did have a literary career, of sorts. I decided that writing might be my pathway to directing. You couldn't be a director, I reasoned, unless someone gave you a job; but you could become a writer with a very simple strategy: you could write. I could try my hand at movie screenplays or short stories. The hundred-plus pages of a motion-picture script intimidated me, so I chose to try my hand at short stories. In the limited time I had after working ten-, twelve-, and fourteen-hour days, I wrote stories that were movie-business oriented, aimed squarely at the readers of a unique magazine, *Rob Wagner's Script*.

Rob Wagner was a brilliant, eccentric man who was prominent in the movie community of the 1920s and '30s. He had been an artist, a scenic designer for stage shows on Broadway and in England, and came to Los Angeles in 1912 as a schoolteacher at historic Manual Arts High School. There he taught art and was the coach of the wrestling team—certainly an odd parley. He taught art and wrestling to celebrities such as General Jimmy Doolittle (who led the air raid on Tokyo in World War II); Lawrence Tibbett, the famous singer; Goodwin Knight, who later became governor of California for several terms; and Frank Capra.

Wagner was a man of many talents. He wrote and directed some of the best silent films, including several silent comedy shorts with

Will Rogers. He was the good friend and confidante of many of Hollywood's elite—Will Rogers, of course, and especially Charlie Chaplin. He was flamboyant, eccentric, and energetic, and in the late 1920s he decided to create a weekly magazine. It was not an ego trip in which he would lose money to get his name on the cover of his own magazine. He did *not* lose money; his list of subscribers and contributors included nearly every producer, director, writer, and performer in Hollywood. Big-time advertisers paid top prices for space in his magazine. Finding time to write after the long hours I worked was difficult, but in the April 3, 1932, issue of *Script*, Rob Wagner printed a story of mine. I was a published author!

So on this rainy Sunday morning in London, I wrote another piece for *Script*. I described the rainfall, the incident on Brick Street, the confrontation between the strumpet and the barkeeper, our visit to the B & D in Elstree, and my visit to the Tower of London. Rob Wagner printed it in his issue of August 5, 1933. I was becoming a veteran writer.

The rain stopped in midafternoon and the sun came out. Joe and I visited Westminster Abbey, then walked to Hyde Park by way of Birdcage Walk and Green Park. We found ourselves at the famous Hyde Park corner where the freest of free speech is permitted—it's even encouraged. The city authorities provided a half-dozen makeshift platforms for speakers. A communist flaunting a big red flag spoke of the violent day when the Communist Party would seize power in Britain. The people of his audience listened politely, mildly interested. On another platorm, a preacher, clearly a mental case, ranted and raved about the doom that was to descend on a sinful world. His audience also listened politely, although a couple of hecklers shouted insults at him. Some of the Britons looked reprovingly at the hecklers. Another speaker argued vehemently for the abolition of the monarchy. The monarchy was revered at that time, but no one in the audience resorted to that traditional American form of protest—a punch in the nose. This was free speech in its purest form, in a nation where the concept of man's rights was born.

There was something disturbing in London, however. Joe and I noticed men in brown shirts wearing Sam Browne–type military belts, with close-cropped hair, affecting a stiff military manner of walking. I wondered whether they were Italian fascists who were visiting London. But the Italians wore black shirts and these men didn't look Italian. We learned then that they were *English* fascists, led by a would-be Führer named Sir Oswald Mosley. The fascists' poison was spreading even to England.

The next morning, Monday, July 17, we were driven to Elstree where I met my sound crew. My boom man was named W. H. E. Lindop. His ancestry was Irish, but he was born in England and had no trace of an Irish accent. He was good-looking, well built, about my age, and proved to be an excellent mike man. My recordist was Lionel Tregellas, a short, stocky, red-haired Australian in his midtwenties. He had an uncle, I was told, who was prominent in the Australian film industry, and Lionel, at his own request, went to England to learn about the British film industry. My cable man was named Straderick—"Straddie," we called him. He was an older man, a Cockney, who had been in the navy during World War I. Joe Walker's crew consisted of his camera operator, Osmond Borradaile, a Canadian; his focus puller (in Hollywood, we'd call him a first assistant cameraman) was a fellow named Harrison, with a gorgeous bright red mustache, the bushiest I'd ever seen.

Joe and I proceeded to make sound and photographic tests with Leslie Howard and Binnie Barnes, our leading lady, who had portrayed Catherine Howard in Alexander Korda's *The Private Life of Henry VIII*. We made a couple of two-shots, a medium shot, a close two-shot, and a couple of close-ups. Binnie Barnes seemed nervous, but Leslie Howard was calm and professional. There was no movement of camera, mike, or people. There was no challenge to my mike man nor to Joe's camera operator. Joe said to me later, "It was like shooting a couple of portraits." Our work that day was no test of how we—Joe with his crew, I with my crew—would function under *real* movie conditions. Consequently, these tests were uneventful and gave no hint of the difficulties to come.

That evening I read my script for our picture, *The Lady Is Willing*. I was appalled. The screenplay had been written by Guy Bolton, an American writer with impressive credits, from a French play by L. Verneuil. I suppose it was intended to be light, sexy (by 1933 standards), and witty, but the central theme was that of a kidnapping, which was hardly a fit subject for comedy at that time. The Lindbergh baby had been taken in March 1932, the ransom was paid in April, and the child's body was discovered in May. Bruno Richard Hauptmann had not yet been arrested.

Even disregarding the temper of the times, I thought the script was bad. Who selected it? Was it Harry Cohn? The man had his flaws, but, as Frank Capra wrote in his autobiography, "Cohn's faults were legion minus one—he was not stupid." It is true that many of the Columbia B pictures of that day were bad, but Cohn had little involvement with the B product beyond an occasional "off with his head" decree to fire some hapless producer or director. In the selection of stories for Columbia's A productions, I considered him to be a discerning judge of story material. Who *did* select the *Lady Is Willing* script? To this day, I don't know.

Tuesday, July 18, was "Moving Day" for us. A truck took our baggage to the place where we would be staying, Radnor Hall, while Joe and I went by car directly to Elstree. That day we ran the rushes of the tests. The photography was pretty good; I thought the sound was not of the best quality, but nobody objected.

Radnor Hall Country Club was located in the little town of Borehamwood, which was about a mile from the studio. It was a century-old manor house, not a castle, probably once the home of a prosperous tradesman. Radnor was called a "country club," although that label was actually a euphemism for "hotel." It was a huge place, completely remodeled into a hotel that catered to long-time guests who came to Elstree to make a picture. Everything about the furnishings were very nice, except that the plumbing was as old as the house, and very cranky. I had a room on the top floor; when I came home from work, I could never get enough water into the bathtub.

Radnor Hall was set on a big piece of land, about four or five acres. They certainly didn't stint on the gardening or the landscaping—the grounds were extremely well kept. The depression in England was probably worse than ours in America, so labor was cheap and Radnor had an abundance of hired help. There was a splendid croquet court on the grounds; when Joe and I first arrived there, we were pretty close to the longest day of the year. We were on D.B.S.T. (Double British Summer Time), which gave us daylight that went beyond ten o'clock at night. So even after we shot a long day at the studio, went back to Radnor, had dinner, and still had time to go out and play a little croquet before we went to bed.

There was a dining room at Radnor Hall; since most of us were long-term residents there, we were given the same tables, day after day. Joe was never quite comfortable with the food, but I liked everything and ate everything that was served to me—and some of Joe's servings, too, as I had at the Park Lane Hotel. It bothered Joe, for instance, that he could never get warm toast for breakfast. It was always stone-cold. When he demanded warm toast, they brought him a new serving, all right—but it was burned black and still cold.

At Radnor, I was introduced to fish for breakfast. I suppose it's traditional in England to have either Yarmouth bloaters or kippers for breakfast. Both are herring, smoked and dried, processed apparently by slightly different methods. "Bloaters" is not a very appetizing designation for a food, but I liked them and often ordered them, and kippers, too, until I noticed that they bothered Joe. They were dark brown and shrunken-looking, and they smelled oily and fishy. Since they were served whole, I guess Joe didn't like their reproachful eyes looking at him. From the time I noticed Joe's reaction, I ordered bloaters and kippers less frequently.

Joe and I were assigned a car and chauffeur to drive us to and from the studio. The car wasn't a taxi; it was brought to us from a nearby garage and was available to take us wherever we wanted to go, at Columbia's cost. It was a standing order that the car would pick us up every morning to deposit us at the studio and then return us to Radnor at the end of the day. From time to time, Joe and I would walk the mile to work. The first morning at Radnor Hall we walked, enjoying the English countryside.

Production began on Wednesday, July 19. It was a frustrating, unproductive day. That evening, Joe commented wryly, "Today, as nearly as I can figure, we shot about one two-hundredths of our picture. I wonder if it gets cold here in winter?"

The second day the entire cast reported for work. Cedric Hardwicke (not yet *Sir* Cedric) was cast as DuPont, a wealthy French swindler; Binnie Barnes as his dissatisfied wife; and Leslie Howard as a French ex-army captain named La Tour, whose military comrades, played by Nigel Bruce, Sebastian Smith, and Graham Browne, come to him for help in recovering money DuPont has swindled from them. It was an all-British cast playing all-French roles.

Relations with our crew were good. Everyone liked Joe Walker. To my mind, it was impossible for anyone not to like Joe. The men of my sound crew were as sharp and willing as any of the soundmen with whom I had worked in Hollywood. Progress, however, was slow and unsatisfactory. The principal reason was Gilbert Miller's inexperience and lack of drive. Diary, July 21: "Progress slow and laborious. Shooting drags, scenes drag. Kibitzers appear—Lewis Milestone, Cyril Gardner (ex-film editor), Columbia executive Nathan Spingold, Harry Cohn. One scene A.M., one scene P.M. Change actor Sebastian Smith to Nigel Playfair for part of Menard. Joe and I to dinner while kibitzers still arguing. Back to studio hour and a half later—they're still at it. Four days' work laid out in advance. Era of great speed in prospect." If there seems to be a touch of irony in the last sentence, it was not unintentional.

Several of the diary references require explanation. First, the appearance of Lewis Milestone: apparently Harry Cohn had some sort of claim on him. A year later, Milestone would direct *The Captain Hates the Sea* for Columbia; perhaps he was already on salary. At any rate, Cohn prevailed upon him to participate in a rescue mission—to "kibitz." What Milestone had done, in the long, angry conference the diary refers to, was to plan, shot by shot, the next four days' work.

By now, Gilbert Miller must have been somewhat disillusioned with becoming a movie director. I had by that time become aware that Miller was not merely a successful theatrical producer but one of the dominant figures of the theater in New York and London. He was immensely wealthy and owned the St. James Theater, where we first met, as well as the Lyric in London and the Henry Miller in New York. I cannot see why, at this stage, he didn't tell Harry Cohn to take his picture and do something unmentionable with it. But he didn't.

I had wondered earlier who selected the script. Now I wondered why Harry Cohn, a notoriously hardheaded character, selected a novice to direct a picture on which he was staking a great deal of personal prestige. I believed that Leslie Howard, having presumably enjoyed a cordial relationship with Gilbert Miller in a series of successful stage productions, had insisted on Miller as his director for the picture. It seemed to be the only explanation that made sense.

Gilbert Miller attempted to shoot the scenes as Milestone had planned them, but our speed increased not one bit. Stress did increase, however, as we fell further behind schedule. On Saturday,

July 22, a problem arose that was with us all through the making of the picture. It was necessary for us to quit at 7:30 P.M. because most of the crew—electricians, propmen, grips—lived in London. They had to get to the Edgware station to take a two-hour train ride into London. If we didn't wrap up by 7:30, they couldn't catch that last train. On Saturday, our crew barely made that last train.

Again, from my diary, July 22: "Joe on the carpet for delay." Harry Cohn and George Seid were picking on Joe for the slowness of our shooting, which was terribly unjust. Joe was always a gentleman, never made excuses, but in commenting to me about his electric gang, he remarked, "Those electricians are nice guys, but they have *no idea* of what those lights are supposed to do!" In Hollywood, at Columbia, every electrician *knew* exactly why he was moving the lights. They could anticipate, and understand why Joe was calling for certain lights to achieve certain effects. On another occasion, Joe said to me, "I'd give anything in the world for George Hager and a couple of rifles." "Rifles" were a type of light with a swirled glass mirror that gave a very useful soft front light. Joe was very partial to the use of rifles for front-light effects, but no such lights were available at Elstree.

For me, accents—and intelligibility—began to be a problem. Leslie Howard presented no difficulty, nor did Cedric Hardwicke or Binnie Barnes. Nigel Bruce, however, was difficult to understand. Diary: "Nigel Bruce (nephew of a duke?) wanted to play it Cockney." For the first time, I had to insist on intelligibility. Nigel Bruce was outraged. He made it clear that he considered me a presumptuous upstart, attempting to impose ridiculous restrictions on actors' use of the King's English. Miller did not intervene, which underscored his lack of leadership. A director must lead; he must take charge. Leslie Howard smoothed over the dispute. Without revealing the source of my directive, he asked for restraint and cooperation. We went back to work. Nigel Bruce had not agreed to modify his accent, but now I could understand every word.

Nigel Playfair was another matter. He did not have what I considered a regional accent; he had what I can only describe as a kind of chewed-up Colonel Blimp delivery. But *Sir* Nigel Playfair had been knighted for acting, and I was obviously far out of line in trying to modify the speech of one so honored. It was my fault, of course—or the fault of my "American ears"—that found him unintelligible. For example, as Menard, he was required to ask La

Tour (Howard), "By guarding her life with your own?" The way Sir Nigel delivered the speech, "by guarding" became, very clearly, "by God"—the *r* was missing, and so was the *ing*. When I explained that at least the semblance of an "r" was needed to make the speech intelligible to Americans, he responded with the longest, most exaggerated rolling *r* I had ever heard. It sounded ridiculous. The cast and crew laughed. Sir Nigel wasn't trying to "show me up," as baseball players say. He was trying his best to do what I asked, which made it even harder for me. I would rather have had to cope with his anger.

Although we were already behind schedule, we didn't work late on Saturday the 22nd; we worked *Sunday* the 23rd. That evening, dog-tired and looking for a little relief, Joe and I ordered our automobile from the garage to go to Edgware to see a movie. We discovered that we *couldn't* see a movie; blue laws were in effect at that time. I was outraged; we had mostly gotten rid of blue laws in California. Even Joe Walker was not amused. Blue laws!

On July 25, Harry Cohn told us a little bit more about the strike in Hollywood. But there was nothing much that was new to report; and he didn't seem to be particularly perturbed about whatever was happening at his studio. At least he didn't display any concern to either Joe or myself.

On Wednesday the 26th, I had lunch at the British Independent Pictures (B.I.P.) restaurant. B.I.P. and B & D were both located at Elstree; they were separate entities, and even had separate lunchrooms, but they were under one roof. A most unusual arrangement.

At Radnor Hall, Joe and I had permanent table seating for breakfast and dinner. Many of the tenants were long-term, like us. We sat at a table alone. At a table close to us were an Englishman and his wife, and there was a troupe of Germans at another table. The early 1930s was the time of the infamous "quota system." If a foreign company made a film in Great Britain using British personnel, they could release one of their own pictures in England. This resulted in the making of many "junk" pictures, or what were called quota quickies. But the German team, like our own, was there at B & D trying to make a pretty good picture. Their director was Carmine Galone, who was obviously an Italian although everyone spoke German at his table. There was also a man named Zimmerman; an Englishman, Arthur Briscoe (probably an actor in the picture); and a woman named Magda Schneider. She seemed

to be a person of importance. Everybody—including Carmine Galone—deferred to her.

The Englishman and his wife at the next table talked a great
deal—that is, he talked a great deal and she listened. He had one of
those mouthful-of-mush, jumbled-up British accents. I strained to
understand him, but couldn't comprehend a word he said. When the
wife answered, I usually understood. She'd say, "Yes, dear," and
that I understood. For weeks I listened, trying to understand a little
of what he said, but never succeeded. On the other hand, at the German table, I understood a surprising amount of what they said. I had
been exposed to the German language when I was a child and there
was a lot of German spoken in our household, but I didn't really
think I had absorbed much. So I was surprised when I began understanding fragments of what they were saying. Among the things
I heard was that they had great respect for Joe Walker—naturally
enough, because he was known worldwide as a great cameraman.
There was not so much admiration for Gilbert Miller, however, and
none at all for Harry Cohn. There were other remarks, some fairly
favorable and some a little unfavorable, and the usual movie talk
gossip. The payoff came when we finished our picture; the Germans were still in production on their film. I would always come
down for breakfast in the morning, meet the Germans, and greet
them in English. But on this morning, just for the hell of it, I greeted
them in German. Suddenly, there was a certain amount of conster-
nation. I could see that they began to wonder what they had said,
and were amazed that the damned American could apparently understand and speak some German. I got a little bit of wicked fun out
of that.

A man who I knew only as Donnie was in charge of everything
at Radnor Hall Country Club. The French have got a name for his
occupation: *concierge*. Donnie was the boss of the kitchen and the
waitresses, and he took care of us when we needed something, like
calling for cars, obtaining maps, and so on. At Radnor, he made
himself very useful and also just happened to be a very nice guy.
But—Donnie drank heavily. I was not used to people who drank
like that, but many British people I encountered *did* drink regularly. I disapproved of it; I had not yet tasted liquor. My father,
who was the quintessential law-abiding citizen, would enjoy an
occasional glass of beer before Prohibition. But when Prohibition
became the law of the land, we never had liquor in our house.

Donnie was very perceptive; he could see that I was disapproving and self-righteous about his drinking, and my attitude apparently bothered him. One evening, he told me why he drank. He had been a schoolboy, just seventeen years old when war broke out. His class of fourteen students all volunteered to enlist—a deadly similarity to Remarque's class of young students in *All Quiet on the Western Front*, who enlisted en masse and were subsequently shattered by the war. Donnie went into the army at seventeen years old, was an officer at eighteen, was wounded twice in 1916, was patched up, and went back to the front. He tapped the top of his head; it made kind of a strange, hollow sound. He said to me, "That's a silver plate. The top of my head was torn off by a piece of shrapnel—and it hurts. It hurts all the time. The whiskey helps a little." I was considerably less disapproving and self-righteous after that.

Lewis Milestone showed up at the studio every day, guiding Gilbert Miller through the daily setups. As the production dragged on, Milestone delighted more and more in "showing off." He was a great storyteller; he had many anecdotes about pictures he'd made and the fantastic things that happened to him. Coincidentally, he was the hero of every single story he told. My diary entry for July 27 tells of one of Milestone's yarns. He directed *Two Arabian Knights* (1927), a very successful silent comedy with Bill Boyd and Louis Wolheim. He made the picture for Howard Hughes, and it won an Academy Award. Milestone proceeded to tell a story about Howard Hughes's bizarre toilet habits—but he managed to make himself the hero of *that* story, too!

My diary also notes on this same day that "Gilbert Miller had a big fight with Binnie Barnes." I believe the argument was over her accent. The way a person spoke was a big issue in Britain then; maybe it still is over there. If you had a regional accent, particularly a Cockney accent, you were considered a second-class citizen. In general, I liked most of the Englishmen I encountered, but there was one fellow I genuinely disliked because of this condescending attitude. He was a secretary or gofer for one of our actors. He regularly came upstairs to my outdated monitoring room. In England, we were still using the CTA mike and we still had the upstairs monitor room.

This particular Englishman liked to sit upstairs and listen to what was happening on the set. I didn't especially like it, but I didn't complain; I wasn't there to be unpleasant to the natives. This person, however, had a bad word for everyone. He sneered at Binnie Barnes because she did not have what he considered an "acceptable" theatrical accent. She once pronounced the word *brutal* and it came out *bwutal*. The chap delighted in pointing out how terrible her diction was, that she didn't really deserve to be a leading lady because she had such a horrible accent. He also criticized Claude Rains. Apparently Rains had made enough of a success in the United States so that this character was jealous of him. He said, "Claude Rains tries to disguise it, but he *really* has a terrible accent!" He would sneer at just about anyone. I have no doubt that when he was away from me, he told people what a oafish colonial *I* was.

But I got rid of him. I encountered the head of the sound department, Overton, and told him that I didn't want to antagonize any of his countrymen, but I didn't like the man's presence in the monitor room. Overton took care of the problem very promptly. I walked up to the monitor room first so it didn't appear that I was throwing the man out. Then Overton walked in and pretended to be surprised that someone else was there. In that supercilious way that some Englishmen talk down to people they consider beneath them, Overton told the man that he was *not* to be in there, should *never* be in there, and, in effect, to get the hell out—all in that elegant English accent.

Every day at the studio proved to be long, frustrating, and difficult; relief came whenever I had a few hours and could explore the beautiful English countryside. During my stay, I made two boat trips, one of them to historic Greenwich. The custom was to take a boat down the Thames, disembark, and stay for an hour looking over the Greenwich observatory and other sites of interest. An hour later, the next boat would return to take the tourists back to London, to Westminster Bridge. For me it was a wonderful experience; on both trips we had guides who were obviously very well educated in English history. They did something interesting: neither guide duplicated the other's work. Although they were working the same stretch of river, they pointed out places of historical interest in a way that never intruded on each other's spiel. These guides were so well spoken and so well informed that I thought perhaps, with the economic depression so severe in England, they were a couple of history professors moonlighting as tour guides.

On another occasion I took a boat upriver to Kew Gardens. I disembarked at Kew Bridge, but it was getting late and Kew Gardens had closed by the time I got there. I spotted a trolley at the end of the line; the motorman and conductor were lounging around, one of them occasionally glancing at his watch to see if it was time to start their run. I went aboard and the conductor, a young fellow about my age, took my fare. I looked at my map and asked him if they went to Chiswick. He replied, "It's *Chizick,*" then he looked at me and exclaimed, "Blimey, a Yank!" They never missed, you know. Then he said in a badgering way, "You one of those Yanks that won the war for us, eh?" I put on my stern, disapproving face, marched into the car, sat down, and looked out the window. He followed me, saying, "Aw, Yank, c'mon, I didn't mean anything, don't take offense. It's just that some of your chaps talk mighty big." But I kept looking out the window, giving him the cold shoulder. It really hurt him; once in a while I could steal a glance and I could see he was still troubled. He hadn't really meant to be nasty; he just popped off. Anyway, I got off the trolley at Chiswick — *Chizick,* that is — and took a bus to Gaumont British Studio at Shepherd's Bush.

I saw something unique at Gaumont: a vertical movie studio. The stages were arranged as floors — one on top of another. It was a terribly inefficient design; the studio had been some kind of an industrial building and had a fair-sized freight elevator, but the elevator wasn't big enough to move sets easily. The sets had to be constructed in very small units, taken up to the appropriate floor, and assembled on the stage.

All was not well back at our Elstree studio. Diary entry, Saturday, July 29: "George Seid deliberately insulting — even short-tempered with Joe." Joe told me that Seid had an incipient ulcer, and blamed his miserable health on the British food he had to eat. Seid had his reasons for being edgy — he was coping with an ulcer, he was far away from home, and Harry Cohn was putting pressure on him for the slowness of production, which was, of course, very unfair — but apparently Seid's way of responding to these oppressive developments was to become insulting to everyone. The diary for this date also indicates a "dreary night of filming until 4:30 A.M." Shades of the Columbia frolic — the good old all-night, Saturday-night marathon that we loved so much back home. But that was one U.S. export that the British weren't going to like very much. The diary entry concludes, "To bed 5 A.M. Sunday."

Diary, July 31: "No scenes shot all morning. P.M. mostly with Hardwicke. Finish 6:30. Rushes very bad." What was bad? Sound? Photography? Action? I don't remember. Perhaps all three. Production went on in that manner: long hours, unsatisfactory results, "kibitzing."

My term "kibitzing" was inelegant but descriptive. It meant that a more or less constant stream of people that would participate, sometimes grudgingly, in play doctoring. Harry Cohn, a persuasive man as well as a powerful one, was able to induce writers, producers, film editors, and assorted meddlers to come to Elstree to perform corrective surgery on our script. On August 1, Laurence Stallings appeared and spent several days discussing the script and rewriting. Roland Pertwee spent much time with us from mid-August onward. I believe that even P. G. Wodehouse appeared, perhaps merely to visit, or perhaps to infuse some lightness and humor into our scenes.

My report for Tuesday, August 1, is a cryptic entry; the diary merely says, "B. Barnes seductive—apple." I don't remember what I meant by that, but I do remember that Binnie Barnes had an aura of sex appeal that was something quite apart from her looks—a little of the same quality that Jean Harlow had. I made a picture with Binnie Barnes much later at Columbia, also with Rosalind Russell. I spoke with Binnie about our adventures in England, and we reminisced briefly about *The Lady Is Willing*. I forgot to bring up the apple or the fact that she was very "seductive" on that picture, so now the incident is lost to the ages.

Also on August 1, I bought a wedding gift for the assistant head of the sound department, a man named Crowhurst. The gift cost three and a half pounds. It was very generous of me—but I should say it was very generous of Columbia, because I charged the wedding present to the studio on my expense account.

Lewis Milestone had been with us since the first week of shooting. He took charge of the doctoring sessions and the advance planning, but otherwise remained in the background. Diary, August 2: "Milestone actively in charge."

Harry Cohn's leverage must have been powerful to persuade him to take over. Milestone was acutely unhappy with his new status. He had been reasonably content in the role of eminent director, giving freely of his wisdom to Miller, the struggling novice; but to be thrust into the firing line was not to his liking. Through my microphone, I heard his bitter complaints at being "shanghaied" into this thankless situation. Production from then on was not pleasant. Milestone did not like Cohn having saddled him with what he must have considered a "turkey." He too was subjected to a certain amount of nagging. When Cohn was on the set, he would nag Milestone about slow progress. When Cohn left, he delegated the nagging to George Seid. So Milestone became a thoroughly disgruntled character.

Bank holiday was a welcome relief from the pressure and frustration of production. For four days, from Friday, August 4, through August 7, we were free. Joe Walker went to attend the motorcar racing at Brooklands. I used the time off to write down my impressions about British filmmaking. I finished an article for *Rob Wagner's Script* and entitled it "The Hollywood of England." Rob Wagner published it in his issue of September 22, 1933. My portfolio of published pieces was growing.

On August 7, I was invited to go with Donnie and a group of his friends to Hampstead Heath. There were eight of us in all, and I was the only American in the group. We went in two cars; I rode with Donnie, who drove not a Morris Oxford nor a Triumph Coventry nor a Vauxhall nor a Riley, all good English-made cars; he drove a Chrysler. August 7 was apparently the climax of the bank holiday. There was a lot of drinking going on during that time, but Donnie drank only moderately since he was going to drive. Hampstead Heath swarmed with revelers. The throngs of Cockneys who came were boisterous, good-natured, mellow with drink, but not at all belligerent or obnoxious. They roamed about singing their own unique songs, perhaps a dozen 'Arrys and 'Arriets (as Londoners described the Cockneys, characteristically leaving off the *h*). The Cockney men had costumes upon which thousands and thousands of buttons were sewn. Mona, one of Donnie's friends, told me that the costumes were a tradition centuries old. The men were linked arm-in-arm, often doing little prancing dance steps. People got out of their way; it was all very good-natured and fun. We went into pubs with historic names: the Spaniard's (which reputedly had been the haunt of Dick Turpin), the Vale of Health, Jack Straw's Castle, and the Bull and Bush. In the ancient pub called the Spaniard's, the doorways were so low that tall people had to duck to enter. In some rooms, I felt that I was close to scraping the ceiling with my head.

We went back to work on August 8. I was mildly surprised that Gilbert Miller had returned. Milestone was in charge; he picked the setups, instructed the actors, decided which takes to print, but permitted Miller to sit in a director's chair and call out "action" and "cut." It was a grotesque situation, one that I believe not even the most short-of-cash B-picture director in Hollywood would have endured. Miller, however, showed no signs of resentment or embarassment. His demeanor from the beginning had been calm, almost placid, and it remained so. And if he had, at any time, expressed a desire to bow out, Harry Cohn would have gone to great lengths to dissuade him. To replace an eminent stage director in midpicture would have been poor public relations and an adverse reflection on Cohn's judgment in selecting him. And I am sure that Milestone would have refused to become the director of record — and probably did.

We were expected to achieve miracles of speed and efficiency under Milestone. My diary tells the sad facts. August 8: "New deal supposed to start. No go. Slow as ever. P.M. — long conferences, no scenes." August 10: "In La Tour set. Slow going. Work until eight. Crew who live in London miss last train from Edgware." Sunday, August 13: "Still in La Tour office. Electricians pull the plug at 7:30 P.M. Sore because they told Boothby [our assistant director] about train, but Milestone refused to stop shooting." When the set suddenly went black at 7:30 and the crew members walked out, Joe and I thought their action was justified. If our crew made that last 8 o'clock train, they still didn't get to London until about ten P.M. I imagine that many of them had sizable walks from the subway station. If they *missed* that last train, a bad situation became worse. Boothby pleaded with Milestone to quit on time, but this was just another instance of Milestone's nastiness; he pigheadedly decided to shoot beyond 7:30. It may have been his anger at being stuck with this project that compelled him to give Columbia some difficulty. Or perhaps his behavior was part of an alibi: the workmen were striking — what could he do?

Our crew was made up of battle-scarred veterans — veterans of years in the picture business and, before that, harsh years in the Great War. Nearly every man in our crew of so-called "military age" had served during World War I, and almost every one of them had been wounded. One of our electricians had received a string of machine gun bullets across his thighs. Another was a survivor of a military catastrophe, the Gallipoli campaign against the Turks, one of the most badly bungled campaigns in military history. This survivor told us that men died there just because water wasn't sent ashore with them.

Straderick, my cable man, had served aboard a battleship in the Battle of Jutland in 1916. I've always been a navy buff, and I found it downright fascinating to hear an account of that great battle from someone who had been there. Straderick was an electrician aboard one of Lord Jellicoe's battleships. His description of the battle was limited by the fact that his battle station was in, what he called, "the generator flat." This was far below the battleship's waterline in a compartment where the ship's generators were housed. Straddie said that every time his ship was hit, "it rang like an enormous gong." I'd never heard that before. Perhaps it was not noticed by the crew topside, who were creating tremendous noise by firing back at the enemy. Straderick probably heard it because he was sealed off from the topside noise, and when armour-piercing shells strike, they penetrate the armour and explode inside the ship. Straddie told me, "I was scared to death. I thought every minute would be my last."

On Saturday, August 19, Joe and I went to the station in Edgware and took the underground (subway) into London. I never got tired of that trip; the names of the places we passed through fascinated me: Burnt Oak, Hendon, Golders Green (I love that one), Chalk Farm, and Camden Town. On this particular trip, Joe and I got off the train at Leicester Square and separated. Joe had heard about a new camera shop and went to check it out, and I went to a shop on Regent Street named Hamley's that called itself "The Finest Toy Shop in the World." I bought some toys and picture books for Eddie Junior and Elsa.

Later we met at a place that Joe had discovered where food was served that pleased him: Apenrodt's, an authentic German restaurant in the heart of London. The food was certainly German—it reminded me of the Sunday dinners my mother used to cook: wonderful, creamy mashed potatoes with a big chunk of butter stuck in the middle; excellent pork roast; and delicious sauerkraut. From Apenrodt's, Joe and I went to Madame Tussaud's Wax Museum. We thought it was a really great show—interesting, stimulating, and it taught a great deal about history if you were willing to learn about it. The wax figures were startlingly lifelike, especially those that were treated to dramatic lighting. One exhibit that was especially dramatic and touching was the tableau from centuries ago, two innocent little princes being abducted and murdered by assassins hired by their uncle, the Duke of Gloucester. Everything about the scene was effective; Joe thought the lighting and the composition were superb.

Sunday, August 20, it was back to work. Diary entry: "Good progress all day." That was a switch! Monday, August 21—back to normal: "Inactivity all morning without a scene done. Rewriting and discussing it." On August 23, we went on location to the Hungaria River Club, at Maidenhead, on the upper Thames. I treated my sound crew to tea (it cost about fifteen shillings) and charged it to Columbia's tab. The little expenditure was worth it for the goodwill. Everything should have gone well at Maidenhead, but it did not. The sun was shining, the setting was lovely, the Thames was a beautiful body of water—but we sat. Diary: "Much waste of time rewriting scenes." Then my diary demands an answer to a question that has been asked ever since the first strips of celluloid began whirring through cameras: "Why can't someone find out a scene is bad before ten thousand dollars (or pounds) worth of payroll and equipment and rolling stock sits waiting on location?"

14

We spent Saturday and Sunday, August 26 and 27, filming scenes at the beautiful Lord Aldenham estate. The grounds were large, perhaps ten acres, with a large rose garden, spacious lawns, and a lake with fish in it. Some members of the crew improvised fishing tackle and caught fish. We were told that at the turn of the century 170 gardeners were employed, but now, in hard times, there were only forty. After our weekend at the Aldenham estate, Harry Cohn departed for California, leaving George Seid in charge.

Monday morning, in a bad mood, Seid attempted to speed up production. He decreed that our picture would—must—finish Wednesday or Thursday and told me to be prepared to sail for home on Saturday. I didn't think we could meet this schedule, and we didn't. His pressure had no discernable effect on Milestone or Gilbert Miller. Nevertheless, I started thinking about my trip home and hit upon what I thought was an excellent idea. Instead of sailing from Southampton to New York in a British ship, I thought I might fly to Paris, spend a few days there, travel by rail across France, board an Italian ship at Genoa, and sail home through the Mediterranean. I told my idea to my friend Donnie at Radnor; he helped me to make plans, inquiring about rail schedules and sailing date from Genoa. My next step was to telephone Harrington, of Northern Transport Company, who was handling our departure. He was most helpful. He would make a hotel reservation for me in Paris, provide me with train schedules, and buy me passage on the Italian superliner, *Conte de Savoia*. It arrived in New York only a day later than the White

Star liner *Majestic*, which I was scheduled to take, and the cost was about the same. It could all be handled nicely; all I had to do was get George Seid's approval. As old Will Shakespeare said, "There's the rub"—and this promised to be a most abrasive rub.

On Tuesday, production was slower than usual. We waited while Roland Pertwee rewrote scenes; and while we waited, Milestone, yarn spinning in fine fettle, told Cedric Hardwicke tales of Charlie Chaplin's eccentricities and how he, Milestone, gave Chaplin sage advice.

We did not work Wednesday—a set was not ready. To add to Seid's problems, a number of scenes we shot on Tuesday were scratched in the lab, and we would have to retake them. Joe and I took the day off; it was our last chance to see London. We did the usual tourist things: the changing of the Horse Guards; then to the Banqueting Hall where Charles I was beheaded; the War Museum, for a fascinating couple of hours; Albert Hall and the Science Museum, where the Wright Brothers, Alcock and Brown, Bleriot, and many other aviators were honored.

On Thursday we reshot the scratched scenes, and after a long, grinding day's work, Milestone decided to break for dinner and film into the night. This was not a simple matter. When we worked late, our assistant director, Boothby, had to hire a bus to take the Londoners of our crew to their homes. He called the vehicle he hired a char-a-banc. I asked him why the vehicles that picked up passengers in London were called buses, while our vehicle was called a char-a-banc. Boothby said he didn't know; perhaps the distinction was made because the char-a-banc was hired for specific occasions. That was certainly not a reason; it was a custom, and adherence to custom was strong in Britain.

After our dinner break, we worked until 11:30. We finished the long day's work on a decidedly sour note. Milestone set up one of his intricate, difficult dolly shots, motivated, I was sure, by his vindictive response to George Seid's pressure. The scene would have been difficult even for a top-notch Hollywood crew. Our people tried hard but blew take after take. Our red-mustached focus puller missed some shots, as did camera operator Borradaile and the grips (chippies) who moved the dolly. Lindop, my boom operator, missed a shot; Milestone was downright insulting to him. In defending Lindop I came close to having what the British call a dust-up with Milestone.

Saturday, September 2, and it seemed that the finish of *The Lady Is Willing* was in sight. George Seid announced that we would wrap up the next day, Sunday, and that I was to sail from Southampton aboard the liner *Majestic* on Thursday, September 7. When I told him of my Genoa–New York plan, his response was an emphatic, outraged no! I pleaded; I might never again have a chance to visit Europe. I promised that my trans-European jaunt would cost Columbia not a single penny, but Seid said roughly, "You be on the *Majestic* Thursday or you go off salary." I knew he couldn't maroon me in England without pay or travel money, but he was close to Harry Cohn and could probably have me fired if I defied him; and so, with a wife, two children, and a mortgage to provide for, I had to give up my lovely plan to sail on the *Conte de Savoia*.

Sunday, September 3, was our last day of production. I presented my thank-you gift to the B & D sound department: an elegant new dartboard for the amplifier room. Binnie Barnes and Leslie Howard were late returning from lunch, which added to George Seid's anger. Again we broke for dinner. Joe and I were invited by Osmond Borradaile to have dinner with him and his wife at his home in Hendon, where we were joined by Alexander Korda's cameraman, Georges Perinal, and his son, Jean. We returned to the studio and shot until long after midnight, but now the mood was festive. From my diary: "Last few scenes shot amid great enthusiasm." I suppose that meant that everyone was heartily glad to be finished. "Fond goodbyes, lots of goodwill to Joe and me." We finished filming at three o'clock Monday morning. Joe and I chose to walk home to Radnor. We were tired, but we were in a mood almost of exaltation, a sense of relief from tension as we walked through the quiet countryside in brilliant moonlight.

I awoke early Monday morning, after about four hours' sleep. It was going to be a busy day. I packed and said my goodbyes to Donnie and my friends at Radnor. A man named Cash, an employee of Northern Transport, arrived and drove me to the studio. Joe was already there, preparing his camera gear to be shipped home. Joe and I and our luggage squeezed into Mr. Cash's noisy, underpowered little twelve-horsepower Austin and were driven to London. We went first to Columbia's offices on Wardour Street, to say goodbye to Joseph Friedman and his people, and to settle our accounts with Mr. Wormser, a pleasant, good-looking young man, an American, who was comptroller of Columbia's London office. I drew a twenty-five pound advance to pay for my going-home expenses; Joe took more; he intended to stay in England for two more weeks.

Mr. Cash and his Austin took me to the Northern Transport offices. Harrington shared my disappointment that Seid had scuttled my Genoa–New York plan. He approved my alternate plan, to spend my remaining time in Paris. He made reservations for a flight to Paris and for lodging at a Paris hotel, the Elysées, which he described as "small, but quite nice."

I walked the short distance to the French consulate to get my visa. My reception there was not particularly cordial. Then, by taxi to Victoria Station, where those of us who were air travelers boarded a bus and were taken to Croydon Airport.

Our airline was Imperial Airways; our plane was a Handley-Page model 42, a large plane for that time, seating thirty-eight passengers. It resembled Britain's World War I bombers, for a good reason. Handley-Page had built England's bombers during the great war, and the HP42 seemed to be based on a Handley-Page bomber design. It was neither a monoplane nor a biplane; it was called a sesquiplane, with a large upper wing and short, stubby lower wing. It was powered by four 550-horsepower Bristol Jupiter engines, two affixed to the upper wing and two to the lower. The interior of the plane was ornate; the walls and seats and ceiling were colorfully decorated, as though the designers wanted the plane to be an aerial version of a crack train such as the *Orient Express*.

From my diary: "The takeoff. Short takeoff and rapid climb. Terrific feeling of power. Croydon from the air—circular dwellings with grounds enclosed, playing fields, English countryside by sunset. Twenty minutes to the Channel, forty-five minutes over Channel." Looking down over the Channel, I saw tiny dark objects—small steamers, trawlers, fishing boats—all trailing long white wakes. That was what Luftwaffe pilots saw, seven years later, when they swooped down to bomb and strafe Britain's indomitable little ships.

Diary: "Cross French Coast at dusk. At 95 mph cruising speed, an hour and a half to Paris. Full moon, lights of Paris, magnificent sight. Pilot gives us an aerial tour, circles the Eiffel Tower; a rare event, says the man in the seat next to me; the weather in Paris is seldom clear enough for such sightseeing."

I cleared customs, boarded a bus to Paris and a taxi to Hotel Elysées, on Rue La Boetie, Champs Elysées. It was, as Harrington described it, "small, but nice." It looked to be quite old. It may have been fairly new when the Prussian Army captured Paris in 1870. I went to my room, but only to leave my baggage. I didn't intend to waste time in Paris with unnecessary activities such as resting and sleeping; there would be time for that on my voyage home.

Near the hotel I found a small family restaurant. Confronted by a menu handwritten in French, I asked my waiter for a translation into English. There was a problem—he spoke no English. I pointed to something in the menu that I thought was beef. It was not beef, but a white, sticky stew that I found inedible. I made do with salad and bread.

I boarded a taxi and went to the Folies Bergère, arriving just in time for the first curtain. I expected to be shocked, as did hundreds of foreigners who attended. A young usherette guided me to my seat. A young woman of Paris—traditionally, she should have been sexy and beautiful, but she was not. I was reminded of a line spoken by an eccentric character in a Columbia Western: "When they was passin' out good looks, Ellie May was out milkin' the cow." Where was the usherette at that critical time? Certainly not milking a cow in Paris. I took my seat, but the usherette pursued me and scolded me in French. I had not given her a tip, and she demanded one, loudly. I gave her a fistful of centimes; she snatched them and departed without a single *merci*.

The show was a musical comedy, French-style, with nudity, but the nudes posed, motionless, like statues, with clouds of gauze, and they seemed no more erotic than statues would have been.

A vaudeville-type act featured a beautiful, statuesque woman who sang songs and told jokes in English, French, German, and Italian, switching languages repeatedly, without missing a syllable. Her various English accents were remarkably well done, and her version of the American cowboy accent was perfect. She could safely have been cast as a Wild West saloon girl in a Buck Jones Western.

The comedy skits were in French. Most of them featured wildly effeminate characters; apparently gay was the stuff of comedy at the Folies.

After the show, I faced a long wait to get a cab. I chose to walk, through some of the ancient, historic streets of Paris, some of them in neighborhoods that seemed downright sinister, but I was probably safer than I would have been in New York, Chicago, or Los Angeles.

The next morning, I had two choices for breakfast at my hotel: "petit dejeuner simple" or "dejeuner complet." I chose the *complet*, for five francs, and *oeufs*, scrambled, for an additional six francs.

I set out to explore Paris. Diary: "Champs Elysées to Invalides bridge; along the Seine to Alexander III bridge, then Petite Palace, Clemenceau statue outside—through Tuilleries to Place du Concorde, Obelisk, Cleopatra's Needle, interesting vistas in all directions. Public piddling places." These were the famous public urinals of Paris. "To Louvre Museé, famed paintings. Cross river by Austerlitz bridge—Voltaire statue on left bank, book stalls along river. Then Métro to Bastille monument. Climb dark stair—queasy high-place sensations on top. Tram to Eiffel Tower. Down from Eiffel, take taxi to Versailles—30 FR! Impressive. Beautiful. Much walking, tired, home by train." I suppose I was stockpiling place names and street names for use if and when I wrote my novel or my screenplay with a Paris locale.

My adventures of the day were not finished. Late in the afternoon I found a pleasant street where Parisians sat at sidewalk cafés, sipped their wine, and watched the world go by. I felt that I should share that experience, so I sat at a table in the late afternoon sunshine. I had never tasted an alcoholic beverage, but when a waiter appeared with a menu, I had to order something. I chose an item—*sauterne*—because I could pronounce it. The waiter brought a small bottle, uncorked it with a flourish, and poured an amber liquid into my glass. It looked like ginger ale, and when I tasted it, it seemed to have no more bite than ginger ale. I sipped, slowly, feeling quite cosmopolitan and worldly. Then, alarmingly, I felt a strange sensation. My head seemed to be floating; the sunlight seemed too bright, and the wine glass and the bottle on my table were slightly out of focus. I tried to rise and knocked over the wine bottle. The contents dribbled on the table and to the sidewalk; the waiter, with a reproachful look, mopped up the spillage. I was horrified; I had sipped so much of the harmless-tasting *sauterne* that I might fall down if I tried to stand up again. I sat for a long time, thinking of dire possibilities—being arrested, perhaps even being in jail when the *Majestic* sailed—without me. Finally, when it was growing dark, I tried carefully to get to my feet. No one seemed to be staring at me, which was reassuring. I took a few tentative steps and slowly began to walk. I walked to my hotel, went to my room, lay on my bed, fully clothed, and fell fast asleep. I awoke briefly at daybreak, undressed, and went back to sleep.

I was awakened at about ten o'clock by band music. From the window of my room I could see marching soldiers and a military band. Something was afoot. I dressed hurriedly, had my *déjeuner* of *pain*, *oeufs*, and *café* and went out on Rue La Boetie to follow the music. I found that from every direction military units were converging on the Invalides, the tomb of Napoleon Bonaparte, where state ceremonies took place. This ceremony, I learned, was the state funeral of a cabinet member, the minister of marine, Georges Leygues.

When the military units converged, they formed an impressive parade. There were cavalrymen in the parade uniforms of the Napoleonic era: brass breastplates, bright-colored uniforms, and plumed helmets. There were infantrymen in their horizon-blue uniforms and a contingent of machine-gunners, their weapons mounted on small carts drawn by dogs. I saw temporary grandstands, apparently for officials and foreign diplomats, at Esplanade Invalides. There were seats available, and I wanted a good view of the spectacle. I used the time-honored tactic: act as though you belong. I approached a gendarme and nodded pleasantly to him. He saluted, a trifle uncertainly. I sat among exotic groups of people: Arabs in native dress, Indians wearing turbans, a man wearing a tasseled fez. The ceremonies were long, and the parade of French military might seemed endless. There were no tanks in the parade, and no planes flew overhead. A few hundred miles to the north the Germans were building tanks and creating a powerful air force.

The next day, Thursday, was getaway day; my voyage home was scheduled from Cherbourg that evening, on *R.M.S. Majestic*. I packed and paid my hotel bill. My tab: 133 francs. The manager managed a smile and wished me a good journey, a welcome departure from the hostile looks some Parisians gave me when they recognized me as an American. Diary: "By taxi to Gare St. Lazare. I'm an hour early. Buy ticket and wander around station, impatient to get going. Departure, noon. Towns as we approach Cherbourg: Evereaux, Conches, Caen, Volognes." Many of those Normandy towns were scenes of fierce fighting in the days that followed D-Day eleven years later. The train took us directly to the immense new Gare Maritime. We were ferried out to the *Majestic* in a small steamer with the unglamorous name *Traffic*. The *Majestic* was truly majestic as we approached her, anchored far out in Cherbourg harbor.

Dinner was ready for those of us who embarked at Cherbourg. I dined alone in a corner of the *Majestic's* impressive dining room.

In my stateroom I found a booklet with a list of first-class passengers and facts about the ship. The *Majestic*, the booklet informed me, was the largest steamer in the world—56,621 tons; length, 956 feet; breadth, 100 feet. I found my name on the passenger list. I was decidedly in the company of the distinguished, the rich, and the famous. Mr. D. Sarnoff was a passenger, as were Count Aurilie Baldeschi- Balleani, Captain Murza Agha of the Indian army, and several members of the aristocratic Biddle family. There were the ladies: Mrs. William Polk, Mrs. J. Taylor. and Mrs. Drexel, each accompanied by a maid, and a Miss Dianne Warner, accompanied by a governess. Mr. H. Yale Dolan traveled with a manservant, but he was one-upped by Mr. D. Milburn and Mr. Charles Steele, each of whom had two manservants. The booklet omitted one interesting fact. The *Majestic* was built not in England but in Germany. A bronze plaque in the grand salon bore the name of Blohm and Voss, shipbuilders, of Hamburg. They built the *Majestic* and turned it over to the British as war reparations payment.

I had a great deal of sleep to catch up on and awakened just in time for lunch. An officer, impressive with zigzag gold stripes on his sleeves, approached me as I ate at my inconspicuous table. He was the chief steward, and he had a favor to ask. He was hesitant and seemed somewhat embarrassed, but he finally told me that he wanted me to move to the chief engineer's table. I was surprised and intrigued. I knew that in ocean-liner protocol ship's officers' tables were reserved for VIPs. The captain's table was first in prestige, of course; the chief engineer's table was ranked third. I was no VIP, I told Mr. Hoey, the chief steward; perhaps there was some mistake. There was no mistake, Mr. Hoey assured me; he would appreciate it if I consented to the move. I agreed, but I wanted to know why I was given the honor. An embarrassing situation existed at the chief engineer's table, Mr. Hoey said. A gentleman at that table spoke a great deal, rather loudly. A British lady—an important British lady, the chief steward emphasized, took offense at the man's nonstop verbiage and demanded that she be removed from the table. I was the only single person available, Mr. Hoey said, and he — and presumably the management of the White Star Line — would be deeply grateful if I consented to fill the embarrassing vacancy. Of course I consented. I was not a VIP or even an IP, but I would have the opportunity to discover whether, as F. Scott Fitzgerald wrote, "The rich are not like you and me."

At dinner I was introduced to my new tablemates: Dr. Alexander Gilligan, of New York, an eminent retired surgeon; another New Yorker, a Miss Wertheimer, handsome and fortyish; a pretty young woman, Mrs. Virginia Edofy; and the nonstop talker, Mr. Carlyle Thorpe. Chief Engineer Evans sat at the head of the table. He was a short, stocky man who spoke with a Welsh accent so pronounced that at times he was completely unintelligible.

I was chagrined to learn that Thorpe was not only a fellow American, he was a fellow Californian, president of the California Walnut Growers Association. He was not rude or profane; he merely talked too much — and too loudly — about himself, his possessions, and his business.

I found Dr. Gilligan to be an interesting person. He had been a leading surgeon in New York for many years and told tales about the practice of medicine in New York City before the turn of the century. On one occasion, all of us at the table — except Thorpe — were interested. When Thorpe began his nightly discourse, the no-nonsense Miss Wertheimer said tartly, "If you please, Mr. Thorpe; we want to hear what Dr. Gilligan has to say." Thorpe didn't seem to be offended — his reaction was of surprise that his words of wisdom were not appreciated, and he subsided — for a time.

Even in as enlightened a time as 1933 it was not customary for women to dine alone, drink alone, or, it seems, walk the deck of a steamer alone after dinner. Miss Wertheimer, plain-spoken and direct, drafted me to walk the deck with her after dinner; sometimes Virginia Edofy joined us. We walked the sun deck, open to the sky in fair weather, and the enclosed promenade deck in rough weather, when waves smashed over the bow of the *Majestic*.

Diary, September 12: "Nantucket Light Ship Tuesday evening. Fire Island Light Ship and Ambrose Light early next morning. About noon, ten tugs push and pull and shove us to a perfect docking. Ashore and deal with snotty customs people." That's what my diary called them; it was a less than elegant description, a throw-back to the language of my growing-up days in Chicago. Today I might write that the customs men were rude or insolent, but "snotty" is what they were, and in that context the word had a fine ring to it.

I boarded a taxi and gave the driver the address of the Colum-bia offices, but this was Thursday, September 13, 1933, the day of a gigantic parade—a show of public support for the New Deal's NRA, the National Recovery Act. A half-million people thronged the parade route; more than fifty thousand people marched in it. There was no way for my taxi to cross Fifth Avenue. I left the cab, stranded somewhere near Madison Square Garden, and phoned the Columbia office. The switchboard operator told me she was alone; everyone had gone to watch the parade. The woman was wonder-fully competent. She understood who I was and what my problem was; she said she would arrange for my railroad ticket—it would be waiting for me at the Grand Central ticket office.

I had much of the day left before train time. I ate lunch at a small restaurant; the proprietor allowed me to leave my baggage under the counter. The parade and the spectators still filled the streets. Di-ary: "Walk back via Fifth Avenue. Big jam of people at Library and at 43rd and Fifth Avenue. Cops clubbing spectators to drive them back. Leave parade. Walk down to East River—small ship-fitting shop, humble little red brick buildings, dingy, boarded-up warehouses. A small square brick dwelling with window-boxes. 'I love you' with initials, chalked on a wall; 'East River Boys' painted on another wall." Graffiti, even then. More diary: "Cob-blestone paving, with grass sprouting between. Across river, huge grim chimneys and cranes. Contrast: poor kids, slums, play along East River—high above them, next to them, Woodstock Tower, rich people, and Tudor House." I know what I had in mind: a story about the slum kids who swam in the East River in the shadow of the luxurious apartment towers. If Sidney Kingsley somehow read my mind, I could sue him. *Dead End* is what I had in mind—and did nothing about, but Sidney Kingsley did.

I retrieved my luggage, braved the danger of being trampled by mounted policemen or being clubbed by policemen afoot, and dashed across the line of march. A taxi took me by a roundabout route to Grand Central Station. My ticket was ready. I was nearly two hours early for train time, and I wandered about Grand Central Station, just as I had at Gare St. Lazare. My train may have been the *20th Century Limited*; my diary fails to inform me. The trip was uneventful and I arrived in Chicago in midafternoon. I went home, to 1111 Cornelia Avenue, the old familiar way: a long, noisy ride by streetcar. I slept again in the tiny bedroom my brother and I had shared. My parents seemed unchanged; my father, as always, was patient, hard-working, and uncomplaining. He'd had a hard childhood; orphaned at the age of eight, he was sent by his sisters, young ladies in their late teens, to a German-language private school for boys. The headmaster was a sadistic tyrant who screamed at the boys in German and whipped them for the slightest infractions. In a halting way, through the years, my father told me bits and pieces of his story. I wish I had listened more. To this day, my heart goes out to that lonely little orphan boy, abandoned by his sisters more than a hundred years ago.

My mother had an equally hard life. Her peasant family emigrated from Germany in the 1880s, when she was six years old. Hundreds of emigrants were packed into the steerage of their slow, unseaworthy ship. Her baby brother died and was buried at sea. At the age of fourteen, my mother went to work in a Chicago sweatshop. She had very little formal education, but she spoke well, wrote well, and had an immense store of common sense—and she possessed a formidable sense of right and wrong.

After three nostalgic days in Chicago, I learned that the strike was over and that Columbia was taking back its strikers. I boarded the Santa Fe *Chief* for the last leg of my trip home. It was not as pleasant as other trips had been. I was concerned about our poststrike future. The strike had been broken by an American Federation of Labor union, the International Brotherhood of Electrical Workers, which was controlled by a Chicago mobster, "Umbrella" Mike Boyle. Boyle sold his strike-breaking services to the Hollywood producers and as an added reward was given the right to force us to join his union. It was a modern version of ancient custom, when the vanquished were paraded in chains and enslaved by their conquerors. The future suddenly seemed not quite bright.

My homecoming to 8749 Clifton Way, however, was a happy one. Elsa was nine months old when I left and, as babies will, progressed greatly in the two months I was away. Eddie Junior was somewhat doubtful about me. Perhaps he thought that after a two-month absence I required some reorientation. When I went to the bathroom, he warned me, "Pick up the seat, stand close, and be careful."

The next day I went to the studio. There was some bitterness about the strike, but all of the back-lot people were back to work. Harry Cohn was a hard man, but he had excellent back-lot personnel; he knew it, was proud of his back lot, and there was no punitive action taken against any of the strikers. That wasn't the case at M-G-M, where the cold, autocratic regime punished the strikers. Some of them, including my brother, didn't get their jobs back for a year or more.

I never saw the finished version of *The Lady Is Willing*. A Columbia producer who did see it told me, "It's the worst picture I ever saw. Maybe it's the worst picture ever made." Of course he exaggerated. At the time, I believed that it was never released, but I learned later that it had a limited release in New York, and that film critic Bosley Crowther gave it favorable comment. Its life, however, was a short and unhappy one; it sank without a trace after a brief New York run. About all that Columbia salvaged from the wreckage was the title, which it used again in 1942. The second *The Lady Is Willing* was a romantic vehicle for Marlene Dietrich and Fred MacMurray.

From time to time, as I waited for my first poststrike assignment, I encountered Harry Cohn in the corridors of Columbia. His greeting to me was usually brusque and hurried. It seemed that he was more brusque and more hurried than he might otherwise have been, as though he was determined to avoid even a passing word about our British adventure.

A week after my return I was assigned to a B film, *Fog*, directed by my least favorite director, Albert Rogell. *Fog* was a murder-mystery story, the action taking place aboard an ocean liner. In the film, a clairvoyant foretells two murders, and then a third, her own. It was written by Ethel Hill and young Dore Schary, who had been recruited by Walter Wanger to come to Hollywood and work for Columbia. After a short tenure at Columbia, Schary went on to an illustrious career: an Academy Award for the screenplay of *Boys Town* and head of production at RKO in 1943 and M-G-M in 1950. *Fog*, however, was not a good script. It should have created suspense and menace, but because of clumsy plotting it did not, and Albert Rogell's sometimes hysterical method of directing did little to help. Young Dore Schary probably got some mediocre writing out of his system during his stay at Columbia.

We finished *Fog* on schedule, fifteen days of filming, some of them ten- and twelve-hour days, generally caused by Rogell's tendency to shout at actors, causing them to blow their lines. What Rogell needed was a crash course in the Capra method: give actors confidence in themselves, and avoid putting pressure on them.

I enjoyed being home again. I was generally too late to have dinner with the children, but Sunday breakfast was an all-family occasion. There were homemade waffles for all, even for baby Elsa, and with my waffle ham or bacon and a three-egg omelette — a delicious, cholesterol-rich breakfast. Had anyone heard of polyunsaturated fats in 1933?

Fog wrapped on October 12, and with only a weekend intervening, we began *Shadows of Sing Sing*, directed by Phil Rosen. Rosen had directed several silent films for Columbia in 1928, then returned in 1930 to direct *El Codiga Penal*, a Spanish-language version of Howard Hawks's *The Criminal Code*. I was the soundman on the Spanish version. It was an odd kind of production. Hawks filmed by day and we — a complete new crew: camera, sound, props, grips, and electricians — shot by night. Rosen's directive was to re-create, as exactly as possible, Hawks's setups and staging. To achieve that, a second script clerk was assigned to the daytime production. Her job was to note in detail every setup, every dolly shot, and to diagram Hawks's staging. With that information, Phil Rosen, working with a Spanish-speaking director, re-created Hawks's work in Spanish. It seemed to me that the Spanish director got good performances from his actors. In *The Criminal Code*, Boris Karloff gave a chilling performance as the killer, Galloway. The Spanish actor selected for the Karloff part was excellent; he generated the same cold-blooded performance that Karloff did. He even sounded like him — in Spanish.

Now I was working with Phil Rosen again. He was even-tempered and efficient in staging and shooting scenes, but he seemed to have no feel for pace. *Shadows of Sing Sing* was poorly written, implausible, and overly melodramatic, but the lackluster pace Rosen gave it robbed it of any chance of being a successful B picture. In reviewing it, "Chic" wrote in *Variety*, "Story is slow in getting under way and a trial scene is equally slow, killing any chance the picture might have." We—sound—were mentioned, with faint praise: "Settings are good, sound fairly so, and dialogue not so good."

While we were shooting *Shadows of Sing Sing*, there were back-lot rumors about Frank Capra's next picture. It was said to be about a bus trip; the title was *Night Bus*. Later, we learned that Clark Gable would star in it and that Carole Lombard would probably be the leading lady. *Night Bus* became *It Happened One Night*. It was scheduled to begin production in mid-November, and I was assigned to it as soon as the start date was announced.

15

The veteran back-lot people at Columbia anticipated production of *It Happened One Night* with complete confidence in Capra. Their loyalty had a solid foundation; he was one of them—he made silent quickies in the Poverty Row days, and his hit films in the early days of sound moved Columbia upward from the lean times of Poverty Row. I was not a veteran of those times, but my confidence was just as solid; it was based on my perception that Capra was a very good director and that he was teamed up once more with Bob Riskin. I felt that we would, without a doubt, make an excellent movie.

I was given my script about three weeks before the start date of *It Happened One Night*. I was troubled by the opening sequence. The film opens with a scene in which Ellie Andrews (Claudette Colbert) quarrels with her father, who has imprisoned her on his yacht, anchored in Miami Harbor. After a bitter argument about her marriage to a man her father called a gigolo, she dives overboard and makes her escape. The scenes were well written, but the sequence was twelve pages long, which meant about eight or nine minutes of film time, too long, I thought. I knew that Clark Gable had been cast as the leading man, Peter Warne, and I was impatient to meet him—in the script and on film.

When the casting of Gable was announced, the reaction of Columbia people was favorable. He was under contract to M-G-M, and in 1931 appeared in eight films. He was cast as a tough gangster in *The Secret Six* and as an equally tough gambler in *Sporting*

217

Blood, in which he charmed women by treating them roughly. In *Night Nurse*, with Barbara Stanwyck, he had one of his most successful roles, again as a rough, hard-bitten character. In 1932 Gable appeared in an astonishing nine releases, including the classic *Red Dust*, with Jean Harlow and Mary Astor. His performance in *Red Dust* established him as a virile, man-of-action leading man. M-G-M owed Columbia a leading man—a star—in exchange for Capra's services when he went to M-G-M on loan; and his project, *Soviet*, was canceled by Mayer. Mayer offered Clark Gable to Cohn, who resisted accepting him "because he was not the first-class actor Mayer promised." Cohn wanted Robert Montgomery, believing that he had the finesse that the role of Peter Warne required; but Montgomery refused the part, and disaster was narrowly averted. Montgomery's Peter Warne would have been about half the size of Gable's. Mayer then insisted that Cohn accept Clark Gable. He had an ulterior motive. After seventeen films in two years, including *Red Dust*, Gable concluded that he was underpaid and asked for more money. To punish him for such insolence, Mayer sold him down the river, so to speak, to Poverty Row—to Columbia. Capra was willing to accept Gable; pressured by Mayer, Cohn grudgingly agreed.

The other half of the casting equation remained; the choice of a leading lady. In his autobiography, Capra tells of offering *It Happened One Night* to Myrna Loy, Margaret Sullavan, Miriam Hopkins, and Constance Bennett. All rejected the role. Many of us at the studio hoped that Carole Lombard would be cast as Ellie Andrews. She was given a script but decided, regretfully, that she was committed to make *Bolero* with George Raft at Paramount. Finally, Claudette Colbert was cast. "I hear she likes money," Cohn told Capra, and when he offered to double her salary, to $50,000, she condescended to accept the role of Ellie Andrews.

We began production of *It Happened One Night* the night of November 13, 1933, in downtown Los Angeles, at the old Greyhound bus depot. Our first scenes were of Colbert, who, aware that her father's private detectives are looking for her, outwits them by having a little old lady buy her a bus ticket to New York. The camera then follows a man who wants to use a telephone, but the phone booth is surrounded by a group of men who apparently have been doing some drinking. One of the men chases the phone seeker away. "Beat it," he says. "History is being made in there. Man bites dog." Capra then cut to a close-up of Gable, on the phone, telling off his editor, in New York, who has fired him. "Listen, monkey-face, when you fired me, you fired the best reporter your scandal-sheet ever had." The scene was not in my script. It took care of a concern I had: I didn't want to wait too long to see Clark Gable, and I felt that an audience would feel the same way. That scene solved another problem: it told us finally what Peter Warne did for a living. In Samuel Hopkins Adams's short story, *Night Bus*, Warne is a chemist, frequently out of work. In their first draft, Capra and Bob Riskin made him an artist, a Greenwich Village character—"a flowing tie, effete kind of guy," Capra described him in his autobiography. In the script I was given, his occupation was changed again; he was described as an inventor. "I fool around with gadgets," he says. "I make up things."

That made three attempts to give Peter Warne an occupation; all were unsatisfactory. Capra credits his friend, producer-writer Myles Connolly, with suggesting that Gable be made a newspa-perman. He quotes Connolly: "Your leading man—forget the chemist or that long-haired Greenwich Village painter. I don't know any vagabond painters, and I doubt if you do. Make him a guy we all know and like. Maybe a tough, crusading reporter, at odds with his pig-headed editor—and when he meets the spoiled heiress—well, it's *The Taming of the Shrew*, but the shrew must be worth taming and the guy who tames her must be one of us."

That was play doctoring at its best. Capra and Riskin did a fast rewrite, which was why my script often differed widely from the scenes we filmed. That was evident when we shot the opening scenes of the picture: Ellie's quarrel with her father and her escape from his yacht. Instead of a twelve page, nine minute sequence, we had a brisk, actionful three minutes; all story points were made, clear and forcefully; the characters of Ellie and her father (Walter Connolly) were firmly established. The sequence ended with Con-nolly's sailors informing him that Ellie had made good her escape. Connolly then ordered a massive effort, by private detectives, to prevent Ellie from getting back to New York. The chase was on; the story was off to a rousing start.

I wondered about the twelve-page version. It seemed to me that Capra and Riskin were too astute as filmmakers to tolerate so long a scene at the beginning of their picture. It may be that the scene was written long in an attempt to make the role attractive to potential leading ladies. Actors—and actresses—have been known to count lines of dialogue to assure themselves that the role offered them is worthy of their talents.

At the bus depot, that first night of filming, Peter Warne is escorted to the bus in royal fashion by his tipsy comrades, who strew rose petals (torn-up newspapers) in his path. Aboard the bus, he discovers that the only available seat is filled by bundles of newspapers. When the bus driver (Ward Bond) ignores his protests, Warne tosses the bundles of newspapers out of the window. The bus driver reacts belligerently. It is a small scene, but it is a beautifully written small scene, important because the audience perceives Peter Warne to be a free spirit, a man of humor and courage. The bus driver says, pugnaciously, "Fresh guy, huh! What you need is a good sock on the nose." Warne: "You may not like my nose, but I do. It's the only one I've got. I always keep it out in the open where anybody can take a sock at it." Failing to intimidate Warne, the driver retires, grumbling. Ellie Andrews, meanwhile, has slipped past the arguing men, and when Warne, victorious, turns to claims his prize, he finds Ellie Andrews firmly seated in it.

Peter, to Ellie: "Excuse me, lady, but that upon which you sit is mine." Ellie is outraged. For a moment she thinks he is referring to her anatomy. Warne continues. "I just put up a stiff battle for that seat. So if it's just the same to you—scram." And so the battle is joined; the love story—and that, inevitably, is what it will be—is off and running, down a twisting, turning, bumpy path.

Capra sets were generally relaxed, pleasant and free of stress. On films such as *Ladies of Leisure* and *Forbidden*, we, the crew, were somewhat subdued, but *It Happened One Night* had a rollicking pace that carried the crew along with it. In his book, Capra writes that in his first meeting with Gable, the actor was belligerent, scornful of Columbia and the *Night Bus* project. That hostile attitude was gone when we shot those first scenes in the bus depot. Perhaps Capra had charmed Gable in preproduction meetings, or it may have been the script that changed his attitude.

Gable's relations with the crew were good. By the end of the bus station sequence he was on a first-name basis with many of the crew. I had heard about the stress of working at M-G-M. A film editor who decided to cut loose from M-G-M and work in the independent field told me he felt as though he was getting out of jail. Gable gave every indication of enjoying himself; he was discovering that making a film could be fun. Claudette Colbert, on the other hand, never lost her cool, disapproving attitude toward Columbia. Joe Walker, in an interview, described her as "standoffish," and my mike man, Buster Libott, called her "snooty." She was, however, thoroughly professional, always on time, always prepared, taking Capra's direction well and adding those creative little bits of acting that every director appreciates. It's hard to believe that she thought that *It Happened One Night* would be a mediocre picture. It may be that having taken an aloof, deprecating attitude she was, as the saying goes, stuck with it. Or perhaps she was cool and standoffish even at her own studio, aristocratic Paramount.

In the script, and in filming, Gable was permitted to be Gable; to speak roughly and behave roughly to Ellie Andrews. On two occasions, he ordered her to shut up; and he repeatedly called her a spoiled brat. That was on film; off-screen he was no gentler. One notable occasion: Gable and Colbert were sitting in the back of the disreputable old jalopy driven by Danker (Alan Hale), who screeched to a stop to pick them up when Colbert made the historic display of her shapely leg. Scenes in the moving vehicle were shot in the studio with the new back-screen process, mercifully faster and less complicated than the old Dunning process. Gable and Colbert could have called for stand-ins to take their places while the process screen was being lined up, but they were comfortable in the back seat of the jalopy. My microphone was near them; I listened in. Colbert said she had heard gossip about Gable's romantic involvement with Carole Lombard and needled him about it. Gable, not a kiss-and-tell man, was silent. I thought I heard a note of jealousy in her needling. After all, Gable was Gable. Their talk turned to Columbia, Capra, and the picture they were making. Colbert made a disparaging remark about the film. Gable made no effort to be gentlemanly. "Are you nuts?" he demanded. "We're making a good movie, a damn good movie. I tell you this little wop's got something!" Colbert didn't talk back, or scold, or walk away—she remained where she was, chastened, in the back seat of the old jalopy. After all, Gable was Gable. The use of an ethnic designation could be insulting—or affectionate. When Gable referred to Capra as a "wop," it was spoken in a spirit of respect and affection.

The definitive scene in *It Happened One Night*, one that audiences remember, is the "Walls of Jericho" sequence. After a day and night of adventurous bus travel, Peter and Ellie's bus encounters a deluge of rain. A bridge is washed out; they are halted at a roadblock. "You won't be able to get through until morning," a policeman tells the passengers. "If any of you people want a place to sleep, there's an auto camp up yonder." Peter calls to Ellie, "Hey, Brat! Come on—we're stopping here for the night."

Ellie is suspicious and resentful, but to escape from the downpour, she follows Peter to the auto camp cabin. There, with a clothesline and a blanket, Peter fashions the Walls of Jericho, which, as related in the Bible, did not fall until Gabriel blew his trumpet. Peter and Ellie go to bed, separated by the blanket between them. From the script, scene 138:

> *Close shot Ellie's side of the room.*
> *She crawls quickly into bed, pulls the covers over her and glances*
> *apprehensively in Peter's direction.*
> *Close shot Peter:*
> *Conscious of her proximity. The situation is delicate and danger-*
> *ous. We get a feeling that the room is atingle with sex. He turns his*
> *gaze toward the blanket. Camera pans to the blanket. It is a frail*
> *barrier.*

The Walls of Jericho scenes were brilliantly written; we filmed them almost verbatim, but the scenes we shot of the events of the next morning varied widely from the scenes in my script. In the script, there was a long, not very interesting discussion about Ellie's abortive marriage to King Westley, the man Ellie's father called a gigolo and whom Peter detests heartily. Instead, we filmed the whimsical doughnut-dunking scene, in which Peter teaches Ellie the proper way to dunk a doughnut. Colbert was doubtful about the scene; she told Gable that it seemed silly and had nothing to do with the story. After a few rehearsals, however, she seemed to accept the offbeat, light-hearted nature of the scene.

That light-hearted mood was shattered when Peter and Ellie hear loud voices outside their cabin. A pair of private detectives knock on their door. Peter quickly devises a strategy. He pretends to be a loud-mouthed blue-collar character. Ellie realizes what he's doing; she nods her understanding. Peter gestures to her to invite the men in and retires behind the blanket. The detectives and Mr. Dykes, the auto camp proprietor, enter. Ellie, to Peter, very sweetly, in a hillbilly accent: "There's some men here to see you,

Sweetheart." Peter emerges from behind the curtain, and when the detectives try to question Ellie, he explodes with a convincing display of good ol' boy anger. Peter: "Hey, wait a minute! You're talkin' to my wife! You can't come bustin' in here like this! I got a good mind to sock you right in the nose!" Ellie gets into the spirit of things. "Don't get excited, Honey," she says. Peter turns his wrath on her, and Ellie begins to cry. Peter: "Aw, shut up! You're just like your old man. Once a plumber, always a plumber. There ain't an ounce of brains in your whole family!" Ellie cries louder. Mr. Dykes protests to the detectives: "Now look what you've done! I told you they were a nice married couple."

Dykes and the discomfited detectives beat a hasty retreat. Ellie and Peter congratulate one another on a pair of superb performances. At that point the script calls for Mr. Dykes to reenter and announce that their bus leaves in five minutes, but Buddy Coleman had committed the assistant director's cardinal sin. He dismissed Dykes, an actor named Oliver Eckhardt, who had one more scene to do. Buddy was mortified and contrite, but Capra was unruffled. "Anybody can do it," he said. "Go out there," he nodded in the direction of Gower and Sunset, "and grab somebody."

We were filming on Stage 6, one of the oldest stages in Hollywood. Profits from *Submarine* and *Flight* had built Stages 3 and 4; profits from *Rain or Shine* had financed the purchase of Stage 6. It was the closest of Columbia's stages to Gower and Sunset, to Gower Gulch. Buddy went "out there" and came back with a Gower Gulch regular, Blackjack Ward. Capra instructed him, "You pull the door open. You're in a hurry. You say, 'Your bus leaves in five minutes.' Mr. Gable says, 'What?' You say it again, louder and faster, 'Your bus leaves in five minutes!' All right, let's try it."

Blackjack Ward tried it; his performance was flawless and we shot it. "Yo' bus leaves in fahve minutes," Blackjack announced. Gable, startled, says "What?" and Blackjack Ward, with a finely crafted escalation of urgency repeats, "*Yo bus leaves in fahve minutes!*" Sir Laurence Olivier could not have done it better.

Some time later Blackjack Ward got into trouble. Like many of the Gower Gulch cowboys, he had his own western gear; cowboy boots, cowboy hat, a gun belt with a holster—and a gun. Blackjack quarreled with another Gower Gulch regular and shot him. The wounded man ran across Gower Street, and Blackjack pursued; he cornered him in back of Joe Roe's restaurant on the southwest corner of Gower and Sunset and killed him.

A plea about the tradition of the Old West might have helped Blackjack Ward's defense: stalwart men of the West facing one another in fair fight on the streets of Hollywood instead of the streets of Laredo. Such a defense, however, had a major flaw: the man Blackjack killed carried no gun, and Blackjack Ward was seen on Gower Gulch no more.

Everything about the making of *It Happened One Night* is memorable to me because, like Gable, I was sure that Frank Capra "had something." To the moviegoing public, a few sequences stand out, one of them the rollicking, spontaneous singing by the bus passengers of "The Daring Young Man on the Flying Trapeze." Claudette Colbert seemed to enjoy the boisterous scene. "Look at her," my boom man said. "She likes it. I guess she forgot that she hates Columbia."

In the story, an amorous traveling salesman, Oscar Shapely (Roscoe Karns) is rebuffed in his attempts to start an affair with Ellie. During the "Flying Trapeze" scene, he does not join in because he has a copy of a newspaper that identifies Ellie as the runaway heiress and tells of a ten thousand–dollar reward for her safe return. He is interested in money, not merriment. When, in the dark of night the bus veers off of the washed-out road and into a ditch, Shapely approaches Peter, who is inspecting the damage. He informs Peter that if he doesn't get a share of the reward, he will spoil what he thinks is Peter's plan.

"What's on your mind?" Peter asks Shapely.

Shapely, confidently, "Half of the ten thousand or I crab the works."

"You're a pretty shrewd guy," Peter tells Shapely. "We better get away from this gang, let's talk this thing over, privately."

Away from the bus, in a wooded area, Peter tells Shapely, "Lucky thing I ran into you; you're just the man I need." Suddenly: "Do you pack a gat? A gat! A gat! A gun!" Shapely's cocksure attitude vanishes. Peter then informs him that he, Peter, is a mobster, operating on the orders of "The Killer," and that the mob is holding Ellie not for a paltry ten thousand–dollar reward but for a million-dollar ransom.

Shapely is utterly terrified. "Say, look," he stammers, "I didn't know it was anything like this . . ."

Peter interrupts roughly. "What's the matter, you getting yellow?" He reaches in his pocket for an imaginary gun. "You can't back out now. You know too much. I ought to plug you right now."

Shapely pleads for his life; Peter relents. "All right, scram," he tells Shapely. "And stay away from that bus!"

"Sure, sure, anything you say." Then, fearfully, "You won't shoot me in the back, will you?"

"I will if you don't get going," Peter threatens, reaching for the gun that is not there. Shapely runs, stumbling and falling, into the dark woods.

Peter and Ellie leave the ditched bus and set out afoot. "Why do we have to leave the bus?" Ellie asks. "Because when Shapely stops running, he's going to start thinking—and talking," Peter replies. "Your father's detectives would be waiting for us at the next town."

Peter and Ellie come to a wide, fast-flowing stream, and moviegoers are given another memorable scene. Peter takes off his shoes and socks, slings Ellie over his shoulder, and wades into the shallow creek. The scene was one of light-hearted whimsy, Capra and Riskin at their best, as Peter and Ellie engage in an argument—of all things—about piggybacking.

"This is the first time I've ridden piggyback in years," Ellie says. "This isn't piggybacking," Peter corrects her. He is right, of course. He is not piggybacking; he is carrying Ellie's delectable 115 pounds slung over his shoulder like a sack of grain.

Ellie persists: "I remember distinctly, Father taking me for a piggyback ride."

The argument continues. "Show me a good piggybacker and I'll show you somebody that's human," Peter says. "Take Abraham Lincoln, for instance—a natural piggybacker."

He thinks he has ended the argument, but Ellie is determined to have the last word. "My father was a *great* piggybacker," she says firmly.

From the script:

Peter raises his eyes heavenward in thorough frustration. He has been carrying his suitcase, now he hands it to her, and with his hand now free, delivers a resounding smack on Ellie's backside. She lets out a yelp. Peter retrieves the suitcase and says "Thank you."

The equally memorable haystack scene followed—Joe Walker's favorite, in which Peter and Ellie bed down for the night on hay pulled down from a pair of haystacks. As Joe photographed it, the setting was idyllic, and the audience is aware that Peter and Ellie, inevitably, are falling in love. The sequence is incredibly romantic; if the Walls of Jericho scene was, as the script says, "atingle with sex," the haystack scene was vibrant with it.

The next morning Peter and Ellie create another classic sequence, the hitchhiking episode. Peter boasts about his hitchhiking technique. "I'm going to write a book about it," he tells Ellie. "It's all in the thumb—it always works."

Peter describes the various thumb techniques—the quick, jerky thumb, the smug, self-confident thumb, the pathetic thumb of someone who is broke, hungry, and badly in need of a ride. Peter goes to the edge of the road to use his magic thumb, but cars whiz by; not one of them even slows down. Ellie says, "Do you mind if I try? I'll show you how to stop a car—and I won't use my thumb."

Ellie hears a car approaching, lifts her skirt, and displays a spectacularly shapely leg. No need to show the driver reacting, no need for a scene showing Peter and Ellie climbing into the car. Instead a foot stamps on a brake pedal, a hand pulls an emergency brake lever, and a tire skids to a screeching stop.

A dissolve, and Peter and Ellie are riding in an ancient Model T Ford, driven by a strange character named Danker (Alan Hale). Capra saw possibilities in Danker's oddball character. In my script, Danker sings a few bars of genuine opera. Capra and Hale went to work, improvising, creating a bigger scene—and creating a weird and wonderful character who burst into song whenever he felt the urge.

As we filmed the scene, he asks Peter and Ellie, "Just married, huh? Hitchhiking? If I was young, that's what I'd do." He bursts into song. "Hitchhiking," he booms, "Down the highway of love! Yessir, down that highway, that good ol' highway of l-o-o-o-v-e!"

Peter interrupts him. "Aren't you afraid you'll burn out your tonsils?" he asks. Danker roars with laughter. "Me, burn out my tonsils? No!" He bursts into song again. "My tonsils won't burn, as down life's highway I turn!"

Gable found Alan Hale's performance irresistibly funny. He fought hard to keep from "breaking up" during rehearsals and takes. It was a tough struggle. Capra finally got a printable three-shot: Danker driving—and singing—Ellie and Peter in the back-seat. Anyone who views the film closely will see Gable trying desperately not to laugh. He grimaces, pretends to whisper to Colbert, looks upward, sideward at the scenery, but never at Danker.

Danker drives to a roadside hot dog stand. It was a genuine hot dog stand, in the small community of Sunland, and the signs were genuine as well: "Hot dogs and hamburgers 10c—popcorn 5c." Danker goes into the hot dog stand, but Peter and Ellie, because they have no money, remain outside. They walk a short distance from the car. Then, a startling turn of events—Danker, the good-natured oaf, is a thief. He emerges from the hot dog stand, sees that Peter and Ellie are not in the car, jumps into the jalopy, and drives off with Peter's topcoat and suitcase on the backseat. Peter yells and dashes after the thief. Peter—and the jalopy—disappear in the distance, and Ellie is left alone, frightened and bewildered.

The filming of the next scenes involved a major script change. In my script Ellie waits for several hours at the hot dog stand. The proprietor, suspicious, calls the local sheriff, who questions Ellie and, when her answers are unsatisfactory, arrests her. At that moment Peter reappears, driving Danker's car, and rescues Ellie.

The scene we did not shoot was intended to be a timing scene, to account for the time it took Peter to pursue Danker, catch him, confiscate his car, and return to Ellie. Apparently Capra decided that the car theft scene had a basic improbability, that Peter could not run fast enough to catch Danker's asthmatic old Ford, and that the timing scene added to the improbability, because the longer Peter was gone, the more unlikely it was that he could catch Danker. Instead, after a dissolve, we find Ellie and Peter in the car, headed for New York. In this new version, there is no attempt to explain how Peter overtook Danker. "How did you get that man to give you the car?" Ellie asks. "I gave him a black eye for it," Peter replies. Other than that, there is no explanation; Capra-Riskin presented it as a fait accompli—take it or leave it—and audiences took it.

A long time later I worked with a British-born writer, Jack Henley, who wrote for Alfred Hitchcock early in Hitchcock's career. Jack told me of an improbable escape in a Hitchcock film. He protested that the escape, as Hitchcock wanted it written, was impossible and that audiences would not believe it. Jack said that Hitchcock put his arm around him in a fatherly fashion: "They will believe it, dear boy," Hitchcock said, "because they *want* our chap to escape." Apparently our *It Happened One Night* audience wanted Peter to overtake Danker, give him his black eye, and confiscate his car.

Capra believed in intercutting, as most directors do, to achieve a change of pace and to keep all elements of the story alive. He used a number of scenes of Ellie's father as he grew more and more concerned about Ellie's safety. While Peter and Ellie are driving toward New York, Capra intercut a scene in which Andrews capitulates to the man he calls a gigolo, King Westley. He tells Westley that he will no longer oppose his marriage to Ellie. In that scene we meet, for the first time, the obnoxious fortune hunter. Portrayed by Jameson Thomas, he is a recycling of the odious Prince Carlos, who was decidedly the wrong man for Carole Lombard in *No More Orchids* and is, without the shadow of a doubt, the wrong man for Ellie Andrews. Ellie's father, however, for the sake of ensuring Ellie's safety, comes to terms with King Westley.

"I haven't changed my mind," he tells Westley. "I don't like you! I never have! I never will! That's clear enough, isn't it?"

King Westley is unconcerned. He is the classic male gold-digger, foppishly dressed, with grease-slick hair and a pretentious little mustache. Andrews's tirade doesn't trouble him—he doesn't want Andrews's approval, only his money.

"All right, you win," Andrews tells Westley. "I admit I'm licked. There's a roomful of reporters out there. Tell them that if Ellie comes home, I won't interfere with her marriage." And so there is a new and ominous development, one that will keep Capra's third-act pot boiling.

That night Peter and Ellie pull up to an auto camp. While Peter is arranging for a cabin, Ellie finds a newspaper that flaunts headlines: "Andrews withdraws objections. 'Everything all right. Come home, darling' says Westley." Ellie hides the newspaper from Peter when he returns. He questions why Ellie insists on stopping for the night when they are only a few hours' drive from New York. The audience senses that Ellie is now deeply in love with Peter and can't face the prospect of losing him.

In the cabin Ellie makes overtures. "Am I going to see you in New York?" she asks. "Nope," Peter replies. "I don't make it a policy to run around with married women." Ellie tries again. "Won't I ever see you again?" Peter explodes. "What do you want to see me for? I've served my purpose. I brought you and King Westley together, didn't I?"

Ellie tries again, but Peter rejects her overtures. Later, when Peter is in bed, Ellie goes around the Walls of Jericho and drops to her knees at Peter's bedside. "Take me with you, Peter," she pleads. "I love you. You can't go out of my life now." Peter is deeply moved but simply doesn't know how to respond. "You better go back to your bed," he tells Ellie. Crushed by what she thinks is Peter's rejection, she sadly returns to her bed.

That was a gigantic improbability. Perhaps the people of Capra's audience could be persuaded that Peter, afoot, could catch Danker in his jalopy, but would they believe that Peter Warne, because of an oversized sense of honor, sends beautiful, desirable Ellie back to her bed, untouched?

I asked Capra about it, half-jokingly. "Is an audience going to believe that your leading man tells Ellie, who just said she loves him, 'Get lost, go back to your own bed'?"

"They've got to believe it," Capra said. "If they don't, we're in big trouble." Then, more seriously, he added, "In almost every story there's a scene in which one word, one logical word, will clear up the misunderstanding, the trouble, the problem. If our guy does the natural thing, grabs the girl, says 'I love you, too' and takes her to bed with him, we've got no third act. And we damn well need a third act."

In the cabin, later, Peter attempts to soften his rejection of Ellie. He calls to her, but she has cried herself to sleep. Peter then conceives a quixotic, improbable plan; he will drive to New York while Ellie sleeps, write his story, and sell it to his editor for a thousand dollars "because a guy who's broke can't ask a girl to marry him." The editor gives him the thousand dollars; Peter starts back to the auto camp. The wife of the owner, however, discovers that Peter and his car are gone. "I wouldn't have known about it until morning if I hadn't taken that magnesia," she tells her husband. They go to Ellie's cabin, wake her up, and turn her out into the night.

The damage is done. Ellie thinks Peter deserted her and left to claim the reward; when Peter, returning to the motor camp sees Ellie in the arms of King Westley, he believes that Ellie has used him merely to get back to her foppish fortune-hunter. And so the stage is set; Capra has his suspense and exciting third act.

Back in her luxurious home, Ellie tells her father that she has fallen in love with the man who helped her on her eventful trip. When Ellie mentions his name, Andrews involuntarily reacts; he has a letter from Peter Warne, demanding a financial settlement. Ellie reads the letter. It is damning evidence that Peter is, after all, a greedy, unprincipled adventurer. Heartbreak, despair, disillusion—apparently nothing can heal this wound. Peter, however, confronts Ellie's father and demands that he be paid. Andrews, naturally, thinks Peter wants the ten thousand–dollar reward. When Peter presents him with an itemized bill for $39.60, Andrews is baffled. "Let me get this straight. You want this thirty-nine sixty in addition to the ten thousand dollars for the reward?" "Who said anything about a reward?" Peter replies. "All I want is my thirty-nine sixty."

Andrews realizes that the man Ellie loves is not a greedy mercenary but an honest man, a man after his own heart. He hands Peter a check for $39.60. "Do you mind if I ask a question? Do you love my daughter?" Peter replies angrily, "A guy that'd fall in love with your daughter ought to have his head examined."

Andrews persists. "That's an evasion. Answer my question. Do you love her?" Peter: "A normal human being couldn't live under the same roof with her without going nuts!" Andrews: "I asked you a question! Do you love her?" "Yes!" Peter shouts. "But don't hold that against me. I'm a little screwy myself!"

Peter storms out. Andrews attempts to talk to Ellie. "I just had a long talk with Warne," he says. Ellie snaps, "I'm not interested," and flounces off to join a coterie of her high-society friends. Andrews is frustrated by his inability to talk to Ellie; worried that she will go through with what he knows will be a disastrous marriage.

This version was a huge improvement over the one in my script. My script version called for Andrews to record, secretly, his conversation with Peter. He induces Ellie to listen to the dictograph recording. Ellie hears Peter declare his love for her. From the script:

Close-up Ellie.
An ecstatic gleam comes into her eyes. Ellie shuts off the machine.
He does love her after all!
Medium shot.
Andrews comes to Ellie.

ANDREWS
There's a car all ready for you at the front gate. If you hurry you can
catch up with him.
Ellie is speechless. She stands motionless, unable to move.
   ANDREWS
But you'll have to hurry.
Close shot Ellie.
*She finally comes out of her trance. Camera pans with her as she
rushes to her father, kissing him gratefully. Camera pans with her
as she exits.*
Close-up Andrews.
Looking after Ellie.
   ANDREWS
(throatily) Good luck to you, baby.

From that scene, after a few shots of Ellie driving a fast car, the
story goes directly to the final scene in which the Walls of Jericho
topple.

The scenes we filmed were a vast improvement over the me-
chanical, gimmicky recording-machine version. Those scenes
were shot at historic Busch Gardens in Pasadena, a large estate
with exotic landscaping and spacious lawns. Capra—and Columbia—set out to make the wedding a gaudy spectacle, with a large
crowd of dress extras—the elite of Hollywood—the men in formal
attire, top hats and tails, the women in beautiful gowns. Newsreel
cameras were on hand, to photograph the flamboyant arrival of
King Westley, who proposed to land his aircraft on one of Busch
Gardens sweeping lawns. Capra stationed a battery of prop newsreel cameras on the roof of my sound truck.

Ellie has been surrounded by her high-society friends, frustrating her father's attempt to speak to her. Someone calls out, "Here
he comes," and there is a rush to greet King Westley. The public-
ity-hungry Westley lands in an autogyro, a strange hybrid aircraft
of that time, half conventional plane, half helicopter. Westley
climbs out of his aircraft wearing top hat and tails and carrying a
gold-headed cane.

Capra needed someone to alert the newsreel man, and he chose
me. Joe Walker turned his camera on my sound truck, the newsreel men on the roof, and on me. Capra directed me to call up to
the men on the roof, "Here they come." I did it in one take, as a
good actor should. A viewer of the film, if he or she doesn't blink,

will see me as I appeared in 1933. My appearance has changed somewhat since then.

And now the big scene, the important scene, was going to be played out where it belonged, as Ellie and her father approach the wedding altar. Suspense was what Capra wanted, and he got it in full measure.

Father and bride-to-be walk between rows of wedding guests. It is Andrews' last chance to appeal to Ellie. "This fellow Warne is OK," he tells Ellie. "He didn't want any reward. All he wants is the $39.60 he spent on you."

Ellie is unmoved. Andrews tries again. "He loves you, Ellie, he told me so. You don't want to marry a mug like Westley."

There is still no reaction from Ellie. They are approaching the altar. Andrews has done all he can. "If you change your mind, there's a car waiting for you at the back gate," he tells Ellie.

Ellie takes her place beside King Westley. The minister intones the wedding rites and King Westley responds, "I do." It is time for Ellie to respond; she has only to say "I do," and the dark deed is done. A moment of painful suspense—suddenly Ellie shakes her head, turns, and plunges through a gaggle of wedding guests like a star fullback smashing through defending linesmen. Ellie runs across the spacious lawns of Busch Gardens, her bridal veil streaming behind her. She finds the car her father left for her, jumps in, pulls the ten feet of her bridal veil into the car, and speeds off.

Andrews is smoking a cigar, immensely self-satisfied. "What happened?" Westley asks him.

"I haven't the slightest idea," Andrews replies.

There remained the payoff, the epilogue, the final triumphant fall of the Walls of Jericho. It is night; Ellie and Peter are in an auto camp cabin somewhere in Michigan. Inside, the lights are on.

"They made me get 'em a rope and blanket," the auto camp proprietor tells his wife. "On a hot night like this?" the wife asks. "What do you reckon that's for?" "Darned if I know," says the man. "I just brung 'em a trumpet—one of them toy things. Hadda go down to the store to get it."

"Sounds crazy to me," says the wife. "What do they want a trumpet for?"

Suddenly the trumpet sounds, there is a quick shot of a blanket falling to the floor, and the lights go out in the cabin. It was a smashing finish, one that audiences longed for.

The world knows how *It Happened One Night* performed in release. It told a love story that all the world embraced; it broke attendance records wherever it was shown and won an unprecedented five Academy Awards: Best Picture, Best Director, Best Screenplay, Best Actor, Best Actress.

I was disappointed when Carole Lombard was not cast as Ellie Andrews. I liked Carole; we developed a kind of bantering friendship during the filming of *No More Orchids*. She was more than a beautiful woman with a truck-driver vocabulary; she was a fine actress and would have responded brilliantly to Frank Capra's directing. I couldn't make up my mind: could Carole have been as good as—or even better than—Claudette Colbert? Joseph McBride, in his book *Frank Capra, The Catastrophe of Success*, made up my mind for me. "For all of the merits of its story and screenplay," he wrote, "and Capra's masterful direction, *It Happened One Night* might never have achieved its great success without Clark Gable and Claudette Colbert. They are so apt as a team that it is impossible to imagine anyone else in those roles." Amen.

16

We wrapped up filming *It Happened One Night* December 22, 1933, on schedule and on budget. 1933 had been a most eventful year: the inauguration of Roosevelt, the Bank Holiday, the Long Beach earthquake, my epochal trip to England and participation in the filming of *Lady for a Day* and *It Happened One Night*.

1934 began quietly. There wasn't much production; I was "carried," kept on the payroll, but required to report to the studio every day. The arrangement allowed me to resume writing stories. I found a place to work: Stage 3, dark and empty except for a few standing sets, one of them a shabby hotel room, where a table and some chairs remained. It was January, and Stage 3 was cold. As I worked, I exhaled frosty breath, the kind of visible cold-weather breath Frank Capra needed so badly for his South Pole sequences in *Dirigible*. The legend of the starving artist, creating his masterpiece in a frigid garret, is a staple of literature. Perhaps I thought that the dank chill of Stage 3 might inspire me.

In the course of about four years, twenty-two of my stories were published in *Rob Wagner's Script*. Whenever something was printed, I sent a copy to Harry Cohn, usually with a request to see him about becoming a director. Sometimes he read the stories; on a few occasions I was able to see him. His response to the short stories was always the same: "Write something we can use. Write a script."

I thought it was a brush-off; actually it was sound advice. I was intimidated by the size of a script—a hundred pages or more—but

I know now that if I had used my after-work time to write screen-plays instead of short stories I could have produced a usable one.

Because we were Capra's crew, Harry Cohn perceived us to be his top sound crew, and what Harry Cohn perceived had the force of law at Columbia. Because of that perception, we were assigned to Columbia's next important film, *Twentieth Century,* starring John Barrymore and Carole Lombard, to be directed by Howard Hawks. It was scheduled to start late in February, and since we were not privileged to wait, as top cameramen were, in well-paid idleness, we filled in with short assignments: retakes, screen tests, and something new at Columbia, two-reel comedies.

Since the advent of sound, Columbia had released a mixed bag of short subjects made by outside producers. Columbia released Walt Disney's early Mickey Mouse and Silly Symphony cartoons; comedy travelogs with John P. Medbury; Mickey McGuire come-dies, starring the young Mickey Rooney; and Sunrise Comedies, produced by the Lambs Club, a group of professional actors. Their two-reelers featured well-known comics: Leon Errol, Ken Murray, Smith and Dale, but they were poorly written, and production val-ues were not up to Columbia standards.

Columbia first attempted to enter the short-subjects field in 1933 with a series of two-reelers called the *Musical Novelties.* They were the creation of a talented man, Archie Gottler, who wrote the scripts, songs, and music and directed the films. Columbia contin-ued making these shorts into 1934 and produced nine *Musical Novelties* in all. They were well made and well cast; Betty Grable appeared in two of them and Lois January in four, but the films suffered a sad fate—the moviegoing public didn't really care for them.

Cohn decided to try a different approach. Mack Sennett was about to close up shop; he hadn't been able to cope with the transi-tion to sound, and Hal Roach, deciding that two-reelers had no fu-ture, was converting to feature films. Many talented people—writ-ers, directors, and comics, refugees from the Mack Sennett and Hal Roach studios—were available. Harry Cohn saw the opportunity. He hired a director from M-G-M, Jules White, to organize a short-subjects department; White did so and Columbia's two-reel come-dies flourished for twenty-five years. And so there was something new at Columbia, slapstick two-reelers. My crew and I worked on several of them, featuring the comedy team of George Sidney and

Charlie Murray. We thought that Sidney and Murray were not funny and that the new man on the Columbia lot, Jules White, had a directorial style even more strident than Albert Rogell's.

I was given my *Twentieth Century* script about two weeks before our start date, February 22, 1934. The script was delightful, with Ben Hecht and Charles MacArthur in top form.

I wondered about the selection of Howard Hawks to direct *Twentieth Century.* I observed him during his filming of *The Criminal Code* and admired his handling of the tense, harsh scenes of prison life. *Criminal Code* was grim drama, and Hawks had directed only drama and melodrama since: *The Crowd Roars,* a motor-racing film with Jimmy Cagney; *Scarface,* with Paul Muni; *Tiger Shark,* starring Edward G. Robinson; and *Today We Live,* a story of romance in World War I. All were important and highly successful films, but there was not a shred of lightness in any of them. I found myself wishing that Frank Capra would direct *Twentieth Century.* The script presented a witty, wickedly sophisticated kind of comedy, far different from the down-to-earth humor of *It Happened One Night,* but I felt certain that Capra could make a great film from this superb script.

That was my thinking when I read the script. Later I learned that Columbia did not select Hawks—he selected Columbia. When Hawks finished *The Criminal Code,* Harry Cohn invited him to come to Columbia whenever he had a project in mind. Hawks had just been through an unpleasant episode at M-G-M. He spent ten weeks in Mexico filming exteriors for the film *Viva Villa.* It was a violent, turbulent time in Mexico; progress was slow and the results were disappointing. When the *Viva Villa* troupe returned, Louis B. Mayer fired Hawks. There was an angry confrontation. Some accounts of the affair say that it came to a brawl, a genuine punch-in-the-jaw fistfight. That tale may or may not be true, but it was true that Hawks left M-G-M and Jack Conway finished *Viva Villa.* Then, a classic rebound—Hawks brought the *Twentieth Century* project to Columbia.

The working relationship of Hawks and Ben Hecht was of long standing. In 1927, when Hawks was a producer at Paramount, he hired Hecht to write the silent film, *Underworld.* In 1930, Hecht wrote *Scarface,* directed by Hawks, his third sound film. *Scarface* was a resounding success, and to this day is regarded as a landmark gangster film.

For a project it was natural for Hawks to think of Ben Hecht, and it happened that Hecht and his writing partner Charles MacArthur had a story, tried and tested—their Broadway play. The pieces fell neatly into place; Hecht and MacArthur agreed to expand the play into a screenplay, everyone agreed that Carole Lombard was ideal for the role of Lily Garland, and Hawks persuaded John Barrymore to take the Oscar Jaffe part. According to Hawks, he told Barrymore the story of *Twentieth Century*. Barrymore was doubtful. "Do you think I'm right for this picture?" he asked. "It's the story of the biggest ham on Broadway," Hawks repled, "and I think you fit that." Barrymore agreed to do the picture.

Almost everyone who read the script described it as sophisticated. Just what is "sophisticated"? Mr. Rubin, owner of a dry-cleaning shop near my home, used to say, "I'll give you a for-instance." I present my for-instance. Oscar Jaffe (Barrymore) is infuriated when his stage director, Max Jacobs (Charles Lane) questions his judgment. "You amoeba!" Jaffe shouts. "You came to me as an officeboy, named Max Mandelbaum; and now, for some mysterious reason, you are Max Jacobs. Out! Get out!"

Jaffe might have called Max Jacobs a snake, a louse, or even a cockroach, and any of them would have fit the situation, but *amoeba,* a one-celled creature, the lowest form of animal life! That was the supreme insult—a *sophisticated* insult—because in an average movie audience, as many of 70 percent of the customers wouldn't know what an amoeba was; they would be puzzled and not amused. The 30 percent of the audience, the *sophisticated* 30 percent who appreciated the outrageous insult, however, would be amused.

We began production of *Twentieth Century* February 22, 1934. It may have been an omen, if one were looking for an omen: our principal sets, the railroad car interiors, were built on Columbia's Stage 6, the venerable stage where the "Walls of Jericho" motel interiors were built. Perhaps some movie magic lingered there.

The first day, when I introduced myself to Howard Hawks, he acknowledged my presence with a curt nod, not brusque or unfriendly, merely businesslike. I had the feeling that a snappy salute may have been in order. I also had the feeling that there would be no rapport, such as I had with Capra, and that it would not be wise to comment on scenes, as I sometimes did with Capra.

When Hawks directed the grim prison drama, *The Criminal Code,* his manner had been reserved and austere. Directing *Twenti-*

eth Century, what is now celebrated as a superb screwball comedy, he was no less reserved and austere. He was cool and businesslike even to his cameraman, Joe August. That was surprising, because Joe August had been the cinematographer on Hawks's first job as a director, the silent films *The Road to Glory* and *Fig Leaves,* in 1926. There must have been a strong bond of friendship between them.

The cast of *Twentieth Century* was excellent. Oliver Webb (Walter Connolly) is Oscar Jaffe's long-suffering business manager. He endures Jaffe's abuse; his reactions to Jaffe's bizarre behavior are a delight to watch. Owen O'Malley (Roscoe Karns) is Jaffe's cynical, hard-drinking publicity man. Another fine performance; whatever Roscoe Karns did invariably was well done. The mousy little deranged man, Etienne Girardot, who plasters the windows of the train with religious messages, is no less than perfect in the role.

From the beginning, the Barrymore-Lombard scenes were fast, furious, and superbly acted—"dynamite," Bus Libott called them. Movie crews tend to become blasé; a couple of superstars may be filming a key scene and crew members take it in stride, not ignoring it but not particularly impressed either—but not the Barrymore-Lombard scenes. They were fascinated by the verve and intensity of the performances and watched, spellbound. A great script, fine actors—the quality was there, but someone had to guide the film to ensure that all the elements were properly used, and for that Howard Hawks must get due credit.

Hawks' shooting method was simple and efficient, not flashy— no intricate show-off dolly shots. He filmed the solid way, using the camera to tell his story as clearly and interestingly as possible, never allowing the camera to draw attention to itself.

The story of *Twentieth Century* is simple. Oscar Jaffe transforms a stage-struck shop girl, Mildred Plotka (Lombard), who he has renamed Lily Garland, into a stage star. He is excessively jealous of her. When she discovers that he has been spying on her, she is enraged, leaves him, and goes to Hollywood, where she becomes a movie star. The greater part of the film then deals with his efforts to lure her back to Broadway—and to him. Those scenes take place aboard the crack train, the *Twentieth Century Limited,* on its run from Chicago to New York.

When Hecht and MacArthur expanded their play into a screenplay, they wrote new scenes in which Oscar Jaffe is shown attempting to make a star of Mildred Plotka. They are some of the sharpest and wittiest in the film. For the theater scenes, Columbia rented the small, elegant Wilshire-Ebell theater. Built in the 1920s, the theater was the property of the Wilshire-Ebell women's club, an organization of high-society ladies of early-day Los Angeles.

In the script, Barrymore is introduced sprawled on the floor of his office, reading a script. Summoned to the set to view a rehearsal, he studies himself in a mirror to make sure he has the proper regal manner. On the stage, he delivers a welcoming speech to his newly assembled cast. In it, Oscar Jaffe leaves no doubt that he is one of the theater world's greatest egos and greatest hams:

"I have been looking forward to this occasion for some time," he tells his adoring cast. "There is nothing in the world like watching a play — watching it come to life, little by little, seeing the living scenes emerge, like genie from a bottle."

I believe that no other actor could have put so much ham, so much ego into those few words. Barrymore's delivery was magnificent; he spoke with intensity that was almost biblical, like Moses demanding that the Red Sea stop blocking traffic and part its waters. Jaffe continues, his words dripping treacle. "Before we begin, I want you all to remember one thing: no matter what I may say, no matter what I may do, I love you all."

The rehearsal begins. Jaffe coaches Lily Garland, transformed only that day from shop girl Mildred Plotka. "You're not Lily Garland any more," he tells her. "You're Mary Jo Calhoun, a shy little girl of the South. Through an open window comes the scent of jasmine — you have just kissed your lover — you come drifting into the room. All right, Mary Jo. Enter the room."

Shy little Mary Jo strides briskly into the room. "No!" Jaffe shouts. "That is the way an *iceman* enters a room, not Mary Jo. Shyly, please."

The rehearsals continue — one disaster after another. When Mary Jo and her father collide during a dramatic scene, Jaffe shouts, "Stop. This is not a scrimmage! Give me some chalk."

Provided with the chalk, Jaffe draws lines for Mary Jo's movements, and soon the entire stage floor is covered with a web of chalk lines. We had a visitor when we were making the chalk-marking scene. Gene Havlick, our film editor and a dedicated sourpuss, came to the Wilshire-Ebell theater to confer with Hawks. He stood near the camera, watching Barrymore as he hopped around the stage like a wounded crow, chalking furiously. In midscene Havlick forgot where he was and laughed aloud. Hawks angrily called "Cut," but when he saw that it was sad-faced Havlick who broke up the shot, he actually smiled. "Thank you, Gene," he said. "I'm glad you liked our scene."

Oscar Jaffe's *Hearts of Kentucky* was clearly a parody of *Coquette*. The similarities were all there: Mary Jo Calhoun of *Hearts of Kentucky* and Norma Besant of *Coquette* were romantic young southern belles. The low-born lover, for each of them, was named Michael; the headstrong fathers of Mary Jo and Norma, obsessed with the family's "honor," kill Michael.

It seems strange that Hecht and MacArthur would lampoon *Coquette;* Helen Hayes, MacArthur's wife, starred in the play. The Hecht-MacArthur satire was neither gentle nor affectionate; much of it was witty, sharp, and wicked. I don't know why Charles MacArthur collaborated in the lampooning of *Coquette*.

Sometime later, I came close to getting an answer. In 1963 I went to Spain to direct a film for Philip Yordan's Security Pictures Company. There was a great deal of film activity in Spain in the 1960s. I often heard the term "filmmakers' paradise"—costs were low and the Spanish bureaucracy was cooperative. I was quartered at the Castellana-Hilton hotel, nerve center of Spanish moviemaking. Everyone came to Rick's in Casablanca, and everyone came to the Castellana in Madrid. Ben Hecht was there, play-doctoring the script for the John Wayne film, *Circus World.* I encountered him in the Castellana lobby. I introduced myself and told him that I grew up in Chicago and as a youth had admired his column in the *Chicago Daily News,* "One Thousand and One Afternoons in Chicago." It is my belief that no one grows so surfeited with praise that he will accept no more. Hecht discerned that my admiration was sincere, and so we sat at a small table and talked. He told me of his early career as a newspaperman in Chicago and New York, and we progressed to his association with Howard Hawks in *Underworld* and *Scarface.* At that point an acquaintance approached; Hecht invited him to join us, and they began a lively discussion—about sleeping pills. They had discovered that in Madrid pharmacies were unregulated. Items could be bought over the counter that were illegal in the United States. Hecht and his friend agreed that their Madrid sleeping pills were wonderful. I waited patiently for the sleeping pill discussion to wear out so that I could get back to

Coquette and *Twentieth Century,* but a bellboy approached and told Hecht that there was a phone call for him. The call was for Hecht to go at once to Barcelona, where much of *Circus World* was to be filmed, and I didn't see him again.

The third act of *Twentieth Century* is wild, weird, and hilarious. In a series of magnificently played scenes, Lily Garland rejects all of Jaffe's efforts to sign her to a contract. She laughs at his threat to shoot himself; Webb and O'Malley also deride his threats—they have heard them many times before. As they leave, the mad little man slips into the compartment. Jaffe, holding the revolver, is not aware of his presence. He begins a Hamlet-like soliloquy. "Messenger of death," he says, addressing the pistol. "Passport to eternity." The little man touches his arm to attract his attention. Jaffe reacts violently. The little man thinks the gun is aimed at him and grabs Jaffe's wrist.

In the club car, Webb and O'Malley assure one another that Jaffe's threat to shoot himself is just one more fake; but suddenly there is a shot, and Jaffe staggers into the club car, wounded. The mad little man follows. "He pointed the gun at me," he pleads. "It was his life or mine."

Jaffe plays the dying man scene to the hilt, but the conductor brings in a doctor, who tells Jaffe that his wound is superficial. "It barely broke the skin," he says.

Garland bursts into the club car, fearing that Jaffe has finally carried out his threat to shoot himself. Jaffe instantly goes into a superb act, abetted by Webb and O'Malley, pretending that he is mortally wounded. "He's dying," Webb tells a tearful Garland. "Sign the contract. It's his last wish." Jaffe speaks up, faintly. "Bury it with me. Next to my heart."

Lily Garland signs. A moment later, Max Jacobs, the amoeba, bursts into the club car with an incredibly rich offer. "Too late, Mandlebaum!" Jaffe shouts in triumph, suddenly alive and well. "Oscar, you fake!" Garland screams, and there is a torrent of screaming and yelling as the *Twentieth Century Limited* speeds through the night.

For the final scenes of *Twentieth Century* we were back at the Wilshire-Ebell theater. Oscar Jaffe addresses Lily Garland and the cast of his new play. "I've been looking forward to this occasion for some time," he says, his voice pure corn syrup. "There's no thrill like launching a new play; but before we begin I ask you to realize one thing—that no matter what I may do, or what I may say, I love you all." Lily Garland doesn't pay attention; she has heard it all, and she is busy admiring herself, the reigning queen of theater and cinema, wearing twenty thousand dollars' worth of furs.

Jaffe summons Garland to come to him. "Don't be nervous, child," he says. Nervous? Child? Garland has starred in a half-dozen Broadway plays and Hollywood movies. "You are not Lily Garland; you are Betty Ann, the ragged little thing they found wandering in the cotton field, and now you come, shyly, into Colonel Merriweather's big house." "Yes, Oscar, I know," Garland says impatiently, but Jaffe cuts her off. "Places, please, for Betty Ann's entrance."

Garland is resentful but obeys. She enters. "Colonel Merriweather, why are you-all looking at me so strange?" she asks in her best corn-pone accent. "Cut!" Jaffe roars. "Let's do this thing correctly! You've been in Hollywood too long; you've forgotten a lot of things! I'll show you how it is done in the theater! Chalk, please!"

Webb produces chalk; Jaffe marks the stage floor. Lily Garland screams at him. "Do you know who I am?" she demands. Jaffe shouts back at her; there is chaos, pandemonium on stage. Owen O'Malley speaks, calm in the eye of the storm. "Here we go again, Oliver, with Livingston through darkest Africa," and as the scene develops into an all-out screaming-match, the picture ends.

17

We finished shooting *Twentieth Century* on March 24, 1934. We didn't wait in salaried idleness for the next important production; that wasn't Columbia's way. Just three days after completing *Twentieth Century*, we were assigned to an unusual kind of short film, *Woman Haters*, one of the final entries in the series of two-reelers that Columbia called the *Musical Novelties*. The films had no conventional dialogue; all words were either sung or recited, in verse, to music. The orchestra was recorded first, before production began. Then, with the playback machine and the cameras locked in sync, the music was played at a low level, for the casts members to sing or recite to. The volume had to be kept low, because the quality of the playback music was not good, but it had to be loud enough for the cast members to keep in rhythm. The level varied from performer to performer. Walter Brennan, who was cast as a Pullman car conductor, needed more playback volume than Marjorie White, the leading lady, or the comedy veterans, Monte Collins, Bud Jamison, and Jack Norton. In re-recording, the poor-quality playback sound was covered up by high-quality prescored music.

I have a reason for remembering *Woman Haters*, because three comedians, billed as Howard, Fine, and Howard, were featured in it. They were not called the Three Stooges; that came later. I wanted to be a director, I hoped to be a director, but in my wildest fantasies I could not have seen myself, eleven years later, as a rookie director, my first assignment a comedy with those wild things, those knockabout characters, the Three Stooges.

There was a three-month interval between the finish of *Twentieth Century* and Capra's next film, *Broadway Bill*. We continued to fill in with tests, two-reel comedies, and quickie films. In 1934, Columbia introduced a new product alignment. Someone in the front office apparently decided that the day of the low-budget Western was ending. Only four Westerns were made that year, down from ten the year before. Their place was taken by what might be called B-minus films, eight of them in 1934, non-Westerns with brutally short eight-day schedules. Bus and I did a couple of them, starring Tim McCoy, directed by short-fused Ross Lederman. Some time later, the front-office people discovered that low-budget Westerns were not dead or dying. In 1935 Columbia was back with a full slate of Westerns, eight of them starring Ken Maynard and three starring a newcomer, Charles Starrett.

Whenever I encountered Capra, he seemed to be in good spirits, as well he might be; *It Happened One Night* was a huge success worldwide. There were rumors that Capra's next film would have a racetrack background and that Clark Gable would star in it. When I asked Capra about the rumors, he confirmed that *Broadway Bill* would be about horseracing. When I asked whether Gable would be in it he said, rather curtly, "We're working on it," and I sensed that his efforts to get Clark Gable were not going well.

The year 1934 is treated rather strangely in Capra's autobiography. In it he takes us from the wrap-up of *It Happened One Night* in December 1933 to his Academy Awards triumph of February 27, 1935. He discusses those fourteen months in less than half a page, almost as though they didn't exist. They *did* exist. We began *Broadway Bill* in the middle of that year, June 1934.

The script, by Bob Riskin, was developed from a short story by Mark Hellinger. Dan Brooks (Warner Baxter) is married to a frosty, selfish woman (Helen Vinson) and works for his father-in-law in father's paper-box factory. His first love, however, is not the paper-box business but horseracing and his thoroughbred horse, Broadway Bill. He leaves his wife to try to win a big race with Broadway Bill. His sister-in-law, Alice Higgins (Myrna Loy), follows him and helps him to surmount a daunting series of obstacles to get his horse into the big race. There are crooked gamblers involved, a jockey is bribed to throw the race, and Broadway Bill wins in spite of it all—but dies after crossing the finish line.

The death of Broadway Bill was not in the first script I read. It probably was Capra's idea, and it saved *Broadway Bill* from being just another happy-ending horse picture; it had shock value and drama, and eventually the story did have a happy ending. Dan Brooks's wife divorces him, Alice Higgins gladly catches him on the rebound, and love conquers all.

There were some interesting repetitions in Bob Riskin's script. In *Platinum Blonde* the leading man, Robert Williams, ignores Loretta Young's charms and treats her like an adolescent teenager. The audience can see that she loves him, but he is blithely unaware of it. In *Broadway Bill* Warner Baxter ignores Myrna Loy in the same way. That makes Robert Williams and Warner Baxter incredibly obtuse, since both Loretta Young and Myrna Loy were not giddy teenage girls but beautiful, desirable young women.

There is another interesting repetition in *Broadway Bill*. In *Lady for a Day*, Riskin created a character named "Happy McGuire," a vinegar-faced, acid-tongued cynic. In *Broadway Bill*, Riskin again created a sour-faced character—again named "Happy McGuire." It was probably no oversight; Capra and Riskin probably intended to use Ned Sparks again, but for some reason Sparks was not cast as Happy McGuire; Lynne Overman assumed the role. Lynne Overman was a competent actor, but Ned Sparks would have been better in the part. It wasn't a matter of acting ability; it was simply the fact that there was no face more sour, no voice more abrasive and sarcastic than Sparks's.

The creation of a character such as Happy McGuire in both *Lady for a Day* and *Broadway Bill* was a shrewd and calculated device by Bob Riskin. In both stories Happy is, in effect, the voice of the audience.

If an audience threatens to rebel against improbabilities in the story, Happy McGuire voices their doubts and their protests. In *Lady for a Day*, when Dave the Dude's preposterous plan to make Apple Annie a grand lady begins to stretch the audience's credulity too far, Happy defuses the threat with his vinegar-tongued sarcasm. In *Broadway Bill*, Happy McGuire again speaks for the audience, sad-voiced, pointing out the hopelessness of Broadway Bill's winning the big race. Happy McGuire is not merely an amusing and colorful character; he is an effective element in Bob Riskin's story structure.

We began production of *Broadway Bill* at Tanforan racetrack, near San Mateo, California. Our first scenes with Warner Baxter and

Myrna Loy revealed a serious and unfixable problem: Warner Baxter was not Clark Gable. He was thoroughly professional, a capable, handsome veteran actor. He had appeared in more than fifty silent films, dating back to 1914; he then continued his career with more than fifty sound films—but he was not Clark Gable. He did not have the quality Gable had, a quality that enabled Gable to do absurd things and make them amusing and acceptable—arguing about piggybacking, for instance, while he carried Claudette Colbert across a stream; giving her lessons in doughnut dunking and hitchhiking and inviting a belligerent bus driver to take a punch at his nose—if he dared. Warner Baxter seemed to be too sensible, too handsome, too much a solid citizen to portray that kind of free spirit, but he tried.

At Tanforan, Capra was again at his best as an organizer and as a commander. We worked at peak efficiency, as we had in the battle scenes of *General Yen* and the riot and circus fire of *Rain or Shine*. Capra also supervised a second unit, directed by Ross Lederman, whose directive was to film camera-car shots of Broadway Bill's big race.

At the end of our first week at Tanforan, Capra invited Joe Walker, Ross Lederman, and me to have dinner with him in San Francisco. We went first to Walter Bell's one-man film laboratory on Howard Street, where Capra worked in 1922. We went down steep stairs; the little lab was below street level. Capra showed us equipment that he had devised: a splicer and a dual rewind. Capra's nostalgia was unusual; generally he was steadfastly forward-looking; and it was touching to see how he looked back, with profound nostalgia, to the days of his struggle from film-lab apprentice to be one of the world's great film directors.

From Ball's lab Capra took us to dinner at Jack's, a famous old restaurant, founded in 1864. Jack's served superb food; it was world-famous, still at its original location on Sacramento Street in San Francisco.

At Jack's, for the first time, I ate escargot. Joe Walker politely declined, but Ross Lederman, a powerful man with a weak stomach, was so revolted by the idea of eating the crawling creatures that he couldn't bear to watch us eat them and left the restaurant. From time to time he peered forlornly through the window of the restaurant to see whether it was safe to return.

There was an ugly incident the following week. A half-dozen of our electricians went to San Francisco to see the sights. Longshore-men were on strike, and as our men walked toward the Embarcadero, a crowd of strikers began to gather. They chose to believe that our men were strikebreakers. They were armed with clubs, baseball bats, and chains. Police were near; they rushed to protect our men. George Hager, Joe Walker's gaffer, told the police that they were union men and offered to show their union cards to the gathering mob. "They don't give a damn about any union cards," a policeman said. "They just want to beat somebody up. You better get the hell out of here."

George Hager told us about it later. "I never ran away from a fight in my life, but there were twenty or thirty of them, six of us, and they had clubs and baseball bats and I saw a couple of knives. It wouldn't have been a fight—it would have been murder."

For long shots at Tanforan, showing capacity crowds, Colum-bia filmed special stock shots during Tanforan's regular racing season. Capra used large numbers of local people to match our ac-tors into those long shots. We were told that Columbia's presence and the money paid to those extras gave an economic boost to the entire region.

Capra wanted to fill the Tanforan grandstand while we filmed scenes with our actors in the foreground. To fill the stands with paid extras would have broken the *Broadway Bill* budget. Instead, our publicity people announced, in newspapers and on the radio, that on the Fourth of July, admission to Tanforan would be free, that there would be horseraces, and visitors would see movie scenes being made. An enthusiastic, orderly crowd filled our grandstand on the July 4. Some races were run; they were not gen-uine races, but Warner Baxter, using our public address system, in-vited our guests to make mental bets. Other members of our cast spoke; Baxter was excellent as an impromptu master of cere-monies. The crowd cooperated nicely; they were quiet when we filmed dialogue scenes, and they cheered loudly on cue.

We filmed the big scene—the climactic scene—in which Broadway Bill wins his big race and dies just over the finish line. A device called a "Running W" was used to crash Broadway Bill to earth in full stride. The Running W is a cruel device. Padded an-klets are secured just above a horse's front hooves and wires are attached to the anklets. Woven steel wire is used; it is strong and flexible, designed to be used as aircraft control wires. The wires are passed through a metal ring fastened under the horse's belly and stretched out, usually to about 150 feet, where the ends are firmly anchored. The horse—the victim of the Running W—is led to a starting point, with enough slack in the wire for him to reach top speed. When he comes to the end of the slack wire his front legs are abruptly jerked from under him, pulled up to the ring under his belly, and in full stride he crashes to earth. I was told that about half of the horses subjected to the Running W were killed. Our horse, the double for Broadway Bill, was not killed, but he limped badly as he was led off. If he was crippled too badly to be used as a racehorse, he would probably be destroyed. The use of the Running W is forbidden now in the United States, but is still permitted in Mexico.

Our final sequence at Tanforan was the burial ceremony of Broadway Bill in the infield of Tanforan racetrack. I listened to Capra's discussion with Joe Walker. He believed that an impressive ceremony would extend the emotional impact of Broadway Bill's death and create a sentimental mood that would carry into the final scenes of the picture. Capra needed all the sentiment and sympathy he could create for the wrap-up of *Broadway Bill*. The final sequence was vintage Capra-Riskin fairy tale.

In that final sequence we learn that two years have passed. J. L. Higgins announces to his daughters and their husbands that he has divested himself of all of his properties—no more Higgins Paper Mill, no more Higgins Iron Works, no more Higgins Bank. The daughters and their husbands are appalled. "What will we do?" one son-in-law cries. "You'll go to work, you'll find a job, that's what you'll do!" Higgins tells him.

At that moment Dan Brooks announces his arrival by throwing rocks through the Higgins's dining room window—a charming way to inform the Higgins clan that he has arrived, "to rescue the Princess from the dark tower!" he shouts. Alice recognizes it as the avowal of love she has been longing for and runs out of the house, into Dan Brooks's arms. The final scene of *Broadway Bill* strains credulity almost to the breaking point. J. L. Higgins, the tycoon, the tyrant, the middle-America Scrooge, cries "Wait for me!" and dashes after them.

In release, *Broadway Bill* did well at the box office. *Variety* noted that in its first week at the Radio City Music Hall, *Broadway Bill* grossed a very impressive $95,000—$5,000 more than *It Happened One Night* earned in its first week at the same theater. Critics were kind to it. Andre Sennwald in the *New York Times* called *Broadway Bill* "a highly ingratiating photoplay, painlessly whimsical and completely engaging. The players who work for Mr. Capra have a habit of performing at the top of their talent. Mr. Baxter is enormously agreeable. Myrna Loy reaffirms our faith in her, both as a light comedienne and as a person."

Otis Ferguson, in *New Republic*: "Anyone familiar with Warner Baxter's sad succession of recent duds might suspect the hand of God in his present transformation; those who saw Clark Gable in *It Happened One Night* will recognize in Baxter's quick, breezy offhand naturalness, the hand of Capra."

"Bige," in hard-nosed, down-to-earth *Variety*, was almost lyrical. In his review of December 4, 1934, he wrote, "If any race track picture has a chance to beat the no-femme draw bugaboo, *Broadway Bill* is the picture—it has a story, a tiptop cast and Frank Capra's direction." That was the first paragraph. The last paragraph: "The effect of capable direction is discernible in every foot of film and appears responsible for the major credit." Sweet praise, from the first paragraph and the last, with not a single quibble or unkind word in the paragraphs between.

It is significant that in almost all reviews Capra gets credit for the good performances of his cast. It is true; Capra did have a way, a subtle, hard-to-define way of getting superior performances from his people. He also had the remarkable ability to make his audiences believe what he wanted them to believe. As Alfred Hitchcock told Jack Henley, "The audience will believe our man can escape because they *want* him to escape." Frank Capra, like Hitchcock, made audiences believe: that long-odds Broadway Bill *could* win his race, that Dan Brooks would suddenly stop being stupid and accept Alice Higgins's love, and that J. L. Higgins would toss away his millions to join Dan and Alice as racetrack vagabonds.

In his autobiography, Capra makes no mention of the filming of *Broadway Bill*, nor does he acknowledge that it did well in release. If he was disenchanted with *Broadway Bill*, it was not apparent during the filming; he gave the film his energetic, capable best. He remained unassuming, approachable, devoid of pretense or ego, even though he was now ranked among the world's foremost directors. I saw no foreshadowing of the dark days of self-doubt that Capra tells of in his autobiography.

18

The Frank Capra who wrote—or cowrote—the autobiography he presented to the world in 1971 seems to be a completely different person from the man of the great decade, 1929–1939. It is incredible that a director who displayed immense skill and self-confidence in that decade would write of the events of 1935 as he did in his autobiography: "I had scaled the Mount Everest of Filmlandia. Nine years after my first childish gags for *Our Gang,* I had knocked off all my challenges. I had licked poverty and ridicule; I had yet to lick a bigger enemy, myself. I had become a pillar of jello, haunted by the fear that my next picture would fail."

Capra describes how his self-doubt caused a psychosomatic illness that became genuine and life-threatening. Max Winslow, a song-publishing partner of Irving Berlin, visited Capra often during his illness. One day Winslow brought a visitor to Capra's sickroom, the nameless, mysterious "Little Man." From Capra's book: "I admitted to Max that I was going to die. About the tenth day, when I was fading fast, Max told me that there was a gentleman in the library to see me." Capra protested but finally agreed to see the man. "I sat down, weak as a cat—just as curious. The little man sat opposite and said: 'Mr. Capra, you're a coward. The talents you have are not your own, *not* self-acquired. God gave you those talents; they are his gifts to you to use for His purpose. And when you don't *use* the gifts God blessed you with, you are an offense to God—and to humanity. Good day sir.'" Later, Capra, regaining his health in Palm Springs, wrote, "I began to gain a pound a day.

What had happened? Who was that faceless little man who told me I was a coward and an offense to God? I didn't know, never would know, never *wanted* to know."

The "little man" episode is one of the strangest tales told in any autobiography, and it seems probable that the encounter never took place. Joseph McBride, in his meticulously researched Capra biography, writes, "Most, if not all, of his fantastic story is an invention." He quotes Chet Sticht, who served as Capra's secretary for nearly forty years. Regarding the mysterious little man: "It doesn't make sense to me," Sticht said. "I never met the little man. It could have been true—but it also could have been an imaginative thing."

We at the studio knew nothing of this. We would certainly have been concerned; Frank Capra was our breadwinner. Jo Swerling and Bob Riskin were working on a screenplay, but it was not to be a Capra film. The script was *The Whole Town's Talking;* instead, we were assigned to *Mills of the Gods,* a B film directed by Roy William Neill.

Mills of the Gods was one more attempt by Columbia to capitalize on May Robson's sudden ascent to stardom in *Lady for a Day.* Robson portrayed a gallant old lady who attempts to save her family's hundred-year-old steel mill from financial ruin. It was a dreary tale of labor unrest and of greedy, uncaring children and grandchildren. Robson, herself a gallant old lady, tried hard to breathe life into the story but failed because of flat dialogue, languid tempo, and uninspired directing.

Bus Libott had a strong, offbeat sense of humor. He decided to rename our film. A singing group, The Mills Brothers, was popular at the time. Bus renamed the film *Oh God, The Mills Brothers.* It was just quirky enough and offbeat enough to delight the crew; they began to use the new title, and Roy Neill, who had wondered why his crew laughed when they found grisly humor in "I didn't think he had the guts" when we made *Wall Street,* now wondered why they couldn't get the name of this film right.

Carnival, directed by Walter Lang, starring Jimmy Durante, Lee Tracy, and Sally Eilers, began production a week after we started *Mills of the Gods.* It was still shooting when we finished; it was behind schedule and trouble plagued. Two cameramen and other crew members had been fired—a jinx picture, our back-lot people called it. We wrapped up *Mills of the Gods* on November

6, and Bus and I were immediately pressed into service to replace the *Carnival* sound crew. I never learned why they were replaced. They may have been the victims of Harry Cohn's arbitrary, ruthless exercise of power, a throwback to ancient days when a monarch from time to time would order a few heads lopped off just to remind the peasants who the boss was.

The *Carnival* script was by Bob Riskin; 1934 was a busy, productive year for him. Because it was a Riskin script, the scenes were well constructed and the dialogue was bright and amusing. Durante and Lee Tracy were excellent in some well-written scenes, but the film, as we shot it, seemed to lack something Capra might have given it, the intangible quality that changed a film from pretty good to very good. *Carnival* wrapped in mid-December, which essentially ended the year for me. Again I didn't attend Columbia's Christmas party Saturnalia. 1934 had been another eventful year—not as adventurous as 1933, but any year in which I participated in making films such as *Twentieth Century* and *Broadway Bill* had to be a memorable one.

1935 began for me with a couple of B-minus films starring Wallace Ford, directed by the tough little man, Lambert Hillyer. In mid-February I was given a script, *Air Hawks,* to be directed by the man I delighted in not working with, Albert Rogell. The leads were Ralph Bellamy and Tala Birell; Wiley Post, a famous flyer in real life, was cast to play himself. The story of *Air Hawks* was pure, double-dipped B material. Two airplane companies are competing for a lucrative air mail contract. Naturally, it was good guys versus very bad guys who play dirty and stack the odds in their favor by creating an infrared death-ray machine. The whole thing had the subtlety and finesse of a Republic serial.

Much of *Air Hawks* was filmed at what is now Van Nuys Airport, a huge facility that now is the busiest general aviation airport in the world. In 1935, however, it was a nearly deserted, forlorn little place with the grandiose name of Metropolitan Airport. In the booming days of 1928–1929, a runway was paved, and hangars and a stubby little control tower were built. Now, in the Depression days of 1935, the control tower was unmanned and the hangars were empty except for a few derelict planes and the pathetic wreck of a plane in which a pilot had been killed.

Our *Air Hawks* troupe had Metropolitan Airport mostly to ourselves. Our planes took off and landed at will, as did an occasional private plane. One day a formation of three Army Air Force bi-planes flew over. They executed what might be called an aerial double-take when they saw what we were doing. They reversed course, circled, and landed. The flyers, three pilots and three enlisted men, came to watch us work. It was all very pleasant and informal. When lunchtime came, the aviators were invited to join us in the chow line. When they took off, they saluted us with a thunderous high-speed pass, three or four hundred feet over our heads.

Early in May we were assigned to *The Black Room,* a Gothic horror story starring Boris Karloff in a dual role, to be directed by Roy Neill. Columbia made a couple of Karloff B pictures in 1932, but the front-office people apparently decided that *The Black Room* would get A treatment, to cash in on Karloff's ascent to horror film stardom in *Bride of Frankenstein.* Roy Neill was given a generous four-week shooting schedule, double that of a B picture, and the budget for sets was as great as that for a super-A film. Columbia's art director, Stephen Goosson, with money to spend, built sets that helped to create, with their grim stone chambers, an atmosphere of fear and foreboding.

The Roy Neill who had plodded through the dull *Mills of the Gods* was a different director on *The Black Room.* The high-walled sets and dramatic archways called for striking photography, and Neill responded with inventive, beautifully composed long shots. His storytelling shots, of people, were no less inventive. Dialogue scenes were filmed in odd, unconventional angles that contributed to the anticipation of ominous events to come. The only conventional setups were the ones that had to be: the split-screen scenes in which Karloff, as Anton, the good brother, talks to his twin, the evil brother, Gregor. The camera could not move, because it had to be securely locked down during both halves of a split-screen setup. Eccentric camera angles were not feasible, because they made it difficult to conceal the split line.

When one-half of the split screen setup was finished, Karloff, as rapidly as possible, changed wardrobe, makeup, and hairstyle. During that time, if the camera was moved or the lights were disturbed, the split line between the halves would be revealed and the whole scene would have to be reshot. Our *Black Room* split screens, however, were excellent, thanks to the skill of our cameraman, Al Siegler, and Karloff's ability to time, accurately, the give and take of his conversations with himself. When *The Black*

Room was released, it was generally recognized that the Karloff split-screen scenes were some of the most skillfully executed of their time. It is my belief that Al Siegler, like Ben Kline, had the talent to be a top-ranked, top-paid cameraman but chose to accept, as Ben did, every job, A or B or B-minus, that was offered to him. In working with Roy Neill he had the opportunity to do some striking, high-quality photography.

Al Siegler was a pleasant, unassuming man and a fine cinematographer, but he had the strange habit of not remembering names. I made three or four pictures with him before he stopped calling me "kid" or "kiddo." On one film, he was given a new assistant, but promptly forgot his name and called him "Buttons" throughout the picture. I didn't mind being called "kid," and Marian Marsh didn't seem to mind when Al Siegler forgot her name and called her "Missy." She knew that Al's close-ups made her look breathtakingly beautiful. She was not permitted to see the rushes, but the camera crew liked her and showed her frames from the laboratory test strips in a little hand-held viewer. Later, in a film with a leading lady who considered herself a star, Al persistently called her "Missy." The lady was not amused. If eyes had launched arrows, they would have pierced Siegler's heart.

When filming began, it seemed to me that the pace was slow and that members of the cast, including Karloff, overacted. As we progressed, I began to see that I might be wrong. The tempo was deliberate because it was in keeping with the mood, the atmosphere of the story. A brisk pace would not have fostered the mood of the tragedy and foreboding that a good horror film demands. I soon changed my opinion, as well, of Karloff's performance. In the beginning I thought that Karloff overacted: far too honorable and kindly as the good brother, and too utterly evil as the bad brother, Gregor. I learned that in a horror film understatement and restrained performances are wrong. Roy Neill and Boris Karloff knew what they were creating—and it worked. Anton, the good brother, is almost angelic; Gregor, the bad brother, is a man of total depravity and evil. Karloff actually gives three excellent performances: as Anton, as Gregor, and as Gregor masquerading as Anton—having murdered his brother, Gregor assumes Anton's identify.

I began to realize that we were making a film that might be very good of its kind, but more than ever I wished that I was working on *The Whole Town's Talking* instead, because we worked long, grinding hours on *The Black Room,* just as we did on Roy Neill's B pictures. Today the film is highly regarded, but when we made it, we, the crew, were interested in down-to-earth considerations, like occasionally getting home for dinner with the family and seeing our children before they were sent to bed. My diary is full of entries like that of Saturday, May 18: "Shooting interior of inn. Break for dinner. Slow going, home midnight." There are many such entries: "May 20, home 11:20." "May 22, graveyard set. Then to stage one for Mocha murder sequence. Well done, but takes much time. Shoot until 11." That pattern was broken on May 29. "Shooting in Black Room. Long, slow session to midnight—midnight meal served, shoot until 4 A.M. Home and to bed by early daylight." At least we didn't work sixty-hour weeks to make a clunker; horror film fans today consider *The Black Room* a classic.

Columbia had high hopes for *The Black Room,* for critical approval as well as for box-office success, but the reviews in the Hollywood trade papers, *Hollywood Reporter* and *Variety,* were devastating. "They murdered us," a member of Columbia's publicity department told me, and they did—brutally. From *The Hollywood Reporter,* July 17, 1935: "Four people are killed without any excitement and certainly no mystery. Mr. Karloff mugs at himself throughout the picture. Marian Marsh looks very beautiful and is called on to do no more. The script was bad to begin with and Neill couldn't do much in the way of direction. Al Siegler's photography is top-notch—too bad it's wasted." In the *Variety* review, "Bon" wrote, "Karloff fans will get a load of their favorite to the saturation point here, but the picture will not get much at the box office—Roy William Neill directed as well as possible a tawdry and obtuse story—as for Karloff, he is his usual self, in practically every sequence of the lengthy, dull proceedings."

Despite critics' negative reviews, *The Black Room* proved to be a hit with the members of the audience who counted most of all: the ticket-buying public. *The Black Room*'s star happened to share moviegoers' sentiments. When Boris Karloff was being interviewed in 1936, he referred to the film as "my favorite picture so far." Television rediscovered *The Black Room* in the 1950s, making it a perennial favorite with a new generation of Karloff fans.

Today, the critical opinion on *The Black Room* has been reversed; connoisseurs of classic horror films hail it as a masterpiece.

J. Robert Nash and Stanley Ralph Ross, in *The Motion Picture Guide,* unequivocally declare that "Karloff is superb. . . . Directed with a great sense of style by Roy William Neill, this Gothic horror is first rate." Phil Hardy, in *The Enclyclopedia of Horror Movies:* "A heavily-styled period piece, more Gothic melodrama than pure horror movie. Neill's direction is solid. Karloff's performance is outstanding throughout." Leslie Halliwell, *Halliwell's Film Guide:* "A neatly produced star vehicle . . . rather splendid."

The ultimate accolade comes from Leonard Maltin's *Movie & Video Guide.* Notoriously frugal in awarding stars, it gives *The Black Room* three of them and tells its readers, "Excellent understated thriller of twin brothers (Karloff) and the ancient curse that dominates their lives. Features one of Karloff's best performances."

19

During the last week of filming *The Black Room,* I was concerned about our next assignment. Two pictures were scheduled to start on June 12, *She Married Her Boss,* starring Claudette Colbert and Melvyn Douglas, directed by Gregory La Cava; and *Atlantic Adventure,* directed by Albert Rogell. *She Married Her Boss* was decidedly an A film; *Atlantic Adventure* was not merely a B but it was an Al Rogell B, which meant it would be a two-week ordeal of long, stressful hours.

No establishment can be completely free of what might be called office politics — not a university, a baseball team, or a movie studio. Some of my fellow soundmen were not happy with my preferred status, and I don't blame them. I think my sound department bosses were trying to even things, and I don't blame them either. *Black Room* finished on Friday, June 8. It wasn't until the following Tuesday, the day before *She Married Her Boss* started, that Bus Libott and I were told that it was our next assignment. Bus believed — and I agreed — that Harry Cohn probably intervened.

Diary, June 12, first day of production: "Cameraman, Leon Shamroy, paunchy, grouchy, profane. Talks like George Seid." I guess that meant he had a New York accent — with a snarl. "La Cava, short, brown-faced, bald; what hair he has is iron-gray. Heavy black brows over deep-set black eyes." His attitude that first morning seemed petulant and short-tempered.

La Cava's emphasis was on tempo. That first morning a scene required a switchboard girl to answer a flood of incoming calls. La

Cava demanded that she answer them at top speed. The young actress was intimidated; she forgot the mechanics of her scene and dealt with several calls without turning any switches or pulling any plugs. La Cava didn't seem to notice the error, but I put aside any notion of calling his attention to it. I decided to wait until I learned how he reacted to suggestions from the crew. Our second assistant director, Milt Carter, was not so prudent; he pointed out the error. He was rewarded by being told that he was fired; La Cava wanted him off of his picture, immediately. Our first assistant director, Norman Deming, persuaded La Cava to relent. Norman was a gigantic young man, about six and a half feet tall. La Cava was about five feet, five inches tall. As Norman Deming pleaded for Milt Carter's forgiveness, he addressed the top of La Cava's bald, brown head.

Bus Libott and I got the message; we wouldn't have the easy camaraderie of a Capra picture, a sense of participating in the filming. There wouldn't be incidents such as the one in *It Happened One Night,* when Capra invited help from the crew. We were filming a "story" scene; Clark Gable entered a Western Union telegraph office to send a telegram to his New York editor. It was an important story scene because it told the audience what Gable's intentions were. To Capra, however, no scene was merely a scene. He exploited Gable's buoyant mood and his impudent charm. As Gable entered the telegraph office, a lighted Western Union sign was in plain view. Gable stared at the sign, then addressed the girl behind the counter. "Send telegrams here?" he asked, brashly.

"All right, you amateur gagmen," Capra called out to the crew. "The girl has to say something to this fresh guy. What does she say?"

Bus Libott spoke up. "She looks him right in the eye and says, real friendly, "I'm just fine. How are all your folks?"

Capra laughed, the crew laughed; we shot it, and whenever I saw it in a theater the audience laughed. It was the kind of zany nonsequitur that Buster loved. Apparently there would be no participation of that kind with Gregory La Cava.

Bus Libott had qualities other than being an amateur gag man and superb boom man; he had the remarkable ability to establish rapport with almost anyone who came on our set. Clark Gable was downright fond of Bus; they were on a first-name basis the first day of production. He made friends with stars and nonstars, with leading ladies and extra girls—particularly extra girls. Colbert recognized Bus as soon as she came on the set. Her disdain for Columbia seemed to be gone, Bus said. The tremendous success of *It Happened One Night* and her Academy Award had changed her opinion of the patch-on-patch old studio on Gower Street. Bus was never shy. At the first opportunity he spoke to Colbert. "That was a pretty good one we made, wasn't it?" he asked. Bus said that for a moment he thought Colbert might go frosty on him but instead she smiled sweetly and said, "Yes, I guess it was."

The title *She Married Her Boss* told the story: Claudette Colbert marries her boss, Melvyn Douglas. Sidney Buchman's script dealt with the events leading to the marriage and the problems the marriage encountered. Colbert, we learn, loves Melvyn Douglas, but he marries her because he needs her business acumen. The script was well constructed, brisk, and witty, very much in the Bob Riskin tradition. And why not? Sidney Buchman and Bob Riskin had the same background: exposure to the New York theater. The producer of *She Married Her Boss* was Bob Riskin's brother, Everett. It is not unreasonable to believe that brother Bob gave his friend, Sidney Buchman, help and advice in writing the script.

There is a recurring theme in *She Married Her Boss;* if Bob Riskin did contribute to the screenplay, it may be his recurring theme: that of obtuse men who ignore beautiful, desirable women who love them. In *Platinum Blonde,* Robert Williams ignores Loretta Young; in *It Happened One Night,* Gable calls Claudette Colbert a "spoiled brat" and drives her from his bed; in *Broadway Bill,* Warner Baxter is unaware that Myrna Loy yearns for him; and now the audience is asked to believe that Melvyn Douglas marries beautiful, desirable Claudette Colbert for her brains, not her body. That was a recurring theme in Bob Riskin's work; now it appeared in Buchman's. Riskin made it work for him, and in Buchman's *She Married Her Boss* it was working again. The film was fast, interesting, and amusing. In her new household, Colbert has to cope with a neurotic, unmarried sister-in-law who tries to break up her marriage, and she encounters a nasty child from a previous marriage. The child, Edith Fellows, in beautifully written scenes, gives an excellent performance as a quintessential spoiled brat. The main story thread, of course, poses the question, "Can Melvyn Douglas see the light, see Colbert as a desirable woman rather than a business asset?" Of course he can, and once again, love conquers all.

I studied directors. I tried to learn what to do from the good ones and what not to do from the others. It was difficult to admire La Cava; he was what I described in my diary as "crabby," but I had to acknowledge that his credits were impressive. When he was about thirty years old, he directed a couple of silent films starring W. C. Fields (*So's Your Old Man, Running Wild*) which were mildly successful with the public. With the advent of sound, he directed a series of films, all well received, with a remarkable diversity of subject matter: *The Half-Naked Truth,* starring Lupe Velez and Lee Tracy, a "delightful comedy," a reviewer wrote; *Private Worlds,* a comedy-drama with Helen Hayes and Brian Aherne; a period piece, *The Affairs of Cellini,* starring Constance Bennett and Fredric March; and, in a complete change of pace, *Gabriel over the White House,* a political fantasy in which Walter Huston, elected president by fraud, is subsequently possessed by the spirit of the angel Gabriel and miraculously brings peace to the entire world.

She Married Her Boss was the kind of brisk, witty comedy that demanded speed. La Cava used a stock phrase to make his point; he used it often: "Keep it flowing. Let it ripple; keep it glib." La Cava's cast members nodded dutifully; they had excellent material to work with and they were talented performers. La Cava's exhortations to keep their scenes flowing, rippling, and glib probably did no harm and may have done some good.

In Hollywood, there are many legends about directors' mannerisms. Many use phrases repeatedly as La Cava did. Frank Capra's favorite was "Each word you hear is the last one." It was useful; I could see and hear the effect. It reminded the actors playing a scene that they must listen to what was said, react to what they heard, and formulate a reply, not merely respond with a line from a script.

Some of La Cava's instructions to his cast members seemed strange. From my diary, June 13, verbatim to his cast: "Keep it filled up with business. No story value here except to show relationship of woman serving man. Keep it glib. Don't let anything stand out—the story value will seep through the scene as a whole." Something seeped through; the scene between Colbert and Melvyn Douglas was fast, sharp, and amusing. Later, La Cava, to his players: "I liked the easy way you played the scene. Throw it away; don't think of anything but glibness and ease." Diary, June 14, La Cava: "Do what you feel—then your reflexes are handling you, which is the theory of it." Diary, July 1: "Lines don't matter. Words don't matter, except sense and feeling—the thing is to get the essence of them—what is said doesn't matter!!" The exclamation points were mine. I recall thinking that if what is said didn't matter, why bother to speak? Shoot a couple of close-ups of actors staring at one another, and allow the essence of the scene to ripple and seep through.

La Cava's instructions did seem to be up in the clouds somewhere. The term *double-talk* was not known in 1935; if it had been, I probably would have used it.

June 26: "Good scene between Colbert and Edith Fellows. How can a kid so young become so good a performer?" July 19: "La Cava in bad temper. No civil answers for anybody." La Cava was said to be a drinker. Perhaps a hangover was making him irritable.

Diary, July 20: "La Cava and Biberman—session of self-congratulation." Herbert Biberman was dialogue coach on our film. He was a New Yorker with stage experience; from time to time Columbia imported such people and gave them experience as potential movie directors, by assigning them to films as dialogue coaches. I resented the New York imports. To put it plainly, I was jealous. I felt that I had earned the right to be given consideration, but I was ignored, while the New Yorkers were given gold-plated invitations, as it were, to train as directors.

Diary, continuation, July 20: "Biberman flatters La Cava, who loves it. La Cava predicts that *She Married Her Boss* will make more money than *It Happened One Night*. Biberman agrees, of course."

We finished production of *She Married Her Boss* July 23. La Cava put on a wrap-up party—with an abundance of liquor. Frank Capra didn't believe in wrap-up parties. When we finished *Broadway Bill* and Buddy Coleman shouted, "That's it, folks—wrap it up," Capra looked at us, the members of his crew, and said, casually, "What do you say we make another picture sometime?" To a chorus of enthusiastic "yeahs" from the crew, he walked out, casually.

Present at La Cava's wrap-up party, among others, were Walter Wanger, Katharine Hepburn, Joan Bennett, Harry Cohn, and Sam Briskin. My diary informs me: "Much drinking by some of crew. La Cava gloriously stewed. Boos and hisses as Cohn and Briskin leave. NG!!!" It definitely was not good, deserving my triple-exclamation points. The boos and hisses were not vicious; they were almost good-natured, like cheers turned upside-down. It was the drinking, of course, but that was no excuse for such flagrant discourtesy. Cohn and Briskin were hard, proud men. The boos and hisses must have hurt them deeply.

Diary, July 29: "La Cava retakes. Talk to La Cava outside stage—friendly and confesses to drunkenness."

That is a remarkable entry, for more than one reason. Why was La Cava suddenly friendly? He had been brusque and distant during most of the filming. And why did he confide in me, a rank-and-file member of his crew? Perhaps I should have written "speaks of" or "mentions" instead of "confesses," but "confesses" is what I wrote, and it must have seemed like a confession at the time. The diary entry is cryptic; at times my entries were so cryptic that I have no idea what I meant by them. I wish I had written more, because I have no recollection of what La Cava actually said in the strange encounter.

In release, *She Married Her Boss* did moderately well. It was in that deadly category "pretty good." It did *not* make more money than *It Happened One Night*.

Audiences laughed at the bright, fast-paced scenes; reviewers were generally kind to the film. Opening grosses in New York were impressive, but the film never gained runaway momentum, as *It Happened One Night* did. I believe that La Cava failed to do what Capra did almost instinctively: humanize his players, make them believable, and cause the audience to care for them and wish desperately for them to solve their problems and live happily ever after.

Working with La Cava reminded me once more of the importance of tempo—the *correct* tempo—for a scene, a sequence, or a film. A picture with a great script and an excellent cast might seem to be director-proof, but it is not; if the pace lags or is rapid where it should not be, the film may fail.

La Cava need not have worried about the "pretty good" label on *She Married Her Boss*. His next film, for Universal, was a huge hit, *My Man Godfrey,* considered one of the best of the great screwball comedies of the 1930s. Perhaps, if I became a director, I should recall the lessons of *She Married Her Boss* and exhort my cast to be glib, let scenes flow and ripple, disregard the words of the script, and allow the essence of the comedy—or drama—to seep through. I never had a chance to ask my good friend, Carole Lombard, how her excellent scenes in *My Man Godfrey* managed to flow, ripple, and cause the comedy to seep through.

Bus Libott, my sound boom operator, knew what our next assignment was to be two days before I did. He knew a girl in the production office who typed the cast and crew lists of films going into production. Our next job was to be *Rich Man's Daughter.* The title was later changed to *She Couldn't Take It,* directed by Tay Garnett, starring Joan Bennett and George Raft. Only two of Columbia's departments were not vulnerable to Bus Libott's intelligence-gathering activities, because Denver Harmon, chief electrician, and Hal Sommers, boss of the grip department, had male assistants. Denver Harmon's assistant was known to everyone as Heavy Franklin, a most appropriate nickname. Al Franklin was not large or fat; he simply looked—and was—heavy.

Chief Electrician Denver Harmon was a rough-hewn man whose career began in Hollywood's earliest days. Electricians, whether they install conduit in high-rise buildings or wrestle heavy lighting units into place on a movie set, tend to be a hard-bitten breed, but when Denver Harmon spoke to his electricians, often at the top of his voice, they listened, respectfully. They knew that their boss often argued, loudly, nose to nose, with Harry Cohn in defense of his men.

There were other interesting men among Denver's electricians. There was Joe Sniff. I assumed that Sniff was a nickname; many of the juicers had oddball nicknames, but Joe really was Joseph Sniff, a little man with big ears, who had a wife who was obsessively jealous. She frequently called Denver Harmon's office to check on Joe, presumably concerned that he was romancing a glamorous movie queen instead of working. The calls were a nuisance, but Denver Harmon, a gentleman encased in a hard shell, gave orders that whenever Joe's wife called, she was to be spoken to patiently and courteously. Another electrician, "Muscat," earned his nickname because he consumed one bottle of Muscatel wine in the morning and another in the afternoon. Muscat's workstation was on the light platforms, called parallels in the studios, which were suspended above the walls of a set. It was hellishly hot on those light platforms. In spite of the wine, Muscat did his job well; he was alert and quick to respond to the gaffer's commands. Muscat's fellow electricians theorized, half in earnest, that the wine Muscat

consumed helped him to endure the searing heat of the light platform, cooling him by evaporating the alcohol in his body.

And there was Ug Wilson. Ug Wilson was a cheerful little man
who looked as though his face had been stepped on by a horse—a
large one. The nickname "Ug," of course, was short for ugly. He
may have had a given name, but no one ever used it. He was plainly
and simply Ug Wilson, boss of Columbia's Iron Gang, the hard-
bitten, hard-muscled electricians who rigged movie sets with
heavy, unwieldy lighting units; then, when filming was finished
and the set was to be taken down—"struck"—Wilson and his men
descended on it and stripped it of lights, cable, and switches.

Wilson's men belonged to the same union and were paid the
same wages as on-the-set juicers, but they lacked the social
niceties to work on the floor of a set. The typical Iron Gang electrician was not prepared to say, with a winning smile, "Miss Colbert, we have to move this lamp. Would you mind?" Or, to a leading man, "Look this way, please, we want to set this key light.
Thank you, sir." For an Iron Gang man to speak in such a genteel
fashion was not possible. As the teenager of today would say, "No
way!" The set riggers were a rough group, but Wilson had no problems with them. He was the boss—they obeyed his orders because
he knew how a set should be rigged and how it could be done efficiently and safely. His men were not merely strong-arm laborers;
they were skilled workmen, and they accorded Ug Wilson the respect he deserved.

I received my *She Couldn't Take It* script a few days before production began. The film was to be a comedy, not quite a screwball
comedy, although it had elements of screwball; it was a romantic
comedy in the Columbia tradition, with an undertone of drama and
genuine peril. The screenplay, by Oliver H. P. Garrett, was well
written and amusing, much in the Bob Riskin manner. It told the
story of a banker, Jason Van Dyke (Walter Connolly), in prison for
an income tax violation, who formed an unlikely friendship with
Ricardi (George Raft), in prison on a bootlegging charge. Van
Dyke found life in prison a respite from problems with his scan-
dal-prone, irresponsible family. Both men have resolved to have
no more problems with the law when they are released. The
banker, impressed by Ricardi's inherent integrity, persuades him
to accept the role of executor of his will. Ricardi accepts, reluctantly, and Van Dyke promptly dies of a heart attack. When

Ricardi is released, he keeps his promise and assumes his duties as executor. The story then becomes *The Taming of the Shrew* or, in the case of the Van Dyke family, the taming of a beautiful shrew, Carol (Joan Bennett) and the task of coping with a selfish, undisciplined family: Carol's giddy, feather-brained mother (Billie Burke), her philandering brother (Lloyd Nolan), and an incredibly hammy ham actor (Alan Mowbray), who is Billie Burke's protégé and houseguest.

The *She Couldn't Take It* script was well written, brisk, and amusing, but it needed a strong finish to provide laughter and excitement. In our script, the writer used a time-honored plot device, one that threatened dire peril, evoked high excitement, and, if done well, would produce a torrent of laughs: a rousing, climactic car chase.

In the world of drama, a chase climax originated long before the automobile was even dreamed of. In ancient times, let us say, our hero's ladylove is in the hands of dastardly villains. Our hero needs help to rescue her. He pleads with the local authorities (Roman Centurions, perhaps), but he is in bad odor with them, and they tell him (in Latin, of course), to get lost. Our hero then steals one of their patrol chariots and leads the enraged Centurions in a mad dash to rescue his loved one. Our script called for George Raft to steal a police car and lead a swarm of vengeful policemen to the rescue of Joan Bennett, held captive by mobsters.

The chase-climax device was so effective and so visual that it was used in some of the earliest silent films. The use of the automobile, for thrills and laughs, goes back to the time when strips of celluloid with sprocket holes were first run through primitive hand-cranked cameras. D. W. Griffith used the spindly vehicles of his day even before he made his historic move to the West Coast. Some of Griffith's chase-to-the-rescue films, such as *A Girl and Her Trust,* still exist, with ancient automobiles careening along the rutted dirt roads of 1911.

From the beginning of production, the filming of *She Couldn't Take It* went well. Tay Garnett, in a smooth, low-key manner, got good performances from his cast. Walter Connolly, as always, was superb, and George Raft, in an effortless way, was convincing as Ricardi. Clive Hirschhorn, the British film critic, wrote, in a review of *She Couldn't Take It,* "Raft gives his usual seamless performance by not seeming to perform at all." "Seamless" is hard to define; Hirschhorn himself probably couldn't define it, but it was an accurate one-word appraisal of George Raft's acting.

Diary, August 3: "Stage one. Interior 'Ham's' dressing room. Alan Mowbray is just plain wonderful as a vain, egotistical ham actor." Monday, August 5, we went to M-G-M to film on Metro's New York street. Diary: "Long wait for Raft. No explanation why. *Mutiny on the Bounty* and *A Tale of Two Cities* filming on the lot. People in costume everywhere; gives the whole M-G-M lot a two-hundred-year-old atmosphere."

On Sunday, August 11, I participated in an event that changed my life. I entered Columbia's annual golf tournament. The event was held at one of the world's great golf courses, Riviera Country Club, in Pacific Palisades, California. It was Depression time, and the cash-starved managers of the historic course were willing to turn it over, at a price, to Columbia's horde of hackers. The gods of golf must have wept bitter tears at the sight of their noble golf course being butchered by a hundred or more unskilled, uncaring hackers. I was one of them. Diary, written next day: "I took a seventeen on the first hole. Total score, 168." My score was probably worse than that. I didn't know the rules; I didn't count penalties for lost balls or balls out of bounds.

The gods of golf may have wept, but they got their revenge; I came away from the tournament hooked, forever, on the wonderful, maddening game of golf. I loved the game and I hated it; sometimes I played well and sometimes badly, always with the dream of playing the elusive perfect game. I even wrote a story about golf for *Rob Wagner's Script*. So, year after year, I signed up for Columbia's annual golf tournament. The events were as traditional as a session of the British House of Lords. Women were never invited to play, and language on the first tee and the tricks played on the golfers had a definitely raunchy aspect. Dinner, followed by presentation of prizes, was the highlight of the evening. Many of the prizes were surprisingly valuable, extorted from Columbia's suppliers, who were told, in effect, to donate valuable prizes—or else.

Harry Cohn made the presentation speeches; they were invariably earthy and profane. His presentation speech in 1935 to Richard Cahoon, one of Columbia's excellent film editors, was vintage Harry Cohn: "Winner, third prize, Dick Cahoon. Come up here, you good-looking bleep bleep bleep." Cahoon, a ruggedly handsome young man, approached the speakers' table. Columbia's executives were seated there, but Dick Cahoon was not abashed. If the president of the United States and the members of his cabinet were present, he would not have been abashed. Cohn: "Take your bleep bleeping prize. Why do you waste your time cutting bleeping film? You ought to be an actor; you're better-looking than any of those bleeping actors that think they're stars and want a lot of money. You come up to the office Monday; I'll make you a bleeping movie star."

Cahoon made exactly the right response. "OK," he said. "Monday morning. Five thousand a week to start." The dining room exploded in a roar of laughter. Briskin and Bischoff and the rest of the Columbia brass joined in. It was a wonderful moment; capital and labor, the bosses and the bossed, joined in a kind of camaraderie in an explosion of rough male laughter.

We resumed filming *She Couldn't Take It.* Diary, Monday, August 12: "Studio full of golf post-mortems. Stage 2—Interior prison library. Good scene, Raft and Connolly." On August 17, there was grim news. Diary: "Wiley Post and Will Rogers crack up in Alaska. Rumors—heard on radio—maybe not serious— later, confirmation, both killed; gloom on set and in whole studio."

We wrapped up principal photography August 22. Diary: "Process shots—slow going. To dinner and back. Work until 10:30 to finish Raft. Studio grapevine says he's getting $2000 per day 'overtime.' End of *Rich Man's Daughter.*" Apparently I was still using the original title.

For the next two weeks my crew and I did small jobs: tests, retakes, a two-reel comedy starring Leon Errol, directed by Del Lord.

My pessimistic friend, Gene Havelick, was the film editor assigned to *She Couldn't Take It.* He told me that Tay Garnett and the producer, B. P. Schulberg, agreed that *She Couldn't Take It* needed an even bigger, more exciting car chase than the one in the script, a car chase that would be a thrilling, laugh-packed climax for the film. Tay Garnett, himself a Mack Sennett gagman in the 1920s, knew the type of finale that was needed and the expert who could pull it off. Additional scenes were written and a director was selected: Del Lord.

In Frank Capra's autobiography, describing his own apprenticeship as a Sennett gagman, Capra wrote, "Del Lord was the highest-paid director on the Sennett lot" and "made the wildest car chases." Mack Sennett, in *King of Comedy,* wrote, "Del had been a racing driver and he came to us as a stunt man. For nerve and invention, Del Lord was about the best man we ever had."

The advent of sound destroyed Mack Sennett and his laugh factory. Jules White's Short Subjects Department was staffed with people from the Sennett and the Hal Roach lots. Charley Chase and his brother, James Parrott, came from Hal Roach. So did Billy Gilbert, Snub Pollard, and James Horne. Mack Sennett talent came to Columbia en masse: Felix Adler, Vernon Dent, Harry Langdon, Andy Clyde, Chester Conklin, Hank Mann, Heinie Conklin, Arthur Ripley, Johnny Gray, Al Giebler, Ewart Adamson, Harry Edwards, Ray Hunt—and Del Lord. Jules White found Del selling used cars in Burbank and recruited him to direct two-reel comedies for Columbia. The Three Stooges had made several two-reelers before Del came to Columbia. They were fairly successful comedies, directed by Lou Breslow, Raymond McCarey, Charles Lamont, and Clyde Bruckman, but when Del Lord began directing them in February 1935, the Stooges' popularity zoomed skyward. When the Stooges came to Columbia, despite their year at M-G-M, they were still essentially vaudeville performers, using stand-up verbal routines; even their hitting and slapping routines were done vaudeville style. Del Lord defined the Stooges' relationship and brought them into the world of sight gags, special effects magic, and outrageous but recognizable stories. And so, Del Lord, already working for Columbia, was selected to direct the *She Couldn't Take It* second unit. He responded by filming a car chase that today is regarded as a classic of its kind.

We began filming on September 5. Diary: "Shooting in Pasadena, first scenes near Devil's Gate Dam. Many moves, lots of excitement—chases, skids—my hunch to move sound truck. Packard hits camera!"

In our story, Raft, doubled by Jack Long, a stunt driver, throws a wrench through the windshield of a police car, inducing the outraged cop to pursue him. In one rehearsal it seemed to me that our sound truck might be a little too close to the action. I found our sound truck driver playing poker in the shade of the grip truck. He moved our sound truck grudgingly. When we shot the scene and Jack Long threw the wrench, his throwing motion gave the steering wheel an unintentional twitch, and the car sped directly toward the A camera, clipped off the front leg of the tripod, and careened directly over the place where our sound truck had been. It happened so quickly the camera crew didn't have time to be frightened. Our assistant cameraman, the redoubtable Freddie Dawson, caught the camera before it toppled forward and saved both the camera and the film of the scene. If our sound truck hadn't been moved, the Packard would have smashed into us. It was possible that Hank Connors, my recording machine operator and I might not have been killed.

The days that followed were filled with high-speed chase shots: camera car running shots, when the camera led the ever-growing number of pursuers. Del Lord loved the comedy of exaggeration— the number of pursuers grew so large that its very size—a quarter of a mile of cars, motorcycles, trucks, even a fire engine—was comic. When Raft took one branch of a road and the pursuers took another, he yelled and gestured to them to correct their mistake. We filmed a "motorcycle spit"—a dangerous stunt. Jack Long, in the speeding Packard, drove straight at a pair of approaching motorcycle officers. Del chose riders with skill and an abundance of courage. We filmed the scene twice, once in a medium shot and once head-on from the camera car. The motorcycle riders displayed great courage and skill; waiting until the last split-second before turning aside. There were other potentially dangerous stunts. In one scene, the speeding Packard hits a peddler's wagon broadside and cuts it in half, leaving the driver of the wagon unhurt, screaming his rage. The angry driver was Walter Brennan. I wondered why Walter Brennan, whom I considered a very good actor, accepted a potentially dangerous stunt job. I knew him well; I had worked with him on several Buck Jones and Tim McCoy Westerns, as well as the Stooges' first Columbia short, *Woman Haters*. He did well in bit parts and was gaining stature as an actor. I hoped that it wasn't financial pressure that induced him to take the dangerous job.

The heart-stopping high spot of our chase came on the last day of shooting. Diary entry: "—then train. Jack Long misses by inches!!" The entry is cryptic, but the double exclamation point is pretty eloquent about how I felt.

The scene was a race with a train, with Jack Long in the stolen Packard crossing in front of it at the last possible moment. We shot the scene in the Simi Valley. There are ten thousand houses there now, but in 1935 it was flat, open range land. A two-lane road paralleled and then crossed the Southern Pacific railroad tracks—a diagonal crossing that could be made at high speed.

When we shot the scene Jack Long seemed to be lagging. I saw Del Lord make a disappointed gesture; to me it meant that he thought the run would have to be aborted. Jack began to gain on the train, but it still looked hopeless. When the Packard drew abreast of the engine cab it still looked as though Jack would have to abort the run or crash, but with a final burst of speed he half-skidded across the track, inches in front of the engine. Inches? Everyone who saw it said there was *no* space between the engine and the Packard.

We were all shaken, even Del Lord, who had devised and directed hazardous stunts for most of his working life. Jack Long drove back, parked the Packard, and lit a cigarette. He laughed when he saw how shaken we were, and held out his hands, one with the cigarette, the other with a lighted match. His hands were rock-steady.

The decision to film the train-car scene last was an eminently practical one. The rest of the chase was safely on film, and if Jack Long and the Packard were demolished, some expert film editing would be employed to convince the audience that Raft won the race with the train.

Later, in 1941, our car chase appeared again in the nation's theaters, in a Columbia two-reel comedy, *So You Won't Squawk,* starring Buster Keaton. The producer, Hugh McCollum, replaced all close-ups of George Raft with close-ups of Buster Keaton, and now we had the man with the Great Stone Face leading our wild, preposterous chase through the streets and the countryside of 1935 Los Angeles.

I knew what my next major assignment was to be before a start date was announced and even before the final draft script was completed.

There had been much speculation about Frank Capra's next picture. *Variety* printed a rumor that Columbia had acquired the novel *Opera Hat,* by Clarence Buddington Kelland, and that Robert Riskin was writing a screenplay. I encountered Capra in Columbia's main screening room. He greeted me and in his bantering way asked, "Are you ready to go again next month?" I assured him I was ready. "*Opera Hat?*" I asked. Capra nodded. "Not a good title. We'll find a better one." He did find a better one: *Mr. Deeds Goes to Town.*

20

Mr. Deeds Goes to Town wasn't scheduled to start until mid-December. My crew and I worked on the usual mix of retakes, tests, and added scenes and a new source of short-duration assignments, Columbia's rapidly expanding program of two-reel comedies. On September 10 we were back with Del Lord, filming a comedy, *Oh, My Nerves!* starring Monte Collins and Tom Kennedy. We went on location to Malibu Lake for two days, with an overnight stay at a rustic inn on the shores of the lake. It is noteworthy that in 1935 the budget of a two-reel comedy provided for location filming and an overnight stay. Ten years later, when I directed two-reelers, budgets were the same but costs had increased, and even short-distance location filming was too expensive, and an overnight stay was completely out of the question.

After the two-reel comedy, we were assigned to a Western, *The Gallant Defender*, starring Charles Starrett, Columbia's effort to create a Western star from whole cloth, as it were. Starrett was a handsome, physically impressive young man with a background of family wealth and Ivy League credentials as a football star at Dartmouth. His sudden elevation from football hero to Western hero, to take his place among the great Western stars—William S. Hart, Tom Mix, Buck Jones, Tim McCoy, Ken Maynard, and John Wayne—was probably the result of Harry Cohn's king-maker urge. Through the years, Cohn attempted to create stars. His most notable effort was his high-pressure campaign to elevate Kim Novak to sex-goddess status, to supplant Rita Hayworth, whom Cohn felt had betrayed him.

275

The Gallant Defender was Starrett's first film for Columbia. In seventeen years, from *The Gallant Defender* in 1935 to his last film for Columbia, *The Rough, Tough West* in 1952, he starred in an amazing 135 of Columbia's low-budget Westerns.

We finished the Starrett Western on October 8. On the ninth, we were assigned to another two-reel comedy, this one with the Stooges, *Three Little Beers*, directed by Del Lord. Many Stooge fans rate it as one of their best.

Three Little Beers was the Stooges' tenth comedy for Columbia, but it was my first since I served as sound technician on the musical two-reeler, *Woman Haters*, in 1934. I found the Stooges vastly different. Directed by Del Lord, with scripts often written for them by veteran Mack Sennett gagman Felix Adler, they now displayed a manic, destructive energy that demolished homes, automobiles, human dignity—and a golf course.

Our first two days of filming were on location at Rancho Golf Course, not far from the Beverly Hills boundary. Rancho had been an exclusive private golf course, but hard times made it possible for Columbia to rent it for two days and inflict incredible mayhem on the beautiful course. Del Lord gave Moe scenes in which he attempts to hit a golfball from a fairway lie. Moe digs up a large divot with every swing and soon the first fairway of Rancho Golf Course was littered with enormous divots. When Curly's golfball lands up in a tree, he retrieves the ball by chopping the tree down. Larry, on an immaculately cared-for putting green, finds what he thinks is a weed. He attempts to pull it up. Our special-effects men had rigged it so that when Larry pulls the inconspicuous little weed, which apparently had endless roots, the entire putting green was torn up. In our film, an actor portrayed an excitable Italian greenskeeper who screamed with outrage as the Stooges destroyed his putting green. We had a real-life counterpart; the Rancho Golf Course greenskeeper. He was not Italian; he did not scream with outrage; he agonized silently, as Moe, Larry and Curly heaped indignities upon his beloved golf course.

On October 12, we filmed scenes of the Stooges loading a mountain of beer kegs on a truck. We shot the scene at the loading dock of old stage seven. A still picture of that scene is one of the most widely seen pictures of the Stooges' activities: Curly is perched on top of a precarious mountain of beer kegs, while Moe and Larry supervise from ground level. Inevitably, in our film, the beer kegs break loose and fall from the truck, and we had what Del Lord called a "barrel chase." Del chose a street on a steep hill, in the Edendale district of Los Angeles, about a half-mile from the site of the old Mack Sennett studio. Del told me he had used the street many times for sequences similar to ours.

The scenes we shot were colorful and exciting—stuntmen leaping over kegs that threatened to knock them down; Moe, frantically running to stay atop a runaway keg, like a lumberjack "birling" to remain upright on a spinning waterborne log; a traffic officer, at the foot of the hill, outraged at the cascade of runaway beer kegs that threaten him and finally knock him down. We filmed two days of interiors; like the barrel chase and the golf course sequences, the scenes were fast-paced, violent, and laugh-packed.

A day after we finished *Three Little Beers*, we started another two-reel comedy with Andy Clyde, *Hot Paprika*, in which Andy quells a revolution in the Central American Republic of Paprika. Making two-reel comedies with Del Lord was pleasant; *Hot Paprika*, directed by Preston Black (Jules White's brother, Jack White), was far from pleasant. When he headed Educational Pictures, Jack White had been Jules's boss; now Jules was Jack White's boss. The brothers quarreled, and production slowed down. Diary, Tuesday, October 15: "Start Jack White Andy Clyde comedy. Unpleasant going. Brothers White argue every setup. Time wasted. Should have been easy day. Work until 11:30 P.M." Diary, Friday, October 18: "Interior Cantina, stage 7. One-legged Earle Bunn back with his Tommy-gun. Stink of gunpowder all day. More quarreling, sinful waste of time. Work until past midnight, then they decide we can't finish. Home about one A.M." We finished *Hot Paprika* with a short day, Saturday, October 19. Diary: "Home 5 P.M. Dinner, dead tired, to bed 7 P.M. with kids still lively."

We, the sound crew, had all of Sunday to rest up, to prepare for our next assignment. On Monday, October 21, we started a B picture, *You May Be Next*, directed by Albert Rogell, whom I did not admire. I tried to avoid the assignment, but Eddie Hahn pointed out that production was booming; every sound channel and every sound crew was needed to keep up with the frantic pace of production. It was true; 1935 was a tremendously busy year at Columbia. About sixty feature-length pictures were made, ranging in importance from films made by Capra, Josef Von Sternberg, and

Richard Boleslavsky to B-minus films and low-budget Westerns directed by Lambert Hillyer, Ross Lederman, and Albert Rogell, and twenty-four of the new two-reel comedies added to the production load. It was exhausting. Crews went from one assignment to another, with only a half-day of rest. Many of our Sundays were spent recovering from participation in the infamous Saturday morning to Sunday morning Columbia Frolic.

When we began production of *You May Be Next*, we found to our surprise, a quieter, less frenetic Al Rogell. Bus and I wondered if someone from the front office had admonished him. We worked only to 7 P.M. that first day. The second day we filmed in Griffith Park, only a few miles from Gower Gulch, but with hidden glades that looked like tropical rain forest. My diary noted that we encountered strong winds, "strong enough to rock the sound truck." Strong winds, in autumn, mean trouble in southern California. Diary, October 23: "Big brush fires. High wind. Many homes burned—Altadena, Mount Lowe and Malibu."

Al Rogell had toned down his hyperactive directorial style, but on October 26 the legendary Rogell returned. During the day we filmed interiors, then journeyed to Long Beach for a night of filming at an impressive place called the Banning Estate. Rogell reverted to type: shouting at cast and crew, making easy scenes into difficult ones. We wrapped up 6:30 Sunday morning. I had driven my own car to the location, and the memory of my drive home frightens me to this day. Fatigued and sleepy, I recalled passing saltwater marshes on the outskirts of San Pedro Harbor. I woke with a start, many miles away, near the Beverly Hills boundary. Fast asleep, apparently, I had coped with traffic and navigated well enough to find myself a few miles from home. Fear caught up to me then. I was so shaken that the last few miles of my trip were an ordeal. I have never found anyone—psychologist, psychiatrist, or know-it-all layman—who could explain what happened to me. Was part of me sound asleep while some obscure part of my brain guided me home safely? My diary is quite matter-of-fact about the incident: "Shot all night. Finish 6:30 Sunday morning. Dangerous drive home."

On November 9 I replaced a mixer who had the flu. The film was *Lady of Secrets*, starring Ruth Chatterton, directed by Marion Gering. Nothing about the film pleased me. The script was heavy-handed and melodramatic. Gering did very little to tone down what seemed to me to be gross overracting. Diary, November 13: "Glen

R. still sick. Take call for Gering picture, stage two, 9 A.M. Stage ice-cold; someone forgot to turn on portable heaters. Chatterton's emotional scenes very hammy—tremolo voice—sounds like an *After Dark* revival. Gering's pacing of scenes slow, and so is filming. Reason: indecision and lack of drive. Late in day Eddie H. tells me I will finish *Lady of Secrets*."

When *Lady of Secrets* was released, "Chic" of *Variety* agreed with what I noted in my diary. He wrote, "A creaky and old-fashioned production of a story hard to swallow; in its dialog and playing it suggests the days when *East Lynne* and *Ten Nights in a Bar Room* were favorites." I had compared the writing and acting to *After Dark*, another old-time play that had been revived to be lampooned.

Mr. Deeds Goes to Town was still three weeks distant. We were assigned to another Western, *The Mysterious Avenger*, with Charles Starrett, again directed by Dave Selman. A new producer was in charge. Harry Decker had been head of Columbia's film-editing department. *Mysterious Avenger* was his first film as a producer. The usual troubles beset us. Dave and Harry Decker chose a quiet Sunday to go location hunting. They picked an ideal location near Iverson's Ranch, but when we arrived to begin filming Monday morning, we discovered that oil wells and an oil-pumping station were our busy, noisy neighbors. We had to pull up stakes and travel several miles to find another location.

When we filmed interiors Dave Selman and Harry Decker made a decision that damaged crew morale and hurt their picture. Crews were accustomed to working late, tired and hungry. They understood that money was saved if they worked late to finish a sequence. It was the custom, however, not to begin a new sequence after six o'clock. Dave and Harry Decker, eager to make their film on schedule and under budget, broke the unwritten rule and began a new sequence. Diary: "Selman and Decker start a new sequence after 6 P.M. Crew angry, hungry, and tired. Slowdown, not deliberate, but who wants to put out for people who don't give a damn about them?" That was a reasonably accurate account of the feeling on the set. Scenes took an agonizingly long time to set up and often, under the pressure of time, were sloppily acted.

Ben Kline, the cameraman, would not sacrifice quality for speed. His work was on the screen; if his photography was poor, no excuses were valid. Bus Libott and I felt the same way. We believed that we were the number one sound crew and couldn't afford a single badly recorded scene, even in a low-budget, carelessly made Western. The result was slow photography and slow sound, and a long, unpleasant session, until nearly midnight, with only a few badly acted scenes done.

We had an early call for location filming the next day. Diary, Tuesday, November 19: "Awoke 5 A.M. Dark and cold. Leave studio 5:45. Dark until halfway through San Fernando Valley. Fields white with frost."

We wrapped *The Mysterious Avenger* on November 27. Bus Libott wondered whether the film would be as corny as the title.

On November 28 I received my invitation to the 1935 Academy Awards Dinner. The guest of honor that year was the noted British writer, H. G. Wells. Betty bought a dress, and I unearthed the formal outfit I bought for the England trip. We attended our first Academy Award celebration Wednesday, December 4, 1935, at the famous Hollywood Roosevelt Hotel. We were seated at a table with a contingent from the United Artists Sound Department; most of our table mates had been my antagonists, responsible for my leaving UA. We were polite to one another. I should have thanked them for creating the cabal that motivated my leaving UA and going to Columbia. Dinner was served; my diary records the meal as "skimpy." Directors Frank Lloyd and Frank Capra greeted the guests. Cecil B. De Mille then spoke at length, verbose and pompous, presumably praising H. G. Wells but managing to get much self-praise into his long discourse. Charlie Chaplin addressed the diners briefly. "Chaplin OK," my diary noted. "Very British." After a series of long speeches praising him, H. G. Wells rose to speak. He paused—a dramatic pause—then said, "Hollywood leaves me speechless," and sat down. There was a strange reaction; I could hear exclamations of disbelief, followed by a buzz of astonished comment. A few people applauded. I joined, whole-heartedly. My ex-antagonists from United Artists Studio looked at me disapprovingly. Diary: "Capra adjourns the dinner. Everyone to the Blossom Room." The adjournment gave many of the guests something they sorely needed: the opportunity to visit a rest room. My wife joined a throng in the ladies' room. She was delighted by what she saw there: great ladies of the screen, among them Norma Shearer, Joan Crawford, Miriam Hopkins, and Anita Louise, waiting in line for the one free toilet because none of them had a dime for the coin-operated ones.

21

I was sleepless the night of the Academy Awards, caught up in the glamor and the excitement of that memorable evening. I had heard, seen, and applauded the great novelist H. G. Wells as he delivered the immortal put-down "Hollywood leaves me speechless" at that Academy Award dinner.

Sleep eluded me. I thought of the past ten years. An incredible series of events brought me to where I now found myself: in my own home, my wife sleeping quietly beside me, my son and daughter asleep in their room. In those ten years my life, as in the past, had been shaped by odd and unpredictable events. My association with Frank Capra was a fluke, an accident, the result of Harry Blanchard's unwillingness to spend a long, cold night on location for *Ladies of Leisure*. The association with Capra gave me preferred status. I was assigned to the best pictures and was assured of a paycheck every week of the year. But I was not content. I had fallen in love with the moviemaking business when I first walked through the Formosa Avenue gate of United Artists studio, and almost from the beginning I had the distant, elusive goal of becoming a director. As 1935 was drawing to a close I wondered whether the new year would be as eventful and exciting as the year just ending. At the time I did not realize that the new decade would be more exciting for me than anything in the past.

The years that followed included great events and great films. The 1930s have often been called the Golden Age of the Cinema, and I participated in the filming of many of the golden ones: Frank

Capra's monumental *Lost Horizon,* his award-winning *You Can't Take It with You,* Leo McCarey's *The Awful Truth,* and Howard Hawks's *Only Angels Have Wings,* the film that began Rita Hayworth's rise to stardom. The Golden Days, however, were darkened by the growing threat of war.

Diary: September 1, 1939: "Second World War begins, France and England reject Hitler's 16 demands. German troops smash into Poland." Then we too were at war. In the beginning, there were bitter defeats. The disaster of Pearl Harbor, the loss of the Philippine Islands. They were bitter days, but we rallied from defeat and with our allies crushed two powerful enemies half a world apart, demonstrating to the world that we were a great and powerful nation.

Columbia, like all the other studios, made patriotic war films during the war. Many of the films glorified the American fighting man. I was the sound technician on one of them, *Destroyer,* with Edward G. Robinson and Glen Ford. We filmed aboard a newly commissioned destroyer, the USS *Abner Read,* during its shakedown cruise. The crew was a mixed lot. Some of them were new recruits; others were survivors of ships that had been sunk in the desperate naval battles of the Solomon Islands. Others had been aboard ships sunk at Pearl Harbor.

We filmed scenes of the destroyer's guns firing at a towed target, depth charge launchings, and antiaircraft firing. The crew was green and it was apparent that much improvement was needed. The destroyer's five-inch guns were inaccurate and nearly sunk the small minesweeper towing the target, and the twenty- and forty-millimeter antiaircraft guns came dangerously close to shooting down the plane towing the aerial target. The ship's captain, an experienced officer, was furious.

Midway through our shakedown cruise our practice mission suddenly was changed to a more serious mission. The USS *Abner Read* was ordered to proceed at full speed to the Santa Barbara area to deal with the reported sighting of a Japanese submarine.

Our dash northward was canceled about an hour after we began, but for a brief time we had the threat of combat with the enemy. Late that evening we returned to the destroyer base in San Diego, sobered by the thought that we might have been in combat.

The USS *Abner Read* had a short life and a tragic fate. In 1942 in the battle to retake the Philippine Islands, the ship was hit amidships by a Kamikaze pilot and was sunk within minutes. There were few survivors. Most of the officers we had met aboard were lost.

In the waning months of the war there was my chance meeting with Frank Capra and his electrifying words, "Go to see Harry Cohn." Cohn gave his grudging permission for me to become a director: "Report to Hugh McCollum." McCollum was a producer in Columbia's short subjects department. That meant that if I became a director, my assignment would probably not be a million-dollar film starring Cary Grant and Rosalind Russell with a generous schedule and a superb script by Bob Riskin but rather a two-reel slapstick comedy with a four-day schedule, frugal budget, and problems with special effects.

When my sound department boss, Eddie Hahn, told me what my new assignment was to be, I was forced to make a difficult decision. I realized that I was taking a big risk leaving the security of a weekly paycheck.

I made the choice. It was do or die. I was going to be a director or, as Harry Cohn elegantly phrased it, "fall on my ass." I expected to be taken off the payroll.

To my surprise I was told that the "front office" had ordered that I be kept on the sound department payroll until further notice. I realized that it was not the front office that kept me on the weekly payroll of the sound department but the tough ruler of Columbia Pictures who gave that order, Harry Cohn. He had instructed my bosses, John Livadary and Eddie Hahn, not to disclose that it was he who had requested that I be kept on the payroll. He probably didn't want his image as a tough, tightfisted tycoon to be destroyed.

As Cohn ordered, I met with Hugh McCollum in his office in the rickety old building attached to Sound Stage 7, which functioned as the short subjects department building. I knew McCollum well. I had been the soundman on several of his two-reel films. McCollum had served for several years as Harry Cohn's secretary and was rewarded by a promotion to producer. I sensed that he was not delighted with the prospect of entrusting a rookie director to make his two-reel films. Cohn's directive was apparently an elastic one. It did not order him to give me a picture to direct. It appeared to be more of a "Use him if you can" directive. I soon discovered that McCollum wanted recognition for his work. It irked him that the Columbia brass paid little attention to the two-reelers.

At Columbia, the two-reelers were next to the bottom rung of the prestige ladder. Only the serials ranked lower than two-reelers. Mac, as I later called him, wanted his two-reelers to be made efficiently and well. He produced one-half of the short subject films. His competitor, a producer-director named Jules White, produced the other half of the program. After several weeks I informed Mac that I was withdrawing from the soundmen's union to devote my full time to directing. Mac questioned my decision, but when I assured him of my determination he shrugged and gave me Del Lord's office next to his. Del had progressed to feature films at Columbia. The next morning I was enjoying the feeling of having my first office, when Mac entered and tossed a couple of old scripts on my desk.

"Rewrite these scripts. Change them around as much as you can so nobody will recognize them but keep the main story lines. They're pretty good. I'll pay you four hundred bucks each. Go to work." I gave those four hundred–dollar scripts my best thousand-dollar effort. I studied them. The structure was crude. I made note of the number of scenes. I timed the scenes with a stopwatch. I marked and counted the gags and laugh lines. I marked each laugh line and gave it a rating of one to five. Reworking those scripts proved to be a priceless education. If I had been given an assignment to write an original script, I might have floundered. But the scripts I was working with had been made into films. As Mac reminded me, the stories were usable. I worked fast and gave each script a maximum effort. Having a tried and true framework with a proven story structure was a great help. I concentrated on changing the locales and of course character names. A drugstore, for instance, might be recognized, so I changed the locale to a restaurant. Most of all, I changed the dialogue.

I discovered, at least to my own satisfaction, that even as a novice I wrote better dialogue than the men who were the star writers of the silent era. That was not ego or an inflated opinion. I did, even as a beginner, write good dialogue. Del Lord, for instance, a master of visual comedy, wrote stilted, clumsy dialogue.

I brought my rewritten scripts to Mac. He read them while I waited. This was a suspenseful and crucial moment for me. I would either go forward or . . . Mac put the pages down and gave me a faint smile. "I'll have a few more changes; we'll go over them later. Now let's see about getting you your money." He not only handed me the checks but new contracts for two more rewrites. It made me feel important to sign those contracts. I soon realized when I read them that the main reason for the contract was to obtain from the writer all rights, in perpetuity, in every means of communication, motion pictures, television (unheard of at that time), and any other media then not discovered. Every writing assignment I had at Columbia required me to relinquish all rights in perpetuity.

Finally, one momentous day, Mac informed me that I was to direct a picture. It was not to be one of his cherished two-reelers. It was wartime and my assignment was a propaganda film for the Office of War Information (OWI). During the war, all the studios, as part of their patriotic effort, cooperated by producing training films for the armed forces and propaganda films for the OWI.

They provided the script and Columbia Studio was assigned the project. This film was to warn of the danger of enemy espionage. The theme was "Loose Lips Sink Ships." Columbia assigned Hugh McCollum to produce. Mac received the script. It had the lurid title *It's Murder*. It was to be shot silent, with voiceover. It told the story of a young soldier who devises a code used in letters to his mother. The purpose of the code is to keep his mother informed of his whereabouts. One of his coded letters informs his mother that he will soon embark upon a surprise invasion of a Japanese-held island. The proud mother tells a neighbor. The neighbor tells a friend who tells a friend. Inevitably, a spy overhears the information. The Japanese learn of the invasion plan and inflict great losses on the American invasion force. The final scene depicts the mother receiving a telegram from the war department informing her of her son's death.

When I read the script, I had my first inspiration as a director. I suggested to Mac that it could be effective and hard-hitting if it had a better ending. I felt that the telegram was downbeat and dull. It had to be downbeat, because that was the whole point of the story—the young soldier had to be killed, but I felt it did not have to be dull.

"Suppose we shoot a scene of the dead soldier, lying face on the beach with the waves gently rolling over him," I suggested.

McCollum approved immediately. "It's a strong finish. Somebody may think it is too strong, but if OWI wants to make a point, this finish sure as hell does it. It will cost about seven hundred dollars to take a crew to the beach and shoot it, but it will be worth it."

"How about the front office, will they O.K. it?" I asked.

Mac replied, "They don't read the scripts. They don't even look at the pictures when they're finished. All they care about is what they cost. Let's shoot it."

We made the picture. It was shot in the style of a newsreel. The film was narrated by an excellent actor, who provided just the right amount of strength and authority to the commentary. The effect for the subject matter was much better than if we had shot the film conventionally with dialogue. Mac was right. The Columbia executives were not interested in seeing our little one-reeler. Some of the Columbia film editors who managed to see our production complimented us. We sent the negative and print to the OWI in Washington. The response came quickly. McCollum received letters from Elmer Davis, the man in charge of the OWI, and Stanton Griffis, a political powerhouse in Washington. Both letters praised our efforts.

This was something new for McCollum — recognition. The letters were no routine thank-you letters. They mentioned details that indicated that they had seen the film. Mac was euphoric with his sudden recognition. The praise delighted Mac and I believe motivated him to assign me to my first writing and directing chore, a two-reel Three Stooges comedy. I was going to be a *real* director — one who was paid to make films people paid to see.

Epilogue: The Story Continues—
Leonard Maltin and Joseph McBride
Interview Edward Bernds

McBride: You once told me you thought *Mr. Deeds Goes to Town* [1936] was "the perfect motion picture story." Why did you say that?

Bernds: The amount of sympathy, empathy, whatever you want to call it, that was generated for Mr. Deeds [Gary Cooper]. The several times I went to see it in a theater, you could just feel the way the audience hoped and wished that he would speak up. You remember the scene when Mr. Deeds is being fitted with the monkey suit, as he calls it? And that little touch of democracy when he says to Raymond Walburn [his valet], "Don't ever get on your knees again"? Robert Riskin was a writer! I think he was one of the greatest writers that ever lived.

Maltin: Do you remember Riskin coming to the set?

Bernds: Coming to the set, but not staying there. Frank Capra was, shall we say, not egotistical but in control of his own destiny. He didn't need any help.

McBride: Of course, the script was in good shape.

Bernds: Oh, yes, when I read that script, it was all there.

Maltin: Through the years, it has been said that Gary Cooper was so low-key that his fellow actors didn't feel he was putting anything out.

Bernds: I thought he was great. He was, of course, the perfect choice for Mr. Deeds. Gable couldn't do it. Cooper just was perfect for the part. I sort of think Robert Riskin wrote it with him in mind.

McBride: You worked with Jean Arthur.

Bernds: Very insecure. Columbia had a system of hiring messenger boys, all under the command of Cap Duncan. He looked like a bank president and sat at the front desk. Instead of a beautiful girl, Cap Duncan was there. He had a staff of messenger boys, and gradually those messenger boys were graduated to assistant directors. During the war, as part of the war effort, they replaced the seventeen- and eighteen-year-old boys with girls. So there were messenger girls. We were making a picture, and one of these messenger girls was watching the scene being filmed. Through the microphone—as you know, a soundman hears a lot of things he shouldn't—I heard Jean Arthur call the assistant director over and say, "I want that girl out of here—she's so darned pretty and I'm so old." Talk about insecurity! The way a good cameraman photographed her, she was beautiful.

Maltin: Did you ever see Capra on the set give direction to his leading actors?

Bernds: Much was done on the set with stand-ins. Capra and his actors would sit around a table, a circle maybe, and discuss it. He would come on the set with a kind of joking manner. He had a great way of fixing a problem with a few words.

Maltin: There were no exterior sets at Columbia, were there?

Bernds: No. Columbia was built around houses that they bought and connected up. It was really a patchwork. With all this conglomeration, there was a little area in the center that we called Columbia Park. The writers' building overlooked it. And sometimes we'd shoot there. I remember six or eight times during my years as a soundman, we went into Columbia Park to shoot close-up scenes on a park bench.

The Columbia Ranch [in Burbank] was wonderful. That was a great acquisition. The sound department was sent out there to determine its feasibility in terms of noise. The Shangri-La set [in *Lost Horizon,* 1937] was built right on the street [Hollywood Way]. One of the problems with the lights at night was that they would disturb the pigeons and they would start making noise. On several shots, the propman would shoot the pigeons and we would get the quiet that way.

McBride: You wrote in your diaries that the first time you recorded Sam Jaffe as the High Lama he was almost inaudible; he was so quiet playing a two-hundred-year-old man.

Bernds: Yes, every time we did it. Capra never demanded a playback. In the early days, you cut a wax recording for the director. But it was a waste of time, and by then we didn't have playback capability on the set. You got to rely on the mixer.

Maltin: Those enormous spectacle scenes in *Lost Horizon*— would you record live sound?

Bernds: We shot everything live. Capra wanted to shoot it that way. We came to be criticized by Harry Cohn for shooting sound with a scene where nothing is heard but footsteps. Unless there was obviously no sound at all, we always shot sound.

Maltin: Tell us about shooting in the ice house for the plane crash scene.

Bernds: On *Dirigible* [1931], Capra had been bothered that they were supposed to be at the South Pole, and no frosty breath was shown. Dry ice will stick to your mouth and burn you, so he had little wire cages built for the actors to use. But Hobart Bosworth swallowed some of the dry ice—lost some of his teeth. On *Lost Horizon,* in the ice house, they used to keep the camera warm by keeping a Barney [a flexible insulation covering] over it. There were no technical problems with the sound. It was just cold. It took a long time to change setups there, so we, the soundmen, spent a lot of time there.

McBride: How was Ronald Colman to work with?

Bernds: The perfect English gentleman. He never warmed up to anybody on the crew. Very professional. Once when we were shooting all night, at midnight, Colman ordered champagne. Not for the crew—not even for Joe Walker [the cinematographer]— but for the elite—Capra, etc. They partook of the champagne, and they did loosen up. Colman and Capra performed for each other. Colman loved the English music hall songs, and he used the Cockney accent and was very good at it.

McBride: What do you think of *Lost Horizon*?

Bernds: I didn't think it was very good. My feelings about it are so personal that I can't be impersonal about it. By the way, the author, James Hilton, visited the set. There are some people who have a peculiar way of walking, as if they are about to fall over. He seemed to be leaning over as he walked, and that is the only impression I have of him. I didn't get to talk to him—I would have liked to. I did talk to Fannie Hurst quite a bit when we made *Lummox* [1930].

Maltin: Let's move on to *The Awful Truth* [1937]. Are the legendary tales of director Leo McCarey making up the story as he went along true?

Bernds: No. Every evening, he would have a conference with the writer. However, he did improvise in ways that were common on the set. I know he was very, very good at comedy and would make the most of every comic opportunity.

Maltin: Tell us about McCarey's way on the set.

Bernds: This was a wonderful, no-tension set. Harry Cohn would come in on the set, but McCarey had such a reputation that Cohn wasn't going to interfere. McCarey would be playing piano on the set and pretend to be thinking. Incidentally, do you know about the thing that caused the tremendous breakup between McCarey and Cohn? Harold Lloyd wanted to come on the lot and see McCarey. Harry Cohn was paranoid about visitors and gave Cap Duncan instructions that no discretion was allowed. So Harold Lloyd came to see McCarey and was turned away. When McCarey found that out, he went livid. He went up to Harry Cohn's office and nobody knows what happened there, but. . . . Cohn needed McCarey because he had lost Capra, so he sent Joe Walker as an emissary to McCarey, who said, "I'll never work for that SOB again."

McBride: When Cary Grant and Irene Dunne would improvise, would that present problems for the sound guys?

Bernds: They improvised at rehearsals. Improvising in takes is not professional. It wouldn't matter much if they improvised lines, but if they improvised moves, you were dead. The mike man had to know what was happening.

McBride: What about overlapping dialogue? How did you handle that?

Bernds: In the early days, real early days, I knew what were the problems. If you had a two-shot, interrupting one another, and then tried to shoot close-ups, it just wouldn't work. You couldn't cut it. You couldn't match the close-ups. I tried to explain that to a director, but he didn't want to listen to the goddamn soundman. I told him to ask the film editor, who told him the same thing. I found out later that Harry Cohn was on the set, listening to the whole thing without letting his presence be known. And I think that reinforced that I was a valuable contributor.

Maltin: Is it true that Cohn had the sets wired so he could eavesdrop?

Bernds: Yes. It is true. He tapped into our sound system. We had only three sound stages at that time. The sound went through the amplifier room, and he could patch in. Harry Cohn heard everything that the mixer heard. The man in the amplifier room told me about it. I didn't want to get anybody into trouble, so I took a few key people off, probably out on Gower Street, and told them.

Maltin: How would you relate to a new director?

Bernds: I'd wait and see if I make my presence known—how I will be received. Now with [Gregory] La Cava, if you tried to make a suggestion or correction with him, you were fired.

Maltin: Columbia let Buddy Coleman, the assistant director, try to direct some Bs. Was he any good as a director?

Bernds: He was Capra's assistant director, which gave him status. He had his faults—he was impulsive, excitable. I could tell you some ridiculous mistakes he made. He had the same exposure to the director as me, but he forgot all those things.

McBride: Did you work on *Golden Boy* [Rouben Mamoulian, 1939]?

Bernds: I shot tests for it with William Holden. He just wasn't right for the part. He should have been Italian, Jewish. Mamoulian directed the test.

Maltin: Did you shoot a lot of screen tests?

Bernds: Oh, yes. Rather than get tied up with B pictures in between major films, I filled in with a lot of little things like screen tests, *Screen Snapshots,* retakes. A big variety of stuff. I enjoyed most of it—*Screen Snapshots* was always a lot of fun.

McBride: When Capra returned to Columbia for *You Can't Take It with You* [1938], after resolving his legal dispute with Cohn, did you think he had changed?

Bernds: Yes. He was different. Showed impatience. I think the fault was Cohn's. But Capra had a sizable ego. They were two strong characters that clashed. I think the film plays well.

Maltin: What was your first impression of Jimmy Stewart?

Bernds: As I recall, he had a wonderful quality. Not very warm on the set—not like Clark Gable.

Maltin: Stewart really came into his own with *Mr. Smith Goes to Washington* [1939].

Bernds: Perfect casting.

Maltin: The sets are magnificent.

Bernds: Capra once said that at Columbia the product may be garbage, but the back lot is pure gold. We had excellent people on the back lot. In those days, they didn't have a lot of money to spend, but the sets were built with a certain amount of class. I believe some critics have commented that Columbia pictures had a "look" that reflected quality in the art direction, the set design.

McBride: Did the U.S. Senate set create problems with the sound engineers?

Bernds: The filibuster scene in the Senate—how were you going to cut that? So I went to Capra. I was always careful never to come on strong. I said, "We're going to have to shoot it with multiple cameras," and he said, "Yeah, I've been thinking about that." So when we shot the filibuster scenes, one camera was on Jimmy Stewart, one on the heckling senators, one on Harry Carey. There was a theory that you shouldn't use more than one mike because it would cause an artificial problem. The sound would be a split-second later, and there would be a mismatch. But I had one mike on each person in the chamber.

McBride: Were you aware that this would be Capra's last picture for Columbia?

Bernds: Yes. Usually when you finish a picture, you have a wrap party, and Capra would go around, saying, "Let's make another picture some time." But this time, he went out without saying much. He went out, it seems to me, with a touch of sadness. The end of an era.

McBride: You once told me that you worked as much as eighty-five hours a week at Columbia, and you felt that the working guys at Columbia were exploited. Did things get better in the later 1930s?

Bernds: Well, at least they paid for overtime. The electricians, grips, propmen got paid for overtime. Assistant directors, script clerks, and soundmen didn't. I got $85 a week for thirty hours or sixty hours. Six days a week.

McBride: Was it hard on your family?

Bernds: We didn't really think so. It was the Depression, and $85 a week was good money. We lived very well. We got one raise before the union came in, and once the union came in, we got more money. I was a fixture at Columbia and stayed there.

Maltin: You came on *Only Angels Have Wings* [1939] after it started.

Bernds: The original soundman—[Lodge] Cunningham—got the flu, I think. So I took it over two-thirds through. Rita Hayworth was a newcomer then, and I thought she was adequate as an actress. I worked with her before then on a couple of Bs.

McBride: Howard Hawks got a good performance out of her.

Bernds: I don't know how Hawks did it. He was even more low-key than Capra. He was austere. I felt like clicking my heels and saluting him.

Maltin: Did you write scripts for short subjects before you started directing them?

Bernds: No. I submitted scripts for the Blondie pictures, and eventually that got me acquainted with the producer.

Maltin: Before we get into that, let's talk about your entrée into the world of shorts. You had recorded sound for shorts with the Three Stooges, Charley Chase, so you already had a feel for how they were done.

Bernds: Yes.

Maltin: What were you most nervous about, most concerned about, starting to direct?

Bernds: Just general trepidation. If I blew it, I was finished, so I was afraid of failure. I saw myself doing it, didn't feel there was anything that would be too difficult for me. I tell you, everybody helped me. Del Lord [the director] wasn't jealous at all that the Three Stooges had been his province. He had graduated to features and expected to stay there. He didn't. He was giving me advice and assuring me that I could do it.

McBride: What was the shooting schedule for a two-reeler?

Bernds: Four days, which was plenty if you were efficient.

McBride: What's the secret of being efficient?

Bernds: Planning your moves—so you don't forget to shoot a close-up and have to come back. To the extent that it's practical, not having to move the camera. The way you plan it has a great deal to do with efficiency.

Maltin: How long would you be working ahead of time to get it ready?

Bernds: As much time as I had. If the script was delivered a week ahead of schedule, I had a week.

McBride: You were on a weekly salary?

Bernds: No. I was paid so much per film.

McBride: And how much was the budget for a short?

Bernds: For the Stooges, I believe the budget was around $35,000. And I didn't get much of it. Columbia exercised a reign of terror when their option was due—so I've heard. Columbia would float rumors that two-reelers were passé, they were going to phase them out; they didn't know whether they were going to exercise the option for the Three Stooges or not, but maybe out of the kindness of their heart they'd reenlist them, so to speak.

McBride: So between 1939, when you did *Mr. Smith,* and 1944, when you directed that war short, *It's Murder,* were you doing feature sound recording?

Bernds: I was a soundman. I worked with Edward G. Robinson, Glenn Ford, and a beautiful girl named Marguerite Chapman.

Maltin: Did you work on *Arizona* [1940]?

Bernds: At Old Tucson, Arizona—Columbia built that. That was a memorable location. I was on the second unit. They had two complete sound units. It was really easy doing second unit, taking an hour to assemble a bunch of cattle and then stampede them.

McBride: How long were you there?

Bernds: Five or six weeks. A long time. What happened there, a lot of guys when they go on location, it's a time for whoopee, for extracurricular activity. Now, we had a whole organization there: a large conference room and several offices, payroll, and everything, with ten or twelve employees. Some of the wives in Hollywood got poison-pen letters, describing in detail what their husbands had been doing. A lot of men got in trouble. I think the FBI was called. It was someone in the office who had access to all the home addresses. He didn't approve of he-and-sheing, because he was inclined to he-and-heing.

Maltin: Did you work on Columbia's two Fred Astaire films?

Bernds: I did both: *You'll Never Get Rich* [1941] and *You Were Never Lovelier* [1942]. Nice guy! Very meticulous about his work. We'd finish one of his scenes and it was perfect, and he'd say, "Do you mind doing it again?"

Maltin: Let's go back to the shorts. The gags were sometimes intricate in these shorts, and they had to go right or you wouldn't get your laughs. Was it just luck that they worked out the first time around, or did you have the ability to do several takes?

Bernds: When you have a gag involving breaking through a brick wall, it looks like a brick wall, but actually it would be much softer. What we called "breakaway," which breaks when you touch it. If the gag fails and you really have to do it again, you do it the next day. If it's the last day of shooting, the schedule was sacred. You never did a fifth day. Time was precious, but not for Jules [White]. He went into overtime all the time.

McBride: How big a crew did you have on those shorts?

Bernds: Almost as big a crew as a feature. The special effects men were assigned only when they were needed.

Maltin: Tell us about some of the tricks you would use, such as frame dropping.

Bernds: If a gag is slow, if there's a little pause that shouldn't be there, you put the film on a moviola. The director will work with the film editor and say, "Let's take out two frames there and try it." That may save the gag.

Wire-belt gags: when you see an actor flying through the air, they have a big belt around their middle, covered by their clothes, with a wire attached. The wire had to be made invisible. If the set-building people knew there was going to be a wire that day, they would put something in with vertical lines so the wire wouldn't show. Otherwise, they would paint the wire with a kind of red color that years of experiment had told them the camera didn't pick up.

Maltin: Was it fun to work with the same people over a period of time?

Bernds: I had to use whomever the production office gave me. If a cameraman happened to be available, I had no choice in that. I didn't get any top-notch cameraman. The propman, a character named Ray Hunt, and the special effects department, they were all pretty good.

Maltin: You had a challenge early on with the Three Stooges, when Curly was not well and you had to shoot around him.

Bernds: That was anxiety time. I couldn't shoot masters [master shots] with the Three Stooges on a Three Stooges film! What should have been a nice brisk three-shot had to be a series of close-ups. You can't shoot just one close-up, because you have to balance them. That was *A Bird in the Head* [1946]. It was the first one I directed, but *Micro-Phonies* was released first [1945]. It was funny. I did five pictures with Curly. *A Bird in the Head,* he was in bad shape. *Monkey Businessmen* [1946], he was a little better. He was down for *Three Troubledoers* [1946]. *Micro-Phonies,* he was in good shape, and he was fine for *Three Little Pirates* [1946]. He was quite unpredictable. We all thought he was hungover, but he had had a small stroke—he had passed out on one of Jules White's pictures.

McBride: How many takes did you do on the Stooges shorts? Did you have to minimize your takes?

Bernds: No. You had to get the picture.

Maltin: *Micro-Phonies* is an awfully good short. It's one of my favorites.

Bernds: I was awfully lucky with that. Hugh McCollum [the head of the shorts department] was smitten with Christine McIntyre. It may seem extraordinary to you, but it may have been platonic. He liked her. And he asked me, rather diffidently, to write a script using Christine and her singing talent—he actually had her audition for me. With that directive, I wrote *Micro-Phonies,* making use of Christine McIntyre's voice, and it worked out all right.

Maltin: You obviously had a stock company of players to call upon. Was it your decision as to who would be right for a certain part?

Bernds: Oh, yes. McCollum came to depend on me for a lot of things. I very soon got the job of creating titles for them all, cooking up crazy titles. I was always careful to defer to him—I'd make the decision his. I never stepped on his toes. I got who I wanted, but we had people who were loyal to us, and we were loyal to them. We used the same people over and over again, because we could depend on them.

Maltin: Did you preview the shorts?

Bernds: It's funny, we previewed the two-reelers but we didn't preview the Blondie features.

Maltin: Did you make changes as a result of the audience reaction?

Bernds: Yes. It was easy to make our audiences laugh. We did preview in relatively unsophisticated places—Huntington Beach, the Alex in Glendale.

McBride: How did you improve as a director?

Bernds: I learned authority. A captain has to have control of a ship, and a director has to have control of the set. I began to relish the authority. I was tough on occasions. I fired a couple of people, and you'd be surprised how that helped my reputation on the set.

McBride: Did the violence in the Three Stooges pictures bother you?

Bernds: I talked to Moe about the poking in the eyes, and this required some courage, to protest something that was his kind of stock in trade. But he said, "Any kid anywhere would hurt another kid, I would feel bad about it. I'd rather not do it." And Moe did not do it. Once in a while, in the heat of battle, so to speak, he would forget himself. Another thing that disgusted me and that I asked him not to do was the nostril pulling. Of course, a lot of the violence, such as the knuckle rapping on the head, was sound effects. Without sound effects, it was nothing.

McBride: Can you provide us with word portraits of each of the Three Stooges?

Bernds: Moe was a gentleman. He loved being an actor. Even after the Three Stooges were finished, he wanted to be an actor, and I cast him in a science fiction picture I was doing [*Space Master X-7,* 1958]. Many fans thought I was doing it out of charity. Well, nothing of the kind. Moe was a wealthy man. He had invested wisely in [San Fernando] Valley real estate. I had the highest respect for him. Jules [White] would not call him in for story conferences, but I did. I wanted to get his opinion on material, and he would give me what he'd call "routines." He'd perhaps recall some vaudeville routine. He was a great help.

McBride: He wasn't at all nasty like his character?

Bernds: I'll always be grateful for what he did, the fact that he cooperated with me in every way. Larry was flighty. I was familiar with his behavior way back when I was a soundman. He'd disappear, going to listen to some horse race on the radio or the World Series. He was a great gambler. Columbia had a resident bookie, and he'd go on all the sets. Not openly. He'd stand back away from the set. The bettors would see him and go and place a bet on a horse race. Larry blew a lot of money. The Stooges shared equally in the salary, and when the series wrapped up, Larry was broke and Moe was a rich man. Larry had a family who were leeches, and a wife who also loved horse racing.

McBride: Was it hard to keep him focused on the set?

Bernds: Yes. But Moe was just the same in real life as he was on film. He'd shake Larry up and tell him off. Curly was funny almost by accident. He was like a huge child and acted like a huge child. Almost like a grown-up baby.

McBride: Was he mentally like that?

Bernds: He was no mental giant. I wasn't aware of it when I was a soundman, but, as I heard later, he drank too much. He drank too much at night, and, of course, his many marriages are a matter of record. I think he had burnt the candle at both ends by the time I worked with him. The early pictures, he was instinctively funny.

Maltin: Curly had a stroke, couldn't work anymore, and Shemp took over. While fans are fondest of Curly, you were fondest of Shemp?

Bernds: Yes. First of all, Shemp was a very likeable, loveable guy, a hard worker, and a delight for a director, because he was always thinking of little things to do. Shemp made a director look good. Shemp was so timid, he would not even drive a car. Not even a few feet for an exit scene. On one film, Shemp was afraid to get the engine running, even to drive it forward, so they put it in neutral and put a rope on the front to pull it out of the scene. He was even afraid to put the brake on, so they had other grips with a rope on the back to stop it. Moe told me that Shemp liked to fish. He went to a pier, but he wouldn't go out on a boat to fish. One time, they were on a small lake and Shemp was fishing from a pier, and they told him he could get into a better position if he got into a rowboat that was tied there. He stepped into the boat, moored to the pier, and got seasick.

Maltin: He picked a strange profession, having to work in roughneck comedies.

Bernds: Well, he was not afraid to get hurt. He wasn't as skillful as Larry and Moe in avoiding getting hurt. I remember one time when he was supposed to make an exit and the door closed on him, he had a cut on his head, with blood, and he said, "What do you know—tomato ketchup." He had to come up with a funny line even while bleeding.

McBride: When you directed the Three Stooges in features, Joe De Rita had joined the trio.

Bernds: Curly got sick and couldn't work. Shemp died. Joe Besser didn't fit in very well. And then along came Joe De Rita. He did the feature-length pictures with the Stooges. Joe De Rita was never truly a Stooge. He was a little bit of a complainer. Moe was very solicitous of him. Joe De Rita didn't want to be slapped. I think he thought he was superior to this brand of comedy. He certainly profited from being with them. He was in *The Three Stooges Meet Hercules* [1962] and *The Three Stooges in Orbit* [1962]. *Orbit* was not that good—the story wasn't good.

McBride: How much were the budgets on those pictures?

Bernds: About 300,000 bucks. *Hercules,* in particular, was very successful. We kidded several things. I always touched up everything I directed, but I don't recall making any changes to the script of that one.

Maltin: Did you have to make any accommodations to the fact that the Stooges were much older?

Bernds: Yes. I was particular with Joe De Rita, because he was so fat. I don't think he was older than the rest of them, but I didn't make him run too much. It would have been very damaging to the schedule if one of them had dropped dead. When it was possible to do so, I would hire doubles.

McBride: How many shorts did you direct before you went into features?

Bernds: I think close to fifty. My first one was in 1945, and my last one was in 1952. Most of them were Stooges pictures—I did twenty-five of them. I also directed Andy Clyde, a wonderful old comic who specialized in being Scottish. I did one with Buster Keaton, *Pest from the West* [1939]; I was the soundman. His director on that was Del Lord, and they had a good rapport. He was very professional—no hint of his "slumming" at Columbia. I took the opportunity to tell him I thought *The General* was one of the funniest pictures I had ever seen. The Great Stone Face broke into a smile and said, "Thank you." In that picture, he had to do something that was uncomfortable, to say the least. We shot it in March 1937, on the oceanfront at Balboa Bay, and there was a gag there that every time he wanted to go back to his yacht, the crew pulled in the gangplank and he walked into the water. That water was cold. Uncomplaining, he went in a total of three times. Perfect discipline. Columbia tried to make a team out of Gus Schilling and Dick Lane, and I made shorts with them. They were excellent, but Columbia didn't think they would take, so we made only three.

McBride: You also directed several of the Blondie pictures.

Bernds: I wrote my way into it. I never wrote and directed the Blondie pictures. I wrote some of them and then I directed some of them. I liked them because they were comedies and I was paid the going rate. Arthur Lake and Penny Singleton got pretty good money because the series had been going a long time. They'd been picking up options. I think the budget was probably $400,000 a picture. We had fourteen days to shoot. A nice schedule. I was shooting about the same number of minutes a day as I was shooting on two-reelers.

Arthur and Penny were problems in different ways. I was told I shouldn't get too friendly with Arthur because Penny would get jealous. Arthur was married to Marion Davies's daughter. Arthur would go to San Simeon each weekend, and he was always late coming back. I begged Bert Kelly [the producer] to have the front office discipline him, have him get to work on time, but anybody to do with [William Randolph] Hearst and Louella Parsons got favored treatment. Also, Arthur did not study his lines. The first time I directed him, I found out he hadn't read the script, much less learned his day's work. He was a quick study, that was true. We had a dialogue coach, and Arthur would cram. But that's no way to do it.

Penny Singleton disliked Arthur, probably because he just wasn't professional. She figured if he was late, she was going to be late. Or she would flaunt the fact that she was on time and knew her lines. In *Blondie's Hero* [1950], there's a fantasy scene. Arthur has a dream he's in combat and wounded, and Penny comes to his aid. The script, which I did not write, called for him to kiss her. The wardrobe lady came to me, and said, "She will not do it." She didn't want him to kiss her. I could have been the big-shot director and said, "You'll do it or else," but I didn't make an issue of it. But when we shot it, Arthur did give her a peck on the cheek, and if you look very closely, you'll see that just for an instant she thought of stopping the scene. She just kind of stops acting for a second or so.

McBride: You did second unit on *Kill the Umpire* [Lloyd Bacon, 1950] and *Woman of Distinction* [Edward Buzzell, 1950]?

Bernds: Yes. *Kill the Umpire,* I did a lot of work on that. I directed night locations for two nights out at Columbia Ranch. Then I did all the chase scenes, all over the [San Fernando] Valley. I did the bicycle chase on *Woman of Distinction.*

McBride: What do you remember about your Columbia western, *Gold Raiders* [1951], with George O'Brien and the Three Stooges?

Bernds: A friend of mine to this day, Bernard Glasser, desperately wanted to be a producer. George O'Brien was a friend of Glasser's—they had served in the navy together—so he had George O'Brien. He paid to have a script written and wanted me to direct for Guild minimum and a share of the profits. We were supposed to have a twelve-day schedule, which was all right, but then Bernard Glasser began to run out of money, and he had to cut down the schedule. Finally—and this is impossible, but we did it—we made a Western in midwinter, between Christmas and New Year's, five days, with exteriors and winter weather. Considering the difficulties, *Gold Raiders* is not bad.

McBride: You left Columbia in 1952 to freelance. Did you have an agent?

Bernds: I tried agents for a while. If you're not a name, you can't really get a name agent. And if you don't have a name agent. . . . I had MCA as my agent for a while and paid them 10 percent of my money for work *I* obtained. When I got to Allied Artists, I had steady work, starting with an ice-skating melodrama—a cheap melodrama—called *Hot News* [1953], followed by the Bowery Boys pictures.

Mc Bride: You did eight Bowery Boys films. Did you have a good rapport with them?

Bernds: Well, not exactly. Leo [Gorcey] was a drinker. I heard him bragging once about how they drove a novice German director crazy. I was determined they wouldn't drive me crazy, but on one occasion I came fairly close. I don't think I'd have hit him, but I grabbed him by the shirt. There would have been no glory—I'm a foot-and-a-half taller than he is. Huntz [Hall] was somber and could be difficult at times.

Ellwood Ullman and I wrote all of the Bowery Boys pictures that I directed. I think they are pretty damn good of their kind. The one saving grace of Leo and Huntz is that they wanted the stuff to be funny. They made trouble on the set, but when it came down to it, they wanted it to be good. I always like to have the first shot in the bag quick. I had Huntz and Leo in the scene rehearsing, and I said, "All right, we'll shoot it." This was first thing in the morning, but Leo was a drinker and he had this gofer named Joe, and he yelled, "Joe," meaning he wanted Joe to bring him a flask. I said, "Joe's not here—let's shoot." He said, "No Joe, no shoot." Maybe he was insecure; maybe he needed the drink first thing in the morning. He got away with it for a number of years. When I shot the last of the Bowery Boys movies, *Dig That Uranium* [1956], it was beginning to show. I told [producer] Ben Schwalb I didn't want to direct the Bowery Boys anymore. He tried one more with another director, and Leo was so bad on that one that they replaced him. But you couldn't replace Leo. He had a quality that was needed.

McBride: What were your favorite films from the 1950s?

Bernds: I did a science fiction picture called *World without End* [1956]. I wrote and directed it, and I really had high hopes for it. The reviews were very kind, and I'm told it made a lot of money for Allied Artists. The original title was *Flight to the Future*. A very successful picture was *The Return of the Fly* [1959]. I consulted with Vincent Price during the writing of the script. He was very professional both in the talks about the script and during the shooting. I enjoyed making the Westerns, which we shot at Iverson Ranch. Iverson Ranch is way up in the northeast part of the San Fernando Valley. I also shot science fiction films there.

Maltin: Is it true that Sam Peckinpah worked as a dialogue director on some of your films at Allied Artists?

Bernds: That's true, yes, indeed. I forget which ones Sam did—I would guess three. But he was a protégé of the guy who directed *Riot in Cell Block 11* [for Allied Artists, 1954], Don Siegel.

McBride: Peckinpah was very young at the time.

Bernds: Yes, very young, very retiring. Later on, when he had the reputation of being a stormy petrel, I found it hard to relate that to the guy I knew, who was kind of self-effacing.

Maltin: Was he helpful to you?

Bernds: Yes, in that he didn't try to second-guess the director. Most of us directors resented [someone else having] the title of "dialogue director." Some of us were pretty vehement in saying, "There's only one director on the set." Well, that's not true, of course; the cameraman is the director of photography, but I would always insist on calling [a dialogue director] a "dialogue coach." They were useful in rehearsing the people. Often the director would be too busy lining up a shot or something, and if he had a competent man there to get the actors together and just make sure they knew their lines and maybe prod them a little bit if they didn't, that was useful.

McBride: Did you have any sense that Peckinpah would become an important filmmaker?

Bernds: No, no. I never got very close to the guy. Well, maybe we just shot too fast to have buddy-buddy talks.

McBride: Did you envy the big-budget directors such as George Stevens and William Wyler?

Bernds: Oh, yes. I had a crack at doing better films at Columbia. But fate took me to where I was, and fate robbed me of a chance. I had done a picture at Columbia, which was pretty damn good— *Gasoline Alley* [1951]—and an executive there, Sam Arnow, was effusive. He was going to talk to Harry Cohn about putting me under contract. I had high hopes. I kept going to producers looking for assignments, and I found a certain coolness. Finally, I found out what happened. Sam Arnow had approached Cohn, but at the wrong time and the wrong place. He talked about *Gasoline Alley,* and Cohn said, "I saw it—it stinks!" Cohn had *not* seen the film, but his impulsive put-down of Arnow made the rounds of the studio, and hurt, badly.

McBride: *Harem Girl* [1952] sounds like a fun picture.

Bernds: It wasn't as good as it might have been. It was produced by Wallace MacDonald, and Wallace MacDonald was a great interferer. He influenced the writing; he interfered with me as the director.

McBride: *Navy Wife* [1956]?

Bernds: It was a fair picture. It wasn't as good as it should be. The script was not very dramatic, not very funny. I guess it was all right.

Maltin: *Reform School Girl* [1957]?

Bernds: I had an interlude there, where I made pictures for AIP [American International Pictures]. Jim Nicholson was the good cop [executive], and Sam Arkoff, the bad cop. They did the bad cop/good cop routine on personnel. There again, I was promised a share of the profits, but the trouble is they keep the books. When they had to get clearance to release it to TV, they had to get my signature, releasing my percentage, and I was able to hold out for $3,500. When it was remade [as a 1994 TV movie], I got $1,600 for use of the title and, roughly, the story. They used the basic idea of the story.

McBride: *Joyride* [1958]?

Bernds: A good picture. I could be proud of that one. We shot it very fast, but I had an excellent cast.

McBride: How do you feel about *Queen of Outer Space* [1958]?

Bernds: A cult picture. It's a little humiliating that people laugh at, not with, it. Ellwood Ullman, Ben Schwalb [the producer], and I tried to put intentional laughs into it. Ben Hecht wrote the story— I think it was only a three- or four-page outline that producer

Walter Wanger brought to Allied Artists—and Charles Beaumont wrote the script. Zsa Zsa Gabor was kind of flighty. She was not very well prepared or very professional. She made trouble. We filled the cast with beautiful girls.

McBride: You also directed the 1954 Cal Tech recruiting film, *Careers for Youth,* with Capra producing. And you got to direct Dr. Robert A. Millikan, the Nobel Prize winner, performing his famous oil drop experiment.

Bernds: I really got to see Cal Tech. I pleaded with Capra not to edit it [Millikan's experiment]—there's a way of using film without cutting it—because I thought that the Millikan lecture was priceless. I was so impressed by this great man. We used Cal Tech personnel. I used a cameraman who was used to photographing scientific experiments. We rented a sound truck, but we had a completely amateur sound crew. The only other professional was the assistant director. Capra did not have much involvement. I never saw the film edited. Capra told me the purpose of it was to assure brilliant or good high school graduates, who were qualified to go on to Cal Tech, that it was not just a grind, that there was fun to be had there.

Maltin: How did you get involved in *Tickle Me* [1965], the Elvis Presley movie you wrote with Ellwood Ullman?

Bernds: Allied Artists made a deal for a Presley picture. Colonel [Tom] Parker [Presley's manager] didn't even want to know about story or anything else. All he wanted was the money, and Allied Artists offered him a huge sum of money for Elvis, so Allied Artists had the commitment for Elvis to do a picture. They gave it to Ben Schwalb to produce, and Ben gave the assignment to write the script to Ellwood Ullman and me. I was supposed to direct it. But it didn't work out that way. Colonel Parker wanted someone Elvis had worked with before, Norman Taurog.

McBride: How did you approach the script?

Bernds: When two people write a script, they should never separate it by saying, "I thought of this," "I thought of that." However, I believe I did have the key to the whole thing. Elvis, a down-and-out rodeo rider crippled by some rodeo accident, takes this job on a ranch. The ranch is owned by a woman—that's all right, he's willing to work for a woman. Except that when he gets out there, he finds out it's a fat farm, a beauty ranch.

McBride: What did you think of Elvis as an actor?

Bernds: I was on the set quite a bit. We shot it on the Paramount lot. Apparently that was one of Colonel Parker's conditions. Allied Artists rented space at Paramount. Elvis was a willing actor. He liked Taurog, and he was cooperative and friendly with everybody. He was not the egotistical big star at all. And in the action scenes, he actually supplied things that were useful, ad-libbing. Where he was supposed to fight a whole troop of bad guys, he had his own buddies doing it, and they created a really good fight routine.

McBride: What personal dealings did you have with Elvis?

Bernds: The one thing I found out when I met Elvis was that he was terribly shy. So the meeting was very formal. He didn't express any interest in the fact that we had written it. When the picture was under way, some high officials of the FBI came to Paramount and wanted to meet Elvis and see him at work. I think there were two of them, and Elvis was so shook up—I guess he behaved himself while they were there, but he quit working as soon as they were gone.

McBride: Why did they want to meet him? Were they investigating him?

Bernds: No, no, no, they were just fans, if you can picture an FBI man as a fan.

Maltin: How do you think *Tickle Me* turned out?

Bernds: It was all right. Norman Taurog did a good job of directing it. Some reviews were good, some fair. It was kind of stylish for reviewers to put Elvis down a little bit.

Maltin: How much television did you do?

Bernds: I spent a whole summer directing Westerns: *Colt .45* and *Sugarfoot*. Will Hutchins was a good actor, a nice guy. Didn't take. For that matter, *Colt .45* didn't take, either. I did a number of TV shows, not one after the other, but from time to time, for Screen Gems. There was really no difference between shooting films and TV, except for TV, you were supposed to shoot a little faster.

McBride: How did you wrap up your directing career?

Bernds: With the Stooges [on *The New Three Stooges,* a syndicated TV series filmed in the summer of 1965]. Norman Maurer [the Stooges' manager and producer of the series] had been a comic book artist before he married Moe's daughter. Norman was a pretty damn good artist. Some of his serious stuff was excellent. It was his idea to make cartoons for television, with live-action sequences [as wraparounds]. That was a hectic thing, shooting a large number [forty] of live-action segments. I wrote 'em all and directed 'em all. They were only short little segments. Of course, writing them was not hard—I just used tried-and-true routines. We worked awfully fast, and the boys were willing to do it. Somebody made an awful lot of money off that.

McBride: Did you have anything to do with the cartoon parts?

Bernds: No. I thought the cartoons were poorly done, and I think Norman thought so too. He tried to invent something that seemed to me not necessary. To shoot live action and then somehow synthesize it into a cartoon which would get away with the intricate figuring of the movement—I never really understood it, and I didn't even see the economy of it.

McBride: What made you retire?

Bernds: I wasn't getting any work. Ellwood Ullman and I decided to offer ourselves as a team to write comedy. Ellwood had a lot of good credits. He had written for Martin and Lewis and Ma and Pa Kettle. I had all my feature credits. The day Ellwood decided to quit, we went to Columbia to be interviewed by a producer. I went into a building where I had once had an office. And here was an arrogant young guy, about half our age, very condescending, wondering what these old guys wanted and explaining to us about the new kind of comedy. When we got outside, Ellwood said, "That does it! When that punk can condescend to us, tell us about comedy. . . . I'm going to call it quits and take my Writers Guild pension." After a bit, I decided too. I got both my Writers and Directors Guild pensions.

Later, after I had been retired for a year or so, Norman Maurer called me. He had got a job with Hanna-Barbera to produce a cartoon series, *Scooby-Doo* [a Saturday-morning series about a Great Dane and four teenage detectives that premiered in 1969 as *Scooby-Doo, Where Are You?*]. Norman wanted me as story editor. He offered me $750 a week and promised me good hours. And every once in a while I could get extra money—I probably could average a thousand a week by putting in one of my own stories. I was flattered that anybody would call me out of retirement for that. Norman was full of enthusiasm, but he was a night person and he chain-smoked. I hate cigarette smoke, and here we were in a closed room full of smoke. He also told me about all the restrictions, all the taboos on cartoons. I spent one day on the show, mostly learning the do's and don'ts. The whole thing was beyond childish.

On the way home, I got to thinking. I had a golf date the next day that I'd have to cancel. I would have to give up my two pensions. I'd have to endure cigarette smoke and long hours. By the time I got home, I decided to hell with it.

Appendix:
The Films of Edward Bernds

This appendix lists all the films directed by Edward Bernds. All titles after 1952 are feature films. Except as indicated, all titles through 1952 are two-reel shorts produced by Columbia. Dates cited for these shorts are official release dates. The films were almost never released in the order in which they were shot; discrepancies between shooting and release dates vary by as much as two years.

1944 IT'S MURDER (one-reel OWI propaganda film, produced at Columbia)

1945 MICRO-PHONIES (with the Three Stooges, released November 15, 1945)

1946 WHEN THE WIFE'S AWAY (with Hugh Herbert, released February 1, 1946)
A BIRD IN THE HEAD (with the Three Stooges, released February 28, 1946)
MR. NOISY (with Shemp Howard, released March 22, 1946)
THREE TROUBLEDOERS (with the Three Stooges, released April 25, 1946)
GET ALONG LITTLE ZOMBIE (with Hugh Herbert, released May 9, 1946)

MONKEY BUSINESSMEN (with the Three Stooges, released June 20, 1946)

HOT WATER (with Gus Schilling and Dick Lane, released July 25, 1946)

PARDON MY TERROR (with Gus Schilling and Dick Lane, released September 12, 1946)

SOCIETY MUGS (with Shemp Howard, released September 19, 1946)

HONEYMOON BLUES (with Hugh Herbert, released October 17, 1946)

SLAPPILY MARRIED (with Joe De Rita, released November 7, 1946)

THREE LITTLE PIRATES (with the Three Stooges, released December 5, 1946)

ANDY PLAYS HOOKEY (with Andy Clyde, released December 19, 1946)

1947 MEET MR. MISCHIEF (with Harry Von Zell, released January 23, 1947)

HOT HEIR (with Hugh Herbert, released February 13, 1947)

SCOOPER-DOOPER (with Sterling Holloway, released February 27, 1947)

FRIGHT NIGHT (with the Three Stooges, released March 6, 1947)

BRIDE AND GLOOM (with Shemp Howard, released March 27, 1947)

OUT WEST (with the Three Stooges, released April 24, 1947)

WEDDING BELLE (with Gus Schilling and Dick Lane, released August 9, 1947)

BRIDELESS GROOM (with the Three Stooges, released September 11, 1947)

HECTIC HONEYMOON (with Sterling Holloway, released September 18, 1947)

WIFE TO SPARE (with Andy Clyde, released November 20, 1947)

WEDLOCK DEADLOCK (with Joe De Rita, released December 18, 1947)

RADIO ROMEO (with Harry Von Zell, released December 25, 1947)

1948 TWO NUTS IN A RUT (with Gus Schilling and Dick Lane, released February 19, 1948)

PARDON MY CLUTCH (with the Three Stooges, released February 26, 1948)

SQUAREHEADS OF THE ROUND TABLE (with the Three Stooges, released March 4, 1948)

EIGHT-BALL ANDY (with Andy Clyde, released March 11, 1948)

THE SHEEPISH WOLF (with Harry Von Zell, released May 27, 1948)

FLAT FEAT (with Sterling Holloway, released June 24, 1948)

HOT SCOTS (with the Three Stooges, released July 8, 1948)

BILLIE GETS HER MAN (with Billie Burke, released September 9, 1948)

MUMMY'S DUMMIES (with the Three Stooges, released November 4, 1948)

CRIME ON THEIR HANDS (with the Three Stooges, released December 9, 1948)

BLONDIE'S SECRET (Columbia feature film)

1949 HE'S IN AGAIN (with Gus Schilling and Dick Lane, released January 13, 1949)

RADIO RIOT (with Harry Von Zell, released February 10, 1949)

WHO DONE IT? (with the Three Stooges, released March 3, 1949)

MICROSPOOK (with Harry Von Zell, released June 9, 1949)

FUELIN' AROUND (with the Three Stooges, released July 7, 1949)

BLONDIE'S BIG DEAL (Columbia feature film)

BLONDIE HITS THE JACKPOT (Columbia feature film)

WAITING IN THE LURCH (with Joe Besser, released September 8, 1949)

VAGABOND LOAFERS (with the Three Stooges, released October 6, 1949)

LET DOWN YOUR AERIAL (with Wally Vernon and Eddie Quillan, released November 17, 1949)

FEUDIN' RHYTHM (Columbia feature film)

1950   PUNCHY COWPUNCHERS (with the Three Stooges, released January 5, 1950)

HIS BAITING BEAUTY (with Harry Von Zell, released January 12, 1950)

DOPEY DICKS (with the Three Stooges, released March 2, 1950)

TWO ROAMING CHAMPS (with Maxie Rosenbloom and Max Baer, released August 12, 1950)

STUDIO STOOPS (with the Three Stooges, released October 5, 1950)

BLONDIE'S HERO (Columbia feature film)

A WOMAN OF DISTINCTION (2nd unit direction on Columbia feature film)

BEWARE OF BLONDIE (Columbia feature film)

THE PETTY GIRL (2nd unit direction on Columbia feature film)

KILL THE UMPIRE (2nd unit direction on Columbia feature film)

A SNITCH IN TIME (with the Three Stooges, released December 7, 1950)

1951   GASOLINE ALLEY (Columbia feature film; also story and script)

THREE ARABIAN NUTS (with the Three Stooges, released January 4, 1951)

THE BEULAH SHOW (television pilot)

MERRY MAVERICKS (with the Three Stooges, released September 6, 1951)

CORKY OF GASOLINE ALLEY (Columbia feature film; also story and script)

THE TOOTH WILL OUT (with the Three Stooges, released October 4, 1951)

THE CHAMP STEPS OUT (with Maxie Rosenbloom and Max Baer, released November 15, 1951)

THE GOLD RAIDERS (Feature film with the Three Stooges for Allied Artists release)

1952   HAREM GIRL (Columbia feature film; also script)

LISTEN, JUDGE (with the Three Stooges, released March 6, 1952)

HEEBIE GEE-GEES (with Wally Vernon and Eddie Quillan, released April 10, 1952)

GENTS IN A JAM (with the Three Stooges, released July 4, 1952)

THE HANK McCUNE SHOW (television pilot for Bing Crosby Enterprises)

THE NEW JOB (television pilot for Alan Young Productions)

ACE LUCKY (Columbia feature film; also script)

1953 CLIPPED WINGS (Allied Artists)

WHITE LIGHTNING (Allied Artists)

PRIVATE EYES (Allied Artists, also coscript)

LOOSE IN LONDON (Allied Artists; also story and script)

HOT NEWS (Allied Artists)

1954 THE BOWERY BOYS MEET THE MONSTER (Allied Artists; also coscript)

JUNGLE GENTS (Allied Artists; also script)

1955 BOWERY TO BAGDAD (Allied Artists; also coscript)

SPY CHASERS (Allied Artists)

1956 WORLD WITHOUT END (Allied Artists; also script)

NAVY WIFE (Allied Artists)

DIG THAT URANIUM (Allied Artists)

CALLING HOMICIDE (Allied Artists; also script)

1957 THE STORM RIDER (20th Century-Fox; also coscript)

REFORM SCHOOL GIRL (AIP; also script)

SPACE MASTER X-7 (20th Century-Fox, 1957)

1958 HIGH SCHOOL HELLCATS (AIP)

ESCAPE FROM RED ROCK (20th Century-Fox; also script)

QUANTRILL'S RAIDERS (20th Century-Fox)

QUEEN OF OUTER SPACE (Allied Artists)

JOY RIDE (Allied Artists)

1959 ALASKA PASSAGE (20th Century-Fox; also script)

THE RETURN OF THE FLY (20th Century-Fox; also script)

1961 VALLEY OF THE DRAGONS (Columbia; also script)

1962 THE THREE STOOGES MEET HERCULES (Columbia)
THE THREE STOOGES IN ORBIT (Columbia)

1966 PREHISTORIC VALLEY (ZRB; also script)

Index

Academy Awards, 280–281
Acquitted, 100
AEO light, 68
Africa Speaks, 137–139
AIP, 303
Air Hawks, 255–256
Alibi, 73–74, 78, 80
All-American Radio Manufacturing Company, 14, 19–20
Allied Artists, 302, 304
American Madness, 151–155
Aquitania, 176–179
Arcadia, California, 128, 130, 131, 133
Arden, Eve, 96
Arkoff, Sam, 303
Arnow, Sam, 303
Arthur, Jean, 288
Arthur, Johnny, 100
Astaire, Fred, 294
August, Joe, 239
The Awful Truth, 290

Badger, Clarence, 167
Baker, Belle, 93, 94, 95, 96
"Bank Holiday," 168
Banky, Vilma, 71
Barnes, Binnie, 188, 190, 192, 195, 196, 198, 205
"Barney," 99, 289
Barrymore, John, 67, 71, 238, 239, 240
Baxter, Warner, 246, 247, 248, 251

Bennett, Joan, 75
Bernds, Edward, Jr., 100, 175
Besser, Joe, 298
Betty Brooks Company, 31–32, 49
Biberman, Herbert, 265
A Bird in the Head, 295–296
Bischoff, Sam, 90–91, 97, 98, 109, 271
Bitter Tea of General Yen, 157–158
The Black Room, 256–259
Blanchard, Harry, 97, 101, 102, 105, 126
"Blondie" series, 293, 296, 299–300
Blondie's Hero, 300
Bonomo, Joe, 141
Borradaile, Osmond, 188, 205
Bosworth, Hobart, 130, 289
"Bowery Boys" series, 301–302
Brandt, Joe, 149
Brenon, Herbert, 83–84
Bridge, Bill, 88
Briskin, Sam, 123, 124, 125, 265, 271
British & Dominions Film Corporation, 184
Broadway Bill, 246–251
Brotmarkle, Win, 102
Brown, Harry Joe, 116
Brown, Karl, 116
Brown Derby, 1

Browne, Earl, 82
Bruce, Nigel, 192
Buchman, Sidney, 263
Bulldog Drummond, 75, 80
Bunn, Earle D., 116, 117, 118, 277
Bunton, George, 35, 36–37, 41, 45–46, 49
Burns, Henry, 23–24, 27
Busch Gardens, 231
Butler, Lawrence, 38–39, 49, 131
Butler, William, 131
Buzzell, Eddie, 155, 158

Cagney, James, 170
Cahoon, Richard, 270
Calcaterra, Joseph, 12–13
Campbell, Howard, 52, 54, 57, 61, 63, 64, 65, 75, 77, 78, 79, 83, 85, 89
Capra, Frank, 1–2, 97, 101, 102, 104–105, 109–114, 119, 123, 124, 126, 127, 128, 129, 130, 131, 132, 134, 135, 143–147, 152–153, 157–158, 169–172, 216–235, 246–254, 271–272, 274, 281, 282, 283, 287, 288, 289, 291, 292, 293, 304
Careers for Youth, 304
Carnival, 254–255
Carpenter, Russell, 119, 125, 126
Carter, Milt, 262
Cawthorn, Joseph, 86
Chasen, Dave, 111
Chatterton, Ruth, 278–279
Chicago, 5–22, 51–57, 213
Chicago Federation of Labor, 54, 56
Chi-Rad, 9, 11
Clark, Wallis, 171
Clyde, Andy, 277, 299
El Codiga Penal, 215
Cohn, Harry, 2–3, 90, 91, 94, 124, 146, 148–149, 151, 157, 162,

163, 164, 165, 174, 175, 181, 183, 184, 185, 186, 189, 191, 192, 194, 197, 198, 199, 203, 214, 218, 235, 236, 237, 255, 265, 267, 270, 283, 289, 290, 291, 303
Cohn, Jack, 149
Colbert, Claudette, 217, 218, 221, 224, 227, 233, 263, 264, 265
Coleman, Buddy, 291
Colman, Ronald, 289
Colorado, 25–28
"The Colorado African Expedition," 137–138
Colt .45, 305
Columbia Park, 288
Columbia Pictures, 1, 89–91, 93–174, 180, 181, 214–286, 288–301
Columbia Ranch, 288, 300
Condemned, 88
Connolly, Walter, 158
Cook, Joe, 108, 109, 111, 112, 114
Cooper, Gary, 287–288
Coquette, 71–72, 80–83, 241
Crane Junior College, 7–8, 9
The Criminal Code, 215, 237
CTA, 69–70, 80, 81, 121, 122, 123, 151, 195
Cummings, Irving, 168
Cunningham, Lodge, 137, 293
Cushway, Charles, 11–12, 14, 15, 16, 18, 21, 35

"dailies," 159
Dangerous Crossroads, 169
Decker, Harry, 279
Deming, Norman, 262
De Rita, Joe, 298–299
Destroyer, 282
Dig That Uranium, 301
Dillon, John Francis, 116
Dirigible, 119–135, 289

Douglas, Melvyn, 263, 264
Dressler, Marie, 170
Duncan, Cap, 90, 288
Dunne, Irene, 290
Dunning process, 133–134
Dwan, Allan, 62, 151, 152
Dyer, Elmer, 119, 133

Elstree, 184, 188, 189, 193, 197, 198
England, 180–206
Eternal Love, 66

Fairbanks, Douglas, 61, 62, 63, 72–73, 78, 82, 85–88
Fellows, Edith, 263, 265
Fields, W. C., 173
Fifty Fathoms Deep, 118–119
Fine, Larry, 297
Fitzmaurice, George, 74
Flight, 97, 105, 114, 127
Fog, 214–215
Foley, Jim, 51
Forbidden, 146–148
Forrest, David, 79–80, 83, 88
France, 206–210
Franklin, Al, 267
Futter, Walter, 137–138

Gable, Clark, 217–218, 219, 220, 221, 233, 246, 262, 291
Gabor, Zsa Zsa, 304
gags, 294–295
The Gallant Defender, 276
Galone, Carmine, 193–194
Garnett, Tay, 167, 269, 271
Garrett, Oliver H. P., 268
Gasoline Alley, 303
Gaumont British, 197
Gering, Marion, 278
Giannini, A. P., 149
Gilbert, Tess, 119
Glasser, Bernard, 300–301

Glendale Airport, 111
Gold Raiders, 300–301
Golden Boy, 291
Goldwyn, Samuel, 74–75
golf, 270, 276
Gorcey, Leo, 301
Goss, Jim, 149
Gottler, Archie, 236
Grant, Cary, 290
Granucci, Charlie, 161
Graves, Ralph, 94, 102, 127, 156
Griffith, D. W., 64, 65, 74
Grigsby-Grunow Company, 51–52
Guilty?, 107

Hager, George, 249
Hahn, Eddie, 105, 107, 174, 277, 283
Hale, Alan, 226
Hall, Huntz, 301
Hanna-Barbera, 306
Harem Girl, 303
Harlow, Jean, 144–145
Harmon, Denver, 168, 267
Havelick, Gene, 271
Hawks, Howard, 237–241, 293
Hayworth, Rita, 293
Hecht, Ben, 237–238, 239, 241–242, 303
Heerman, Victor, 100
Henley, Jack, 227, 251
Herstein, Lillian, 8
Hill, Sam, 61
Hilliard, John, 89
Hillyer, Lambert, 141, 169, 255
Hilton, James, 289
Hoefler, Paul, 137, 138, 139
Holden, William, 291
Hollywood Speaks, 155
Holt, Jack, 117–118, 123–124, 125, 126, 127, 135, 156, 167, 168

Horn, Camilla, 67, 71
Howard, Leslie, 184, 188, 190, 193, 205
Howard, Moe, 297
Howard, Shemp, 298
Howard, Tom, 108, 111, 112, 114
Howard, Fine, and Howard. *See* The Three Stooges
Humberstone, Lucky, 62
Hunt, Ray, 295
Hurst, Fannie, 290
Hutchins, Will, 305

Ince, Ralph, 96, 97
The Iron Mask, 61, 63, 72–73
It Happened One Night, 216–235, 262
It's Murder, 285–286
Iverson Ranch, 139–140, 173–174, 302

Jaffe, Sam, 289
James, Harry, 36, 37, 38, 39, 42, 43, 44, 45, 46, 49
Jeffries, Jim, 108
Jones, Buck, 107, 139, 141–142, 173
Joyride, 303

Kaifer, Fred, 110, 111
Karloff, Boris, 256–259
Keaton, Buster, 274, 299
Kelly, George, 119
KELW, 35–49
Kenton, Erle, 95, 99, 116–117
Kill the Umpire, 300
Kline, Ben, 140–141, 168, 279
Krasna, Norman, 162

La Cava, Gregory, 261–262, 264–266, 291
Ladies of Leisure, 101–105, 109, 111, 112, 114, 146

Lady for a Day, 169–173, 186
The Lady Is Willing, 188–205, 214
Lady of Secrets, 278–279
Lady of the Pavements, 64, 65, 74
Lake, Arthur, 300
Lakehurst Naval Air Station, 123–126
La Rocque, Rod, 71
Landsberg, Bathsheba, 8, 18, 31, 39, 41, 49
The Last Parade, 117
Lederman, D. Ross, 139, 150, 246, 248
Levee, Mike, 75
Libott, Buster, 151, 156, 239, 254, 261, 262, 267, 279
Lindop, W. H. E., 188
Livadary, John, 90, 97, 98, 102, 105, 106, 119
Lloyd, Harold, 290
The Locked Door, 74, 101
Lombard, Carole, 159–161, 218, 221, 233, 239
Long Beach earthquake, 168–169
Lord, Del, 272–274, 275, 276–277, 284, 293
Lost Horizon, 288–290
Lubitsch, Ernst, 66
Lummox, 83–85, 290

MacArthur, Charles, 238, 239, 241
MacDonald, Wallace, 116, 303
Malibu Lake, 101–102
Malmgren, Russell, 5–6, 7–8, 9, 100, 106, 137
Mamoulian, Rouben, 291
Mann, Ned, 131
Marquardt, Maynard, 5–6, 54
Marsh, Marian, 257, 258
Marshall, E. K., 20
Maurer, Norman, 305, 306
Maxfield, J. P., 78–79

Maxwell, Edwin, 86
McCarey, Leo, 290
McCollum, Hugh, 283–286, 296
McCoy, Tim, 150, 246, 273
McIntyre, Christine, 296
Menjou, Adolphe, 146–147
Mencken, H. L., 6
Metropolitan Airport, 255
Mexicali Rose, 99, 117
Micro-Phonies, 296
Milestone, Lewis, 64, 191, 195, 198, 199, 200, 203, 204
Miller, Gilbert, 184, 191, 194, 195, 200, 203
Millikan, Dr. Robert A., 304
Mills of the Gods, 254
The Miracle Woman, 143
Mr. Deeds Goes to Town, 274–275, 287–288
Mr. Smith Goes to Washington, 292
Mitchell, Everett, 15
Mole-Richardson, 99
Monkey Businessmen, 296
Moran and Mack, 39
Movietone, 68
moviolas, 106, 295
Mowbray, Alan, 269, 270
Murder on the Roof, 98
Murray, Charlie, 237
Musical Novelties, 236.
The Mysterious Avenger, 279–280

Natheaux, Louis, 116
Neill, Roy William, 96–97, 118–119, 254, 256
Nelson, Sam, 113, 119, 129
Newmeyer, Fred, 142
The New Three Stooges, 305
New York Nights, 64, 72
Nicholson, Jim, 303
No More Orchids, 160–161

O'Brien, George, 300–301
O'Brien, Pat, 159
Oh, My Nerves!, 275
Only Angels Have Wings, 293
Orson, Peggy, 37, 41

Parker, Colonel Tom, 304, 305
Peckinpah, Sam, 302
Personality, 100
Pertwee, Roland, 198, 204
Pest from the West, 299
Phonophone, 68
Pickford, Mary, 66, 71–72, 78, 80–82, 85–89
Platinum Blonde, 143–146
Playfair, Nigel, 192–193
Presley, Elvis, 304–305

Queen of Outer Space, 303–304

radio, 5–6, 11–21, 34–50, 51–57
Rain or Shine, 107–114
Rauland, E. N., 14, 16, 18
Rauland Manufacturing Company, 11–21
Reform School Girl, 303
The Return of the Fly, 302
Rhein, George, 119, 120–121
Richards, Billy, 37–38, 39–40, 42–43
Riesenfeld, Hugo, 75–78
Riskin, Everett, 263
Riskin, Robert, 2, 143, 144, 145, 152, 170, 172, 219, 246, 247, 255, 287, 288
Rob Wagner's Script, 186–187, 235, 270
Robson, May, 170–172, 254
Rogell, Albert, 214–215, 255, 277–278
Rominger, Glenn, 137, 143

Roosevelt, Franklin Delano, 156,
    157, 165, 168
Rosen, Phil, 215
Rowe, Tommy, 52–54
Royal Romance, 116
"Running W," 249–250

Schary, Dore, 214–215
Schneider, Magda, 193
Schwalb, Ben, 120, 121, 301, 303
Scooby-Doo, 306
Screen Snapshots, 291
Security Pictures Company, 241
Seid, George, 181, 183, 192, 197,
    199, 204, 205
Seitz, George, 98
Selman, Dave, 101
Sennett, Mack, 236–237, 271–272
Shadows of Sing Sing, 215
Shamroy, Leon, 261
She Couldn't Take It, 267–274
She Married Her Boss, 261–266
short subjects, 236–237, 272,
    294–299
Sidney, George, 236–237
Siegler, Al, 256, 257
Singleton, Penny, 300
Sloane, Paul, 156–157
Sniff, Joseph, 267
Song of Love, 93–95
So This Is Africa, 161–165
sound systems, 68–69
So You Won't Squawk, 274
Space Master X-7, 297
The Squealer, 116
Stanwyck, Barbara, 74, 99, 101,
    102, 104–105, 117, 146, 148,
    218
Starrett, Charles, 275–276
Stewart, James, 291–292
Sticht, Chet, 254
Strayer, Frank, 100
Subway Express, 142

Sugarfoot, 305
Swerling, Jo, 129, 155, 156, 159,
    168

Talmadge, Norma, 64
Taming of the Shrew, 85–88
Tanforan racetrack, 247–250
Taurog, Norman, 304, 305
Taylor, Sam, 81–82, 85
Tetzlaff, Ted, 96
Thomas, Jameson, 160
Three Little Beers, 276
The Three Stooges, 245, 272,
    276–277, 294, 295–299
The Three Stooges in Orbit, 299
*The Three Stooges Meet Her-
    cules,* 299
Three Troubledoers, 296
Tickle Me, 304–305
Toms River, 120–125
Tregellas, Lionel, 188
Twentieth Century, 237–244

Ullman, Ellwood, 301, 303, 304,
    306
United Artists, 61–89

Vale, Eugene, 105
Van Nuys Airport, 255
Velez, Lupe, 65
Virtue, 158–159
Vitaphone, 68

Wagner, Rob, 186–187
Wainwright, Stuart, 35, 36, 37,
    42, 43, 46, 47, 48
Walker, Joseph, 95, 101, 104,
    113, 119, 122, 124, 129, 131,
    143, 160, 175–178, 181,
    182–191, 193–194, 199,
    201–202, 205–206, 231, 248,
    249, 250, 289
Wall Street, 96–97

War Correspondent, 156–157
Ward, Blackjack, 223–224
Washington Merry-Go-Round, 159
WCFL, 54–57
Wells, H. G., 280
WENR, 14–18
West, Roland, 73, 78
Westerlin and Campbell, 7, 8
Western Electric Variable-Density Sound System, 68–69
Westerns, 107, 139–142, 150, 173–174, 246, 275–276, 300–301, 305
Westover, Winifred, 83–84
Westphal, Frank, 15
Wheeler and Woolsey, 161–165
When Strangers Marry, 167–168
White, Jules, 236, 277
Williams, Robert, 143, 144, 145

Wilshire-Ebell Theatre, 240, 242
Wilson, Ug, 268
wire-belt gags, 295
Witt, Harold, 57–61
WLS, 52–54
W9CAN, 14
Wodehouse, P. G., 198
Woman Haters, 245, 273
The Woman I Stole, 168
Woman of Distinction, 300
World without End, 302
Wright, Maurice, 132

Yordan, Philip, 241
You Can't Take It with You, 291
You'll Never Get Rich, 294
You May Be Next, 277–278
Young, Loretta, 143–144, 145
You Were Never Lovelier, 294

ADT-5708

Armstrong

TK
7807
B47
M7
1999

11/3/99
S.O.